SCENIC DRIVING

COLORADO

D0369342

SCENIC **DRIVING** SERIES

FIFTH EDITION

SCENIC DRIVING

COLORADO

Exploring the State's
Most Spectacular Back Roads

STEWART M. GREEN

Guilford, Connecticut

All the information in this guidebook is subject to change. We recommend that you call ahead to obtain current information before traveling.

Globe
Pequot

An imprint of The Rowman & Littlefield Publishing Group, Inc.
4501 Forbes Blvd., Ste. 200
Lanham, MD 20706
www.rowman.com

Distributed by NATIONAL BOOK NETWORK

British Library Cataloguing in Publication Information available

Library of Congress Cataloging-in-Publication Data available

ISBN 978-1-4930-3598-4 (paperback)
ISBN 978-1-4930-3599-1 (e-book)

∞™ The paper used in this publication meets the minimum requirements of American National Standard for Information Sciences—Permanence of Paper for Printed Library Materials, ANSI/NISO Z39.48-1992

Printed in the United States of America

*I dedicate this book about my beloved home state of Colorado
to my mother and father—Mildred and Ralph Eric Green—
for encouraging me to pursue my writing career;
for keeping me in pencils and paper as a young writer;
for having more books than television programs in my childhood home;
and for unwavering love and support.*

Contents

The Scenic Routes

Climbers ascend the last pitch of John Otto's 1911 route to the summit of Independence Monument in Colorado National Monument.

About the Author

Stewart M. Green, a Colorado native, is a freelance photographer, writer, and publisher based in Colorado Springs, Colorado. He travels the US and the world working on projects for Globe Pequot Press and other publications. Stewart has written and photographed many books for FalconGuides and Globe Pequot Press, including *Rock Art, Rock Climbing Colorado, Rock Climbing Utah, Rock Climbing New England, Scenic Driving New England, Scenic Driving Arizona, Rock Climbing Europe, Best Climbs Moab, Best Climbs Rocky Mountain National Park,* and *Best Hikes Near Colorado Springs*. His work also appears in many catalogues, advertisements, and national publications. Stewart is also a senior climbing guide at Front Range Climbing Company in Colorado Springs.

Acknowledgments

Colorado, my home state, remains a place of beauty and mystery—for now. It's a place of pristine views and wide-open spaces. But it is also slowly shrinking. No longer is Colorado a great frontier and an enclave of wilderness. Now, like most of the American West, it's a collection of wilderness areas, a few untouched places, and uncluttered scenic views dismembered from a greater eco-community. It's a special land that needs, more than ever before, to be loved, respected, and preserved. *Scenic Driving Colorado* celebrates Colorado's unique history, natural diversity, and gorgeous beauty.

Nature and guidebook writers have a serious responsibility to address environmental ethics, to interpret natural history, and to bring historical sensitivity to their subjects. By educating and sensitizing visitors, newcomers, and longtime residents to the beauty, wonder, and fragility of a place, a writer and a book can instill a sense of reverence, pride, and preservation in its users. *Scenic Driving Colorado* helps educate its readers by interpreting and caring for this wonderful place. Bring that respectful ethos with you as you travel its ribbons of highway and remember that we are a reflection of this world.

Over the last few years I've explored over 10,000 miles across Colorado to research, update, and fact-check the manuscript for this new 5th edition of *Scenic Driving Colorado*, formerly *Scenic Routes & Byways Colorado*. I spent nights along the scenic drives under star-studded skies, in roadside motels and hotels, and with friends scattered around the state.

My thanks to FalconGuides for the opportunity to write and photograph the first edition of *Scenic Driving Colorado*—a book we had talked about doing for 10 years—back in the early 1990s. And more thanks and applause to Globe Pequot Press for keeping the book in print and bringing this new edition to bookshelves and tablets everywhere.

A special thanks to Amy Lyons, Globe Pequot's travel editor, for republishing the book in its new format. My sincere thanks and appreciation to the current editorial and art staff at Globe Pequot, including Sarah Parke, for all their skilled work on this stunning new edition.

Thanks also to the USDA Forest Service, Bureau of Land Management, and National Park Service naturalists and rangers who reviewed and corrected portions of both the original and revised manuscripts to ensure their accuracy.

Much of this book was rewritten and researched at La Baguette in downtown Colorado Springs, my office away from home. Thanks to Joe and Robin Frodge

Sunrise brightens an armada of clouds above Picture Canyon at the Comanche Grasslands in southeastern Colorado.

and their great staff for putting up with me at the back table almost every morning. If you stop by for coffee and baguettes, look for me and say hi!

And finally, a big thanks to Ian and Bee Green for our special relationship and friendship, as well as their encouragement, belays on rock climbs, and campfire wisdom and comedy while I researched and wrote the first edition 25 years ago. *Scenic Driving Colorado* continues to be a great adventure on the road.

Introduction

Colorado—it's a state of majestic landscapes, startling panoramas, and an amazing ecological and topographical diversity. It's a land of uncompromising beauty, dominated by lofty, snow-capped peaks; creased by precipitous canyons and broad valleys; and rimmed by distant horizons, mesas, and buttes. Colorado offers a land of extreme contrasts—sere desert and verdant meadow; urban sprawl and rural solitude; granite cliff and aspen woodland; whitewater rivers and dissected arroyos. The timeless landscape out there, beyond the highway's edge, is filled with hidden places and undiscovered wonders.

Colorado, the eighth-largest state, stretches across North America's midsection. This giant, rectangular 104,091-square-mile state bestrides the Continental Divide, the great twisting spine that separates the Atlantic and Pacific watersheds. It's a land of immense topographical variety that ranges from a 3,350-foot low point on the Arkansas River near the Kansas border to the boulder-strewn summit of 14,439-foot Mount Elbert high in the Sawatch Range.

In between lies a stunning geography dominated and tempered by its mountain ranges. Geographers divide Colorado into three main physiographic provinces: the Great Plains, the Rocky Mountains, and the Colorado Plateau. Each distinct province is defined by its geology or earth structure, which, coupled with different climates, dictates the state's diverse ecology, the complex web of relationships between plants and animals and the changing land.

Prairie, Peak, & Plateau

The Great Plains, covering 40 percent of Colorado, sweep eastward from the abrupt mountain escarpment to the Kansas border. It's a misnomer to call this region a plain. This lean land is characterized by undulating hills and interrupted by rock-rimmed mesas, buttes, and escarpments. The broad Arkansas and South Platte River valleys and angular canyons carved by the sparse Purgatoire, Apisapha, and Huerfano Rivers seam the short-grass prairie. Wide fields, watered by snowmelt-laden rivers and groundwater aquifers, are planted with wheat, corn, sorghum, sugar beets, and other crops, while cattle and antelope roam the drier ranges.

The Rocky Mountains abruptly begin where the Great Plains end. The horizontal, 10,000-foot-thick sedimentary rock layers that floor the prairie sharply tilt into steep hogbacks like those seen at Garden of the Gods and Red Rocks along the eastern edge of the mountain uplift. Most Coloradans live in large cities scattered along this transition zone. The Continental Divide, separating water from the Atlantic and Pacific watersheds, dominates Colorado's Rocky Mountains, part of the world's longest mountain chain.

The Rockies twist from Alaska to Mexico but reach their climax in Colorado, with more than 50 separate mountain ranges that include 53 of America's 67 14,000-foot peaks with 300 feet of prominence in the lower 48 states and another 1,728 ranked summits that top 11,000 feet. The mountains, raised over the last 70 million years, were shaped by volcanism, faulting, and earthquakes and sculpted by huge glaciers and swift rivers and streams.

Colorado is the mother of rivers, with the Animas, Arkansas, Blue, Cache la Poudre, Colorado, Conejos, Cucharas, Dolores, Eagle, Fryingpan, Gunnison, Mancos, South and North Platte, Purgatoire, Rio Grande, San Juan, San Miguel, Uncompahgre, White River, and Yampa originating in snowy alpine cirques. Rich mineral deposits, including gold, silver, zinc, lead, copper, and molybdenum, lurk in the Rockies and lured 19th-century prospectors who left a historic legacy of roads, trails, mines, towns, and place-names on the mountains.

The Plateau region, part of the 150,000-square-mile Colorado Plateau which is also in Utah, Arizona, and New Mexico, includes the western quarter of Colorado. It is a brilliantly colored land of horizontal sedimentary layers, including Wingate and Navajo sandstones, dissected by erosion into deep canyons, mesas, and cuestas. Deep canyons carved by the Yampa, Green, Colorado, and Dolores Rivers slice through the layer-cake rocks. Folding and faulting created huge basins, rolling uplands, and rocky hogbacks in this arid area.

Colorado's Natural History

Colorado is an ecological melting pot, a place of unbelievable natural diversity, a place that thrills and startles the naturalist. Famed nature writer Edwin Way Teale wrote in his classic book *Journey into Summer*, "Before us now extended all of Colorado, a state that, like Florida and California, holds endless interest for the naturalist."

The Rocky Mountains mold and temper the state's plants and animals, dictating their responses with variable temperatures, precipitation patterns, and elevations. Short-grass prairie, interrupted by a mosaic of farms, blankets the eastern plains. Verdant ribbons of cottonwoods, willows, and underbrush line sinuous rivers and creeks. Pygmy woodlands of piñon pine and juniper trees scatter over dry mesas and desert canyons. Dense evergreen forests of ponderosa pine, Engelmann spruce, lodgepole pine, and Douglas fir trees coat mountain slopes, while ancient bristlecone pines, dwarfed by wind and weather, huddle at timberline on snow-shrouded peaks. Immense golden groves of quaking aspen shimmer across the mountains under autumn's bright sun. Alpine tundra, a fragile ecosystem of grass and flowers akin to those of northern Canada and Alaska, covers the harsh mountainsides above timberline, and above on the mountain summits stretches a chilly world of shattered rock, permafrost, and long winters.

Natural Wonders & Historic Sites

Colorado offers the traveler not only incomparable scenery, but also a host of natural wonders, historic sites, and outdoor recreation. The state boasts Rocky Mountain, Great Sand Dunes, Black Canyon of the Gunnison, and Mesa Verde National Parks, some of the nation's most popular parklands, as well as Colorado, Dinosaur, Hovenweep, and Florissant Fossil Beds National Monuments; Curecanti and Arapaho National Recreation Areas; and Bent's Old Fort National Historic Site.

There are many other significant natural areas and historic places, like the 15 designated National Natural Landmarks, including the Garden of the Gods, Summit Lake, Slumgullion Earthflow, and the Spanish Peaks, and 25 designated National Historic Landmark sites such as Durango-Silverton Narrow Gauge Railroad, Pikes Peak, Leadville Historic District, and Telluride Historic District.

Forty-two state parks are managed for both water- and land-based recreation. Eleven national forests and two national grasslands spread across almost 14.5 million acres of public land, while the Bureau of Land Management offers an additional 8.3 million acres for recreation and multiple uses. There are 42 designated wilderness areas that protect and preserve much of Colorado's scenic beauty and diverse habitats for future generations of both Coloradoans and the other animals that inhabit the peaks, plains, and plateaus.

Colorado also offers more than 8,000 river-miles and 2,000 lakes for anglers and rafters to pursue their watery pleasure. Hikers can follow the 486-mile-long Colorado Trail as it threads through seven national forests and six wilderness areas between Denver and Durango. Numerous stony tracks invite mountain bikers and four-wheel-drive enthusiasts to sample the backcountry.

Scenic Driving Colorado finds the best of Colorado's splendid landscapes and recreational offerings. Its 30 drives traverse more than 2,300 miles of remote highways and off-the-beaten-track back roads that offer access to Colorado's scenic landscapes, ecological diversity, colorful history, and outdoor activities. Travelers cross lofty mountain passes on Independence Pass and Trail Ridge Road, twist

The West Spanish Peak towers above a dike of volcanic rock along the Highway of Legends in southern Colorado.

through deep rock-walled canyons along the Dolores and Cache la Poudre Rivers, follow the historic Santa Fe Trail, marvel at Mesa Verde's long-deserted Ancestral Puebloan cities of stone, and climb to lofty mountain aeries atop Pikes Peak and Mount Evans on the highest roads in the United States. On these scenic drives, travelers leave urban sprawl behind and take to the open road.

Colorado Driving Adventures

These drives are only the start of a grand Colorado adventure. Most of them are paved highways, but some are genuine back roads. Beyond the blacktop and the book hide more scenic drives. After exploring the prime roads detailed here, the intrepid traveler can seek out new tracks. Some of the best include Owl Creek Pass, Ophir Pass, Engineer Pass, the Divide Road on the crest of the Uncompahgre Plateau, Hagerman Pass, Boreas Pass, the twisting road between Buford and New Castle, the Deep Creek Road above Dotsero, and some of those lonely prairie roads like CO 71 and the Elbert Highway.

All of the drives in *Scenic Driving Colorado* are the author's choice as the state's best scenic, recreational, steering-wheel adventures. Many of the drives or parts of the drives are designated as official Scenic Byways and Back Country Byways by the US Department of Agriculture Forest Service and the Bureau of Land Management (BLM). Others are part of the state of Colorado's Scenic and Historic Byways program, established in 1989 to provide recreational, economic, and educational benefits to Coloradoans and visitors. These highways, nominated by local partnership groups, are designated by the Colorado Scenic and Historic Byways Commission for their scenic, historic, cultural, recreational, and natural features.

Two highways—the San Juan Skyway and Trail Ridge Road—are designated as All-American Byways and are among the most scenic drives in America, with only 29 other highways nationwide receiving this honor. Another six Colorado roads are listed as National Scenic Byways.

Being Prepared

Be prepared when driving Colorado's scenic highways, routes, and byways. Make sure your vehicle is in good working condition and the spare tire is properly inflated. Follow the speed limit, particularly on winding mountain roads, stay in

Blanca Peak and Little Bear Peak, both "Fourteeners," lift snowy crowns above Los Caminos Antiguos Scenic Byway in the San Luis Valley.

your lane, and watch for blind corners. Maintain a safe speed and pull off to allow faster cars to pass.

Fickle weather creates changeable driving conditions. Violent summer thunderstorms can impair vision and create hydroplaning situations. Snow and ice quickly slicken mountain highways. Carry tire chains, a snow shovel, and extra clothes when traveling in winter. Many high passes require tire chains in winter. Hot summer temperatures and steep mountain slopes can overheat your car. It's best to pull off the road and allow the engine to cool down. Carry extra water in case of breakdown. It's best to top off your gas tank before embarking on remote roads. Know your vehicle and its limits. And above all—use common sense.

The scenic drives cross a mosaic of public and private lands. Respect private property rights by not trespassing. Forest Service and BLM maps designate public lands. Federal laws protect paleontological, archaeological, and historic sites, including fossils and bones, Native American sites and artifacts, and historic buildings and structures. It's best to utilize existing campgrounds and campsites to mitigate human impact. Remember to douse all campfires and tote your trash out.

Take a Colorado Drive

Colorado—it's a word that resounds with images as clear as a mountain stream. Snow-capped peaks rise sharply against an azure sky at sunrise. A muddy river runs between dusky red sandstone cliffs, its glassy surface reflecting sun and shadow. Dark whiskery forests of spruce and fir clot a shaded ravine. An abandoned prairie homestead lies open to the blazing sun and dissecting spring winds.

Colorado is out there, along the highway shoulder, beyond the white lines. Follow the scenic roads and drive without destinations. Stop, look, and linger. Every highway bend, every scenic overlook, every canyon crook, and every alpine pass yields a glimpse into the beauty, wonder, and awe of Colorado's natural soul.

Colorado Overview

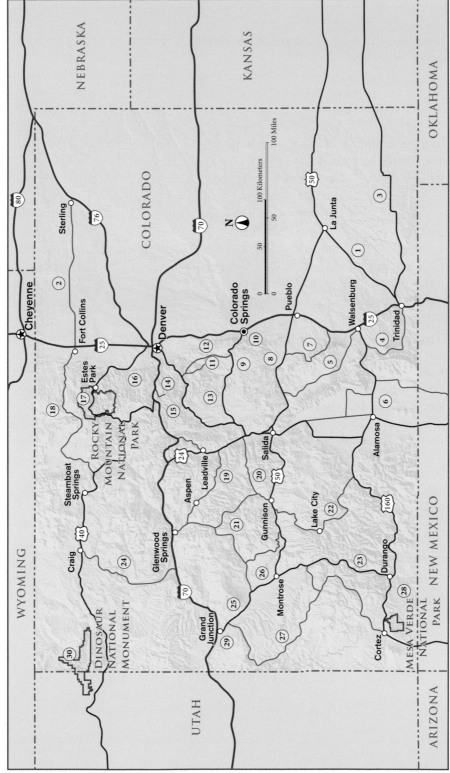

Map Legend

Interstate Highway/ Featured Interstate Highway	———90———	/ ———90———
US Highway/ Featured US Highway	———89———	/ ———89———
State Highway/ Featured State Highway	———22———	/ ———22———
Local Road/ Featured Local Road	——————	/ ——————
Unpaved Road/ Featured Unpaved Road	— — — — —	/ — — — — —
Trail	- - - - - - - - - -	
Railroad	+++++++++++++	

Airport	✈	Picnic Area	🎋
Boat Ramp	🚤	Point of Interest	▯
Bridge	⌣	Rapids	∥
Building or Structure	■	Ranger Station	🏠
Campground	▲	Route Number	⑩
City	◉	Ski Area	⛷
Geyser/Spring	⌐	Small State Park, Wilderness or Natural Area	▲
Historic Site	🏛	Town	○
Lodge	🛏	Waterfall	≋
Marina	⚓	Wildlife Management Area	🦅
Museum	🏛	Visitor, Interpretive Center	⑦
Pass	) (		

Mountain, Peak, or Butte ▲ Deseret Peak 11,031 ft.

River, Creek, or Drainage

Body of Water

State Line — — — — —

National Park	▭	Wilderness Area	▭
National Forest	▭	Misc. Area	▭

Santa Fe Trail Scenic & Historic Byway

La Junta to Trinidad

General description: This 80-mile-long scenic drive, following the old Santa Fe Trail, crosses the high plains between La Junta and Trinidad.

Special attractions: Santa Fe Trail, Bent's Old Fort National Historic Site, Comanche National Grassland, El Corazon de Trinidad National Historic District, Baca House–Bloom Mansion–Santa Fe Trail Museum (Trinidad), scenic views, hiking.

Location: Southeastern Colorado. The drive runs from La Junta and US 50 to Trinidad and I-25.

Route name and number: Santa Fe Trail Scenic and Historic Byway, US 350.

Travel season: Year-round.

Camping: No campgrounds along the drive. Primitive camping is permitted on the Comanche National Grassland. Nearby campgrounds are at Trinidad State Park and in San Isabel National Forest.

Services: All services are in La Junta and Trinidad. No services along the drive.

Nearby attractions: Highway of Legends Scenic Byway (Scenic Drive 4), Raton Pass, Trinidad State Park, Stonewall Gap, Cokedale National Historic District, Spanish Peaks Wilderness Area, San Isabel National Forest, Ludlow Monument, Comanche Grasslands (see Scenic Drive 3), Purgatoire Canyon.

The Route

The limitless prairie stretches out beneath the blazing sun to a distant line of mountains perched on the horizon. Dusty arroyos, chiseled by quick runoff from occasional summer thunderstorms, seam broad valleys flanked by rock-rimmed cuestas and undulating hills covered with tawny short-grass prairie. A few intermittent creek beds twist north to the Arkansas River, their water dwindling into sand and reappearing as occasional bitter pools nestled in sandstone canyons. Southeastern Colorado is a land of little rain, fierce temperature ranges, and a leaping vault of azure sky. It's a supple, muscular land, an arena of light and space that reminds us that untamed corners still exist.

These rolling plains are Colorado's underdog landscape, a lost place forgotten and almost unseen by those intent on greener mountain pastures. But this brown land south of the Arkansas River is blanketed by a sea of short-grass prairie, a delicate and complex ecosystem, and a history older than the US. Folsom hunters trod the land 10,000 years ago in pursuit of big game; Comanches and Pawnees battled over its buffalo and water holes; Spanish battalions crossed its bleak wastes

Santa Fe Trail Scenic & Historic Byway

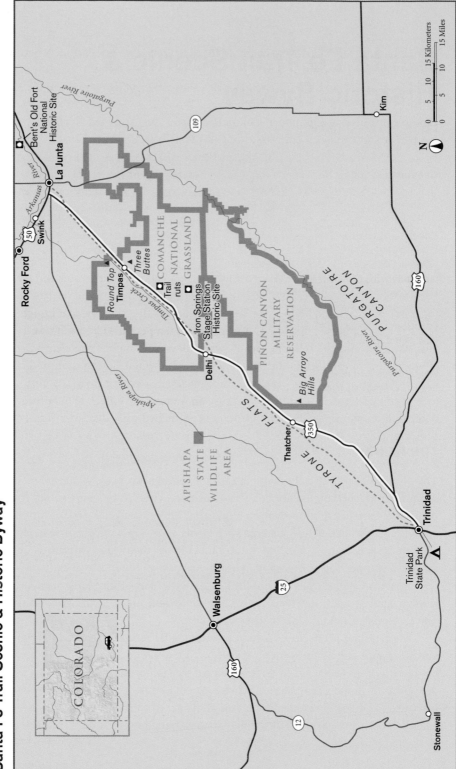

in search of golden Cibola, and in the 1840s the caravan wheels of traders bent for Santa Fe creaked across this land.

The Santa Fe Trail Scenic and Historic Byway, traversing 80 miles of US 350 between La Junta on the Arkansas River and Trinidad at the foot of the Rockies, explores this diverse and hidden Colorado corner. The byway route follows the old trail that once connected Missouri with the distant Mexican colony of Santa Fe in northern New Mexico. This description is only part of the entire Santa Fe Trail Scenic and Historic Byway, a 187-mile designated Colorado historic byway that runs from the Kansas border to La Junta then southwest on the byway section described here.

Southeastern Colorado is a land of little rain, and what rain does fall usually drops from violent summer thunderstorms that brew over distant mountains. Annual precipitation ranges between 12 and 15 inches. Summer brings hot weather, with daily highs climbing into the 90s and above. Carry water and wear a hat if you walk anywhere. Watch for the ubiquitous rattlesnakes; they teem among the area's boulders and bluffs. Late September begins the cool down, although hot weather can persist into late October. Expect temperatures in the 70s and 80s. Winter is mild, with light snowfall, warm days, cold nights, and clear skies, although storms can lock in the land in a blizzard of white. Spring is unpredictable. A persistent wind gnaws at the high rangeland, sweeping clouds of dust across Timpas Creek and rattling dry grass on hummocky hills. Light showers dampen the ground, and by May, green grass sprinkled with wildflowers carpets the land. This exquisite bloom lasts but a few weeks before the blast of summer sun arrives to desiccate the prairie.

La Junta & Bent's Old Fort

La Junta, a small town straddling the Arkansas River 64 miles east of Pueblo, is at the junction of US 50 and US 350. La Junta, Spanish for "the junction," was founded in 1875 at the convergence of the Kansas Pacific and Santa Fe railway lines. But its history as a trading center goes back to Bent's Fort, a trading post established in 1834 just east of today's La Junta by brothers Charles and William Bent and Ceran St. Vrain.

Trade with Santa Fe and its remote Mexican colony began in 1821 with Mexico's secession from Spain and the fall of trade barriers. Missouri trader William Becknell crossed the prairie in 1821 to that lonely northern outpost of a newly independent nation and found an eager market for his trade goods. On his journey to Santa Fe, Becknell had followed the Arkansas River into Colorado and coaxed his mules over rocky Raton Pass, finding the route impractical for wagons.

On his second trip, Becknell left the Arkansas and cut across waterless plains to the Cimarron River to establish the Cimarron Cutoff.

A Missouri resident later recalled Becknell's triumphant return: "When the rawhide thongs of the saddlebags were cut, the Spanish dollars rolled into the gutters, causing great excitement." Speculative traders soon found it was cheaper to ship goods to Santa Fe from Missouri than from Mexico City, and by 1827 the New Mexico trade had firmly established the 900-mile-long Santa Fe Trail, western America's great road of commerce.

The Bent brothers and St. Vrain cashed in on the lucrative Native American trade in eastern Colorado with their adobe castle perched on the cottonwood-lined banks of the Arkansas River. William Bent concentrated on Native American goods, while Charles Bent and St. Vrain specialized in the lucrative Santa Fe and Taos trade. The Cimarron Cutoff route on the Santa Fe Trail was fast and popular, but mounting Native American attacks and the lack of a reliable water supply forced an increasing number of merchants to follow the longer, but safer, Mountain Branch up the Arkansas River to Bent's Fort. Here they could rest and purchase supplies before heading southwest up arid Timpas Creek to the rough track over Raton Pass.

The Bent, St. Vrain & Company mercantile firm thrived until the late 1840s, when the enterprise began to unravel. Charles Bent, then the first American governor of the New Mexico Territory, was killed in the 1847 Taos Revolt by rioting Pueblo Indians, and shortly afterward a cholera epidemic swept along the river, decimating both Anglos and Native Americans. The US Army, fighting a war with Mexico from 1846 to 1848, also requisitioned part of Bent's Fort, overgrazed surrounding pastures, and used up what little firewood remained around the fort. In frustration, William Bent abandoned and torched the fort in 1849 and moved downstream to build Bent's New Fort at Big Timber.

The old fort site lay open to the sun and sky until the mid-1970s, when the National Park Service, using original plans and scale drawings made in 1846 by army topographical engineer Lieutenant James W. Abert, rebuilt the massive adobe fort. Now **Bent's Old Fort National Historic Site** offers a glimpse of frontier life in the 1840s. At the adobe-walled fort, interpreters clad in period clothes, including a trader, blacksmith, Mexican laborer, and mountain man, keep the legacy of Bent's Fort and the Santa Fe Trail alive today. The fort lies a few miles northeast of La Junta on CO 194.

Bent's Old Fort recreates 1840s frontier life along the Santa Fe Trail.

Along the Santa Fe Trail

The drive begins in western La Junta at the intersection of US 50 and US 350. Head south on quiet residential streets on US 350. The road bends southwest and leaves the town behind after a mile. US 350, nicknamed the National Old Trails Highway, was a major transcontinental highway between New York and Los Angeles in the days before the interstate highway system was built in the 1950s.

The trace of the **Santa Fe Trail** itself, from Franklin, Missouri, to Santa Fe, New Mexico, is now preserved as a national historic trail. The 80-mile section between La Junta and Trinidad follows the Mountain Branch of the Santa Fe Trail. Here the old trail offered passage to trade caravans and later stage, freight, and mail lines, before the completion of the railroad in the 1870s. Travel along this segment generally took about four days. The entire trail stretched 1,200 miles from its beginning at Franklin, Missouri, to the Plaza in Santa Fe, New Mexico. The **Santa Fe National Historic Trail,** designated in 1987, remembers the historic trading route, its colorful characters, and the diverse cultures, including Native American, Mexican, and Spanish, that inhabited the trail corridor. Visitors today can follow highways and roads along the old trail, visiting historic sites that allow glimpses back to events, waterholes, settlements, commerce, landmarks, and military forts.

The highway gradually ascends a tilted plain. Short grass coats the flat ground and only occasional windmills mark the desolate plain. At about 5 miles an unassuming granite marker sits along the fence on the road's west side. This marker, one of many placed along the trail by the Daughters of the American Revolution (DAR), indicates where the trail crossed today's highway. Sharp eyes can discern wagon wheel ruts etched into the ground west of the marker.

Trail ruts, found along much of the drive, appear as long, furrowed depressions and are usually heavily vegetated. When traveling flat country like this, wagon caravans spread out three and four abreast, creating wide rutted areas. In 1844 teamster Josiah Gregg wrote, "The wagons marched slowly in four parallel columns, in broken lines, often at intervals of many rods between. The unceasing *crack, crack,* of the wagoners' whips, resembling the frequent reports of distant guns, almost made one believe that a skirmish was actually taking place between two hostile parties." Wagons traveled single file on steep ascents, gouging deep swales into hillsides that have eroded into sharp arroyos.

Unlike other Santa Fe Trail sections in Colorado and Kansas, the trail stretch followed by this drive remains much as it did when wagons inched across the wide expanse. Eighteen-year-old Susan Shelby Magoffin traveled the trail from Independence, Missouri, to Santa Fe with her trader-husband Samuel Magoffin in 1846, a boom year when more than $1 million in goods was hauled over the trail.

Magoffin kept a journal recounting her daily experiences that has become a classic tale of the Santa Fe Trail. On Saturday, August 8, she wrote about the trail section southwest of the fort: "The dust is very great, and the vegetation so perfectly parched by the sun that not a blade of *green* grass is to be seen."

After 13 miles the highway drops over a tawny bluff above **Timpas Creek,** its dry meanders dotted with cottonwoods. Both the highway and Santa Fe Trail follow the Timpas Creek drainage to its headwaters, some 40 miles to the southwest. Distant views unfold west from the bluff top. The Wet Mountains and Spanish Peaks, over 70 miles away, float on the shimmering horizon like far-off blue clouds. The twin Spanish Peaks, called *Wahatoya* (Breasts of the World) by the Ute Indians, were long a crucial landmark for the Native Americans, Spanish, and Santa Fe Trail travelers.

The Three Buttes, another trail landmark, lift pointed summits above the cluster of trees marking the abandoned townsite of Timpas. Susan Magoffin traveled here on Sunday, August 9, noting, "Mountains are coming in sight this morning—we are winding about among large stone hills which finally run into mountains, two of which appear in the distance. . . ." You can find this view by turning north on CO 71 and driving 0.5 mile to a parking area for **Sierra Vista Overlook.** A short walk leads to the overlook atop a bluff and a commanding view of the country along the Santa Fe Trail as it runs southwest. From here you can hike a 3-mile section of the Santa Fe National Historic Trail marked with stone posts to Timpas Picnic Area.

Timpas & Comanche National Grassland

The road begins a gradual descent into the broad Timpas Creek valley and enters the Timpas Unit of Comanche National Grassland, with over 440,000 acres. The area, a patchwork of public and private lands, encompasses a diversity of habitats within the grassland ecosystem. The grassland is managed by the USDA Forest Service and spreads across southeastern Colorado. Originally Comanche Indian territory, the area was overgrazed by early cattle barons and later divided by homesteaders into 40-acre tracts. But dry soil and bad farming and conservation practices created the Dust Bowl here and in surrounding states in the 1930s. In 1938 the federal government began reacquiring the homesteads and retiring them from cultivation.

Today the Forest Service has reclaimed much of the grassland. Plentiful animals inhabit the high plains, including both mule and white-tailed deer, pronghorn, black bear, opossum, mountain lion, black-tailed prairie dog, jackrabbit, snapping turtle, Texas short-horned lizard, and prairie, massasauga, and pygmy rattlesnakes. The area offers excellent bird habitats, with more than 235 bird species recorded. Common birds seen on the drive include turkey vulture, red-tailed hawk, American kestrel, western meadowlark, and raven.

The highway passes the ghost town of **Timpas,** an old stage station and railroad stop established in 1868. Clusters of elms and cottonwoods surround its abandoned school, houses, and weather-beaten stockyard. The site was a stagecoach station between 1869 and 1871 on the Metcalf Ranch.

You can explore the area at **Timpas Picnic Area** by turning right or northwest on CR 16.5. After crossing the railroad tracks, turn right into the parking area. Several covered picnic tables with grills (charcoal only) make a good lunch stop. Timpas Creek was the first water source encountered on this trail section after leaving the Arkansas River. An 0.5-mile nature trail loops out to the creek, passing stone markers that indicate the trace of the Santa Fe Trail. The trail is ideal for watching prairie wildlife. You can also hike 3 miles northeast, passing stone markers that mark the old trail, up to Sierra Vista Overlook.

The drive runs up the valley flank, cresting a low hill north of Three Buttes. Soft, rolling hills broken by arroyos and shallow canyons surround a roadside overlook. A sandstone rim fringes distant bluffs, and junipers scatter across their talus slopes. The Southern Overland Mail Company stagecoach route threaded through the Three Buttes, leaving eroded ruts below the gap. Another DAR trail marker sits a couple miles down the road near milepost 51.

Following the valley floor, the highway dips across Lone Tree Arroyo, Hoe Ranch Arroyo, and Sheep Canyon Arroyo. Eleven miles from Timpas, the drive intersects Iron Springs Road (CR 9). The Santa Fe Trail crosses this gravel side road a half mile south.

Iron Springs Stage Station Historic Site sits a little farther south of the trail by two stock tanks. Iron Springs, capped by a concrete box, supplies water to the tanks. Nearby lies the foundation of the station barn, a low mound marking the adobe remains of the station itself, and the stubby outline of the stage corral. The station, built in 1862 by Henry C. Withers, was burned by Cheyenne Indians in 1864. The stage station allowed for a change of horses and a chance for passengers to stretch their legs and get a meal. One early traveler, Episcopal bishop Joseph Talbot, arrived here at four in the morning after a 10-hour night ride from Bent's Fort. He noted, after dining on a "greasy breakfast of antelope," that the station was a "miserable, dirty place." Trail ruts are still visible north and west of the parking area.

In 1872 the Atchinson, Topeka & Santa Fe Railroad came through, replacing the old stage route. The Iron Springs Station closed and Bloom, a new railroad stop, arose west along today's highway and railroad.

Past the site of Bloom, the highway bends south, crosses Taylor Arroyo, and leaves Comanche National Grassland. The road climbs away from Timpas Creek

The sun rises over rolling stone hills along the Old Santa Fe Trail near Timpas.

to the deserted railroad town of **Delhi** and its single house. Cresting the hill, the road again enters the broad Timpas valley. High cuestas edged with sandstone and darkly dotted with junipers flank the highway. The Spanish Peaks and the snow-capped Culebra Range loom straight ahead.

Thatcher, the next ruined town encountered, began as a stage station called Hole-in-the-Rock and became a bustling railroad town after the Atchison, Topeka & Santa Fe Railroad pushed through in 1872. The town flourished as a cow-shipping center and was named for M. D. Thatcher, a well-known southern Colorado rancher and banker. The town's fortunes soared in the early 20th century after a helium plant was built near local helium wells. Over 400 people lived here during World War II. The gas, used to inflate dirigibles, took orders from around the world until airplanes made them obsolete. After that, the town slowly declined. The lavish train depot closed in 1965, and shortly afterward the post office shut its doors. Now the town basks under the hot sun, empty but for a few remaining residents. Wind sifts across stone foundations and adobe walls crumble, unprotected from years of rain. A rusted car door and sagging fences are scattered across weed-filled front yards. The town high school, once full of promise, has largely vanished beneath prairie dust and cholla cacti. As late as 1990, however, much of the ghost town remained among leafy elms.

A short side trip turns west at the only intersection in Thatcher. Head down the gravel road past the school to a narrow wooden bridge spanning Timpas

Creek. Look north up the shallow rocky canyon. Hidden there is one of the prominent Santa Fe Trail landmarks on the highway—**Hole-in-the-Rock.** This deep tinaja, carved by flash floods into solid sandstone bedrock, kept water through even the driest times and was a welcome sight in trail days. Susan Magoffin wrote, "This road is very badly supplied with water." Her party camped here for a couple of days after their cattle ran off. She described the well as "a large 'hole in a rock' filled with clear, cold water, and to which a bottom has never as yet been found." The hole, on private property, is now dry and usually filled with wind-blown sand. The well was later used for railroad engines, which led to it drying up at the beginning of the Dust Bowl in 1929. A ruined stone barn at the ranch just east of the bridge is the remains of the Hole-in-the-Rock Overland Stage Station's barn.

Thatcher to Trinidad

The highway runs southwest from Thatcher up a broadening valley among undulating hills. Fisher Mesa, a flat-topped landmark north of the New Mexico border, rises beyond the road. The drive reaches a wide-rounded ridge above the Timpas Creek headwaters and heads down a gently tilted plain covered with short-grass prairie. The highway sweeps through a couple more mostly abandoned towns—Tyrone and Model—before dropping down into the Purgatoire River valley. The 234,896-acre **Piñon Canyon Maneuver Site,** lying east of Tyrone and Thatcher, is used by the US Army for tank and military training.

The drive's last 15 miles border the **Purgatoire River,** passing pastures and fields of pinto beans, alfalfa, and sugar beets. The Purgatoire River, running 150 miles from the Culebra Range to the Arkansas River, is a river of history and character. The river's original name, *El Rio de las Animas Perdidas en Purgatorio* (the River of the Lost Souls in Purgatory), was shortened by Anglos to Purgatoire River and given a French spelling. Cowboys mangled it to "Picketwire." The river, after passing Trinidad, hastens through lonely red rock Purgatoire Canyon east of the drive.

Above the river, US 350 intersects US 160, and 5 miles later enters 6,025-foot-high **Trinidad.** The road bends through the town's old downtown before ending at I-25. The summit of Raton Pass and the New Mexico state line lie 13 miles to the south, while Walsenburg sits 37 miles to the north. The Highway of Legends Scenic Byway (see Scenic Route 4) begins on Trinidad's west side.

Trinidad, lying at the foot of Fisher's Peak, was an important Santa Fe Trail town. Founded in 1859 at the base of rough Raton Pass, the community was named *Santisima Trinidad,* or "Most Holy Trinity." Sheepherder Gabriel Gutierrez first settled here on the river's south bank, and soon other settlers drifted in. Trinidad, a favorite haunt of mountain men and desperadoes, acquired a rowdy reputation that was reinforced after the Battle of Trinidad on Christmas Day 1867. Racial friction between Anglo and Hispanic settlers escalated from a wrestling match to an all-out riot. Soldiers, called in from Fort Lyon, quelled the violence and imposed martial law. Later the town flourished when the vast coal reserves along the river to the west were mined for Pueblo's steel plant.

Much of downtown Trinidad, with its narrow, bricked streets, is preserved as **El Corazon de Trinidad National Historic District.** The **Trinidad History Museum,** a Colorado Historical Society complex that includes the **Baca House, Bloom Mansion, Santa Fe Trail Museum,** and the Historic Gardens on a city block, depicts life in pioneer Trinidad, local historical characters, and the Santa Fe Trail, including a display of covered wagons used on the trail. The Louden-Henritze Archeology Museum at Trinidad State Junior College illustrates the area's diverse archaeological resources and exhibits Native American artifacts. A replica of the **Trinchera Shelter,** a prehistoric rock shelter in eastern Las Animas County, depicts ancient life, including artifacts like yucca sandals, braided rope, grass mats, projectile points, potsherds, and bones preserved in the cave's dry sand.

2

Pawnee Pioneer Trails Scenic Drive

Ault to Sterling

General description: This 125-mile-long drive traverses the Pawnee National Grassland, passing ranch lands, abandoned homesteads, and undulating high plains.

Special attractions: Pawnee National Grassland, Pawnee Buttes, Crow Valley Recreation Area, Sterling Overland Trail Museum, wide views, photography, bird watching, hiking, mountain biking, camping.

Location: Northeastern Colorado. The drive begins in Ault, 14 miles east of Fort Collins and I-25, and ends at Sterling and I-76.

Route name and numbers: Pawnee Pioneer Trails Scenic Byway; CO 14; Weld CR 77, 120, 390, 112, 111, 107, 110, 113, 110 1/2, 115, 127, and 129; Grasslands Road 685.

Camping: Crow Valley Recreation Area, 24 miles east of Ault at Briggsdale, is the only developed campground along the drive. Primitive camping is permitted elsewhere on the grassland. Watch for high winds and flash flood areas.

Services: All services in Fort Collins, Ault, and Sterling. Limited services in Raymer.

Nearby attractions: Fort Collins, Cache la Poudre National Wild and Scenic River, Lory State Park, Roosevelt National Forest, Rocky Mountain National Park, Estes Park, Trail Ridge Road (Scenic Drive 17), Cheyenne (Wyoming), Fort Morgan Museum, Fort Vasquez State Historic Site, Centennial Village (Greeley).

The Route

Northeastern Colorado is a spare, austere landscape, a sparsely populated province of undulating hills that break into badlands, short-grass prairie that recedes to a flat eastern horizon, and trickling streams that dwindle into sand, only to reappear later in occasional muddy pools surrounded by cottonwoods. Native Americans once roamed its vastness, camping along the meager creeks and hunting vast buffalo herds. Later homesteaders tilled the dry soil but grew only loneliness and frustration.

Still, the prairie remains a refuge from today's urban sprawl and a place of exquisite beauty. Its buttes and mesa rims gleam white in summer's noonday sun; dancing heat waves shimmer across the plain, revealing rumpled sky mirages. Evening brings smoky shadows and immense, billowing thunderheads tinged pink and rose with sunset. Out here the prairie traveler develops a new appreciation for simple forms and a devoted adoration of this elemental earth of clay, sky, and wind song.

Pawnee Pioneer Trails Scenic Drive

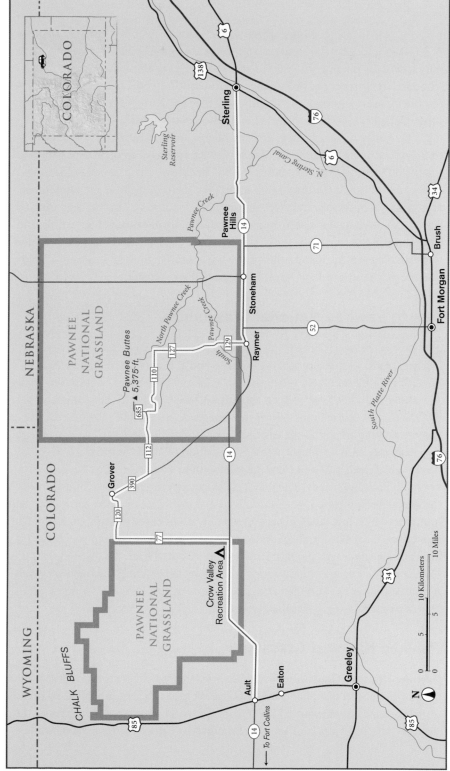

Fickle, unpredictable weather dominates along the drive. Summer days are hot, with highs ranging into the 90s and above. Heavy thunderstorms, coupled with hail, regularly occur on summer afternoons. Rain makes the drive's dirt back roads temporarily impassable, muddy, and slippery. Watch for lightning on the exposed, higher elevations such as the Pawnee Buttes Overlook and trail parking area. Autumn days, from mid-September to early November, are pleasant and warm. Winter brings snow. Severe blizzards cause deep drifts along the back roads, and melting snow closes dirt roads. Check with the grassland office for road conditions and closures. Long warm periods in midwinter melt the snow, dry the roads, and make for excellent traveling conditions. Spring, beginning by late March, is characterized by rainstorms, heavy spring snows, high winds, and warming temperatures. Much of the prairie's 12 to 15 inches of annual precipitation falls between April and June. May, with greening grass and carpets of wildflowers, makes an excellent travel time across the grassland.

Ault to Pawnee National Grassland

The Pawnee Pioneer Trails Scenic Byway, a designated Colorado Scenic Byway, begins in **Ault,** 14 miles east of Fort Collins and I-25 on CO 14. Take I-25 exit 269A for CO 14 east. Ault, established in 1888 and named for Fort Collins miller Alexander Ault, has long been an agricultural town. It is a friendly, unassuming place with neat frame homes along tree-lined side streets and tall grain silos that line the railroad tracks on the east side of town.

Ault, elevation 4,950 feet, sits at the junction of US 85 and CO 14. Scenic drivers head east on CO 14 from the intersection. The drive's first leg runs east for 24 miles to Briggsdale. The first 5 miles run across gentle farmland seamed by the sleepy meanders of Spring, Lone Tree, and Owl Creeks. Corn and wheat fields, interrupted by white farmhouses and windbreaks of cottonwoods, elms, and Russian olives, form a pastoral roadside border. After 5 miles the highway tilts up a long hillside and leaves the farmland behind. Ahead stretch tawny, rolling hills blanketed by short grass and subdivided by long fence lines. The highway bends northeast for 6 miles and then straightens eastward. At just over 13 miles, the blacktop enters Pawnee National Grassland.

Pawnee National Grassland

Pawnee National Grassland is an immense (193,060-acre) swath of prairie managed by the USDA Forest Service. This remote land was first inhabited by prehistoric big-game hunters some 11,000 years ago. Later nomadic plains tribes—the Pawnee, Apache, Arapaho, and Cheyenne Indians—traversed the plains while hunting bison. The first known European to visit the area, Don Pedro de Villasur, arrived in 1720, and French fur trappers regularly crossed it while trading with local Native Americans.

Anglo homesteaders arrived here in the late 1800s after the 1862 Homestead Act opened western lands to any able-bodied American willing to work 160-acre tracts. Early settlers plowed lands along the few perennial rivers and streams, while latecomers homesteaded the marginal dry land. The dryland farmers, initially successful, suffered after 1920 because of low wheat prices, drought, and bad farming practices. The Dust Bowl and Great Depression of the 1930s forced the mass migration of homesteaders from their 160-acre dream parcels. The federal government began buying back the damaged lands and restoring them with a semblance of their original grass cover. The recovered lands were returned to cultivation and grazing or administered as multiple-use national grasslands by the Forest Service.

The Pawnee National Grassland, divided into two large units, is a patchwork of both public and private land. A Forest Service map, detailing the different lands, is a necessity for exploring beyond the area's gridwork of county roads. Be sure you are on public land; otherwise, obtain permission from the landowner. Most of the grassland is managed for livestock grazing as well as wildlife habitat. Oil and gas deposits, tapped by producing wells, underlie the grassland, particularly at the Keota Oil Field south of Grover and north of Raymer. The US Department of Agriculture also operates the 15,600-acre Central Plains Experimental Range for research on grassland ecology, range cattle nutrition, and the use of fertilizers and herbicides.

After entering the grassland, CO 14 rolls east, dipping through dry arroyos walled with clay. Wind-driven tumbleweeds stack against barbed-wire fences, lonely windmills rise against the sky, and elms shade the occasional ranch house. The road drops into broad Crow Valley and reaches Briggsdale, an almost deserted town of a half dozen streets south of the highway. Frank Briggs, a local real estate man and farmer, platted the townsite in 1909. **The Briggsdale Museum,** housed in the old schoolhouse, depicts the area's homestead history.

Briggsdale's claim to fame is the Briggsdale Meteorite, a 5-pound hunk of outer space junk that originated in the Asteroid Belt between Mars and Jupiter about 4.6 billion years ago. The meteorite was found by a farmer in the 1940s near Briggsdale and then donated to the Denver Museum of Nature and Science by Robert Heath from Fort Collins in 1948. The rock was later sliced like a bread loaf and sections doled out to various museums, including the British Museum of Natural History. Most of the 87 meteorites discovered in Colorado were found by farmers plowing fields on the eastern plains.

Crow Valley to Grover

The drive turns north at Briggsdale on paved CR 77. **Crow Valley Recreation Area,** the only developed camp and picnic ground along the drive, sits 0.2 mile up CR 77. Shady campsites are scattered among cottonwoods and elms. The area also offers restrooms, water, a ball field, and a group picnic area. The campground makes an excellent base to explore the surrounding grasslands on foot and mountain bike. An auto birding tour route threads along Crow Creek in the shallow valley. The **Lee and Dorothy Rhodes Farm Implement Museum** is a fenced display of antique farm machinery, including various plows and a windmill, on the grounds of the recreation area.

Pawnee National Grassland, sitting on the edge of the Central Flyway, offers excellent birding opportunities, particularly in May and June when numerous migrant species nest in the varied habitats. Noted ornithologist Roger Tory Peterson called the grassland his favorite Colorado birding area. More than 225 species, including golden eagle, horned lark, black-billed magpie, western meadowlark, American goldfinch, burrowing owl, and the lark bunting, Colorado's state bird, live on the area's grassy plains, sandstone cliffs, moist creek bottoms, and wooded draws. Grassland mammals also thrive here. Common species are pronghorn and mule deer, coyote, badger, prairie dog, and jackrabbit. Hikers should watch for rattlesnakes. They commonly inhabit dry, rocky slopes on buttes and mesas, often sunning on ledges and boulders.

The narrow road runs due north up the edge of shallow Crow Valley. Ancient cottonwoods line the creek bed, and ranches and farms scatter across the rolling hills. The snow-capped Front Range rims the western horizon with sculpted peaks. Flat-topped Longs Peak, the 14,259-foot high point of Rocky Mountain National Park, looms in the southwest sky. After 10 miles a low-browed escarpment of sandy cliffs fringed by green forest etches the eastern valley rim. The road passes an abandoned farm, its weather-beaten house and barn now the haunt of owls and lizards. An upturned, rusted refrigerator lies on the ground amid elms and tall grass.

The drive turns east on paved CR 120 15 miles north of Briggsdale and passes an empty two-story house surrounded by junked cars and a plowed field. CR 120 bends north and east past farmland in broad Crow Valley, and 7 miles later rolls into Grover, "Home of the Pawnee Jackrabbit."

Grover to the Pawnee Buttes

Shady gravel streets fill **Grover,** an off-the-beaten-track village. The small **Grover Depot Museum** in the old railroad station houses displays of local artifacts and grassland ecology. Grover, platted in 1888, was a stop along the Burlington Railroad from 1887 to 1973. Women took over the mayor's office and town council in 1929 to control gambling and bootlegging. Since 1923, Grover has hosted an annual rodeo, now called the **Earl Anderson Memorial Rodeo,** on Father's Day weekend. The event, dubbed the "Biggest Little Rodeo in the West," is one of the smallest rodeos sanctioned by the Professional Rodeo Cowboy Association and attracts top cowboy competitors. The weekend includes a parade on Main Street, Rodeo Dance in the Community Building, and a pancake breakfast at the Fire Hall.

On the far eastern edge of Grover, CR 120 dead-ends into CR 390. Turn right, or southeast, on this gravel road. The drive assumes a new character for the next 40 miles to Raymer, threading eccentrically along numerous dirt roads that crisscross the prairie. Keep a careful eye on the road signs and you'll stay on the drive route. If you blunder off, however, it's hard to get lost. Almost all the roads run north and south or east and west, eventually intersecting some major road.

CR 390 runs southeast alongside the abandoned Chicago, Burlington & Quincy Railroad right-of-way. The railway, originally a branch line between Cheyenne, Wyoming, and Sterling, came through in the late 1880s. During the halcyon days before World War I and the Dust Bowl, the towns and homesteaders along the track flourished with the railroad. Grover and neighboring Keota to the south offered daily passenger service, and the railroad shipped area grain to market. Locals even planned to chisel a new county called Pawnee out of eastern Weld County in 1912, but Grover and Keota argued so bitterly over which would be the county seat that the entire proposal was scrapped. Oil wells, part of the Keota Oil Field, dot grass fields along the road. A wall of tumbled bluffs, the edge of an eroded upland called the High Plains Escarpment, looms to the east.

Just past a low hill 6 miles southeast of Grover, the road intersects CR 112. Turn east on CR 112. The road, passing a ranch, twists through dry hills. After 2 miles it climbs onto a broad ridge studded with prickly pear cacti and yucca. **Sligo Cemetery** sits atop the rounded shoulder. Numerous pioneer graves dating from the early 1900s spread over this lovely hillock. Mostly young children and toddlers make up the cemetery's residents. Nameless plastic markers from Adamson Mortuary designate their remote graves. A purple cloth rose, torn and tattered by the ceaseless wind, lies half-buried in dust beside one faded plaque.

The road dips east from the cemetery ridge and enters the southern edge of a broad valley. Cliffs and deep ravines fringed with juniper stretch along its flat-topped rim. The valley narrows as the road runs east. Five miles from the graveyard, CR 112 intersects CR 107. Jog south and east on CR 107 over steep hills. After almost 2 miles the road intersects Grasslands Road 685. This marked route heads north onto a wide, rolling ridge for 1.5 miles to the **Pawnee Buttes Trailhead.**

An abandoned grain elevator recalls Grover's heyday as an agricultural hub in the early 20th century.

An excellent picnic area with restrooms and shaded tables is at the trailhead. An overlook, another 0.5 mile farther north, yields one of eastern Colorado's most dramatic views.

The Pawnee Buttes to Raymer

The twin monolithic **Pawnee Buttes,** forming distinctive landmarks, rise out of North Pawnee Creek's broad, grass-filled valley. James Michener renamed them the Rattlesnake Buttes in his Colorado-based novel *Centennial* and called them the "two sentinels of the plains." Sandstone deposited on an ancient seafloor some 125 million years ago forms the horizontal layers on the 300-foot-high twin buttes. Over the last 10 million years, wind and water erosion attacked soft sediments between the overlook's rimrock pedestal and the buttes a mile to the east, chiseling these towering monuments from the soft rock. The Arikaree Formation, a layer of sandstone and conglomerate, makes an erosion-resistant cap atop the softer clay-like Brule Formation beneath.

The area surrounding the buttes and overlook is a well-known fossil locale. As early as 1871 paleontologists came to dig fossilized mammal skeletons dating from Miocene and Oligocene times, some 30 million years ago, in the area's deep arroyos and steep mesa slopes. The fossils here, similar to those in South Dakota's Badlands, include small hooved animals, giant megafaunas such as the rhinoceros-like *Titanothere* and the clawed horselike mammal *Chalicothere,* other ancestral horses, and turtles. The **Denver Museum of Nature and Science** displays several mammal skeletons found here.

The Pawnee Buttes Trail, winding 1.5 miles down from the trailhead to the base of the 5,325-foot West Pawnee Butte, offers an excellent introduction to the grassland ecology. While most of the short-grass prairie was altered by decades of overgrazing, much has returned and resembles the historic grassland that was once the hunting ground of the Pawnee tribe. Blue grama and buffalo grasses dominate the dry prairie, while taller grasses still flourish in moist ravines unreached by grazing cattle. Prickly pear cacti scatter in clumps along the trail, and junipers cloak rocky hillsides. A stand of limber pines, probably a relic from wetter, glacial times, grows in Dave's Draw west of the buttes. The trail makes a good mountain bike excursion, although it's all uphill coming back.

The trail continues past the west butte to 5,375-foot East Pawnee Butte, which is climbed by a short scrambling route up rotten rock slopes on its east side. West Pawnee Butte is surprisingly one of Colorado's more difficult technical peaks to climb, with its only route ascending a vertical mud wall on its north side with aid-climbing techniques.

The drive returns west from the picnic area and trailhead to CR 112, which immediately bends south on CR 111. The byway jogs around for the next few miles, following a single road that changes numbers almost every mile. After a mile, turn east on CR 110 for another mile, north on CR 113, and then east on CR 110 1/2 for a mile. Turn south on CR 115 and after 0.5 mile east again on CR 110. The drive runs straight east, skirting rolling hills and dropping across dry swales. The Pawnee Buttes play hide-and-seek behind a broken bluff to the north for a few miles before the road breaks into the open on a broad valley edge.

CR 110 dead-ends into CR 127 a few miles later. An abandoned homestead, surrounded by gangly elms, sits on the lonely corner. The drive turns south on CR 127. The dirt road sweeps over the undulating landscape, dipping through Igo Creek's valley and climbing over sandstone rimrock. Scattered oil wells and windmills fringe the hillsides, and the buttes poke above the northwestern horizon. Thick grass and shallow pools of water fill South Pawnee Creek's lush valley before the track ascends a rise and reaches Raymer and CO 14.

Raymer to Sterling

Raymer is another one of those old homestead supply towns that prospered at the turn of the 20th century. The town, platted by the Lincoln Land Company, was named for Burlington Railroad engineer George Raymer. The USPS post office and zip code directory call it New Raymer to avoid confusion with Ramah to the south, while the state highway map still calls it Raymer.

The drive turns east on paved CO 14 and traverses open grasslands and fenced farm fields. **Stoneham,** an 1888 railroad town, lies 11 miles from Raymer. Grain elevators, two churches, and a few houses mark this roadside hamlet. The drive leaves the Pawnee National Grassland almost 5 miles east of Stoneham and climbs over a low broken mesa called the **Pawnee Hills.** The road descends sharply through littered sandstone blocks to the broad Pawnee Valley. The sandy creek bed, lined with cottonwoods, winds southeast to the South Platte River. After gently climbing out of the valley, the highway enters farm fields irrigated by Platte water. Fields of corn and bright sunflowers border the blacktop.

The road tilts downward, crosses the North Sterling Canal, and enters the 3,935-foot-high town of **Sterling.** This pleasant town, on the fertile South Platte River floodplain, is an agricultural hub. The town started as a post office on rancher David Leavitt's property in 1872. He named it for his Illinois hometown. Sterling grew quickly a few years later after the Union Pacific Railroad pushed through to Denver. The **Overland Trail Museum,** just east of town by I-76, is a worthwhile stop. The museum interprets the trail's colorful history and displays artifacts such as branding irons, horse-drawn farm machinery, and a stone duplicate of old Fort Sedgewick, a U.S. military outpost from 1864 to 1871. The drive ends in Sterling. Continue east from the town over the river to exit 125 on I-76.

3

Comanche Grasslands Scenic Drive

Trinidad to Springfield Loop

General description: This 192-mile-long drive explores the Comanche National Grassland and the scenic prairie and mesa country between Trinidad and Springfield.

Special attractions: Comanche National Grassland, Picture Canyon, Carrizo Canyon Picnic Area, Mesa de Maya, short-grass prairie ecosystems, Native American rock art sites, birding, wildlife observation, hiking, camping, mountain biking.

Location: Southeastern Colorado. The drive begins just east of Trinidad and I-25 at the junction of US 350 and US 160, and heads east on US 160 to Springfield. It turns south on US 287/385 to Campo and heads west on a series of gravel county and grassland roads back to Kim and US 160.

Route numbers: US 160 and US 287/385; Baca CR J, 13, M, 8, P, 3, and Q; and Las Animas CR 30.0, 211, 34.0, and 36.0.

Travel season: Year-round. The drive's gravel back roads between Campo and Kim can become impassable after heavy summer thunderstorms and when winter snow melts. Watch for thick mud and slippery roads. Inquire at the Springfield USDA Forest Service office for current road conditions.

Camping: No designated campgrounds along the drive. Limited dispersed camping is permitted, however, at the parking areas at Withers Canyon Trailhead, Picketwire Corrals, and Carrizo Creek, Timpas, Vogel Canyon, and Picture Canyon picnic areas.

Services: All services are in Trinidad and Springfield. Limited services are in Kim and Campo.

Nearby attractions: El Corazon de Trinidad National Historic District, Trinidad State Park, San Isabel National Forest, Spanish Peaks, Santa Fe Trail, Purgatoire Canyon, El Capulin National Monument (New Mexico), Bent's Old Fort National Historic Site.

The Route

The undulating plains stretch eastward across southeastern Colorado from the bold, snowy escarpment of the Culebra Range. The swelling land rolls with a lean musculature, lifting into rounded hills and low-browed mesas or breaking into sharp arroyos and sinuous hidden canyons. Out there on the tawny prairie lies the land of the flattened horizon, the land of the rising sun. It's a minimalist landscape. Everything is spare and lean, stripped of its veneer and laid bare under the blazing sun. Brittle grasses huddle in windswept clumps, prickly pear cacti clench together like tightly closed fists, and cottonwoods rustle along intermittent creeks. Under the yawning sprawl of sky and space, the prairie is reduced to simple forms—straight-arrow horizons, roads bordered by three strands of barbed wire

Comanche Grasslands Scenic Drive

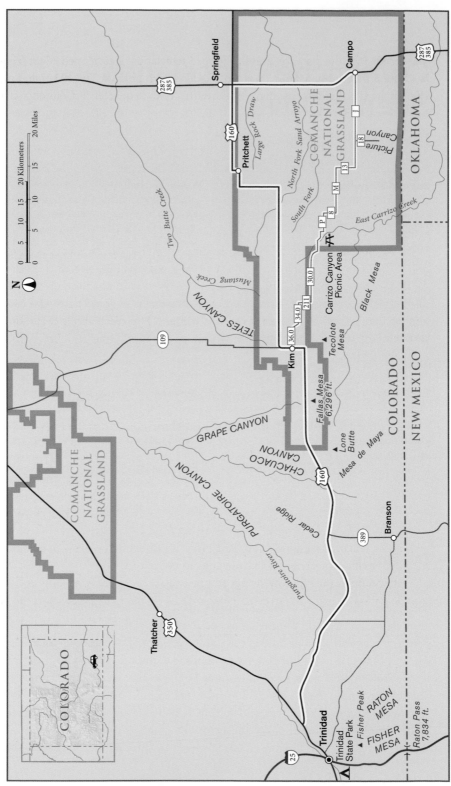

COLORADO

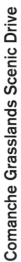

that recede into the distance, and flat-topped tablelands, their sloped edges fringed in juniper, that bump against the azure sky like worn pillows. The 192-mile-long Comanche Grassland scenic drive explores this remote quarter of Colorado, crossing sun-baked prairie, dipping through shallow canyons, and finding its secret places.

Southeastern Colorado is an arid land, with chilly winters and hot summers. Annual precipitation is low, bordering on desert amounts in some areas. The Springfield area receives 15 inches of rain annually. Much of the precipitation comes in intense summer thunderstorms, with the swift runoff flooding down arroyos and canyons. Gravel back roads on the drive during or after thunderstorms can become muddy and impassable. Summers are hot. Expect daily highs in the 90s and above. Autumn and spring are more reasonable times to drive the roads. Temperatures range between 60 and 90 degrees. Wind often tempers spring days. Winters are cold and dry, with occasional heavy snowstorms that quickly melt. High temperatures range from 30 to 60 degrees with cold nights. Use caution when driving the gravel back roads in winter. Blizzard conditions arise during swift-moving storms, and melting snow and ice can turn gravel and dirt roads into impassable mud.

The Purgatoire to Comanche National Grassland

The drive begins 5 miles east of Trinidad at Beshoar Junction at the intersection of US 350 and US 160. Turn east on US 160. Springfield, the end of the drive's first leg, lies 114 miles away. The vanished town of Beshoar, named for an early Trinidad resident, sat here along the Colorado & Southern Railroad at the end of the 19th century. The paved highway runs east through low hills. Occasional pastures, hay fields, and ranch houses border the blacktop. Fishers Peak and **Raton Mesa,** dark with evergreen forest, form a broad escarpment to the south. This long, high mesa, reaching a high point of 9,627 feet, is capped by 11 layers of erosion-resistant basalt, deposited as lava from ancient volcanoes.

After 6 miles the highway swings southeast past the Mooney Hills, a low, rounded mesa etched with arroyos. Three miles later the road sweeps past the hills and across a broad basin seamed with Frijole Creek, an intermittent stream arising on the mesa flank to the south. Mesa de Maya huddles darkly on the eastern horizon.

The road winds over Frijole Creek, a tamarisk-lined thread of muddy water in a brown clay arroyo, and parallels the **Purgatoire River** for a few miles. The 196-mile-long Purgatoire River, beginning at the confluence of its North and Middle forks near Weston, courses across southeastern Colorado from snowmelt-fed creeks high on the crest of the Culebra Range west of Trinidad. The river keeps

The scenic drive, following US 160, runs east from Trinidad and the lofty Culebra Range.

the French spelling of its name, a reminder of the itinerant fur trappers that traversed this wild country in the 19th century. The river's original name—*El Rio de las Animas Perdidas en Purgatorio* (The River of the Lost Souls in Purgatory)—was acquired after the members of a 16th-century Spanish expedition, murdered by Native Americans on the riverbank, died without the last rites of their Catholic faith. Cowboys later corrupted the Spanish to "Picketwire," a name applied to part of the river's 40-mile-long canyon that slices across the prairie north of the drive. The river empties into the Arkansas River near Las Animas to the northeast.

The river twists through low hills, passing occasional cottonwoods on its banks, a half mile north of the highway. After a couple miles the river bends northeast and enters Purgatoire Canyon through abrupt portals of Dakota sandstone. A piñon pine and juniper woodland fills the canyon and spills onto the rim.

The highway ascends a gradual rise onto a broad, barren plain. It dips across Salt Creek's shallow valley at 19 miles, passing black sandstone boulders mirrored in pools of clear water. Trinchera Creek, draining north to the Purgatoire like the other creeks here, lies a couple of miles farther east; it's a deep canyon sharp with cliffs and coated by sparsely spaced junipers. The road climbs northeast onto a high tableland, with expansive views back west to the long ridge of the Culebra Range and the twin Spanish Peaks to the northwest. After crossing Trementina Creek, another canyon filled with cliffs, water, and thick grass, the highway ascends through a juniper forest and reaches its junction with CO 389 at a place dubbed Walt's Corner. A classic store, now a gallery surrounded by marvelous views and a few trees, sits at this lonely intersection on a rolling grass plain. The wooden front porch has a pay phone, bench, and soda machine that says: "Refreshing Ice Cold Drinks." A right turn on route 389 leads due south to Branson by the New Mexico border.

The dark bulk of **Mesa de Maya** dominates the highway view as it runs east. Cliffs of basalt deposited as lava flows cap the high flat-topped mesa, and a forest of juniper and piñon pine spills over its ragged flanks. No roads traverse this mostly wild upland, the home of mule deer, coyotes, and range cattle. Early Native Americans inhabited the mesa and the canyons along the drive beginning some 6,000 years ago. Traces of their passage include rock art panels pecked onto smooth rock slabs, projectile points and stone tools, broken pottery shards, and manos used for grinding seeds. Meadows of tall buffalo and grama grass blanketed the mesa top and its shallow valleys more than 100 years ago, attracting cattlemen to its lush pastures in this land of little rain in the 1870s.

The highway runs over undulating plains before dropping into abrupt Chacuaco Canyon. Chacuaco Creek, rising from mesas on the New Mexico state line to the south, excavated this long cliff-lined gorge. Water trickles through the wild canyon almost all year, creating a haven for mammals and birds.

The asphalt climbs out of the canyon onto another dry plain and arches northeast around Mesa de Maya. The road dips through several dry, rocky canyons that drain north from the mesa. A ghost village of abandoned stone houses sits on a canyon rim below the mesa, cattle poking through their empty rooms. Distant views unfold west from here. Rows of mountains—the Culebra Range, Spanish Peaks, Raton Mesa, Sierra Blanca, and the Wet Mountains—parade across the horizon, their snow-capped summits gleaming in the sun like whitewashed castles.

Comanche National Grassland

The highway enters the **Comanche National Grassland,** a sprawling spread of 443,081 acres managed by the USDA Forest Service and divided into the Timpas Unit south of La Junta (see Scenic Route 1) and the Carrizo Unit along this scenic drive. The story of the national grassland began in 1884 when Baca County's first homestead patent was granted. Thousands of homestead patents in southeast Colorado were issued from 1884 to 1926, with the homesteaders required to plow 40 acres of each 160-acre homestead. The homesteader's plow, along with farming marginal agricultural lands and severe overgrazing in this semiarid region, caused the Dust Bowl of the early 1930s here and in neighboring states, including

Oklahoma and Texas. The federal government began buying back damaged farms and ranches, retiring the land from cultivation and allowing families to relocate in other areas. More than 11 million acres were acquired and rehabilitated, with 4 million acres designated as national grassland in 1960 and assigned to the Forest Service. Crumbling stone homesteads, abandoned windmills, and empty cross-roads stores are all that remain of Colorado's homestead era on today's Comanche Grassland.

The highway bends straight east after entering the grassland. The ruins of **Tobe** sit in the field to the north. The town, established in 1910 and named for resident Tobe Benavides, was more of a post office than a town. When the filling station/post office closed its doors in 1960, Tobe folded. The only remnants now are stone foundations scattered among grass and cacti.

The long, low rim of Mesa de Maya looms south of the road as it runs due east across a featureless plain coated with short grasses. Six miles from Tobe the drive passes 6,296-foot-high **Fallas Mesa,** a barren escarpment riddled with ravines. Dalerose Mesa, broken by canyons and cliffs, lies farther south, while broad Tecolote Mesa sits to the southeast. The drive turns north at 65 miles and enters Kim a mile later.

Kim to Springfield

Kim, named for Rudyard Kipling's orphan boy hero, was established in 1918 by Olin D. Simpson when he built a general store and post office on the corner of his homestead. The 5,690-foot-high town now serves as a ranching and agricultural center. Frame houses line neat side streets, cattle graze on the edge of town, and a cemetery makes a final resting place. The town offers an RV park, gas, groceries, and the Kim Outpost, the town's only café. Try one of their cowboy burgers and fries and chat with local ranchers. Picnic tables sit in a roadside park.

The drive continues north along US 160 and swings east after a couple of miles. CO 109 intersects the drive here and continues north to La Junta. US 160 travels 50 miles from here to Springfield, passing over a mixture of federal and private land. This is flat, dry country, broken by fences and occasional irrigated fields.

Pritchett, the only real town along this section, sits 36 miles east of Kim. The town rises out of the plain like a mirage, its skyline of trees and housetops dominated by three towering grain elevators. Boarded-up shops line the main street, a reminder of more prosperous times. The town, established in 1920, marked the western end of an Atchison, Topeka & Santa Fe Railroad branch. It was named for railway director Dr. Henry Pritchett. The highway goes east from Pritchett past farms and ranches and reaches US 287/385 14 miles later. A roadside picnic area and a truck stop sit at the junction.

Springfield lies a mile to the north, looming as Pritchett, above the endless sweep of the prairie. Grain elevators form the highest point for miles around. Elms, maples, and cottonwoods shade the town streets. Springfield, the seat of Baca County, was established in 1887 by the Windsor Town Company and named for townsite owner Andrew Harrison's hometown of Springfield, Missouri. The town has since flourished as an agricultural hub. A Forest Service office, lying just north of the highway intersection, dispenses information and directions to points of interest on the Comanche Grassland. Also, check out the Springfield Museum with a large collection of area newspapers dating to the late 1800s and artifacts and history of Baca County.

Springfield to Campo

The journey's next leg runs south 20 miles from Springfield to Campo on US 287/385. The road crosses a high plain divided into farms and ranches. A clutch of houses huddles along the highway in Campo, an old farming community aptly named with the Spanish word for "field." Campo lies 9 miles north of the Oklahoma border. The town flourished in the 1920s, with the First State Bank, gas station, rooming house, a café, a couple drilling rigs, and *The Campo Enterprise,* a weekly newspaper. Campo's barber shop was run by Mr. Warlick, who walked 7 miles from his home west of town every other Saturday to give shaves for a dime and haircuts for 15 cents. Later the town had a roller skating rink, grocery store, and, in 1951, the Gem Theater, which burned down 3 years later.

For the drive's last leg, turn west on 4th Street/Baca CR J at the Campo Café, the town's only restaurant. The road turns to gravel after it bumps across railroad tracks and passes a grain elevator. The drive's last 53 miles follow numerous gravel back roads over the Comanche National Grassland back to Kim and US 160. The dusty road courses west past farms, fields, pastures, cattle, and windmills. Baca CR 18 intersects CR J after 10 miles. Turn south for a side trip to Picture Canyon, one of southeastern Colorado's hidden treasures.

Picture Canyon

Follow CR 18 south for 5 miles and turn right down a marked lane into upper Picture Canyon. The road twists down the broad canyon and after a couple of miles reaches the road's end. A picnic area with three tables spreads along the base of tall sandstone cliffs. A 2.6-mile hiking trail, following an old road, drops down into the canyon.

Ragged cliffs, forming abrupt canyon walls, are broken by side ravines and eroded into promontories, buttresses, and arêtes. After 0.5 mile the canyon makes a sharp bend west. Pools of water surrounded by tall grass and cottonwoods spread along the creek bed. A couple of panels of Native American petroglyphs, marred by modern vandalism, sit along the shaded cliff base.

The Picture Canyon trail continues north up a side canyon, scales its slope onto a low mesa, and heads west to a spur of Holt Canyon and a natural arch. The trail wends east and drops through Hell's Half Acre back to Picture Canyon. Watch for rattlesnakes in the grass and on the rocky canyon sides when hiking during the warmer months.

Picture Canyon, along with other southeast Colorado canyons, has long attracted settlers. Early Native Americans found shelter in shallow caves, harvested the area's diverse plants, and hunted game. Native American campsites from the Late Archaic period (AD 1–500) scatter under the canyon's overhanging shelters. Later inhabitants, the Apishapa culture, lived here after AD 1000, planting crops on the moist canyon floor and building small villages atop the canyon rims. The rock art that gave the canyon its name probably came from nomadic plains tribes like the Apaches and Comanches.

An interesting archeological site in Picture Canyon is **Crack Cave,** a single, narrow, 15-foot-long passage in a sandstone cliff. In 1976 a hiker discovered that the rising sun on both the spring and autumn equinoxes illuminates the passageway with a shaft of land that lands directly on a hump on the north wall that is inscribed with runic lines. Later Bill McGlone, a rock art enthusiast from La Junta, translated the lines using ogam; they read "The sun strikes on a certain day, Bel" and "People of the Sun." Bel is traced back as the ancient Celtic sun god, celebrated at Beltane on the summer solstice, but also revered by the ancient Babylonians. The cave is now gated and only opened for viewings at the equinoxes.

Clues to this puzzling mystery of Colorado archeology are also found on the canyon's west side, south of a bend. Here, etched onto the soft sandstone wall, are a series of vertical lines incised into the rock. Some ancient-language scholars say the lines are ogam (also spelled ogham), a type of Celtic writing used as long ago as 2000 BC in the British Isles. This strange writing is found at more than 50 sites in southeastern Colorado and the Oklahoma panhandle. Some of the translated writings include compasses, sundials, traveler's messages, directions, and information about the area's latitude, equinoxes, and planting seasons.

One theory holds that Irish monks traveled to Iceland, eastern Canada, and even Mexico over a thousand years ago, lending some credence to the idea that early Celtic wanderers roamed this area. Most archaeologists, however, are skeptical about the Celtic influence, saying not enough evidence exists to substantiate

Sandstone hoodoos and cliff bands line the rim of remote Picture Canyon near the Oklahoma border.

the theory. And so the ogam writings in southeastern Colorado remain a tantalizing, unsolved mystery.

Carrizo Mesa to Kim

Head back north on CR 18 to Baca CR J and continue west on it. The rest of the drive crosses grassland, broken by shallow ravines, windmills, and occasional cottonwood-lined watercourses. After 5 miles turn north on CR 13 and at 3 miles turn west on Baca CR M. This runs west 5 miles to Baca CR 8. At this lonely intersection sits the old Kirkwell Post Office, now used for storage by the Kirkwell Cattle Company. The post office operated from 1917 to 1921.

Turn north on CR 8 and after a couple of miles, head west on Baca CR P. **Carrizo Mesa,** a low-slung tableland rimmed by shattered basalt cliffs, sits to the west. Canyons dark with junipers and piñon pine slice into the mesa, and Potato Butte forms a sharp summit atop the flat mesa. Baca CR P dead-ends at Baca CR 3 above Carrizo Creek. Turn north on CR 3 for 0.5 mile and then west on Baca CR Q.

CR Q twists over a low ridge and dips down alongside Carrizo Creek in a wide valley. Rounded hills studded with juniper and cliff bands line the creek. Immense cottonwoods shade the trickle of water. Cottonwoods are the tree of the plains. These tall, broad-trunked trees, growing along creeks, signified water, shade, and firewood to early pioneers and Native Americans. Native American children made toy tepees with the wide triangular leaves, and the sweet inner bark was used as winter horse feed. Cottonwood bark also had medicinal uses, particularly for upset stomach from bad water—an occupational hazard that cowboys called the "gypwater quickstep." Nineteenth-century cattle baron Charles Goodnight, whose Hereford empire stretched into southeastern Colorado, called the bark tea "a hell of a drink, a wonderful astringent, and a bitter dose. But it is a sure shot."

The drive wends up along the creek's arroyo and passes a ranch house and barn shaded by huge cottonwood trees. The road bends northwest, edging along below Carrizo Mesa. It becomes a single-lane track for a couple of miles before joining improved Las Animas CR 30.0. This narrow road rolls west from the mesa over prairie toward Tecolote Mesa. This mesa, also rimmed with cliffs, stretches darkly on the western horizon. CR 30.0 ends and bends north on Las Animas CR 211. The drive jogs north and west for 10 miles, following CR 211 past Pintada Creek's bouldery valley and over broad dry ridges to Kim. The drive ends back on US 160 at Kim's cemetery. A left turn heads 65 miles back to Trinidad and I-25, while a right turn goes to Springfield via US 160 or La Junta on CO 109.

4

Highway of Legends Scenic Byway

Walsenburg to Trinidad

General description: The Highway of Legends Scenic Byway forms a 117-mile-long open loop between Walsenburg and Trinidad on the eastern slope of the Culebra Range.

Special attractions: Lathrop State Park, La Veta, Francisco Fort Museum, Great Dikes of the Spanish Peaks, Spanish Peaks Wilderness Area, Cucharas Pass, Culebra Range, Cordova Pass, Monument Lake, Stonewall, Picketwire Valley, Cokedale National Historic District, Trinidad Lake State Park, Trinidad historic sites, camping, fishing, hiking, scenic views.

Location: South-central Colorado. The drive begins in Walsenburg, off I-25, and runs west on US 160 and south on CO 12 to La Veta. The byway continues on CO 12 to Trinidad and I-25. A spur road goes over Cordova Pass to Aguilar.

Route name and numbers: Highway of Legends Scenic Byway, US 160, CO 12, FR 415.

Travel season: Year-round.

Camping: Four San Isabel National Forest campgrounds—Cucharas, Blue Lake, Bear Lake, and Purgatoire—lie off the drive. Others are Lathrop State Park (103-sites) Trinidad Lake State Park's Carpios Ridge and South Shore Campgrounds (73 sites). The Monument Lake Resort, owned by the city of Trinidad, has a campground, rooms, and cabins.

Services: All services are in Walsenburg, La Veta, and Trinidad. Limited services are in Stonewall and Cuchara.

Nearby attractions: Santa Fe Trail Scenic Byway (Scenic Drive 1), Wet Mountain Valley, Comanche National Grassland, Capulin National Monument, San Luis Valley, Great Sand Dunes National Park, Wet Mountains (Scenic Drive 7), Graneros Gorge.

The Route

The 117-mile-long Highway of Legends Scenic Byway skirts the wooded eastern flank of the Culebra Range in southern Colorado. The twisting crest of the Culebras imposes a lofty barrier between the sweep of prairie to the east and the San Luis Valley, a broad intermontane basin, to the west. The range, even still untraversed by any roads, is mostly private land, the remaining legacy of sprawling early Spanish land grants. The area's numerous Spanish place-names also linger on the land. *Culebra,* the Spanish word for "snake," was first applied to a creek on the range's western slope and later given to the mountain range.

The scenic drive, beginning in Walsenburg, ascends the fertile Cuchara Valley to the 9,941-foot summit of Cucharas Pass before dropping south through forests

Highway of Legends Scenic Byway

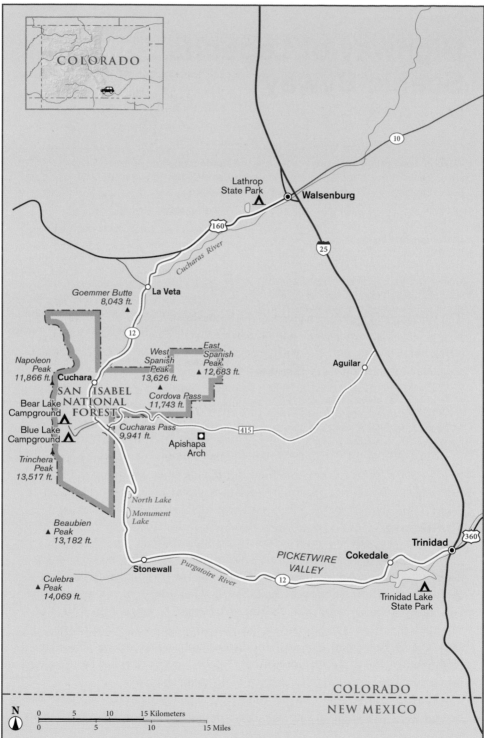

COLORADO

Lathrop State Park

Walsenburg

10

160

25

Cucharas River

Goemmer Butte 8,043 ft.

La Veta

12

West Spanish Peak 13,626 ft.

East Spanish Peak 12,683 ft.

Aguilar

Napoleon Peak 11,866 ft.

Cuchara

SAN ISABEL NATIONAL FOREST

Cordova Pass 11,743 ft.

Bear Lake Campground

Blue Lake Campground

Cucharas Pass 9,941 ft.

415

Apishapa Arch

Trinchera Peak 13,517 ft.

North Lake

Monument Lake

Beaubien Peak 13,182 ft.

PICKETWIRE VALLEY

Cokedale

Trinidad

360

Culebra Peak 14,069 ft.

Stonewall

Purgatoire River

12

Trinidad Lake State Park

COLORADO

NEW MEXICO

N

| 0 | 5 | 10 | 15 Kilometers |
| 0 | 5 | 10 | 15 Miles |

and meadows on the range flank to the Purgatoire River's broad valley west of Trinidad. A spur segment of the drive travels over Cordova Pass to Aguilar.

The highway is open year-round, with each season lending a distinctive flavor to the drive experience. Summers are pleasant, with high temperatures ranging from 70 to 90 degrees along the drive. Afternoon thunderstorms regularly build above the mountains, dousing the road with rain and hail. September and October, the autumn months, bring warm days and cool nights. Expect golden aspen groves in late September and occasional rain showers through October. Temperatures can be hot on the drive's lower elevations. Winter days are chilly, with highs in the 30s and 40s. Snow falls heavily in the upper Cuchara Valley and on the pass. The lesser amounts in the low valleys quickly melt under the warm winter sun. Spring begins in April with warming days and melting snow. Look for breezy afternoons and rain or sleet storms.

Walsenburg & Lathrop State Park

The Highway of Legends, a national forest scenic byway, begins in **Walsenburg** just off I-25. The town nestles in the Cucharas River's broad valley amid dusty, piñon pine-covered hills. Walsenburg began in 1859 as an early Mexican hamlet, named *La Plaza de los Leones* (The Square of the Lions) for prominent early settler Don Miguel Antonio Leon. When the pueblo incorporated in 1873, citizens renamed it for local shopkeeper Fred Walsen. After the Denver & Rio Grande Railroad pushed through in 1876, Walsenburg boomed as one of Colorado's largest coal producers. The remains of over 50 mines still litter the area. Town points of interest include the historic Huerfano County Courthouse, built with limestone blocks in 1904, and the nearby **Walsenburg Mining Museum,** with exhibits detailing the coal miner's life and the replica of a mine shaft. The museum, open May through September, is housed in a historic jail behind the courthouse.

The drive begins in downtown Walsenburg. Head west on US 160, the Navajo Trail. After passing houses and the town park and swimming pool, the highway swings past slag heaps and abandoned mining ruins. The road crosses the Cucharas River, climbs a steep hill, and after 3 miles reaches **Lathrop State Park.** This small state park, with 1,594 land acres and 320 water acres in Martin and Horseshoe Lakes, offers 103 sites in Piñon and Yucca Campgrounds, picnic facilities, a nine-hole golf course leased to Walsenburg, boating, swimming, and fishing. The lakes yield trout, crappie, bass, channel catfish, and perch to anglers. Lathrop has a couple of good hikes. The handicap-accessible Cuerno Verde Trail makes a 3-mile loop hike, while the Hogback Trail loops north from Martin Lake for almost 2 miles, climbing onto a scrubby volcanic hogback. Gnarled junipers spring from the bedrock amid barrel cacti, yucca, and rabbitbrush. Distant views unfold along the ridgeline: Pikes Peak, almost 100 miles to the north, lifts its broad shoulders beyond the Wet Mountains, the barren prairie sweeps eastward to a Kansas horizon, and to the south loom the Spanish Peaks.

The highway runs west from Lathrop along the northern edge of the broad Cuchara Valley. Low hills, coated with a pygmy forest of piñon pine and juniper, flank the road on the north, while the wide valley stretches south to forested foothills below the Spanish Peaks. Open rangelands, broken only by fence lines and a twisting grove of cottonwoods along the river banks, fill the valley floor. Perennial blue grama and needle-and-thread grasses sod the spacious pastures, while shrubby saltbush, snakeweed, and rabbitbrush cover the drier slopes. A small roadside Catholic shrine, with a statue of the Virgin Mary and many votive candles, is tucked into a sandstone alcove at 6 miles on the north side of the highway. The drive turns southwest onto CO 12 a few miles farther west. US 160 continues west over La Veta Pass to the San Luis Valley.

The Spanish Peaks & La Veta

CO 12 follows an undulating, grassy bench sprinkled with ranches and grazing cattle above the Cucharas River. The **Spanish Peaks** continue to dominate the southern skyline. The Spanish Peaks, designated as a National Natural Landmark, are preserved in a 19,226-acre wilderness area. The higher west peak reaches 13,626 feet, while the east peak is 12,683 feet.

These jutting twin peaks were conspicuous landmarks to travelers on the Great Plains. Early explorers often confused the Spanish Peaks with Pikes Peak far to the north. Jacob Fowler noted them in 1821: "We Head a full view of the mountains, this must be the place Whare Pike first discovered the mountains, Heare I took the bareing of two that ware the Highest." Native Americans, Spaniards, French trappers, and Santa Fe Trail traders called them a host of names—Pikes Peak, Las Cumbres Españoles, Las Dos Hermanas, The Two Sisters, Les Tetons, Les Mamelles, and Wahatoyeh or Huajatolla. *Wahatoyeh,* a Pueblo Indian word still used, loosely translates as "Breasts of the World."

The wild Spanish Peaks host an improbable fable of a lost gold mine. The legend originates with Coronado's 1541 trek across southeastern Colorado in search of mythical Quivara, a gleaming city of gold. Three priests were left behind to convert the natives, and two died at their hands as martyrs. The third, Fray Juan de la Cruz, journeyed to Huajatolla after hearing of wealthy Native American mines there. According to the legend, he found the gold, enslaved Native Americans to remove it from the hidden passages, and journeyed south to Mexico with gold-laden mules. The priest and his treasure, however, disappeared, never to be seen again. Persistent rumors of the lost Spanish gold echoed across southern Colorado

The snow-capped Culebra Range looms beyond Goemmer Butte and the town of La Veta.

for the next three centuries, but no trace of the gold or the fabulous mine was ever uncovered. Indeed, no geologic evidence suggests that the Spanish Peaks or their immediate neighbors ever yielded any precious metals.

After 4 miles the blacktop drops down to the river bottomlands and a mile later enters the town of **La Veta.** This lovely village spreads among ranch land at the feet of the Spanish Peaks. The town was originally established as a trading post and fort by Colonel John Francisco and Henry Daigre in 1862. A post office opened at the site, known as Francisco Plaza, in 1871, and when the Denver & Rio Grande Railroad came through in 1876, the town of La Veta arose. The name means "the vein" in Spanish and probably refers to the numerous volcanic dikes slicing across the Spanish Peaks.

The **Francisco Fort Museum,** operated by the Huerfano County Historical Society at the original site, makes an informative stop in downtown La Veta. The museum displays coal mining equipment, an old saloon, a barbershop with poker-playing dummies, a medical office, a blacksmith shop, a collection of old carriages and wagons, and an excellent collection of historical documents and letters, including an 1853 letter by practicing attorney Abraham Lincoln and Kit Carson's will. Also at the museum is a huge, shady round-leaf cottonwood planted in 1878 by Colonel Francisco. La Veta offers a variety of visitor accommodations and several restaurants.

La Veta to Cuchara

The drive leaves La Veta on the south and runs along the Cucharas River. Goemmer Butte, an 8,043-foot-high volcanic plug or conduit of a long-extinct volcano, rears to the west. Its cliffed summit rises 500 feet above the valley floor. The road descends into the grassy valley, crosses the river at Three Bridges, and swings southwest below scrub oak–covered slopes.

Six miles from La Veta, the highway passes under **Devil's Stairsteps,** an abrupt volcanic rock dike that stair-steps south from the highway. This dike, as well as prominent Profile Rock to the east and other rock walls, is part of the Spanish Peaks' great dike system. The buff-colored igneous rock dikes formed, along with the Spanish Peaks, some 35 million years ago. During that period of geologic unrest when the Rocky Mountains began to rise, two blisters of molten rock pushed their way upward, buckling the sedimentary surface layers. As the strata bulged, long cracks radiated out from the molten blisters like spokes on a bicycle wheel. Liquid magma filled the cracks before the entire mass slowly cooled into classic volcanic rocks like the granite and granodorite that compose the Spanish Peaks. Erosion later attacked the old sedimentary layers and exposed the harder, more erosion-resistant igneous rocks, leaving the page of geologic history seen today. More than 400 separate dikes fan out from the peaks, with the longest stretching 14 miles. The dikes range up to 100 feet high and vary in width from 1 foot to 100 feet.

As the highway runs southwest, the valley slowly narrows with high ridges looming overhead. The snow-capped Culebra Range towers to the west. After a few miles, the road passes through a gap cut through the **Dakota Wall,** a sandstone hogback that stretches along the Front Range from Wyoming to New Mexico. The highway roughly follows the hogback from here to Stonewall. New Mexican locust trees, Colorado's only native locust, line the asphalt and offer colorful pink blossoms in early summer. The road enters San Isabel National Forest and a couple of miles later rolls into 8,468-foot high Cuchara.

Cuchara & Cucharas Pass

Cuchara, established in 1916, is something of a ghost town today. The village sits near the head of a spectacular valley, surrounded by thick forests of spruce, pine, and fir. This spoon-shaped valley gave the name Cuchara ("spoon" in Spanish) to the town, river, and valley. Cuchara thrived in the 1980s as a ski resort until the savings-and-loan scandal, and the ski slopes closed. Much of the town folded up with the resort, leaving only a few cafes and lodges. Vacation cabins sprinkle throughout the valley around Cuchara. Spring Creek Picnic Area and Trailhead, with 3 picnic sites and a restroom, lies on the south side of Cuchara.

The drive steadily climbs the valley south of Cuchara and after a couple of miles reaches FR 422. This short dirt road climbs west along Cucharas Creek to a pair of gorgeous forest-lined lakes cupped in a basin beneath the Culebra Range crest. At road's end are 15-site Blue Lake and 15-site Bear Lake Campgrounds beside their respective lakes. An excellent 2-mile trail climbs south from the spruce and fir forest at 10,500-foot Blue Lake to the alpine tundra atop the rounded summit of 13,517-foot Trinchera Peak. The Cucharas River begins at the confluence of Cucharas Creek and the South Fork at the junction of FR 422 and route 12.

The highway twists up steep, aspen-blanketed slopes above the South Fork of the Cucharas River and reaches 9,941-foot **Cucharas Pass.** The dense forest along this drive section yields a textbook example of plant succession. The thick transitional aspen woodland is slowly being replaced by a climax spruce-fir forest. Autumn is gorgeous along here, with dark spruce sprinkled among golden groves of quaking aspen. Meadows, ringed by dark woods, surround the highway and a stock corral on the broad pass summit. Henry Daigre, one of La Veta's founders, built a road from La Veta to Stonewall along an old Native American path in 1865. Today's highway follows his old track over the pass, but it wasn't paved until the 1960s.

The Cordova Pass Segment

A 35-mile-long extension of the Highway of Legends Scenic Byway runs east from the top of Cucharas Pass to Cordova Pass, and then down to I-25 at Aguilar. This road segment, added to the scenic byway in 2002, is a welcome addition to the Highway of Legends as an alternate route with different views and beauty than the main scenic drive.

To drive this route, head east from Cucharas Pass on FR 415. The unpaved road climbs 6 miles to the summit of 11,743-foot **Cordova Pass.** A picnic area with restrooms is located here, along with some short, easy-going trails that explore the subalpine environment. A longer trail leaves the parking area and meanders through grassy meadows and woods of lodgepole pine and Engelmann spruce on a ridge to a timberline lookout below West Spanish Peak, with views from Pikes Peak over 100 miles to the north to high plateaus in New Mexico to the south. Intrepid hikers can continue up the steep west ridge another few miles to the peak's 13,626-foot summit and its grandiose views of mountains and prairie.

The scenic byway passes through Apishapa Arch, a short tunnel piercing a volcanic dike.

Cordova Pass was named for Jose de Jesus Cordova, a prominent southern Colorado citizen in the early 20th century. Cordova, a three-term Las Animas County commissioner, pushed for funding to build a road between Cuchara and Aguilar. It was finally approved in 1928 and was finished in 1934 by the Works Progress Administration and the Civilian Conservation Corps. Cordova died in 1929 and didn't see the road completed, although it was dedicated to his memory.

From the summit, you can either return to the main scenic highway or continue east to I-25. This winding road runs another 29 miles along the Apishapa River. One of its best features is **Apishapa Arch,** an immense stone archway spanning the road that was blasted through one of the volcanic dikes that radiate from the Spanish Peaks. The lower road section twists past ranches along the willow- and cottonwood-lined river. It's especially pretty in early October when autumn's golden leaves color the stream corridor.

Cuchara to Stonewall

CO 12 runs south from the pass along the Culebra Range's eastern flank, traversing rolling hills and dipping through shallow valleys. A variety of ecosystems cover the hillsides, with mixed fir and spruce forest blanketing the moist, north-facing slopes and ponderosa and limber pines and Gambel oak covering the drier, south-facing hills. Open aspen-lined meadows break the woodland mosaic.

The road horseshoes around **North Lake,** an 840-acre state wildlife area and reservoir, 7 miles from the pass. Peaks of the Culebra Range—13,488-foot Cuatro Peak, 13,406-foot Mariquita Peak, and 13,350-foot De Anza Peak—lift snowy ridges to the west. The Dakota Hogback forms an abrupt wall above the lake and highway. North Lake, with a boat ramp at its north end, offers fishing and boating.

Just past the lake, CR 34 heads 4.5 miles west up the North Fork of the Purgatoire River to 23-site Purgatoire Campground. This pleasant camping area, with 10 tent sites, is tucked into a valley filled with spruce, corkbark fir, and quaking aspen at the foot of the Culebras.

Monument Lake lies in a shallow valley a mile farther south. A turn at the southern end of the narrow, mile-long reservoir leads to Monument Lake Campground, operated by the city of Trinidad. This popular recreation area, called Monument Lake Resort, offers camping, an adobe lodge with 22 rooms, 13 cabins, a restaurant, trout fishing, boating, and hiking. The resort is open from mid-May to mid-September. The drive continues south, crossing Whiskey and Romain Creeks before dropping down Wilkins Creek to Stonewall and the upper Purgatoire River canyon.

Stonewall, at 7,460 feet, is a quiet ranching and vacation village settled in 1867 by early rancher Juan Guitterez. The town is named for an immense stone wall of Dakota sandstone. This tilted hogback, part of the Dakota Hogback seen near La Veta, was deposited along ancient beaches some 70 million years ago during the Cretaceous period. The formation, widespread over much of Colorado, was later uplifted during the rise of the Rocky Mountains. Culebra Peak, the range high point at 14,069 feet, forms Stonewall's western skyline. CO 12, upon entering Stonewall, swings past a cliff and passes through a gap that breaches the sandstone escarpment.

Picketwire Valley to Trinidad

The drive turns east at Stonewall and enters Stonewall Valley and then **Picketwire Valley,** a broad swale carved by the Purgatoire River. The name "Picketwire" is a bastardized version of the river's French name, Purgatoire. The Spanish first named the muddy river *El Rio de las Animas Perdidas en Purgatorio,* or "The River of the Lost Souls in Purgatory." The 196-mile-long Purgatoire, its headwaters on the Culebra divide west of Stonewall, twists east and northeast onto the prairie before merging with the Arkansas River near Las Animas. The river officially begins at the confluence of its North and Middle Forks a few miles downriver from Stonewall.

The drive's 30-mile leg from Stonewall to Trinidad crosses dusty plateau country. Low rock-rimmed mesas, creased with shallow canyons and dry arroyos, loom above the valley. The drive passes through a succession of old Hispanic villages and homesteads. Vigil Plaza lies 5 miles east of Stonewall. Weston, first called Los Sisneros, started as a 1880s ranch and was later renamed for pioneer farmer Sam Weston. An adobe structure on the town's east side is part of the original Sisneros Ranch. Farther east are the ruins of Cordova, Medina, and Valasquez plazas and San Juan, all old family communities. Segundo, an old town of old stone buildings and low-slung adobe houses, sits along the river. Valdez sits a mile east. It headquartered the Frederick Mine, which, with over 30 miles of tunnels, was one of Colorado's largest underground mines until it closed in 1960. Huge piles of red mine tailings are heaped alongside the road.

A few miles east of Valdez, the highway turns north from Picketwire Valley and climbs through low hills to Reilly Canyon and **Cokedale National Historic District.** Cokedale, spread over hillsides amid colored tailings, was established in 1906 as a company town by the Carbon Coal and Coke Company. Numerous historic homes and buildings are scattered throughout the hamlet, and lines of coke ovens lie south of the highway. Coke, a refined form of coal that burns hotter, was shipped from the town ovens to Leadville and other smelters.

The drive climbs through low hills and drops past 2,680-acre **Trinidad Lake State Park.** The park's centerpiece is a 900-acre, 3-mile-long reservoir built for irrigation and flood control. Archaeological sites include a tepee ring, a circle of stones that once surrounded a nomad's tent, at Carpios Ridge Picnic Area. Forty-eight archaeological sites lie beneath the lake and on surrounding ridges, while six mining towns lie submerged under the lake's green waters. The reservoir offers great fishing, as well as boating, waterskiing, board-sailing, and camping.

Trinidad, the drive's end, is 3 miles east of the reservoir. The highway drops back into the Purgatoire's valley and passes through Jansen, a town that was the eastern terminus of the Colorado & Wyoming Railroad during the area's mining heyday. Trinidad, one of Colorado's oldest and most historic communities, sits at the foot of Raton Pass. The town sprang up as a stop on the Mountain Branch of the old Santa Fe Trail. Wagon trains could rest here before climbing over the steep, rough pass into New Mexico. Gabriel Gutierrez, the town's first settler, built a cabin on the river's south bank in 1859. The town later flourished as a ranching and transportation center fueled by years of prosperous coal mining. The town, protected as **El Corazon de Trinidad National Historic District,** boasts several excellent historic sites, including the Trinidad History Museum with the Baca House, Bloom Mansion, Historic Gardens with flowers, herbs, and vegetables, and the Santa Fe Trail Museum. Trinidad offers all visitor services and is the gateway to the Comanche National Grassland to the east (see Scenic Route 3). Hop on Interstate 25 in Trinidad to return north to Pueblo, Colorado Springs, and Denver.

5

Sangre de Cristo Scenic Drive

Texas Creek to Walsenburg

General description: This 86-mile-long scenic highway runs south along Texas Creek from the Arkansas River into the Wet Mountain Valley and the historic town of Westcliffe. The drive, bordering the Sangre de Cristo Mountains, continues south into the broad Huerfano River valley before ending at Walsenburg.

Special attractions: Arkansas River, McIntyre Hills Wilderness Study Area, Wet Mountain Valley, Westcliffe, Silver Cliff, Sangre de Cristo Mountains, ghost towns, Huerfano River Valley, Walsenburg, scenic views, fishing, hiking, wildlife.

Location: South-central Colorado. The drive, following CO 69, runs from US 50 26 miles west of Cañon City southeast to Walsenburg and I-25.

Route number: CO 69.

Travel season: Year-round. Winter storms and blizzards can temporarily close the highway. It's advisable to carry chains and a shovel if the weather is threatening.

Camping: No public campgrounds along the highway. Campgrounds are in the San Isabel National Forest, including Lake Creek Campground (11 sites) west of Hillside and Alvarado Campground (50 sites) southwest of Westcliffe. Other forest campgrounds are in the Wet Mountains. Dispersed camping is at Lake de Weese State Wildlife Area.

Services: All services are in Westcliffe and Walsenburg. Limited services in Texas Creek, Hillside, and Gardner.

Nearby attractions: South Colony Lakes, Crestone Peak and Needle, Hermit Pass, Arkansas Headwaters State Recreation Area, Grape Creek Wilderness Study Area, Cañon City, Temple Canon, Hardscrabble Pass, Marble Cave, Sierra Blanca, Medano Pass, Highway of Legends Scenic Byway (Scenic Drive 4), Great Sand Dunes National Park.

The Route

CO 69 rolls down the broad Wet Mountain and Huerfano River valleys for 86 miles from the Arkansas River to Walsenburg on the western rim of the Great Plains. The excellent route, flanked by the lofty **Sangre de Cristo Mountains** on the west and the swelling Wet Mountains on the east, travels an unpopulated land rich in spectacular views, lush with verdant grasslands and pastures, and alive with early Spanish and mining history. The highway is a friendly back road, used mostly by locals who salute oncoming traffic with a wave.

The Sangre de Cristo Mountains, one of the longest ranges in the Rocky Mountains, stretches over 150 miles from Salida to Santa Fe in New Mexico. The sierra's midsection in southern Colorado is called the Culebra Range. Above the scenic drive and the Wet Mountain Valley, the Sangre de Cristos form an awesome escarpment of sawtooth peaks that soar into the azure sky. Four 14,000-foot peaks—Crestone Needle, Crestone Peak, Humboldt Peak, and Kit Carson

Sangre de Cristo Scenic Drive

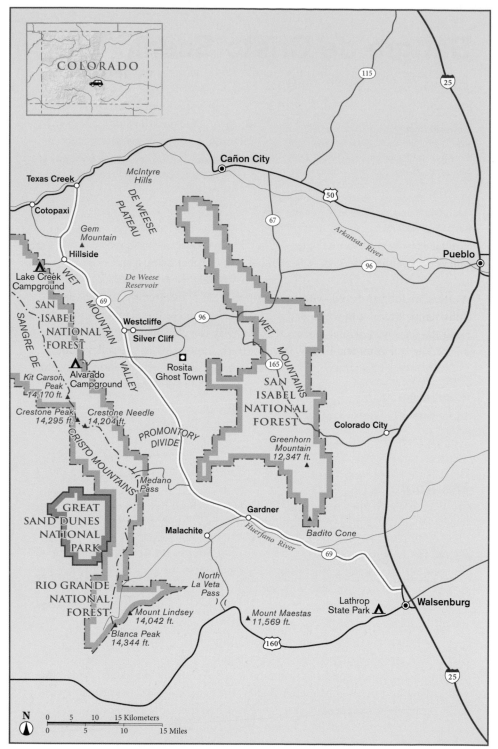

COLORADO

Cañon City

Texas Creek

McIntyre Hills

Cotopaxi

DE WEESE PLATEAU

115

25

50

67

Arkansas River

Pueblo

96

Gem Mountain

Hillside

De Weese Reservoir

WET MOUNTAIN VALLEY

Lake Creek Campground

SAN ISABEL NATIONAL FOREST

69

Westcliffe

96

WET MOUNTAINS

Silver Cliff

165

SANGRE DE

Kit Carson Peak 14,170 ft.

Alvarado Campground

Rosita Ghost Town

SAN ISABEL NATIONAL FOREST

Crestone Peak 14,295 ft.

Crestone Needle 14,204 ft.

PROMONTORY DIVIDE

Greenhorn Mountain 12,347 ft.

Colorado City

CRISTO MOUNTAINS

Medano Pass

GREAT SAND DUNES NATIONAL PARK

Gardner

Badito Cone

Malachite

Huerfano River

69

RIO GRANDE NATIONAL FOREST

North La Veta Pass

Lathrop State Park

Walsenburg

Mount Lindsey 14,042 ft.

Mount Maestas 11,569 ft.

Blanca Peak 14,344 ft.

160

25

N

0   5   10   15 Kilometers
0   5   10   15 Miles

Peak—cluster along the skyline southwest of Westcliffe. Sierra Blanca, an abrupt massif containing another four "Fourteeners," sits farther south.

Although the Sangres are only 20 miles wide, no highways cross their rugged crests. The few passable gaps, including Medano, Mosca, and Hermit Passes, have been well-traveled routes for centuries. The range supposedly received its Spanish name *Sangre de Cristo,* or "Blood of Christ," from the Spanish explorer Valverde, who upon sighting the peaks bathed in morning alpenglow fervently exclaimed, "Sangre de Cristo." Most of the range is protected in the 220,803-acre **Sangre de Cristo Wilderness Area.** This area, the fourth largest in Colorado, was established in 1993.

Summer and fall are ideal times to drive the route. Summer days are warm, with temperatures ranging from 90 degrees near Walsenburg to the 70s at Westcliffe. Heavy thunderstorms regularly build up over the mountains and douse the valleys on summer afternoons. September and October bring a succession of clear, crisp days. Warm temperatures are occasionally broken by rain and low clouds. Winters are long and cold, with snow lasting from November to April. Expect chilly temperatures and wind. Bad road conditions, including ice and whiteouts, occur during severe winter storms. The highway is a glorious drive after a winter storm. The sun glimmers in the clear sky, fresh snow blankets the valley floor, and wind sweeps gossamers of snow off the high mountain ridges. Spring is cool and breezy. Daily high temperatures range from 30 to 60 degrees, and unsettled weather brings frequent storms.

Texas Creek

The drive begins 26 miles west of Cañon City at **Texas Creek,** the junction of US 50 and CO 69. Turn south on CO 69. The highway climbs south alongside Texas Creek in a steep-walled canyon broken by jumbled boulders and a scattered piñon pine and juniper woodland. The abandoned rail bed of the Westcliffe Branch of the Denver & Rio Grande Railroad parallels the highway in the canyon. The line, built in 1900, served Westcliffe and its prospering ranches. A previous narrow-gauge line that hauled silver ore down Grape Creek was torn up by the Denver & Rio Grande in 1890 after a series of disasters and a downturn in the area's silver boom.

The road steadily climbs up the canyon, passing placid ponds formed by beaver dams. The first view of the Sangre de Cristo Range is 2 miles up the drive. The rough **McIntyre Hills** rise east of the highway, forming a rugged maze of deep canyons and sharp peaks. This remote region, traversed only by a few trails, was studied for possible wilderness designation by the Bureau of Land Management but finally rejected. The hills offer excellent hiking adventures with abrupt stair-stepped canyons and plentiful wildlife including mule deer, bighorn sheep, and mountain lion.

By 6 miles, ponderosa pines begin mixing in the piñon forest, lifting their rounded crowns above the low piñons. A mile later the highway climbs away from the creek onto the northern Wet Mountain Valley, a high sagebrush plain dotted with ponderosa and piñon pines below the looming mountain escarpment. At 10 miles the drive reaches green pastures filled with grazing cattle and wide hay fields.

The Wet Mountain Valley

The **Wet Mountain Valley,** considered one of Colorado's prime ranch lands, flanks the Sangre de Cristos for over 30 miles from here to Promontory Divide. The broad valley, reaching 15 miles in width, is drained by Grape and Texas Creeks. The valley is rich in history. The Ute tribe frequented the valley, drawn by plentiful game and a salubrious summer climate. One early prospector remembered that "many a howling war dance has disturbed the midnight air of this pleasant valley."

Spanish explorers and miners scouted the region, leaving legends of mysterious lost gold mines and treasure troves hidden in mountain caverns. In 1806 Lieutenant Zebulon Pike, on his quest to explore the southern Louisiana Purchase, traversed the valley en route to the Rio Grande and his capture by Spanish soldiers. The first Anglo settlers were a group of 397 German immigrants who colonized the valley on a communal basis. These farmers and artisans failed due to inexperience at irrigation and at high-altitude farming. Most left for Denver and Pueblo, but those who hung on to their land eventually prospered. Descendants of these early immigrants still live and ranch in the valley.

After entering the northern Wet Mountain Valley, the highway passes **Hillside,** one of those one-store towns that you don't even notice if you blink, before swinging back along Texas Creek on the valley's east edge. Hillside was on its last legs and headed for extinction until Chris and Tara Seegers bought the whole town, all nine acres, in 2014. Chris, who grew up in Westcliffe, often drove through the town when he was a university student but never thought about it until one day he saw a "For Sale" sign stuck by the side of the highway.

Despite living in Texas, he took the plunge and the area's 100 or so residents, mostly ranch families, were happy he did since the post office and its 81232 ZIP code stayed alive. The historic post office is Hillside's liveliest place, with local ranchers stopping their pickup trucks to sip cups of coffee brewed by postmistress Barb Koch, talk about the weather, and pick up their mail. The Seegers renovated

A rancher checks his horse in the Wet Mountain Valley below Crestone Peak and the Sangre de Cristo Mountains.

a few rustic cottages that welcome overnight guests and plan to use other places in Hillside for weddings, bluegrass concerts, and yoga classes. The white-sided Hillside Hall, built in 1921, was a lively dance hall in the 1920s. Westcliffe residents paid a dollar to ride a special train to Hillside for weekend dances.

Past Hillside, turn right on CR 198 and climb west to 11-site Lake Creek Campground in **San Isabel National Forest.** The drive continues south through a shallow canyon lined with volcanic cliff bands and ranches. Dense willow thickets border the tumbling creek, and pines coat low surrounding hills. After 5 miles the highway emerges onto the valley floor. A spectacular panorama opens to the south: The Wet Mountains rim the valley on the southeast; the landmark Spanish Peaks poke their snowy heads above the southern horizon; and the Sangre de Cristo Mountains march across the western skyline. The high peaks of the southern Sawatch Range on the Continental Divide glimmer to the north. The highway runs past 8,549-foot Beckwith Mountain, an abrupt hogback broken by cliffs east of the asphalt, and after a few miles crosses meandering Grape Creek, the valley's main drainage. Westcliffe, at 7,888 feet, sits 3 miles south on a rounded bluff above the creek.

Westcliffe & Silver Cliff

Westcliffe, the gateway to the Sangre de Cristo Mountains, was founded in 1885 by local landowner Dr. J. W. Bell, who named the picturesque community for Westcliffe-on-the-Sea, his English birthplace. The town, seat of Custer County, has long outlived its neighbors Silver Cliff, Querida, and Rosita. All three were mining boom towns in the late 19th century. Westcliffe, however, grew and thrived as a supply center for area ranchers and as a railhead. After the great Silver Crash of 1893, Westcliffe still prospered while its neighbors faded away. The Denver & Rio Grande Railroad came to town in 1900 but was abandoned in 1937. Westcliffe today is the county's center of commerce and offers all services to travelers, including restaurants.

Just east of Westcliffe is its twin town, **Silver Cliff.** While it's mostly a suburb of Westcliffe, it is worth stopping at the Silver Cliff Cemetery on some dark and stormy night to have a look at its mystery lights. Since 1882 the lights have been seen, usually on dark cloudy nights. The blue, white, and gray lights reportedly appear as twinkling Christmas tree lights, fireflies, and floating orbs that sometimes dart, flicker, pulsate, and hover. One account from 1956 said the lights were the size of basketballs. The mysterious lights have been thoroughly investigated and there is no logical explanation. Visit yourself and make up your own mind—restless spirits, bioluminescence, foxfire, or UFOs?

Westcliffe and Silver Cliff are renowned for stargazing, with a cloud of stars pricking the black night sky. In 2015 the towns were the first in Colorado to receive the coveted **International Dark Sky Community** designation by the International Dark Sky Association. The Wet Mountain Valley is perfect for starry nights with its high elevation and distance from city light pollution from Colorado Springs and Pueblo.

One of the best stargazing spots is on the Bluff, a hill on the west side of Westcliffe that overlooks the valley and the Sangre de Cristo Mountains. It's the perfect place to watch the familiar constellations and planets follow their stately procession across the sky. A dozen or so people congregate here on clear nights to stargaze and there are usually a few telescopes that let you get up close and personal with the craters and mountains on the moon, Saturn's colorful rings, the Andromeda Galaxy, and the Great Cluster in Hercules, a shimmering ball of thousands of stars. Summer is the best time to observe the Milky Way, our home galaxy. The area is perfect to see meteor showers like the Perseid in early August, the Leonid in mid-November, and the Geminid in mid-December.

CO 69 runs south from Westcliffe past verdant ranches. After 3 miles the highway intersects Schoolfield Road. A turn west leads 6 miles straight across the valley into the Sangre de Cristo Mountains and 50-site Alvarado Campground. This

9,000-foot-high campground makes a cool summer base camp for exploring the valley and mountains. The **Comanche** and **Venable Trails** lead west up from a trailhead at the campground to forested valleys, waterfalls, alpine lakes, and high peaks.

Rosita

For a side trip, head east on CO 96 from Silver Cliff for a few miles to a right turn on CR 341 to 329 which leads to the ghost town of **Rosita,** nestled among summer cabins and ranchettes in the scrubby hills east of the valley. Silver was found here in 1870; by 1872, when rich claims that yielded as much as 145 ounces of silver to the ton were found, the silver rush was on. Rosita, along with nearby Querida and Silver Cliff, arose around rich mines and lived and died by their earthen fortunes.

Rosita epitomizes the boom and bust mining cycle. Founded after a rich find in the winter of 1872–73, Rosita quickly became one of the Colorado Territory's largest towns. Rosita swelled with miners who dug the ore and teamsters who hauled the silver through deep canyons to Pueblo and the nearest railhead. By 1875 the town boasted a population of 1,500, a two-story school, Townsend's Brewery, three churches, a bank, the Pennsylvania Reduction Works for ore milling, a newspaper, a post office, and hotels, as well as doctor and real estate offices. The mines began a slow decline in 1876, and Rosita was usurped by a new boom town, Querida, a few miles north. The decline furthered in 1878 when horn silver was discovered in Silver Cliff. Much of Rosita was destroyed in an 1881 fire and never recovered. The town lingered on as a well-preserved ghost of its former self well into the 1960s, when the post office was finally closed down.

Rosita, used as a film set for a few movies, including *Saddle the Wind, Cat Ballou,* and *Continental Divide,* is now a forgotten, windswept corner of Colorado's colorful history. Only a few crumbling buildings remain of this faded rose along the dusty back road. The Rosita Cemetery tells the poignant story of the town's rise and fall.

Return to Westcliffe to continue the scenic drive.

Sangre de Cristo Mountains

The 17-mile-long highway section through the upper Wet Mountain Valley from Westcliffe to the crest of the Promontory Divide is simply spectacular. The broad valley, crisscrossed by arrow-straight side roads, is divided by barbed-wire fences into fertile ranches dotted with grazing cattle.

The **Sangre de Cristo** range pierces the western skyline, its abrupt escarpment of ragged peaks broken by plunging glacier-carved cirques and thickly wooded canyons. Five 14,000-foot peaks dominate the range here: 14,295-foot

The Sangre de Cristo Mountains, with seven "Fourteeners," lifts its rugged spine beyond the scenic drive.

Crestone Peak, 14,204-foot Crestone Needle, 14,170-foot Kit Carson Peak, 14,087-foot Challenger Point, and 14,065-foot Humboldt Peak.

The Crestone peaks, named for their resemblance to a cock's comb, were the last of Colorado's 53 "Fourteeners" with at least 300 feet of prominence to be ascended, when Albert Ellingwood and Eleanor Davis led a party up them in 1916. Kit Carson Peak was named for the famed western scout, and Humboldt Peak for Alexander von Humboldt, a renowned 19-century geographer. **Challenger Point** was named in 1987 in memory of the seven astronauts killed after the Space Shuttle *Challenger* disintegrated after takeoff in January 1986. Nearby Columbia Point, a 13,986-foot subpeak of Kit Carson, was named for the astronauts who died after the Space Shuttle *Columbia* fell apart on reentry in 2003.

The peaks are often approached and climbed from the Wet Mountain Valley via South Colony Road and FR 313 up South Colony Creek. Uplifted 270-million-year-old Paleozoic sediments including sandstone, shale, conglomerate, and limestone compose the bulk of the range, although ancient granite forms the southern Sierra Blanca section.

The Sangre de Cristo Mountains, besides being an enclave of wildlife and wilderness, are rife with legends. One of the best myths concerns **Marble Cave,** called by the Spanish *El Caverna del Oro,* or "The Cavern of Gold," a deep cave high above the timberline on the windswept flanks of Marble Mountain south of the Crestones. Mountain mythology relates that Spanish conquistadores used the cave as a stash for ill-gotten gold mined by Native American slaves. An old Maltese cross painted on a rock wall marks the cave's entrance. The cave makes an unpleasant exploration, reaching a depth of 300 feet, including a vertical 80-foot pit, a year-round average temperature of 34 degrees, 95 percent humidity, and snowdrifts that reach far into the cave. The first explorers in 1929 found a crude ladder and hand-forged hammer thought to be at least 200 years old. The gold, if it was there at all, vanished long before.

CO 69 runs south on gravel benches above meandering Grape Creek and gently climbs toward 8,500-foot Promontory Divide, a low ridge that separates the Wet Mountain Valley from the Huerfano River drainage. As the road climbs, the surrounding country dries, with sagebrush hills replacing the fertile valley floor. Wild country stretches in every direction from atop the divide. The highway drops south from the divide along Muddy Creek, a shallow trickle lined with willows and cottonwoods in a shallow valley. Piñon pine–covered hills flank the valley. Eight miles from the divide summit, the drive passes Medano Road, a 22-mile, four-wheel-drive track that climbs over 9,950-foot Medano Pass and drops down to the Great Sand Dunes National Park and Preserve and the San Luis Valley. Past the turn the highway bends southeast down Muddy Creek's broad valley. The creek meanders through deep flash flood–carved arroyos on the valley floor. Low mesas studded with piñon pine and juniper trees flank the drive.

Gardner to Walsenburg

After 59 miles, the scenic drive reaches **Gardner,** an old southwestern settlement perched at the confluence of Muddy Creek and the Huerfano River. The town, named for pioneer farmer Herbert Gardner, retains a frontier spirit with old adobe houses shaded by towering cottonwoods. A spur road, CR 550, heads southwest up the river through Malachite and Redwing and climbs up a four-wheel-drive trail to the San Isabel National Forest boundary and a trio of Fourteeners—14,344-foot Blanca Peak. 14,042 Mount Lindsey, and 14,042-foot Ellingwood Point. A good hike begins at the end of the 4x4 track and climbs to gorgeous Lily Lake tucked against the Sangre de Cristo crest. Another side road, follow CR 580 ascends to the summit of 9,714-foot Mosca Pass. An old Ute trail drops west from the pass summit to the Great Sand Dunes.

Gardner Butte, a rough volcanic plug broken by cliff bands, looms east of Gardner. The Wet Mountains, topped by 12,347-foot Greenhorn Mountain, form the ragged northern horizon. Broad outwash plains below the range, cloaked with sagebrush and scattered piñon pines, sweep up to the range's steep forested slopes. Greenhorn Mountain is named for Cuerno Verde, a Comanche chief killed

The historic Hope Lutheran Church, built in 1917, rises above a playground in Westcliffe.

in a violent battle between the Comanches and the Spanish in 1779. The mountain's southern flank is part of the 23,087-acre Greenhorn Mountain Wilderness Area, a rough region with remote canyons, soaring ridges, and few trails. A great six-mile hike is to Apache Falls, one of Colorado's highest waterfalls, tucked in a canyon on the east side of Greenhorn Mountain. Find a detailed description in the FalconGuide *Hiking Waterfalls in Colorado.*

The scenic route follows benches above the Huerfano River, passing through the old Mexican town of **Farista.** The town, originally called Fort Talpa, was established in 1820. A few miles to the east, the highway runs through the abandoned town **Badito** at the far southern edge of the Wet Mountains. The range terminus is topped by distinctive Badito Cone, a volcanic vent.

The road twists through a narrow gap carved through uplifted sandstone layers by the muddy Huerfano River below the cone. The old Taos Trail, a path used by American traders and Spanish soldiers, cuts through Badito en route to Sangre de Cristo Pass and Taos. A Spanish fort was built a few miles south of here in 1819 to protect the pass from an American invasion. Past the gap the highway climbs away from the river and onto the edge of the treeless Great Plains. The drive's last 15 miles roll across short-grass prairie, over piñon-dotted mesas, and past an old bituminous coal mine. The drive drops down to I-25 just north of **Walsenburg.**

6

Los Caminos Antiguos Scenic Byway

Alamosa to Cumbres Pass

General description: This 152-mile-long scenic byway traverses the San Luis Valley between Alamosa and Cumbres Pass. The drive passes historic sites, Rio Grande, Great Sand Dunes National Park and Preserve, desert hills, valley farms, and aspen forests.

Special attractions: Alamosa, Great Sand Dunes National Park and Preserve, San Luis State Wildlife Area, Zapata Falls, Medano-Zapata Ranch, Fort Garland Museum and Cultural Center, Sangre de Cristo Heritage Center, Stations of the Cross, Jack Dempsey Museum, Rio Grande, Pike's Stockade, Cumbres & Toltec Scenic Railroad, Cumbres Pass, Rio Grande National Forest, autumn colors, fishing, hiking, scenic views, camping.

Location: Southern Colorado. The drive begins in Alamosa and travels north on CO 17, then east on Six Mile Lane and south on CO 150 to US 160. It heads east on US 160 to Fort Garland, south on CO 159 to San Luis, and west on CO 142 to Romeo. It turns south on US 285 for 7 miles to Antonito and then west on CO 17 to Cumbres Pass and the New Mexico border.

Route name and numbers: Los Caminos Antiguos Scenic Byway; CO 150, 159, 142, and 17; US 285 and 160; Six Mile Lane.

Travel season: Year-round. Heavy snow can temporarily close the highway over La Manga and Cumbres Passes.

Camping: Mogote, Aspen Glade, Elk Creek, and Trujillo Meadows campgrounds lie along CO 17 west of Antonito in Rio Grande National Forest. Campgrounds are also at San Luis State Wildlife Area (51 campsites) and Piñon Flats Campground (88 sites) at Great Sand Dunes National Park and Preserve .

Services: All services are in Alamosa, Blanca, Fort Garland, San Luis, and Antonito. Limited services in Manassa and Romeo.

Nearby attractions: Sierra Blanca, Penitente Canyon climbing area, San Isabel National Forest, Spanish Peaks, South San Juan Wilderness Area, Monte Vista National Wildlife Refuge, Alamosa National Wildlife Refuge, Silver Thread Scenic Byway (Scenic Drive 22), Taos, Chama, Rio Grande Gorge, Carson National Forest (New Mexico).

The Route

The 152-mile Los Caminos Antiguos Scenic Byway, a designated Colorado Scenic Byway, traverses the San Luis Valley between Alamosa and Cumbres Pass in southern Colorado. The San Luis Valley, an intermontane basin roughly 100 miles long and 60 miles wide, reaches from Poncha Pass to the New Mexico border. The valley, three times the size of Delaware, rolls out like a giant carpet patterned with fields, pastures, and sagebrush flats to the mountains which encircle it.

Los Caminos Antiguos Scenic Byway

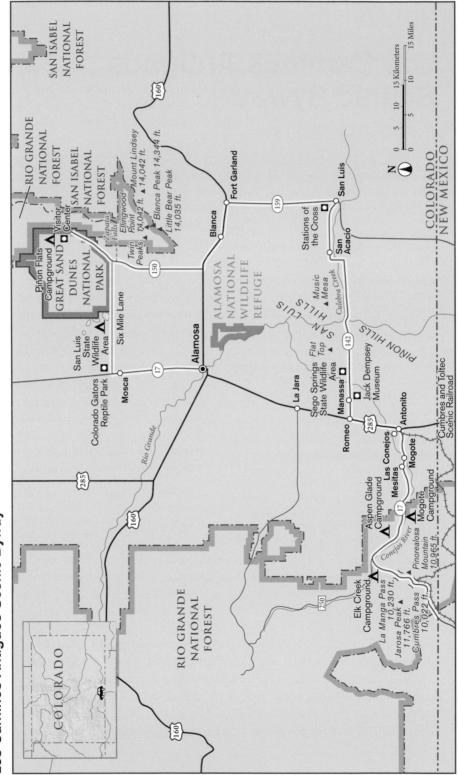

The Sangre de Cristo and Culebra Ranges form a steep mountain wall on the valley's eastern border. The jagged escarpment, including ten 14,000-foot peaks, makes a formidable barrier that is crossed by only one paved road and two four-wheel-drive tracks. The **San Juan Mountains** form a lower but equally impassable barrier to the west. The Rio Grande, southern Colorado's river of history and character, breaks out of the San Juans at Del Norte on the valley's western edge, then meanders across the San Luis Valley between banks thick with cottonwoods and willows before plunging down a wild cliff-lined gorge into New Mexico. This superb scenic drive passes old towns and historic sites, skirts the Great Sand Dunes National Park and Preserve, threads across volcanic hills, follows the sparkling Conejos River, and climbs through fir and spruce forests to the summit of 10,022-foot Cumbres Pass, a stone's throw from New Mexico.

The San Luis Valley, lying at elevations above 7,500 feet, is classified as desert, with an average precipitation of only 10 inches. The valley, the driest part of Colorado, lies in the rain shadow of the San Juan Mountains. Storms laden with Pacific moisture unload on the San Juans, but by the time the clouds reach the valley, most rain has already been wrung out. The bulk of the year's meager moisture generally falls in torrential afternoon thunderstorms during July and August. The San Juans west of the valley are Colorado's wettest region. Heavy snows fall on the mountains, including an average 267 inches atop Cumbres Pass. In contrast, the town of Manassa to the east receives only 18 inches of snow each winter. Summer and fall are the best times to travel the highways. Summer days are warm and sunny, with highs generally in the 70s and 80s. Autumn brings cooler days and bright skies. Winters are frigid, with temperatures often falling below zero and snow lingering on the valley floor. Spring months are cool and windy, with occasional rain and snow showers.

Alamosa to San Luis Lakes

The drive begins on the east side of Alamosa in the center of the San Luis Valley at the junction of US 160 and CO 17. **Alamosa,** the largest city in the valley, was established in 1878 as a railroad town. It was named for the large cottonwood groves along the Rio Grande. It flourished with the railroad, becoming the region's main agricultural and mining center. The town's economy depended on freight. At the temporary end of the railroad, shipments of goods reached out to Santa Fe and northern New Mexico as well as the mining areas in the San Juan Mountains to the west. After the railroad extended westward, Alamosa became the center of a prosperous farming and ranching economy, which continues today. Points of interest include a fabulous collection of Native American pottery at the **Luther Bean Museum** on the Alamosa State University campus and **Splashland** hot springs a mile north of town on highway 17. Splashland boasts a huge outdoor pool with thermal water between 88 and 96 degrees.

Two of the best nearby points of interest are the 11,169-acre **Alamosa National Wildlife Refuge** and the 14,804-acre **Monte Vista National Wildlife Refuge.** The two large wetland areas are rich habitat for migratory waterfowl. Many bird species, including whooping cranes, sandhill cranes, snow geese, egrets, and bald eagles, either stop or nest at the refuges. Self-guided tours can be taken year-round. A visitor center is located at the Alamosa refuge, which is 3 miles east of Alamosa on El Rancho Road off US 160.

From Alamosa head north on CO 17 through agricultural land dotted with fields and houses. After almost 14 miles you reach the village of **Mosca,** a small community named for Mosca Pass in the Sangre de Cristo Mountains to the east. The pass was named for Luis de Moscoso Alvarado, a Spanish conquistador who assumed command of Hernando de Soto's multi-year exploration of the southern United States area after de Soto's death in 1542. Alvarado, however, never set foot in Colorado.

Turn right (east) just north of Mosca on Six Mile Lane (CR LN 6N), following signs for the Great Sand Dunes National Park and Preserve. Three miles north of this turn on CO 17 is the **Colorado Gators Reptile Park,** one of Colorado's most unusual ranches. Warm water, spewing at 87 degrees from geothermal wells, allows alligators to flourish here in several man-made pools. The original farm was purchased in 1977 to raise tilapia, an African perch, in the warm water. In 1987 a hundred baby alligators were added to eat dead fish. An admission fee is charged.

Drive east on Six Mile Lane toward the tawny sand dunes. At 8 miles you reach the turnoff to **San Luis State Wildlife Area.** This quiet area is composed of a couple of lakes surrounded by low sand dunes stabilized with rabbitbrush and saltbush. The park's main geographic feature is shallow, 890-acre San Luis Lake, a popular summer recreation area for anglers and boaters. To the north is a wildlife area with marshy wetlands and Head Lake. Both provide valuable wildlife habitat. The lake, one of the largest in the San Luis Valley, is significant as a resting point for migrating shorebirds, waterbirds, gulls, and terns. Over 150 bird species have been identified at the park, including sandhill and whooping cranes, grebes, avocets, snowy egrets, white-faced ibis, herons, and bald and golden eagles. For recreationists, the park offers picnic sites, a ramp for only hand-launched boats, fishing, birding, 9 miles of hiking and biking trails, and pleasant 51-site Mosca Campground. The lake is often empty so plan accordingly. Spectacular views of the Sangre de Cristo Mountains abound from the park and its lakes.

Medano-Zapata Ranch

Continue driving east on Six Mile Lane. The land surrounding the road is part of the **Zapata Ranch,** 103,000 acres of undeveloped land that includes the western part of Great Sand Dunes National Park and Preserve as well as adjoining Baca National Wildlife Area. This region, one of the largest biologically intact undeveloped landscapes remaining in Colorado, is an important repository of natural diversity and beauty.

The Nature Conservancy acquired the property in 1999 at a price below market value because the land's owner wanted that biodiversity protected. The arid terrain belies the abundant groundwater that helps support a wealth of plant and animal life, including a free-roaming herd of bison on the ranch and 78,697-acre Baca National Wildlife Refuge west of the national park, more than 200 bird species, deer, elk, pronghorn, and some rare and endemic insect species, including the circus beetle, the antlike flower beetle, and the Great Sand Dunes tiger beetle.

North of Great Sand Dunes National Park and Preserve is the 97,000-acre **Baca Ranch,** another piece of the San Luis Valley's unspoiled lands that was acquired by the Nature Conservancy in 2002. With more than 151 square miles, the ranch encompasses a large part of the Sangre de Cristo Range, including 14,170-foot Kit Carson Peak. The Baca Ranch, part of the Luis Maria Baca Grant No. 4, an 1824 Mexican land grant, is part of the largest land preservation effort in Colorado history.

After bumping over a cattle guard, look for a large parking area on the right or south side of the road. Park and follow a short paved trail to a fenced hump with informative signs. This makes a good orientation stop to the ranch and sand dunes area. The display details Folsom man's habitation of the San Luis Valley and provides information on the San Luis Lakes, Zapata Falls, and the bison herd.

Great Sand Dunes National Park

Continue east on Six Mile Lane until it dead-ends at CO 150. Take a left turn to visit 149,028-acre **Great Sand Dunes National Park and Preserve** and one of America's most unusual dune fields. The highway runs north across scrubland and enters the park after a couple of miles. Continue past the fee station and through an area that was burned by fire in April 2000. The human-caused fire burned 3,120 acres, but only 200 acres of forest. Stop at the park visitor center on the left for orientation, interpretive displays, and maps.

The Great Sand Dunes, nestled in a deep alcove on the eastern edge of the San Luis Valley, holds the tallest sand dunes in the Western Hemisphere. The dunes, rising over 700 feet above the valley floor, have a sandy volume estimated at 8

Kit Carson Peak, Crestone Peak, and Crestone Needle tower above Star Dune, one of the national park's highest sand dunes.

cubic miles, enough sand that it would be almost 5 inches deep if evenly spread across Colorado's 103,766 square miles. The dune field, covering 39 square miles, has an oval shape that is kept from advancing eastward by the abrupt mountain escarpment and Medano Creek.

The San Luis Valley receives less than 10 inches of annual rainfall, making it a true desert as well as Colorado's driest region. The dune field began to form 20,000 years ago, when great ice sheets marched south across North America. During that period glaciers were scraping out Colorado's peaks and valleys, and snowmelt-laden rivers rushed into the San Luis Valley. As the climate warmed and dried up, glacial sand and silt were deposited along the Rio Grande. Wind and time did the rest of the work, with centuries of brisk wind scouring the valley floor and sweeping the sand across the valley into a natural pocket below the mountains. The wind, forced to rise over Medano and Mosca Passes, dropped its load of sand. The dunes today are still part of this ongoing process. The dune field now, however, is growing in volume rather than size.

The Great Sand Dunes are also a fascinating study in natural history. The dunes are not nearly as lifeless as they appear at first sight. Sunflowers spring from the sand in August. Indian ricegrass wavers under the ripple of wind. Cottonwood trees, half buried in sand, avoid suffocation by sending out new roots. A delicate tracery of beetle tracks thread across the dunes. And kangaroo rats, which never drink water, plug their burrow entrances with sand to avoid midday heat and await the cool of nightfall. Insects are among the brave creatures that choose to live among the inhospitable dunes. Three species—the circus beetle, Great Sand Dunes tiger beetle, and giant sand treader camel cricket—live only on the dunes and in the eastern San Luis Valley.

The dunes are an exhilarating playground for park visitors. Many clamber to the highest ridges, High Dune and Star Dune, before bounding back down in giant steps. Some put on skis and schuss down the gritty slopes. Others splash about in Medano Creek. If you do climb the dunes, remember to wear shoes because surface temperatures can soar to over 140 degrees—hot enough to burn your soles. Also bring sunscreen, a hat, and plenty of water in summer. You can pick your own path; there are no trails across the dunes. Hiking up the ridgelines is much easier than hiking in a straight line up steep slopes. Worthy hiking objectives are 8,617-foot Star Dune, the highest sand dune in North America with a height of 750 feet from the valley floor to its knife-edge summit, and a 2.5-mile round-trip hike up High Dune, a 650-foot-high dune that is the highest in the park. If you have the time, get a free overnight permit and camp among the dune hollows, especially during the full moon.

There are other trails in the park, including Dunes Overlook Trail (1.15 miles one-way), which explores "escape dunes" east of the creek and a ghost forest of smothered trees; Montville Nature Trail (0.5 mile); the historic Mosca Pass Trail (3.5 miles one-way); and Castle Creek Trail (2.5 miles).

Since the dune field is a wilderness area, no motorized or off-road driving is allowed except for the 12-mile Medano Pass Primitive Road, a four-wheel-drive track that follows Medano Creek to Medano Pass. Campers at the 88-site Piñon Flats Campground (open April through October) enjoy marvelous views of the dunes. Primitive backcountry campsites are along Medano Pass Primitive Road. Other activities include a visitor center and ranger-led talks and walks. Check at the center for scheduled activities and insider tips for visiting the sand dunes.

Sand Dunes to Fort Garland

The next drive section heads south from the national park along CO 150. South of the park on the west is the historic **Zapata Ranch.** This area, listed on the national historic register in 1993, is owned by the Nature Conservancy. The ranch, established in 1879, included a stagecoach station, store, and post office. The ranch boasts one of Colorado's largest bison herds with over 2,000 head, as well as hiking trails, ranchland vacations, and a hotel that hosts workshops, field trips, students, and researchers.

Zapata Falls hides in a deep cleft in South Zapata Creek's narrow canyon east of the byway. Turn east on the marked dirt road (BLM Road 5415) at mile marker 10.5 and drive 3.6 miles to a parking area and trailhead. The steep, rough road gains 1,000 feet and may be impassable for some vehicles. A 0.5-mile hike up North Fork Zapata Trail (#868) leads through a piñon pine and juniper woodland to the waterfall, which cascades down a series of cliffs. The falls formed as water from a retreating glacier pooled behind a rock dike. Eventually a weakness was created in the dike and the water eroded its way through the rock, leaving today's waterfall. Besides the falls, you find excellent views of the sand dunes and the valley from this lofty height. Zapata Falls Campground, with 23 nonreservable campsites, is near the trailhead. For detailed information on visiting Zapata Falls, check out FalconGuides' *Hiking to Waterfalls in Colorado.*

If you're the adventurous sort, you can stay after dark at the Zapata Falls area and perhaps witness a strange visual anomaly. Under the right conditions, small yellow lights, like those on a Christmas tree, appear in the dark and float in the air, sometimes moving in a playful manner, sometimes hovering, and often blinking.

Continue south on CO 150 across a broad sagebrush-covered apron below the mountain massif of the Sierra Blanca. This massif soars more than 7,000 feet above the flat valley to airy ridges and rocky summits. **Blanca Peak,** a sacred mountain of the Navajo Indians, is the range's high point and Colorado's fourth-highest peak at 14,344 feet. The other "Fourteeners" in this group are 14,035-foot Little Bear Peak, 14,042-foot Mount Lindsey, and 14,042-foot Ellingwood Point, named for pioneering Colorado climber Albert Ellingwood. Blanca, Little Bear, and Ellingwood are usually climbed from Lake Como on the west side of the range. It's accessed via an unmarked dirt road that begins on CO 150 3 miles north of US 160. The dirt road eventually becomes an axle-breaking, rock-filled four-wheel-drive route that has been called Colorado's roughest road. Most climbers park low on the road and hike to the lake and peaks.

When CO 150 reaches US 160, the main east-west route in southern Colorado, turn east and drive 10 miles to Fort Garland. The drive passes through **Blanca,** a small community of old adobe and stucco buildings. The town was founded after a land drawing in 1908 brought a mass of people here with the chance to draw for large lots of land. Problems with water rights and unproductive soil have kept the village from growing.

Fort Garland, 47 miles west of Walsenburg, sits at the intersection of US 160 and CO 159. Now a sleepy little crossroads, Fort Garland started out in 1858 as an army fort to protect settlers from marauding bands of Utes. Colorado's first permanent settlements, established in the early 1850s in the San Luis Valley, lay on newly acquired territory ceded by Mexico after the Mexican-American War. The military built Fort Massachusetts, Colorado's first military post, in 1852 northeast of Fort Garland.

The poor location and stagnant water, however, prompted the army to relocate the garrison to Fort Garland a few years later. The new fort, named for Brigadier General John Garland, maintained order in the valley until the Utes were moved westward in 1880. The post was abandoned in 1883. Famed scout, Native American fighter, and soldier Kit Carson commanded the fort in 1866–67 before dying two years later at Fort Lyon. Soldiers considered a post at remote Fort Garland to be a type of involuntary exile.

One visitor wrote that he was "struck with commiseration for all the unfortunate officers and men condemned to live in so desolate a place."

The old fort, a grassy parade ground surrounded by low adobe buildings, is now open year-round as a state historic site that preserves a slice of Colorado's colorful past. Exhibits at the **Fort Garland Museum and Cultural Center,** run by History Colorado, include a re-creation of the commandant's quarters during Carson's tenure and displays of military life, Hispanic folk art from the San Luis Valley, the Civil War in the West and the Battle of Glorieta Pass, and the Buffalo Soldiers. The museum is open daily from March 1 to October 31.

Fort Garland to San Luis

From Fort Garland, drive south on CO 159, passing farmland watered by deep artesian wells and wide sagebrush-covered flats. Scrubby, broken mesas rimmed by ancient lava flows border the drive to the east, forming low foothills below the alpine crest of the Culebra Range. Most of these hills were subdivided as part of the 172,000-acre Forbes Trinchera Ranch, the largest private land holding in Colorado, but they were originally part of the million-acre Sangre de Cristo Land Grant given by the Mexican government to Stephen Lee and 13-year-old Narcisco Beaubien for eventual colonization in 1843. After the two were murdered during a Taos Indian uprising two years later, the land passed to Beaubien's father, Charles, owner of the Maxwell Land Grant near Trinidad. Much of the grant was acquired in 1863 by William Gilpin, Colorado's first territorial governor and a land speculator, and used for grazing. Much of the Forbes Ranch property was burned in the Spring Creek Fire, one of the largest forest fires in Colorado history, in the summer of 2018.

The **Culebra Range** forms a ragged mountain wall east of the scenic drive. This 32-mile-long range twists south from La Veta Pass into New Mexico. Much of the range, topped by 14,053-foot Culebra Peak, remains wild, uninhabited country where visitors are unwelcome. The Maxwell and Sangre de Cristo land grants kept the mountains out of the public domain, and even today most of the Culebra Range is private property. Hikers pay $150 apiece as of 2018 for the privilege of crossing the private land to climb Culebra Peak. Hikes are limited to specific days and months and all ascents require advance reservations on the Cielo Vista Ranch website.

After 15 miles the highway drops down into Culebra Creek's broad, shallow valley and reaches **San Luis,** Colorado's oldest town. Historians acknowledge the community as the first continuously occupied town in today's Colorado, although Taos resident George Gould established a nearby settlement in 1842. The original San Luis, called San Luis de Culebra, was built 0.75 mile south of today's town on the Sangre de Cristo land grant in April 1851 by six Spanish families. The original town was a collection of low-slung adobe buildings huddled around a central plaza for protection from Native Americans; the surrounding arable land was divided into ranches and farms. A canal diverted water from Culebra Creek, establishing Colorado's first water right.

Today San Luis, part of the Plaza de San Luis de la Culebra National Historic District, boasts strong civic pride and a sense of community. Many local ranchers and farmers descended from the original settlers. The excellent **San Luis Museum and Cultural Center** displays southern Colorado's classic Hispanic culture and includes a brilliant collection of santos, or carved religious icons. The museum, run by History Colorado, is in the Old High School, a historic building erected in the early 1930s in Pueblo Revival-style architecture.

The Stations of the Cross Shrine, following a 1.4-mile trail up a dark basalt mesa northwest of San Luis, depicts the last hours of Christ's life in a series of dramatic bronze sculptures by sculptor Huberto Maestas. The trail ends at the beautiful, domed Capilla de Todos los Santos, or All Saints Chapel, atop the mesa. The shrine attracts numerous pilgrims who walk the path and ruminate on their faith.

The Rio Grande, San Luis Hills & Manassa

The drive turns west onto CO 142 at the Stations of the Cross trailhead. The road runs alongside a low mesa rimmed with basalt blocks and coated with sagebrush. Verdant hay fields, watered by Culebra Creek, fill the wide valley south of the blacktop. After 8 miles the highway passes through **San Acacio.** Only a few houses and abandoned buildings remain in this town, founded in 1853. Early settlers battled the Utes here in the name of San Acacio, a Spanish soldier canonized as Saint Acacius.

A mile past the town, the drive bends south and runs across a creek floodplain for 2 miles before turning west again on an almost arrow-straight road. The **San Luis Hills,** a small range of rough volcanic knobs, hills, and mesas, rears to the north and west, forming a wall gray with sagebrush and mottled with piñon pines and junipers. The highway heads across brushy flats toward the hills for 9 miles and reaches the Rio Grande tucked into a shallow cliff-lined canyon.

The **Rio Grande,** the second-longest river in the US at 1,887 miles, arises on the Continental Divide west of the San Luis Valley. The river winds across the valley to this crossing, where it begins cutting into basalt layers. Farther south it enters a deep gorge and plunges into New Mexico. This upper section offers good canoeing through quiet, steep-sided canyons. The cliffs and open spaces attract numerous raptors, including bald eagles, common winter residents.

The highway crosses the Rio Grande on a long bridge and begins climbing over rolling benchlands to a wide saddle between the Piñon Hills on the south and Flat Top, a mesa to the north. Several connected groups of low, barren mountains—South Piñon Hills, Piñon Hills, Flat Top, and Brownie Hills—compose the San Luis Hills. The hills, rising as much as 1,000 feet over the surrounding valley, are the eroded remnants of the volcanic deposits that form the San Juan Mountains. The steep slopes are blanketed in sagebrush, saltbush, and rabbitbrush and dotted with piñon pines and junipers; they house numerous wildlife species, including mule deer, pronghorns, coyotes, bobcats, and eagles. Pristine grasslands thrive on the upper elevations. Hikers can park anywhere along the highway here or take one of the side roads to access the backcountry. A good hike climbs to Flat Top's broad summit and yields marvelous views of the valley and surrounding ranges.

The highway crests the saddle and begins a gradual descent to the Conejos River valley. After 4 miles the road reaches the valley floor and crosses Rio San Antonio, a small stream densely lined with narrow-leaf cottonwoods and willows. The highway swings around a low hill and crosses the Conejos River a mile later. Farms and hay fields cover the moist floodplain, with cattails and sunflowers lining marshland along the highway. A dirt road goes north for 0.5 mile to **Sego Springs State Wildlife Area.** The area, lush with ponds and tree-lined Conejos River, is an excellent birding area, especially in late autumn when migrating birds rest in cottonwood trees. The area is closed from February 15 to July 15 for nesting waterfowl.

Past that turnoff, the drive enters **Manassa,** a well-kept rural community with wide streets and orderly clapboard houses. The town, established in 1878 by Mormon colonists, is famed as the 1895 birthplace and childhood home of heavyweight boxing champion Jack Dempsey. Dempsey, who fought as a teenager in surrounding mining camps as "Kid Blackie," won the crown at age 24. Nicknamed "The Manassa Mauler," Dempsey is considered the best heavyweight in the first half of the 20th century. The **Jack Dempsey Museum,** a one-room cabin where he grew up on Main Street, displays boxing memorabilia and family photos.

Two miles west of Manassa, the drive enters Romeo and intersects US 285. Just a few miles north of the drive and this intersection is **Pike's Stockade** at Sanford, off CO 159 East. The stockade is a replica of the fort built by Lieutenant Zebulon Pike and his soldiers in January 1807 while exploring today's southern Colorado, including the San Luis Valley. The group, after crossing Medano Pass, passed the Great Sand Dunes and explored south along the Rio Grande and Conejos River. They built the makeshift fort as protection from the severe winter weather and against Native Americans. The American flag was raised above the fort on January 31. The stockade, however, was on Spanish soil and within a month the group was arrested by Spanish dragoons and escorted to Santa Fe and then Chihuahua, Mexico; they were released after a year. The replica fort, made of cottonwood logs, measures 36 feet square with 12-foot-high walls and has projecting pickets and a moat for added security. The replica was built by the Colorado Historical Society using notes from Pike's expedition diary.

Conejos to Antonito

From Romeo, US 285 runs south over farmland, crosses the Conejos River again, passes the turnoff to the village of Conejos, and reaches Antonito after 6 miles. **Conejos** is well worth a visit. The town, first settled by Major Lafayette Head and 84 Hispanic families in 1854, soon rivaled San Luis, with numerous settlers, productive farms, and Colorado's first church, dedicated by Bishop Lamy of Santa Fe in 1863. The beautiful Our Lady of Guadalupe Church dominates the town with its twin domed towers. Conejos thrived as a commercial center until 1881, when the Denver & Rio Grande Railroad bypassed the town and founded Antonito just down the road. Conejos became a footnote in Colorado history when the state's last hanging took place there on July 16, 1889.

Antonito began in 1881 as a railroad stop. The line originally planned on stopping at Conejos, but high land prices and difficulty in obtaining a right-of-way prompted the Denver & Rio Grande to build a new town. The narrow-gauge railroad, now known as the **Cumbres & Toltec Scenic Railroad,** ran from Alamosa through Antonito and west over Cumbres Pass to Durango. A branch called the Chile Line went south from Antonito to Española. The town quickly became the south valley's business hub, with warehouses, hotels, saloons, bordellos, and banks.

Antonito, with a population of about 800, retains its old charm and remains a ranching and farming community. Its most popular attraction is the 64-mile railroad between Antonito and Chama. The Cumbres & Toltec Railroad, America's longest narrow-gauge line, twists along the Colorado and New Mexico border and passes through scenic Toltec Gorge. The train runs daily from early summer to late fall.

A famed Antonito landmark on State Street east of US 285 is **Cano's Castle,** a unique folk art "castle" with four buildings: the King, Queen, Rook, and Knight's Horse. The place was built by Vietnam veteran Dominic Espinosa, nicknamed "Cano" from "Chicano." He started building the Castle in 1980 after his late mother, Margarita, told him to get rid of his growing collection of beer cans in the backyard. Using the project to stay clean and sober, Cano built it using over a million cans, mostly beer cans (which he says he never took a sip from), thousands of tires, and hundreds of shiny hubcaps, which adorn the outside walls. If you stop by and Cano is outside, he might give you a tour of the Castle and tell you how God is his inspiration. Oh, he will also tell you that the murderous Espinosa brothers were his great uncles, but more about them below.

Over a million cans, mostly beer cans, were used to construct Cano's Castle, an unusual Antonito landmark.

The Espinosas & Las Mesitas

At the train station on Antonito's south side, US 285 turns south toward New Mexico. The scenic drive continues west on CO 17. Past Antonito, the road runs through a succession of small, old towns—Paisaje, Mogote, and Las Mesitas. All three towns were first established in the 1850s as settlers spread out from Conejos across the fertile bottomlands along the Conejos River.

Paisaje is best remembered as the home of the crazy **Espinosa brothers.** The duo, Felipe and Julian, claimed that a vision told them to kill "gringos." In the spring of 1863 they went on a brutal rampage, murdering numerous Anglos in the South Park area. A posse surprised the pair near Cripple Creek, and Felipe was killed in a shootout. In his diary they found an entry revealing that the brothers had sworn to kill 600 men. A $2,500 bounty was put on the escaped Julian, and soldiers at Fort Garland mobilized to find him, dead or alive. In September army scout Thomas Tobin tracked Espinosa and his nephew to Cucharas Pass, where he shot them at their evening campfire. Tobin collected his reward after bringing the outlaw's head to the fort commandant.

After crossing the Conejos River, the highway swings through **Las Mesitas.** Adobe houses and small ranches mark the town today, along with the gutted roadside ruins of San Isadore church. The church burned down in 1975, leaving its massive walls open to the sun and rain. From here the canyon narrows and the road runs west beneath a high mesa. Scattered piñon pines and junipers mix with sagebrush on its steep slopes. The highway passes through Fox Creek and a mile later enters **Rio Grande National Forest.** Mogote Campground, with 40 campsites on two loops, nestles among ponderosa pines and tall cottonwoods along the Conejos River at 8,300 feet.

Conejos River to Cumbres Pass

The highway runs alongside the river for the next 10 miles, passing into a deep canyon lined with volcanic cliffs and dense forests. The **Conejos River,** draining from 13,172-foot Conejos Peak, is one of Colorado's least known yet wildest rivers. Excellent trout fishing in Gold Medal waters, great wildlife habitat, and its undammed flow provide recreation for anglers, kayakers, and naturalists.

Aspen Glade Campground, with 28 single and 4 double campsites, sits just past the first roadside aspen grove. Numerous stands of golden aspens gild the hillsides along the drive in late September. Keep an eye out for wildlife, including bighorn sheep, elk, and mule deer. The canyon widens into a broad, glaciated valley 20 miles from Antonito. FR 250 continues up the valley, passing several campgrounds and lakes to Platoro, an old 1880s mining ghost town. The scenic drive

A coyote prowls through January snow at Great Sand Dunes National Park.

crosses the river, passes the turnoff to 31-site Elk Creek Campground, and begins the final climb.

Today's highway follows an old Native American trail over La Manga and Cumbres Passes. The Overlook wayside site makes a great stop with its scenic viewpoint after the highway begins its steep climb out of the valley. The road switchbacks up through aspen and spruce forest on the western flank of 10,561-foot McIntyre Mountain and after a few miles follows La Manga Creek to the grassy 10,230-foot summit of **La Manga Pass.**

The highway drops south along a creek to Rio de Los Pinos in a broad valley, swings around Neff Mountain above the railroad tracks, and climbs to the summit of 10,022-foot **Cumbres Pass.** Just before the summit, a road heads northwest to Trujillo Meadows Reservoir and Campground. A small railroad station sits in the spruce forest atop the pass. The low mountains between La Manga and Cumbres Passes offer excellent cross-country skiing in winter, with plentiful snow and gorgeous scenery. The drive continues southwest, dropping over rolling hills studded with crags and covered with meadows and forest before quietly ending at the Colorado–New Mexico border. Chama, a picturesque New Mexico town, sits 8 miles south of the byway.

Wet Mountains Scenic Drive

Florence to Colorado City

General description: This 58-mile drive, part of the Frontier Pathways Scenic Byway, traverses the Wet Mountains between Florence and Colorado City, passing historic sites, ragged canyons, and recreational areas.

Special attractions: Florence, San Isabel National Forest, Hardscrabble Canyon, Bishop Castle, Lake Isabel, Greenhorn Mountain, camping, hiking, fishing, aspen colors, rock climbing.

Location: South-central Colorado. The drive begins in Florence 5 miles south of US 50 at the junction of CO 115 and 67. The highway runs south, joins CO 96 in Wetmore, and intersects CO 165 at McKenzie Junction. The drive ends in Colorado City at exit 74 on I-25 south of Pueblo.

Route name and numbers: The Greenhorn Highway; CO 67, 96, and 165.

Travel season: Year-round.

Camping: Five national forest campgrounds—Ophir Creek (31 sites), Davenport (12 sites), La Vista (29 sites), Southside (8 sites), and St. Charles (15 sites)—lie along the drive. Primitive camping is permitted on national forest land. Greenhorn Meadows Park in Colorado City offers camping.

Services: All services are in Florence and Colorado City. Limited services in Wetmore, San Isabel, and Rye.

Nearby attractions: Sangre de Cristo Wilderness Area, Westcliffe, Cañon City attractions, Gold Belt Tour Back Country Byway (Scenic Drive 8), Royal Gorge, Pueblo attractions, Lake Pueblo State Park, Lathrop State Park, La Veta, Spanish Peaks, Highway of Legends Scenic Byway (Scenic Drive 4).

The Route

Far away, across the dusty prairie, the Wet Mountains lift above the western horizon like a humpbacked blue cloud. Early pioneers, inching across the Great Plains in wagon caravans, saw a promise in those dreamlike mountains. Up there, beyond the dry land of short grass, yucca, and rattlesnakes, lay a cool oasis lush with wind-ruffled pine forests, wildflower-dotted meadows, and sparkling streams of clear water. A party of early Mormon emigrants, on reaching this mountain outpost, reveled in the wooded slopes and rain-laden clouds after their months-long trek over what was then called "The Great American Desert." They named them the Wet Mountains—oddly enough, a name also given by the Spanish and Native Americans.

The Wet Mountains, the southern vestige of the Front Range, make a broad arc from the Arkansas River west of Cañon City to the Huerfano River at Badito. The range, composed of Precambrian granite and metamorphic rocks, formed when a fault uplifted those old rocks and thrust them onto younger sedimentary

Wet Mountains Scenic Drive

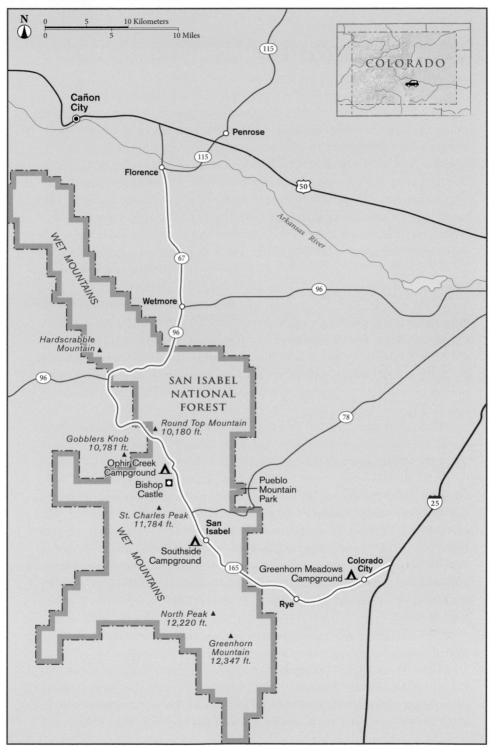

layers. The range summits are from 9,000 to over 12,000 feet, with 12,347-foot Greenhorn Mountain the highest point. Creeks slice into the ancient bedrock, creating abrupt, cliff-lined canyons and shallow, grassy valleys.

The Wet Mountain scenic drive, part of the Frontier Pathways Scenic Byway, begins in Florence in the Arkansas River valley and wends through canyons and valleys for 58 miles before emptying onto the prairie at Colorado City. Weather along the drive is generally pleasant year-round. Summer temperatures range from the 90s at the lower elevations at Florence and Colorado City to the 70s in the mountains. Immense thunderstorms build over the Wet Mountains and the neighboring Sangre de Cristo Mountains on summer afternoons. Expect localized heavy rain. Autumn days are warm and clear, with golden aspens sprinkled on the hillsides. Winter sets in by early November, and snow locks the upper reaches until April. Spring is short and unpredictable, with periods of rain, snow, and sun.

Florence to Wetmore

Florence is 5 miles southwest of US 50 and Penrose and 10 miles east of Cañon City at the intersection of CO 115 and 67. The town lies on the south bank of the Arkansas River in a broad, arid valley hemmed in by the Pikes Peak massif to the north and the Wet Mountains to the south. The river, after bursting from the mountains and the Royal Gorge at Cañon City, gently braids across a wide channel lined with cottonwoods.

Florence, founded in 1860, was first named Frazerville for Joe Frazer, who developed coal mines south of town and planted the first apple orchards here. The town was renamed for the daughter of local oilman James McCandless in the 1870s. Besides seams of coal, oil deposits underlie the Florence area. A. M. Cassiday drilled the first well in 1862 in nearby Oil Canyon, where an oil spring bubbled to the surface. The oil field, called the Florence Pool, is the second oldest in the US. Well No. 42, considered the oldest continuously operating oil well in the world, has pumped out over a million gallons of crude since it was drilled in 1889. A stroll down Main Street is a step back in the past with over a dozen antique shops, restaurants, and galleries. Main Street was also the setting for the fictional town of Holt in the 2017 film *Our Souls at Night*, based on the novel by Kent Haruf.

The drive starts east of downtown Florence on CO 67, heading south. The straight road runs across a gently tilting plain seamed with shallow valleys and scarred by deep arroyos. The highway crosses a succession of dry creekbeds—Cocklebur, Newlin, and Mineral Creeks. Cottonwoods, indicating underground water, border the creek beds, and low scrubby mesas, fringed with tawny rimrock and scattered junipers, form low ramparts. Round-shouldered Pikes Peak looms to the north above the wide Arkansas River valley. After 7 miles the road climbs onto a flat, barren bench surrounded by low-browed hills. The Wet Mountains, a high escarpment of green forested peaks and canyons, towers to the west and south.

A state historic marker at 9.5 miles commemorates the area's earliest settlements. The first was El Cuervo (The Raven), a Native American trading post built by Maurice LeDuc a mile west of the marker near the mountain base at the junction of Adobe and Mineral Creeks. Colonel Henry Dodge of the First Regiment of United States Dragoons noted a camp of 60 Arapaho tepees at the post in 1835.

The pueblo of Hardscrabble was established in 1844 at the confluence of Adobe and Hardscrabble Creeks a few miles north of the marker and used as a trading post for Native Americans and trappers. The village was visited by explorer John C. Fremont in 1845. Twenty-five trappers with Native American wives and children lived there. Fremont stopped by again in late November 1848 during his disastrous fourth expedition in search of a transcontinental railroad route along the 38th parallel. Few people inhabited the village, most having moved to Pueblo after Native American attacks. Richard Kern, an expedition member, described Hardscrabble in his journal as the "summer resort of hunters." The expedition lingered only two days, buying and shelling 130 bushels of corn and dining on chicken and pumpkin before heading west to the San Juan Mountains.

The highway continues south, passing a lone ponderosa pine and running 2 miles to **Wetmore** on Hardscrabble Creek's gravel banks. Frances and William Wetmore bought an old homestead here and surveyed, named, and established the town around 1880. It served as a stagecoach station on the line between Pueblo and the Wet Mountain Valley. CO 67 dead-ends here at CO 96. Turn west or right on CO 96.

Hardscrabble Creek

The highway bends south onto a bench above **Hardscrabble Creek** in a broad valley. The valley edge gently rises west toward the Wet Mountains, where tilted sandstone layers form rocky hogbacks against a soaring mountain wall. Rounded hills cloaked in oak and pine trees flank the valley's east side. As the road runs south, the valley narrows and deep forests of scrub oak and ponderosa pine mix with open meadows. Tall cottonwoods shelter the creek below the road. A wildfire tore through this area in 2012, torching a few houses and burning scattered sections of the woodland alongside the highway. A couple other fires in the dry summer of 2018 burned woodlands along the drive here.

At 15 miles the drive enters San Isabel National Forest. A half-mile later the road swings west into North Hardscrabble Canyon's abrupt defile. FR 306 begins here and runs south and west up South Hardscrabble Creek. Near this road junction sits a rock face inscribed with famed frontiersman Kit Carson's name and his wife Josefa Jaramillo's initials.

The highway heads west up the canyon, cutting through sandstone hogbacks and passing steep side canyons. Bighorn sheep and mule deer graze in open meadows along the drive. As the road climbs, the canyon steepens and narrows. Ponderosa pines, piñon pines, and junipers scatter over the warm north slopes, while deep forests of spruce and fir darken the south side. A picnic area sits partway up the canyon along the creek.

Peaks, including rough 10,402-foot Hardscrabble Mountain, tower above the canyon floor. Tilted layers of metamorphic rock form bands of cliffs and break into sharp buttresses, pointed pyramids, and blocky castles. The origins of the name "Hardscrabble" are lost, but local legend says the name came after Utes massacred settlers in Pueblo on Christmas Day 1855. The Native Americans, pursued by soldiers, fled up the creek and had a "hard scrabble" to elude capture.

At 19 miles the canyon narrows and the highway twists through road cuts. The creek below tumbles over boulders, forming frothy cascades. A pullout at Rattlesnake Gulch is a good picnic stop. A trail climbs the steep gulch, passing numerous climbing crags and boulders. The canyon widens above the gulch, the road grade abates, and narrow-leaf cottonwoods densely line the creek. McKenzie Junction, the intersection of CO 96 and 165, sits in the widening, grassy valley. The drive turns south on CO 165, while CO 96 heads west for 16 miles to Westcliffe.

Greenhorn Highway & Bishop Castle

CO 165, the **Greenhorn Highway,** runs 35 miles from the CO 96 junction to Colorado City. The road climbs south up Hardscrabble Creek's south fork, a shallow valley fringed with pine and fir forest, aspen groves, and meadows. The road steadily ascends and reaches 9,379-foot Wixson Divide after 5 miles. This broad saddle, surrounded by grassland and open forests, lies below 11,121-foot Wixson Mountain to the west.

The drive drops down another valley, crosses South Hardscrabble Creek, and begins climbing another shallow valley to the summit of Bigelow Divide. Edging south above Bigelow Creek, the drive passes old ranch buildings and bends west up Middle Creek. Ophir Creek Campground, with 31 sites, is tucked into a wooded valley along the creek, where the highway makes a hairpin turn.

"Every man wants a castle," said Jim Bishop, "and I have mine."
Starting in 1969, he built Bishop Castle with over 50,000 tons of local stone.

The Ophir Creek Road (FR 360) heads west up Ophir Creek here and reaches the Wet Mountains range crest. To climb 12,347-foot **Greenhorn Mountain,** the twin-summited high point of the Wet Mountains, follow the Ophir Creek Road to a left turn on Greenhorn Mountain Road (FR 403) and follow the winding dirt road along the crest to the road's end at Blue Lakes and the Greenhorn Trail Trailhead. It's 24.3 miles from the highway to the trailhead. The excellent hike to Greenhorn's summit is 5.2 miles round trip and requires 3 to 5 hours of hiking. Expect spectacular views of the tawny prairie, the Spanish Peaks, and the southern Sangre de Cristo Mountains. Hike details are in *Climbing Colorado's Mountains* from FalconGuides.

The drive climbs out of the valley, slices through several road cuts, and reaches **Bishop Castle.** The castle, a marvelous stone building rising out of the forest above the highway, is testimony to the ingenuity and labor of Jim Bishop

Greenhorn Mountain, the high point of the Wet Mountains, offers wide views across southern Colorado.

and the support of his late wife Phoebe Marie Bishop. Bishop, starting at age 25 in June 1969, began building the castle from his imagination.

Today, without blueprints, Mr. Bishop continues to craft arches, turrets, towers, a fire-breathing dragon, and huge rooms from local cobbles, boulders, and mortar. The main tower soars 160 feet into the sky. This marvelous structure, looking less like a traditional medieval castle and more like a storybook fantasy castle in *Lord of the Rings*, attracts more than 100,000 travelers a year. Jim, a wiry man with strong hands, calls the castle "the largest one-man project in the world" and says it's "a tourist attraction without being a tourist trap." The castle, owned by the nonprofit Bishop Castle Foundation, donates money raised from donations for newborn heart surgery. Admission is free and the castle is open year-round.

Past Bishop Castle the highway runs south, across Davenport Creek, over Greenhill Divide, and into Willow Creek valley. At the valley base sits **San Isabel,** a small resort with lodging, restaurants, and supplies. Lake Isabel nestles in the broad valley beyond the town, its deep blue water attracting anglers. The 40-acre lake, formed by St. Charles Dam, impounds the St. Charles River. High forested ridges and rounded peaks studded with granite crags loom above the aspen-fringed lake. A parking area on the east side of the highway and one on the lake's north shore allows angler and hiker access to Lake Isabel. A turn south of the lake leads to the national forest's Lake Isabel Recreation Area with 73 campsites in Southside, La Vista, and San Isabel campgrounds and a large picnic and day use area.

The drive intersects the twisting Old San Isabel Road a mile past the lake. Here the highway begins winding downward, dipping through shallow canyons and passing groves of aspen. Greenhorn Mountain towers above the drive. As the highway descends, steep ridges and slopes, scaled with a dense conifer forest, rise above the blacktop. This wild land of woods and canyons is part of 23,087-acre Greenhorn Mountain Wilderness Area.

Rye to Colorado City

As the road descends the mountain flank, the vegetation changes from moist spruce, fir, and aspen forest to a drier woodland of ponderosa pine and scrub oak. The highway leaves the national forest 6 miles from San Isabel and traverses high, rolling foothills coated with scrub oak and open grassland. Sandstone-rimmed cuestas, or upturned mesas, seamed with canyons break from the hills and drop eastward. After a few miles the road passes grazing cattle and pastures and bends into **Rye.** This quiet town, established in 1882, was named for surrounding grain fields. It serves today as a ranching center.

Apache Falls, a 100-foot-high horsetail waterfall pouring over a cliff, is south of Rye. Reach it from the Bartlett Trailhead at the end of FR 427. It's an 11-mile hike with lots of elevation gain and loss but the falls at trail's end is magical. For the trail details, consult *Hiking Colorado's Waterfalls* from FalconGuides.

The drive runs east from Rye along the north side of the Greenhorn Creek valley. Fields scattered with hay bales and cattle lie alongside the creek. Higher mesas rimmed with Dakota sandstone and covered with pine and oak rise north of the asphalt. The road and creek continue descending eastward, and the climate and hills steadily dry. By the time the road reaches the valley floor, short grass, yucca, and cactus dominate this Upper Sonoran life zone. Greenhorn Meadows Park, with a cottonwood-shaded campground, sits along the creek.

The nearby **Cuerno Verde** monument memorializes the Comanche chief killed near here. Cuerno Verde or Green Horn was a war chief who wore green-tinted horns on his war bonnet. He died on September 3, 1779, after his Comanche forces had engaged in a series of battles with Spanish troops led by Juan Bautista de Anza. Anza took the green horns from the battlefield and presented them to the Spanish Viceroy, who in turn gave it to the King of Spain who gave it to the Pope. Cuerno Verde's horns are now displayed in the Vatican Museum in Rome. While Anza called him a "scourge" and noted the atrocities of the Comanche, modern-day Comanches say he was only protecting their land and people from the Spanish invaders.

Passing over low, scrubby hills, the highway climbs to **Colorado City,** one of the state's newer communities. The town, called Crow Junction in the 1880s, was founded in 1963 as a resort and commercial enterprise and named for the Colorado City Development Company. Now it's a placid crossroads with visitor services, a golf course, and Beckwith Reservoir, offering fishing and boating. The drive ends at a spacious and clean highway rest area at I-25's exit 74. Pueblo lies almost 25 miles to the north, while Walsenburg sits 24 miles to the south. Graneros Gorge, just south of the interchange, is a spectacular canyon sliced into grassy hills east of the interstate highway.

8

Gold Belt Tour Back Country Byway

Cañon City to Cripple Creek Loop

General description: This 64-mile-long open loop drive, part of the Gold Belt Tour Back Country Byway, follows Phantom Canyon and Shelf Roads through canyons on the south slope of Pikes Peak.

Special attractions: Indian Springs Trace Fossil Site, Beaver Creek Wilderness Study Area, Cripple Creek and Victor National Historic Districts, Cripple Creek & Victor Narrow Gauge Railroad, Window Rock, Shelf Road Climbing Area, Garden Park Fossil Area, Red Cañon Park, Cañon City attractions, hiking, rock climbing, camping, fishing, wildlife, mine ruins, photography.

Location: Central Colorado. The drive follows Shelf Road north from Cañon City to Cripple Creek, then turns south on CO 67 to Victor and down Phantom Canyon Road to US 50 near Florence.

Route names and numbers: Shelf Road, Phantom Canyon Road, CO 67, Fremont CR 9, Teller CR 88.

Travel season: Year-round. Snow and mud may temporarily close the roads during winter. Watch for slick roads after summer thunderstorms. Both roads are narrow—often only one lane wide with tight turns. Do not drive vehicles over 25 feet wide, including motor homes, large campers, and travel trailers, on the drive.

Camping: Private campgrounds are in the Cripple Creek and Cañon City areas and at Indian Springs. Two campgrounds operated by the Bureau of Land Management (BLM) are at the Shelf Road Climbing Area. National forest campgrounds are in nearby Pike National Forest.

Services: All services in Cañon City, Cripple Creek, Victor, and Florence.

Nearby attractions: Royal Gorge Park, Temple Canyon Park, Arkansas Headwaters State Park, Mueller State Park, Florissant Fossil Beds National Monument, Pikes Peak, Beaver Creek State Wildlife Area, Elevenmile Canyon, Colorado Springs attractions, Lake Pueblo State Park.

The Route

Pikes Peak, towering to 14,115 feet, anchors the southern Front Range and forms a distinctive landmark for travelers. Canyons slice into its bedrock southern slopes, forming deep defiles separated by high, forested ridges. This rugged country remains one of the Front Range's wildest and least-accessible landscapes. It's a bold, sculpted land overlooked by pink granite bastions and inhabited by bighorn sheep, mountain lions, falcons, and rattlesnakes. This 64-mile-long scenic drive makes an open loop between Cañon City and Cripple Creek on two narrow gravel roads—Shelf Road and Phantom Canyon Road—that thread through precipitous canyons on Pikes Peak's southern slope.

Gold Belt Tour Back Country Byway

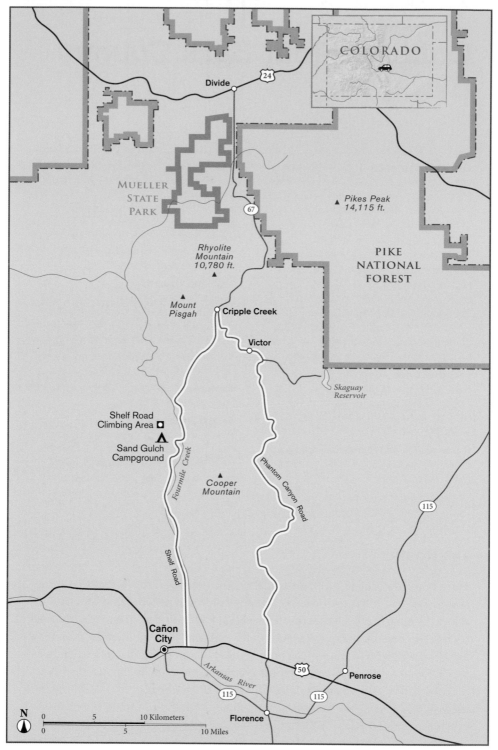

The roads, part of the Bureau of Land Management's **Gold Belt Tour Back Country Byway,** offer an out-of-the-ordinary scenic driving experience. Both are winding dirt and gravel tracks that often narrow to a single lane for miles at a time in deep canyons or on exposed slopes. Frequent pullouts allow passing on narrow sections. Neither road is well maintained, and each is often rough and corrugated, particularly after heavy rain. Shelf Road's shelf section should not be driven after rain or during snowmelt; its clay surface becomes extremely slippery and there is no guardrail to stop a slip to oblivion. *Trailers, motor homes, or vehicles over 25 feet in length should not be used to travel either road.* Drive defensively on the roads. Always expect another car on blind corners, don't speed, and remember that uphill traffic has the right-of-way.

The drive is open year-round, with each season offering its own flavor. Summers tend to be hot in the lower elevations, with highs regularly climbing into the 90s near the Arkansas River valley. The pleasant upper-elevation temperatures range from 60 to 80 degrees. Expect thunderstorms on summer afternoons. Autumn days are warm and clear, with occasional showers. Winter brings variable weather. Mild winter weather rules in the lower elevations, with days as warm as 50 degrees and light snowfall. Snowpack and ice slicken shaded road sections near Cripple Creek and Victor from November to February. Spring brings warm, breezy weather along with rain and snow showers.

Morrison Formation & Garden Park Quarry

The Shelf Road drive segment begins in east Cañon City. Turn north on Raynolds Avenue from US 50. A Colorado state scenic drive sign reading "Gold Belt Tour" marks the turn. Head north on Raynolds for 0.7 mile through a residential neighborhood. When the street ends, bend left on Pear Street for 0.1 mile and then turn north on Fields Avenue and drive past fenced pastures, subdivisions, and Harrison School. The street quickly leaves Cañon City behind and climbs a low, flat hill topped with homes and drops through shale hills past a lumber mill to merge with Red Canyon Road (CR 9) and enter into Fourmile Creek's canyon.

The paved road swings past a ranch and tall cottonwoods, and at 4.5 miles enters a cliffed portal carved through tilted Dakota sandstone cliffs above the creek. The canyon quickly deepens, with the sandstone layer capping the canyon rim. Slopes below the rim cascade down to the road with a veneer of fallen boulders and scattered piñon pine, juniper, and rabbitbrush. The first oil well west of the Mississippi River was drilled in this canyon in 1862.

The drive winds along benches on the creek's western margin. Native American petroglyphs decorate one roadside boulder. A BLM picnic area with an information kiosk about dinosaurs sits partway up the canyon. The road continues up

Shelf Road twists through rocky Helena Canyon above Fourmile Creek.

the shallow canyon. Steep slopes of colored shale and mudstone stair-step back to the higher sandstone rim above the creek. These unassuming soft rock layers, called the **Morrison Formation,** hold one of Colorado's most astounding natural wonders—a dinosaur graveyard.

The Morrison Formation, a thick widespread layer of sandstone, mudstone, siltstone, and shale, was deposited on a vast, swampy floodplain along the edge of a retreating sea during Jurassic times, almost 150 million years ago. Wide rivers and streams, flowing from distant mountains and volcanic peaks, sluggishly meandered across a broad basin. Trees lined the riverbanks and backwater ponds, and life flourished on the fertile, subtropical landscape. The most prominent residents of this ancient land were giant dinosaurs. The rivers and swamps swallowed their bones after death, slowly entombing, petrifying, and preserving the remains until small Fourmile Creek exhumed the bones in another age.

Dinosaur bones hide in the Morrison Formation all over Colorado and Utah, including Riggs Hill near Grand Junction, the famous quarry in Dinosaur National Monument, near Morrison outside Denver, and at the **Garden Park Quarries** along Shelf Road. The area's first finds came to local school superintendent O. W. Lucas in March 1877. Lucas, an amateur botanist studying local plants, found several fossil fragments, including a 5-foot-long leg bone weathering out of the strata. He sent off samples to eminent Philadelphia paleontologist Edward D. Cope, who promptly dispatched excavators to the Garden Park site.

Over the next few years, Cope and rival Yale scientist Othniel C. Marsh dug into the soft shale and mudstone slopes and found a staggering number of gigantic, almost complete dinosaur skeletons. The first stegosaur, the official Colorado state fossil, came from the Garden Park quarries, as well as camarasaur, diplodocus, and allosaur remains. The area also yielded bones from numerous small dinosaurs, plants, and trees. The Denver Museum of Nature and Science continues to probe the Garden Park Quarries. A state historic marker, sitting near the canyon's northern end, commemorates the Garden Park Quarry and its buried treasures. The area is protected as the BLM's **Garden Park Fossil Area,** a Colorado Research Natural Area, and as a National Natural Landmark.

The drive swings across Fourmile Creek beneath low bluffs and climbs into Garden Park, a long, broad valley flanked by rolling hills and steep mountains. The road traverses the valley for almost 5 miles, passing hay fields, fenced paddocks with grazing cattle and horses, and the cottonwood-lined creek. Mule deer and wild turkeys often congregate in the open fields along the creek in early evening.

The drive passes the entrance to **Red Canyon Park,** a 600-acre Cañon City parkland, just after crossing the creek halfway up the valley. The park, a maze of upturned sandstone layers, fringes the base of Rice Mountain on Garden Park's western edge. This primitive, off-the-beaten-track park offers eroded hoodoos and spires, long sweeping escarpments chiseled from red sandstone, a maze of hiking trails that thread among the formations, and picnic tables with a mountain view.

Shelf Road to Cripple Creek

The road continues north past a couple of ranches into dry hills studded with piñon pines and junipers. At 12 miles the University Wall looms to the east, lifting its leaning limestone rampart above Fourmile Creek's shallow gorge. The road passes a stylish ranch house and climbs onto an almost level plain coated with short grass and surrounded by low woods. Just east of here inside the canyon rim lie two small caves—Marble and Fly Caves—in limestone cliffs. Wilson Cave hides farther up Helena Canyon.

Prominent limestone cliff bands rim the low hills and canyons north of the road at the northern end of Garden Park. These short, sharp cliffs comprise **Shelf Road Climbing Area,** one of Colorado's best sport-climbing areas, with over 1,500 established routes. Two turns lead to the best crags. The first goes through a gate and bumps northwest across a pasture to a campground and parking area for The Gallery and Sand Gulch. A tenth of a mile north is a marked BLM road that climbs north to The Bank and The Dark Side, two long cliff bands in Trail Gulch. Some of the area's best climbing routes, including Thunder Tactics, Heavy

Weather, and Back to the Future, ascend The Bank's blond limestone walls. Almost all of the area's routes are protected with permanent bolts and anchors. See FalconGuides' *Rock Climbing Colorado* for information on climbing access, cliff sectors, and routes at Shelf Road.

Shelf Road twists down a slight canyon with piñon pines, junipers, and boulders tacked to the hillside. The track emerges onto a 4-mile-long shelf road hacked from a steep slope between cliff bands in Helena Canyon. This spectacular road section offers stunning scenery, dramatic drop-offs below the passenger windows, and a white-knuckle grip for inexperienced mountain drivers. Most of the road is single lane, with only the occasional outside pullout for passing.

The road edges along the shelf, only leaving the main canyon to dip into Trail Gulch. Fourmile Creek, dashing over worn boulders and bedrock, riffles far below the road in a somber granite gorge. Above the shelf stretches a band of limestone broken into varnished black faces and tawny overhangs and arêtes. Steep slopes littered with boulders and cholla cacti cascade below the cliffs to the roadside. The Ordovician period sandstone deposited atop the Precambrian granite below the road preserves traces of some of the world's oldest known vertebrate life. Small blue dots are revealed through a microscope as fossilized platelets of *Agnathid* fish that swam here in an ancient ocean over 500 million years ago.

Shelf Road follows the track of an 1892 toll stage road that ran from Cañon City to the new gold camp at Cripple Creek. The uphill ride took six hours and required 18 horses in teams of six. Stages paid tolls on each rig's number of horses at both ends of the shelf itself. The lower toll keeper's cabin ruin lies on a spacious bend on the canyon floor just after the shelf road begins.

After 3 miles the road begins a gentle descent through a mixed conifer forest and a mile later reaches the canyon floor and crosses the creek. The drive winds up the east side of the creek in a broadening canyon for a couple of miles before reaching a long stack of tailings excavated from the Carlton Drainage Tunnel. The 6-mile-long tunnel, bored in 1941, drained water that had collected in gold mines north of Victor. Past the tailings the drive turns away from Fourmile Creek and enters a steep canyon carved by Cripple Creek.

Shelf Road follows Cripple Creek for the next 8 miles. The road corkscrews up a deep canyon flanked by granite cliffs and talus and scrub oak–covered slopes. The creek trickles over boulders and past small groves of quaking aspen. **Window Rock,** an unusual granite arch, towers over the road a couple of miles up the craggy canyon. Watch for bighorn sheep grazing across these boulder-strewn slopes. Higher up, the canyon widens and becomes a shallow, grassy valley and passes several old mines before intersecting CO 67 just south of the town of Cripple Creek.

Cripple Creek

Cripple Creek and its sister city, Victor, lie in the fabulously wealthy Cripple Creek Mining District, a collapsed volcanic caldera rimmed with sparkling veins of gold. Local cowboy Bob Womack first found gold in nearby Poverty Gulch in 1890. His claim, the El Paso Lode, sparked a gold rush to the Pikes Peak region. Almost overnight a town sprang up and by 1900 more than 50,000 people lived in Cripple Creek, making it Colorado's fourth-largest city at the time. During the boom years the district's 500 mines yielded over $340 million in gold at the prevailing price of $20.67 per ounce or over $37 billon at 2012 prices. The area mines eventually yielded more gold than the California and Alaska gold rushes combined.

Today active mining continues in the Cripple Creek & Victor Gold Mine, a deep open-pit mine east of Cripple Creek, and geologists say a fortune in gold still

Casinos and shops line Bennett Avenue where miners once walked in downtown Cripple Creek.

lies underground. Cripple Creek, now preserved as a National Historic District, offers numerous attractions, including the Cripple Creek District Museum, the Cripple Creek & Victor Narrow Gauge Railroad, the Old Homestead brothel, and gambling casinos.

The **Old Homestead House Museum** is certainly one of the most interesting places to visit in Cripple Creek. The Old Homestead was an elegant brothel established by Pearl de Vere, a beautiful 30-something redhead, in 1896 with crystal chandeliers, wallpaper from Paris, two bathrooms, newfangled electricity, and four classy working girls in the Creek's boisterous red-light district. Men who wished to visit needed letters of recommendation as well as a big bankroll to cover the $250 required for an evening date. Unfortunately, Madam Pearl took a large draft of morphine in 1897 as a sleeping aid and never woke up. She was buried in a Parisian gown in the Mount Pisgah Cemetery; her wooden grave marker, now in the Cripple Creek museum, was replaced in the 1930s by a heart-shaped marble tombstone. The brothel, however, stayed open until 1917, then was a boardinghouse and a casino before it was opened as a museum in 1958.

Victor: City of Mines

The drive turns south in Cripple Creek on CO 67, winding 5 miles to **Victor** through aspen, spruce, and pine forests. Dramatic views unfold along this lofty highway stretch of the snow-capped Sangre de Cristo Range and the broad Arkansas River valley. The highway passes the Carlton Mill, part of the Cripple Creek & Victor Mine, owned by the Newmont Mining Corporation.

The road bends through a road cut and enters 9,729-foot Victor, nicknamed the "city of mines." The slopes of Battle Mountain, looming north of town, are studded with colored mine tailings from famous mines like the Ajax, Portland, and Independence. The Gold Coin Mine operated within Victor itself. Victor, also a National Historic District, remains a mining town at heart, with old brick buildings, frame houses, and a working-class ethic. The best way to see the historic town is on the **Downtown Victor Trail.**

Besides exploring Victor on foot, several interesting trails in the area access old mining areas. Head north from Victor on Portland Avenue (CR 81) to the Vindicator Valley Trailhead. The excellent **Vindicator Valley Trail,** a two-mile loop, passes the location of the town of Independence and the ruins of several large mines that boomed in the 1890s. Informative signs along the trail detail mining history, railroads, and area towns. The **Little Grouse Mountain Trail** just west of Victor switchbacks up a rounded hill to great views of the mining district and distant mountains.

The drive meanders through downtown Victor before bending onto Phantom Canyon Road at the town's far southeast corner.

Phantom Canyon Road

The unpaved **Phantom Canyon Road** runs 31 miles south to US 50. The road initially loops across high benches and rolling hills covered with meadows, aspen groves, and spruce and pine forests. A left turn, just outside Victor, on CR 861 leads east 6 miles to 715-acre **Skaguay Reservoir State Wildlife Area.** The popular 84-acre lake, tucked in a wooded valley, offers trout and pike fishing and primitive camping.

A rugged hike descends 5 miles down the rough **Beaver Creek Trail** along West Beaver Creek below the reservoir's dam to the ruins of the **Skaguay Power Plant.** The power station provided electricity to Victor and its mines on Battle Mountain. Work on the red-brick power plant building and the dam began in 1899. A wooden and metal pipeline descended over 5 miles from the dam to the power plant to generate pressure to spin 4 turbines for electricity. An engineering error, however, extended the piping too low so there was only enough pressure to turn 3 turbines. The plant opened in 1901 and provided electricity until a 1965 flood, caused by the failure of a dam near Gillette upstream, plugged the wooden pipe with debris. The power plant ruin is an architectural gem in the middle of nowhere, with 25-foot-high walls, Romanesque arches, and decorative brickwork. The site also boasted a laundry, cabins, a store, dance hall, saloon, and gambling tables.

Phantom Canyon Road, a narrow dirt road, traverses the abandoned rail bed of the old Florence and Cripple Creek Railroad, "The Gold Belt Line." The railroad carried raw gold ore from Cripple Creek's mines to 9 reduction mills in Florence. At Alta Vista the road begins a slow descent for a few miles before dropping steeply into Phantom Canyon. The train originally climbed the Wilbur Loop on 4 percent grades out of the canyon with helper engines.

After reaching upper Phantom Canyon, the road bends south and follows the canyon floor past granite crags, aspens, and pine-covered hills. The road gently winds down the canyon alternately widening and narrowing. Fifteen miles down, the canyon pinches off to a narrow slot, with Eightmile Creek and the road twisting below tall granite cliffs. Beyond, the canyon widens and drops steeply below the road as it edges across dry mountain slopes. After crossing a steel bridge built in 1897, the road reaches a BLM information booth and the parking area for access to the adjoining **Beaver Creek Wilderness Study Area** on the east. This proposed 28,069-acre wilderness area encompasses the rugged, rocky canyons of East and West Beaver Creeks, which drain south from Pikes Peak's southern slopes. The wild area is seldom visited, home to large mammals, including black bear and mountain lion, and is a renowned native cutthroat trout fishery.

A trail into the west side of the WSA begins by the parking area and heads northeast up a shallow canyon, passing the remains of the pioneer Holbert Cabin. The best way to explore the area is the 7-mile **Beaver Creek Loop Hike,** which follows the Beaver Creek, Trail Gulch, and Powerline trails in a lollipop loop. It begins from a trailhead in Beaver Creek State Wildlife Area at the end of Teller County Road 123 east of the scenic drive. For trail details, consult *Best Hikes near Colorado Springs* from FalconGuides.

The narrow road continues down the canyon past the abandoned townsite of Adelaide, an 1890s train watering stop. As the road descends, the canyon deepens and becomes drier. Piñon pine, juniper, cactus, and yucca replace the spruce, fir, and pine forests of higher elevations, and the creek slows to a trickle among cottonwoods. The road runs through two tunnels built in 1895 after floods destroyed the original track alignment. A mile past Tunnel #1 the canyon walls slacken, the mountains become rounded, and the drive runs through a narrow gate hemmed in by tall rock walls. The canyon widens and the road bends west along a sandstone hogback and then south into a broad valley flanked by the mountain uplift and the Dakota Hogback. The road becomes paved and swings past the turn to **Indian Springs Trace Fossil Natural Area.**

This 113-acre national natural landmark, on private land, exhibits surface trails on sandstone of 460-million-year-old arthropods. The area, once a mudflat in a tidal lagoon, preserves some 25 different kinds of markings left by diverse animals including a brachiopod; the walking, foraging, and burrowing tracks of an ancestral horseshoe crab; walking and swimming tracks from a giant trilobite; and evidence of a jawless armor-plated fish, one of the world's first known vertebrates. The site's owners conduct tours and offer a private campground for overnight visitors.

The drive passes through a deep notch chiseled into the hogback, twists through a shallow canyon, and climbs onto a broad bench above Sixmile Creek. The scenic drive runs south through a typical Upper Sonoran ecosystem with short grass and cholla cacti, and ends a few miles later at US 50. Cañon City sits 4 miles to the west, while Florence lies 3 miles south on CO 67 along the Arkansas River.

9

Pikes Peak Highway

Cascade to the Summit of Pikes Peak

General description: The 20-mile-long paved Pikes Peak Highway, a toll road, climbs to the summit of 14,115-foot Pikes Peak, Colorado's 31st-highest mountain.

Special attractions: Scenic views, hiking, rock climbing, Bottomless Pit, Glen Cove, tundra plants and above-timberline ecosystem, Barr Trail, Pikes Peak Cog Railroad, fishing.

Location: East-central Colorado. Pikes Peak towers over Colorado Springs and the surrounding Front Range 70 miles south of Denver. The scenic highway begins in Cascade off US 24 about 5 miles west of Manitou Springs.

Route name and number: Pikes Peak Highway, FR 58.

Travel season: The road is usually open from May through October, depending on the weather and snow conditions. Call the tollgate at (719) 684-9138 for more information.

Camping: No camping is allowed along the highway. Campgrounds are in Pike National Forest at The Crags, Elevenmile Canyon, north of Woodland Park on CO 67, and along Rampart Range Road. Private campgrounds are in Colorado Springs.

Services: No services on the drive, except for food at Glen Cove and the Summit House. Limited services at Cascade and Green Mountain Falls at the highway's base. Complete services are in Colorado Springs, Manitou Springs, and Woodland Park.

Nearby attractions: Colorado Springs attractions, Air Force Academy, Garden of the Gods Park, North Cheyenne Cañon Park, Red Rock Canyon Open Space, Cheyenne Mountain State Park, Cripple Creek, Florissant Fossil Beds National Monument, Pike National Forest, Lost Creek Wilderness Area, Mueller State Park, Royal Gorge, Gold Belt Tour Back Country Byway (Scenic Drive 8), Rampart Range Road (Scenic Drive 12).

The Route

Pikes Peak stands high above the tawny Colorado prairie like a strong, silent sentinel. From its base, the peak lifts over its low, forested neighbors, rising almost 8,000 feet from Colorado Springs to its snow-capped 14,115-foot summit. The great peak has long been a beacon for travelers. Its distinctive outline, seen from over 100 miles away, was a landmark to the Ute Indians, early explorers and trappers, traders on the Santa Fe Trail, and prospectors and settlers heading west during the 1850s rush to northern Colorado's gold fields.

The peak is perhaps America's most famous mountain. More people reach its 60-acre summit—via Barr Trail, the Pikes Peak Cog Railroad, and the Pikes Peak Highway—than any other high peak in the US. The highway, ascending 20 miles to the summit, is one of Colorado's highest and best drives. The paved road offers expansive views and dramatic scenery.

Pikes Peak Highway

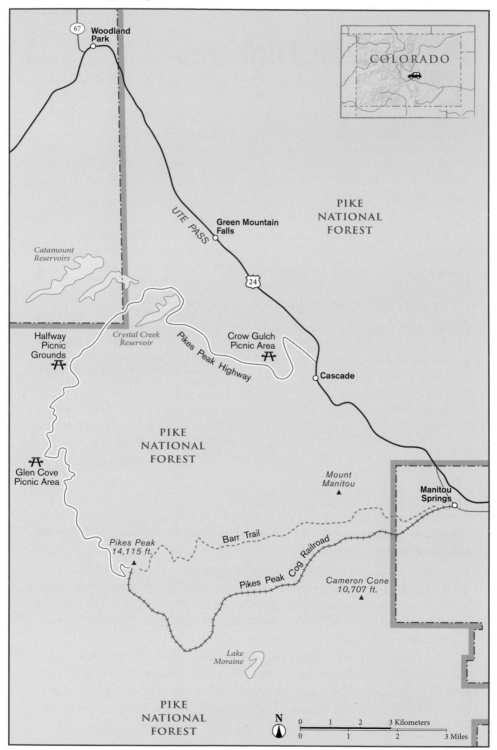

COLORADO

67 Woodland Park

PIKE NATIONAL FOREST

UTE PASS

Green Mountain Falls

24

Catamount Reservoirs

Crystal Creek Reservoir

Halfway Picnic Grounds

Pikes Peak Highway

Crow Gulch Picnic Area

Cascade

PIKE NATIONAL FOREST

Glen Cove Picnic Area

Mount Manitou

Manitou Springs

Barr Trail

Pikes Peak 14,115 ft.

Pikes Peak Cog Railroad

Cameron Cone 10,707 ft.

Lake Moraine

PIKE NATIONAL FOREST

N

0   1   2   3 Kilometers
0   1   2   3 Miles

Pikes Peak began attracting tourists in the 1870s, who trekked on foot or mule to its lofty summit above the new resort community of Colorado Springs, founded in 1871 by General William Jackson Palmer. The first road, a rough 17-mile carriage track, reached the summit in 1889, allowing visitors to ride in relative comfort to the top. But the completion and popularity of the nearby Pikes Peak Cog Railroad in 1891 forced the wagon route to close by 1905.

In 1913 Cripple Creek mining magnate Spencer Penrose joined with Charles Noble, a retired railroad man, and petitioned the Department of Agriculture to build a new road for automobiles to the peak's summit. Naysayers said no automobile had enough power to climb the peak, but on July 17, 1913, two Denver men drove a Buick Bear Cat up the carriage road to the summit in four hours. In 1914 the federal government gave Penrose a permit to build the road, warning him it would cost as much as $25,000. The highway, completed in 1915, climbed 6,746 feet on an average 6 percent grade to the peak's apex and ended up costing over $250,000.

Penrose started the **Pikes Peak International Hill Climb** auto race, the world's highest auto race, in 1916 to give needed publicity to his expensive road. The race tradition continues every July. The Hill Climb, nicknamed the "Race to the Clouds," has a variety of classes, including race cars, motorcycles, stock cars, and trucks, that speed up a 12.43-mile track with 156 turns from mile marker 7 on the Pikes Peak Highway. The first winner in 1916, Rea Lentz, crossed the finish line at 20:55.60. Vehicle and engine advances shaved minutes off the fastest race time, with a new record of 7:57.14 set in 2018 by French driver Romain Dumas in an electric Volkswagen.

The Pikes Peak Highway operated as a toll road until 1936, but Penrose never turned a profit on his investment due to the road's expensive maintenance. The deteriorating road was free until 1948, when Colorado Springs received a permit from the National Forest Service to operate the highway. Because of costly maintenance, the city of Colorado Springs, which operates the highway under permit from Pike National Forest, charges a toll for all travelers.

The Pikes Peak Highway

The **Pikes Peak Highway** is one of the most expensive roads to maintain in the US. As much as 7 million cubic feet of snow is removed from the highway every spring. Melting snow also damages and erodes the road surface. After a lawsuit filed by the Sierra Club in 1998, the road was eventually paved to the summit to control erosion and sediment deposition along the roadside and in drainages below the highway. As much as 1.5 million tons of gravel had been dumped on the road since 1970, which left a legacy of choked watercourses, including some

The Pikes Peak Highway edges up steep slopes high above the Rampart Range and the distant Great Plains.

harboring endangered native cutthroat trout, and damaged fragile wetlands and vegetation. The paving, which was finished in 2011, is allowing Pikes Peak's ecosystems to recover and also provides for a better driving experience.

Allow at least two to three hours for the 40-mile round-trip. Drivers should make sure their vehicles are in excellent operating condition. Use lower gears when ascending and descending the peak to avoid overheating and riding the brakes. The Pikes Peak Patrol checks brakes at Glen Cove for excessive brake heat on busy days and weekends. Use the numerous highway pullouts for sightseeing and to allow faster traffic to pass. The highway is narrow in places, clinging to steep slopes. Stay on your side of the road, do not cut corners, avoid passing on blind corners, and stay within the speed limit. Uphill traffic has the right-of-way. The Pikes Peak Patrol regularly traverses the highway and provides road assistance. *Travelers with cardiac and respiratory problems should not make the ascent.*

The highway is open from 7:30 a.m. to 8 p.m. from late May to early September; through September it's open from 7:30 a.m. to 7 p.m.; and from October 1 to late May, the highway is open from 9 a.m. to 5 p.m. The highway is closed on Thanksgiving and Christmas days. The highway may be closed or partially closed due to bad weather, usually snow and ice, which make the road unsafe. Call (719) 385-7325 to confirm if the road is open or closed.

The Pikes Peak Highway travelers should be prepared for all weather conditions. Snow often falls on the highway, leaving a muddy and slick surface. The weather atop the peak is usually cool and breezy. While summer temperatures in Cascade at the drive's start are often in the 80s, it can be as cold as 30 degrees on Pikes Peak's summit. Be prepared by bringing warm clothes and a raincoat. Autumn days are generally brisk and clear.

Ute Pass

The Pikes Peak Highway begins off US 24 in 7,379-foot-high Cascade, 5 miles west of Manitou Springs. Exit west off US 24 and follow signs to the highway tollgate almost a mile from Cascade. The road begins climbing immediately up steep mountain slopes thickly clad in ponderosa pine, Douglas fir, and Engelmann spruce. The highway reaches **Camera Point,** the first overlook, just under a mile from the tollgate. This lofty point yields a spectacular view down Ute Pass to Colorado Springs and the distant prairie. Look across the deep valley to see areas on the Rampart Range that burned during the massive Waldo Canyon fire in June 2012.

Ute Pass is not a pass at all, but rather an abrupt canyon sliced into the Front Range escarpment that separates the Pikes Peak massif from the Rampart Range. The canyon, carved by Fountain Creek, follows the weakened line of the almost 60-mile-long Ute Pass Fault. Ute Pass has long offered an easy passage from the plains into the mountains. The Ute Indians regularly followed a trail down the pass from their mountain strongholds to the mineral springs at Manitou Springs and the rich hunting grounds east of the Front Range. A freight road was built up the pass in 1872 to better serve the South Park mining camps, and the Colorado Midland Railroad, a standard-gauge line between Colorado Springs and Aspen, was completed in 1887. The railroad, with tunnels and old rail bed still existing in lower Ute Pass, climbed 4 percent grades up the pass to Divide. The pass was a dangerous place in the 1860s, with numerous robberies and murders.

Cascade Creek to Glen Cove

The road swings west from the viewpoint and quickly enters Cascade Creek's hanging valley. The highway twists up a shallow canyon. Immense granite boulders, scattered hillsides of pine and fir, and groves of quaking aspen line the highway. **Crow Gulch Picnic Area,** with restrooms and tables, sits at the mouth of Crow Gulch on the road's north side at 3 miles.

Beyond, the highway climbs away from Cascade Creek, reaches 9,000 feet, and drops north above 136-acre **Crystal Creek Reservoir.** Most of Pikes Peak is part of the Colorado Springs watershed. Numerous dams plug the mountain's creeks to form sparkling reservoirs. Trout fishing is allowed at Crystal Creek Reservoir as well as nearby North and South Catamount Reservoirs. The three lakes form the 2,267-acre **North Slope Recreation Area;** fishing is only allowed from the bank or a nonmotorized boat. The **Crystal Creek Reservoir** area has a large parking lot, picnic sites, and hiking trails along the lake's 3.3-mile shoreline. Mountain bikers can ride about 10 miles of trails on gravel roads, logging roads, and singletrack trails. Bike trailheads are at the North and South Catamount Reservoir parking lots.

After crossing the reservoir spillway, the highway passes a viewpoint and the large parking lot above Crystal Creek Reservoir. This is a good stop to stretch your legs and take in a grand vista of Pikes Peak. On the west side of the parking lot, make sure you visit the carved wooden statue of Sasquatch, the red-haired man-creature of the Rockies, and get a selfie with the big guy. Numerous reported sightings of Colorado Sasquatches date back to the Native Americans, who called them guardians and elder brothers after spotting them on holy mountains. Pike National Forest, surrounding Pikes Peak, is apparently Sasquatch territory, with many local sightings at places like Green Mountain Falls near the highway start and at The Crags behind the peak. Keep your eyes peeled while driving up Pikes Peak—you don't want to be the guy that ran over one!

As the drive crosses rounded gravel ridges, **Pikes Peak** towers to the south, an abrupt wall of ragged cliffs, buttresses, cirques, and ridges. Steep gullies coated with snow and ice plunge down the peak's north face. Pikes Peak, composed of billion-year-old Pikes Peak granite, is a huge batholith, a mass of once-molten rock that cooled under the earth's crust as the core of a mountain range. The granite later lifted as part of the ancestral Rocky Mountains eroded, and then rose again as today's peak. Glaciers chiseled and sculpted Pikes Peak's distinctive features over the last million years. Thick glaciers perched on the mountainside, carving out huge cirques on the peak's east flank, including the Crater, North Pit, and Bottomless Pit. The last of the glaciers disappeared about 11,000 years ago.

Pikes Peak and the surrounding mountains, composed of ancient granite, are renowned for their exquisite minerals and gemstones. Some that have been found include smoky quartz, topaz, amethyst, amazonite, fluorite, and zircon crystals. Delicate blue topaz crystals are found on the steep cliffs above Glen Cove on the highway, while foot-long smoky quartz crystals hide in pockets. Pikes Peak, while not a volcano, has had volcanic episodes on its western slopes. Rich gold deposits hide in the Cripple Creek mining district southwest of the peak in the caldera of a collapsed volcano.

The highway climbs southward over humpbacked ridges broken by shallow canyons toward the looming peak. At almost 10 miles the road reaches

10,000 feet and passes the Halfway Picnic Grounds. Past here the highway begins switchbacking across steep forested slopes and 3 miles later reaches **Glen Cove** just below tree line at 11,425 feet. Glen Cove lies in a north-facing alpine cirque carved by a hanging glacier. Granite crags and boulders litter the steep mountainsides above the cirque floor. Steep snow-filled couloirs, including Little Italy, attract extreme skiers in May and early June. The Glen Cove Inn serves meals and has a gift shop.

The drive reaches timberline past Glen Cove. Timberline marks the upper limit of forest. This snowy, windswept transition zone between the subalpine spruce and fir forest and the treeless tundra is characterized by stunted, twisted trees including Engelmann spruce, subalpine fir, limber pine, and bristlecone pine. At this elevation, the trees grow slowly because of extreme temperatures and the short growing season.

Elk Park & Devils Playground

Past timberline the highway climbs steeply up a flattened ridge. **Elk Park,** a grassy knoll with a parking area, lies a mile past Glen Cove. A marvelous view of the peak's rugged north face and surrounding mountains and valleys spreads out below this timberline viewpoint. A trail, following an old road, heads southeast from here and drops into North Pit, an abrupt glacier-carved cirque, and then heads southeast to Barr Camp on the east flank of the peak.

The road edges up the mountain flank for the next 2 miles, gaining almost 1,000 feet of elevation on eight twisting switchbacks. This airy road section is particularly treacherous for both cars and drivers. Remember to keep to your side of the highway on the sharp turns. Use lower gears when ascending to keep a constant speed and avoid overheating, and when descending to keep brakes from overheating. Pump the brakes to reduce speed rather than applying continuous pressure.

At the top of the switchbacks sits 16-Mile Turnout. This overlook offers spacious views to the north across the South Platte River country. Beyond the river basin stretches the snow-capped Front Range, including 14,264-foot Mount Evans and 14,060-foot Mount Bierstadt. The Tarryall Range lifts a jagged brow of broken rock outcrops and rough summits to the northwest.

Devils Playground spreads south from the pullout. A good hike heads west along a rounded ridge to a couple of scenic viewpoints, including the small rocky peak above the wide parking area. This 13,070-foot-high unranked summit, called Devils Playground Peak, is the high point of Teller County, which includes the western slopes of Pikes Peak. The 7-mile-long Crags Route, the standard ascent trail used by mountaineers to climb Pikes Peak, comes up from The Crags on the northwest slopes and crosses Devils Playground here before paralleling the road to the summit.

The Devils Playground area, named because lightning likes to play on the exposed ridges here, is a great place to explore the delicate alpine tundra ecosystem. The climate and growing season on this ridge are the same as that in northern Canada and Alaska. Despite the climatic rigors, including a below-freezing mean annual temperature, a frost-free season that is at most two months long, and winds exceeding 100 miles per hour, numerous plants and shrubs thrive at this elevation. July and August bring a carpet of petite colorful wildflowers to these mountain heights—greenish white Arctic gentians, yellow paintbrush, spiked elephant flowers, brilliant alpine sunflowers, and many others. More than 250 plant species grow above timberline in the Colorado Rockies. Most are small perennials that not only endure but also thrive in this stark land of never summer.

From the large Devils Playground parking lot, the highway uncoils across Pikes Peak's long northern ridge. The road slowly climbs above 13,000 feet and passes a couple of spectacular viewpoints. The first overlooks the deep chasm of **North Pit,** its steep walls littered with soaring granite crags and buttresses. Past the North Pit view the highway swings around a rocky knob and reaches the **Bottomless Pit** overlook at 13,200 feet. The cirque falls away below the viewpoint. Long rock ribs plunge north from the peak's summit to the distant cirque floor. Vertical cliffs, stained with snowmelt and cracked by ice, line the abyss far below.

The highway's final 2 miles slowly scale the boulder-strewn western slope of the peak's final rock pyramid, edging across precipitous slopes. After the last switchback and the last incline, the road ends on the peak's level 60-acre summit. This lofty sky-island rises more than 2.5 miles above sea level at 14,115 feet.

Pikes Peak Summit

Pikes Peak was called "Long Mountain" by the Arapahos. Black Elk, an Oglala Sioux medicine man, had a vision of the sacred peak at the age of nine as the cloud home of the six Grandfathers that represented *Wakantanka,* the Great Spirit of the Sioux religion. Pikes Peak was also sacred to the Ute Indians, who called the mountain *Tava,* a Ute word that means "sun."

Lieutenant Zebulon Pike first spotted the peak that bears his name from far out on the Colorado plains on November 15, 1806. He recorded the occasion in his journal: "At two o'clock I thought I could distinguish a mountain to our right, which appeared like a small blue cloud." Pike dubbed it Grand Peak and calculated its elevation at 18,851 feet. Pike and a small party of soldiers were dispatched by President Thomas Jefferson in 1806 to explore and determine the southern

More people stand on the summit of Pikes Peak every year than any other high mountain in the United States.

boundary of the newly acquired Louisiana Purchase, a vast swath of pristine land that swept from the Mississippi River to the Pacific coast.

Pike and three of his ill-equipped men later left their Arkansas River camp in today's Pueblo and attempted to scale Grand Peak. Freezing temperatures and a blizzard conspired to defeat the feeble effort. Pike noted in his journal that "the summit of the Grand Peak, which was entirely bare of vegetation and covered with snow, now appeared at the distance of fifteen to sixteen miles from us, and as high again as what we had ascended, and would have taken a whole day's march to have arrived at its base, when I believe no human being could have ascended to its pinnacle."

The peak was first ascended by Anglo-Americans on July 14, 1820, when botanist Dr. Edwin James and two companions from Major Stephen Long's "Expedition from Pittsburgh to the Rocky Mountains" ascended its east flank. In the process the trio started a major forest fire after leaving a smoldering campfire.

In 1858 20-year-old Julia Archibald Holmes became the first white woman to ascend Pikes Peak. On the summit she penned a letter to her mother, saying: "In all probability I am the first woman who has ever stood upon the summit of this mountain and gazed upon this wondrous scene, which my eyes now behold . . . all, and everything, on which the eye can rest, fills the mind with infinitude, and sends the soul to God."

Not much has changed over the last 170 years; magnificent panoramas still spread out below the rocky summit in every direction. To the east, the peak's escarpment sweeps down to low forested mountains, jewel-like reservoirs and lakes nestled among ridges, and the urban sprawl of Colorado Springs. Beyond stretches the brown prairie, its grasslands reaching the Kansas horizon. The Spanish Peaks, twin landmarks on the Santa Fe Trail, and the serrated crest of the Sangre de Cristo Mountains glisten in the sunlight like alabaster towers in the south. The Continental Divide, Colorado's mountainous spine that divides the Atlantic and Pacific watersheds, marches across the western rim. Clear days yield marvelous views northward to Longs Peak in Rocky Mountain National Park more than 100 miles away, while Denver's skyscrapers huddle in a broad basin below the mountain uplift.

The breathtaking views from Pikes Peak's summit inspired "America the Beautiful," the nation's unofficial anthem. Katherine Lee Bates, a visiting English professor at Colorado College, rode to the summit in a wagon in the summer of 1893. The view inspired her to write: "Oh beautiful for spacious skies, for amber waves of grain, for purple mountain majesties above the fruited plain. . . ." She later recalled, "The opening lines of the hymn floated into my mind as I was looking out over the sealike expanse of fertile country spreading away so far under those ample skies."

The **Pikes Peak Summit House** sits on the eastern edge of the summit, with a snack bar, gift shop, and historic Peak photographs. Most visitors like to have their photo taken standing in front of the official summit sign on the west side of the Summit House. Work began in June 2018 on the new Pikes Peak Summit Complex, a modern and sustainable visitor center with 38,000 square feet of space for interactive exhibits, sheltered viewing areas, rooftop terraces, and enhanced shopping and dining. The new summit house is scheduled to open in late 2020.

The summit house is famed for its "world famous" doughnuts made with a special, secret recipe that overcome the challenges posed by the high altitude. After the US Army abandoned its weather station on the summit in 1888, the mayor of Manitou Springs saw an opportunity to capitalize on tourist hunger and began selling coffee and doughnuts. The doughnut recipe, using flour, water, evaporated milk, and the secret ingredient, was perfected by 1916 and has remained the same ever since. Over 700 of the famed treats are made every hour until 5 in the afternoon when the deep fryer shuts down. While you're enjoying the alpine views, nip inside the summit house and buy a single 350-calorie doughnut or a whole bag and enjoy with coffee in your new Pikes Peak mug.

While you're up there, take a walk around the edge of the summit plateau and enjoy the marvelous distant views. Below you to the east spreads Colorado Springs, glinting in the sun, and beyond stretches the limitless prairie to a Kansas horizon. You can also pick out half of Colorado's 53 ranked "Fourteeners," or 14,000-foot peaks, on a clear day, from Longs Peak to the north, to the Maroon Bells to the west, to Blanca Peak and Culebra Peak far to the south. Make sure to bring warm clothes since the summit temperature is usually cold, especially if it's windy.

The **Barr Trail,** a 13-mile National Recreation Trail, drops east from the Summit House, swinging down the broad East Face and over forested mountains to Manitou Springs almost 8,000 feet below. The strenuous Pikes Peak Marathon follows the trail over two days every August, with an ascent-only race on Saturday and the grueling 26.2-mile round-trip race on Sunday. The round-trip course record, set in 1993 by local runner Matt Carpenter, is an astounding 3 hours and 16 minutes. The **Pikes Peak Cog Railway,** the highest in the world, also ends at the Summit House. The 8.9-mile railway climbs from its Manitou Springs depot to the summit on grades as steep as 25 percent. As of 2019, the future of the cog railroad is in limbo and closed. The owners plan to rebuild the entire railway and put new cars in service, with a completion date after 2020.

After sipping your coffee and munching on a famous doughnut, follow the highway back down the peak to Cascade, 20 miles away. Let your vehicle's gears do the work and don't ride the brakes, and remember that the views are just as good going down as coming up.

10

North Cheyenne Cañon & Lower Gold Camp Roads Scenic Drive

Colorado Springs

General description: A 9-mile drive through North Cheyenne Cañon Park and along historic Gold Camp Road in the mountains above Colorado Springs.

Special attractions: North Cheyenne Cañon Park, Starsmore Visitor and Nature Center, Columbine Trail, Mount Cutler Trail, Helen Hunt Falls, Helen Hunt Falls Visitor Center, Silver Cascade Falls, mountain biking, hiking, rock climbing, scenic views.

Location: East-central Colorado. The drive is on the southwest side of Colorado Springs. Begin at the junction of North and South Cheyenne Cañon Roads. To access from I-25, take Exit 140 onto South Tejon Street and head southwest up Tejon and Cheyenne Boulevard to the canyon entrance.

Route names: Lower Gold Camp Road, North Cheyenne Cañon Road.

Travel season: Year-round. North Cheyenne Cañon Road is sometimes closed in winter due to ice and snowfall.

Camping: No camping along the drive. Nearest public campground is at Cheyenne Mountain State Park (61 sites) off CO 115 south of Colorado Springs. Campgrounds also are in Pike National Forest at The Crags, Elevenmile Canyon, north of Woodland Park on CO 67, and along the Rampart Range Road. Private campgrounds are in Colorado Springs.

Services: No services on drive. Complete visitor services are in Colorado Springs.

Nearby attractions: Colorado Springs attractions, Cheyenne Mountain Zoo, Section 16 Trail, Garden of the Gods, Pike National Forest, Rampart Range Road (Scenic Drive 12), Pikes Peak Highway (Scenic Drive 9).

The Route

The 9-mile-long North Cheyenne Cañon and Lower Gold Camp Roads scenic drive ascends a steep, rocky canyon carved into the Front Range southwest of Colorado Springs and then edges above the canyon back to the city and US 24. This short but lovely drive offers lofty viewpoints, a couple of waterfalls, and solitude on the edge of one of Colorado's largest cities, along with superb hiking trails.

The canyon road segment is a paved, two-lane road. The Gold Camp Road segment is a narrow, gravel road. Numerous pullouts allow for safe passage around oncoming vehicles and for scenic views. Recreational vehicles or those towing a trailer should not be used for the drive. The drive is open year-round,

North Cheyenne Cañon & Lower Gold Camp Roads Scenic Drive

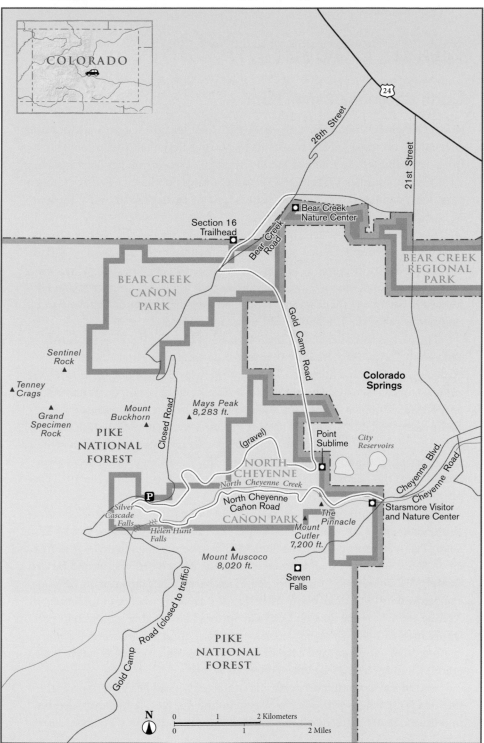

COLORADO

☰ 24

26th Street

21st Street

Bear Creek
Nature Center

Section 16
Trailhead

Bear Creek Road

BEAR CREEK
CAÑON
PARK

BEAR CREEK
REGIONAL
PARK

Gold Camp Road

Sentinel
Rock ▲

Colorado
Springs

▲ Tenney
Crags

▲ Mays Peak
8,283 ft.

Point
Sublime

City
Reservoirs

▲ Grand
Specimen
Rock

Mount
Buckhorn ▲

Closed Road

PIKE
NATIONAL
FOREST

(gravel)

NORTH
CHEYENNE

North Cheyenne Creek

Cheyenne Blvd.

Cheyenne Road

P

North Cheyenne
Cañon Road

Silver
Cascade
Falls

CAÑON PARK

The
Pinnacle

Starsmore Visitor
and Nature Center

Helen Hunt
Falls

Mount
Cutler
7,200 ft.

▲ Mount Muscoco
8,020 ft.

Seven
Falls

Gold Camp Road (closed to traffic)

PIKE
NATIONAL
FOREST

N

| 0 | | 1 | | 2 Kilometers |
| 0 | | 1 | | 2 Miles |

except after severe winter storms, when the North Cheyenne Cañon Road is closed. Allow an hour to drive the route.

North Cheyenne Cañon Park

North Cheyenne Cañon Park, a spectacular Colorado Springs city park, is a deep cleft chiseled through pink granite cliffs by North Cheyenne Creek tumbling down from its headwaters on rounded Mount Almalgre. The canyon has been a popular local destination since 1885, when Colorado Springs purchased 640 acres for a city park. Early residents often brought visitors here by carriage to marvel at the granite bastions and the raw natural beauty.

The 1,855-acre park, the largest in the Colorado Springs city park system, is tucked into the forested mountains on the southwest side of the city. The park, easily accessed by the paved road that winds up its twisting floor, offers over 20 miles of hiking and mountain biking trails, as well as two visitor centers and two waterfalls. North Cheyenne Cañon, renowned for hummingbirds that flit about in summer, is called the Hummingbird Capital of Colorado.

The park is listed on the National Register of Historic Places as the **North Cheyenne Cañon Park Historic District** for its scenery, natural attractions, archeological sites, and numerous historic structures. These human-made features include stone bridges, retaining walls, historic hiking trails, and the Bruin Inn site near Helen Hunt Falls. The listing also recognizes that the Cañon's history and environment reflect the growing interest in conservation in the late 19th and early 20th centuries as well as the growth of tourism and recreation in the United States. Construction of the Short Line Railroad, now the Gold Camp Road, decimated forests along the rail line so Pike National Forest reforested the park in 1913 by planting over 700,000 trees in 3 months.

The drive begins on the southwest edge of Colorado Springs at the junction of North and South Cheyenne Cañon Roads. The start is easily reached from I-25 via South Tejon Street and Cheyenne Boulevard. Before starting the drive, park in a lot on South Cheyenne Cañon Road and visit the **Starsmore Visitor and Nature Center** (719-385-6086). This visitor center for North Cheyenne Cañon Park is situated in a historic stone house that originally sat at the corner of S. Nevada Avenue and Cheyenne Road in Colorado Springs before being moved to its present location in 1992. The center offers park information and maps, an indoor climbing wall, dioramas, and a hands-on mineral exhibit, as well as nature programs, a junior ranger program, and special events.

The **Lower Columbine Trail** begins at the center and heads west, parallel to the road. This 4-mile trail, open to hikers, mountain bikers, and horses, divides into three distinct segments. It finishes at the Upper Columbine Trailhead near

Helen Hunt Falls in the upper canyon. A fun 2-mile round trip-hike begins at Starsmore and follows Columbine Trail alongside North Cheyenne Creek for a mile to Mid-Columbine Trailhead, then returns to the visitor center. The wide trail is easy to follow and offers fine views of the cliff-lined lower canyon. The upper 3-mile section of Columbine Trail from the midway trailhead to the upper one twists along scenic slopes high above the creek and road.

At the Y-road junction, turn right onto North Cheyenne Cañon Road. The road winds west up the deepening canyon. Tall ponderosa pines, narrow-leaf cottonwoods, and thickets of scrub oak line North Cheyenne Creek on the left. After 0.5 mile, the road makes the first of three wide, looping meanders beneath the north-facing granite cliffs of Mount Cutler, and after 0.8 mile it reaches a wide parking area next to Graduation Boulder, a massive creek-side boulder on the left.

The Pinnacle, a looming 250-foot-high granite precipice, towers to the south. This formation, along with surrounding rock pinnacles and faces, is popular with local rock climbers. Do not attempt to climb any of the canyon's rock formations without a rope, proper climbing hardware, and technical climbing experience. The granite can be rotten and crumbly in places, and it's easy to scramble into dangerous places. Consult the comprehensive guidebook *Rock Climbing Colorado* from FalconGuides for climbing information and route descriptions in North Cheyenne Cañon.

All the rock in the Cañon and the surrounding Pikes Peak massif is Pikes Peak granite, a rough, coarse-grained pink granite originally deposited almost a billion years ago when it bubbled up under the earth's crust into an immense batholith. The rock slowly cooled into granite far underground over millions of years. This rock core became part of the Ancestral Rocky Mountains and later the Rocky Mountains. As the mountains rose, eons of erosion stripped away all of the surface layers above, eventually exposing the ancient granite bedrock. Weathering, mostly water erosion and frost wedging in winter, has chiseled this relatively soft granite into today's canyon, cliffs, buttresses, and spires.

The road swings west beneath pointed Longfellow Pinnacle on the right and the west face of The Pinnacle to the left. At 1.1 miles is the parking area for the **Columbine Trail.** The trail climbs onto the canyon's dry northern slopes here and continues west to Helen Hunt Falls. At 1.6 miles is the parking area on the left for the very popular 1-mile-long **Mount Cutler Trail.** The trail legs it uphill to the summit of 7,200-foot-high Mount Cutler and marvelous views across Colorado Springs. The trail is for hikers only.

The drive continues west up the floor of the canyon, passing granite monoliths jutting above hillside pines. The rocky summit of 8,020-foot Mount Muscoco rises to the south as the road climbs Mine Hill at 2 miles. Several picnic areas with tables scatter along the road before it reaches **Helen Hunt Falls** at 2.7 miles. The

Helen Hunt Falls Visitor Center, housed in a replica of the old Bruin Inn, an early hotel beside the falls, is open from Memorial Day to Labor Day. Helen Hunt Falls is a picturesque 35-foot-high waterfall named for Helen Hunt Jackson, a 19th-century writer who lived in the region. A short path climbs to a bridge above the falls.

Helen Hunt Jackson (1830–1885) wrote a couple best-selling books that advocated for Native American rights. *A Century of Dishonor,* published in 1881, depicted the mistreatment of native peoples and broken treaties by the US government. In 1884 her passionate book *Ramona* portrayed the life of an orphan Native American girl in California just after the Mexican-American War and her mistreatment and abuse. She died of stomach cancer in San Francisco a year later and was buried on a 1-acre plot on a clifftop above Seven Falls in nearby South Cheyenne Cañon, where a plaque and stone pile still marks her original grave site. Helen Hunt was later disinterred and her remains moved to Evergreen Cemetery in Colorado Springs.

Continue hiking from the top of the waterfall along a wide trail that switchbacks up to **Silver Cascade Falls,** a pretty waterfall spilling down a granite slab. It's best admired behind fenced overlooks. The slick, water-polished slabs are treacherous to walk across; more than 30 visitors who have ventured beyond the fences have been killed by falling on the smooth rock. Above the cascade is Silver Cascade Slab, a large sweep of granite with a dozen climbing routes, and a section of the Gold Camp Road, including Tunnel 3, which is closed to auto traffic.

Just beyond the Helen Hunt Falls parking area at a tight switchback is the upper trailhead for the Columbine Trail. Continue up the paved North Cheyenne Cañon Road until it ends at 3.4 miles at the **Powell Parking Lot and Trailhead,** a large gravel parking lot at the road's junction with the Gold Camp Road. The middle section of the Gold Camp Road from here to its junction with the Old Stage Road to the south is closed to vehicle traffic. The road is a popular hiking and mountain biking trail that leads to the Seven Bridges Trail, Buckhorn Cutoff Trail, and the St. Marys Falls Trail.

Powell Parking Lot is also the trailhead for the **High Drive,** a now-closed road that climbs north to a pass between Mount Buckhorn and 8,283-foot Mays Peak before dropping into the Bear Creek Cañon drainage. The 3.3-mile-long, one-way road-trail, open to hikers and mountain bikers, offers spectacular views of towering Grand Specimen Rock and Sentinel Rock on the eastern slope of Tenney Crags. It ends at Lower Gold Camp Road near the Section 16 Trailhead. The High Drive was permanently closed in 2015 by the US Forest Service to lessen sediment

Helen Hunt Falls, named for a famed 19th-century writer, tumbles over granite bedrock in North Cheyenne Cañon.

deposition in Bear Creek, which harbors one of the last remaining genetically pure populations of greenback cutthroat trout, the Colorado state fish.

Lower Gold Camp Road

The scenic drive goes right or east at Powell Parking Lot and descends the **Lower Gold Camp Road** for 6 miles to the west side of Colorado Springs and US 24. The narrow, dirt road heads east, edging above steep slopes on the north flank of North Cheyenne Cañon. After 0.6 mile the road narrows down to one lane and plunges through Tunnel #2. Note the tunnel roof is still black from locomotive smoke, a reminder of the tunnel's history.

The original Gold Camp Road, following an old railroad bed, meandered 31 miles along the south slopes of Pikes Peak between Colorado Springs and Cripple Creek. Cripple Creek was, in the 1890s, the world's richest gold camp. The mountainsides above the town yielded millions of dollars of gold ore that was hauled down to mills in Colorado Springs and Cañon City for refining. Three railroads served the booming gold district. The most famous of these lines to Cripple Creek was the Colorado Springs & Cripple Creek District Railway, otherwise dubbed the Short Line.

Many of the early Cripple Creek gold barons, living on Wood Avenue in Colorado Springs, were protective of their prosperous monopoly on Cripple Creek's commerce. So when Irving Howbert, president of the First National Bank in Colorado Springs, proposed a new railroad to Cripple Creek, it was not difficult to find interested investors. Thus in 1901 the Short Line was born. The line, also nicknamed "the gold-plated railroad," boasted the best rolling stock, track, and equipment available in its day. The railroad ran through nine tunnels on a 3.8 percent grade from the mill in Colorado City to the way station at Summit, making it one of the steepest standard-gauge railways in the world.

Eventually the price of gold bottomed out. Competition with the Colorado Midland Railroad for haulage of the last reserves was too much, and the Short Line folded. The last train left the great gold camp in May 1920. Shortly thereafter businessman W. D. Corley saw the rail line's potential for tourism and paid $370,000 for the rail bed. He promptly tore up the tracks and made it a toll road—the Gold Camp Road. The road became public in 1936.

The Gold Camp Road between Colorado Springs and Cripple Creek still follows the original railroad bed, although the 8-mile section between the top of the North Cheyenne Cañon Road and the Old Stage Road is closed to vehicular traffic because of unstable tunnels.

Three of the railroad tunnels on the Gold Camp Road have garnered attention from ghost hunters since 2000. The troubled tunnels creep out our rational mind. By day they are innocent holes burrowed through ridges but at night they become echoing chambers filled with ghastly victims. Most of the stories about the haunted tunnels are far-fetched urban legends, especially since before the 1990s there are no stories about hauntings. Myths recount how a school bus filled with children was crushed when Tunnel 3 collapsed on them in the 1980s, the shrill whistle of a ghost train rattling up vanished tracks, a walking specter inside Tunnel 2, and dusty handprints found on cars after exiting the tunnel. Another legend says black-robed Satanic worshippers carried torches and marched through the tunnels on dark nights in the 1970s and 1980s.

The thing is that none of these stories appear to be true. The collapse on Tunnel 3 on the school bus—it never happened. The tunnel was closed in 1987 after timbers inside rotted away and iron fencing has blocked both entrances after a 2006 fire burned the remaining supports, but a look inside the tunnel reveals no collapsed sections. Most of the peculiar ghostly events can be explained by fertile imaginations that run wild on dark and stormy nights. The Lower Gold Camp Road, however, has had its share of auto accidents. Local authorities say 11 wrecked cars still rest below the road. The curvy section north of Point Sublime, now protected by a stout guardrail, was notoriously dangerous with numerous fatalities caused by vehicles plummeting down gravel slopes.

Scenic views abound as you follow the Gold Camp Road above the canyon. When President Teddy Roosevelt rode the line in August 1901, he stated theatrically that the trip "bankrupts the English language." The road edges across steep slopes and twists through Tunnel 2 to an overlook on the right with scenic views south to Mount Muscoco, a rocky peak that rises above the canyon, and down North Cheyenne Cañon. You pass through Tunnel #1 after 1.6 miles and 0.5 mile later reach an overlook at **Point Sublime** on the right that looks straight down into the rocky heart of North Cheyenne Cañon below.

Past the viewpoint, the road slims down to a single lane and edges around several sharp curves onto the wooded east flank of Mays Peak. After the road widens and becomes paved, there is another spectacular overlook offering a spacious view of Colorado Springs and the prairie stretching beyond to a flat horizon. This is an excellent view in the early evening when the city lights twinkle across the basin.

The drive heads north through copses of scrub oak and tall ponderosa pines. Secluded houses lie alongside the drive. The road eventually bends west and twists into the mouth of Bear Creek Cañon. At a three-way junction, keep straight on Gold Camp Road. The road passes a shallow canyon filled with granite buttresses and reaches a parking area on the left for the popular **Section 16 Trail** in **Red Rock Canyon Open Space,** a Colorado Springs parkland.

A quarter-mile later the road passes through upturned sandstone layers of the Dakota Hogback and reaches a stop sign at the intersection of Lower Gold Camp Road and 26th Street, marking the end of the scenic drive.

A left turn on 26th Street leads 2.5 miles down to US 24 and the Old Colorado City Historic District. A right turn on 26th Street drops down to the **Bear Creek Nature Center,** an El Paso County natural area that offers a fine introduction to the ecology of the Pikes Peak region. The center is great for kids and families with interpretive programs, hands-on displays, special events, and several miles of friendly trails along Bear Creek and across oak-covered hillsides.

The Short Line, passing through Tunnel 1, hauled gold ore and passengers between Cripple Creek and Colorado City in the early 20th century.

South Platte River Roads

Woodland Park to Deckers to Pine Junction

General description: This 72-mile drive runs north from Woodland Park to Deckers, where the road divides and forms a loop that follows the South Platte River and the river's North Fork to the historic town of Buffalo Creek and the drive's end at Pine Junction.

Special attractions: Pike National Forest, Manitou Lake, South Platte River, Buffalo Creek, Pine, North Fork National Historic District, fishing, camping, picnicking, rock climbing, hiking, Colorado Trail, mountain biking, scenic views.

Location: Central Colorado. The southern access is the junction of CO 67 and US 24 in Woodland Park, 20 miles west of Colorado Springs. The northern access is from US 285 at Pine Junction about 25 miles west of Denver.

Route numbers: CO 67; Jefferson CR 126, 96, and 97; Douglas CR 40 and 67.

Travel season: Year-round. Roads are open all winter, although snow and ice accumulate in shaded areas.

Camping: Ten national forest campgrounds—Red Rocks Group Campground, South Meadows (64 sites), Colorado (80 sites), Painted Rocks (18 sites), Lone Rock (19 sites), Wigwam (10 sites), Kelsey (17 sites), Platte River (10 tent sites), Osprey (13 tent sites), and Ouzel (13 tent sites)—are along the drive. Dispersed primitive camping is allowed on Pike National Forest, unless otherwise posted.

Services: All services are in Woodland Park. Limited services at Pine Junction, Pine, Buffalo Creek, and Deckers.

Nearby attractions: Lost Creek Wilderness Area, Mount Evans Wilderness Area, Rampart Range Road (Scenic Drive 12), Devils Head, Mount Evans Scenic Byway (Scenic Drive 14), Guanella Pass Scenic Byway (Scenic Drive 15), Denver area attractions, Colorado Springs area attractions, Cripple Creek, Florissant Fossil Beds National Park, Pikes Peak Highway (Scenic Drive 9), Mueller State Park, Rampart Reservoir Recreation Area.

The Route

The South Platte River, arising on the Continental Divide's snowy peaks above Fairplay, twists 360 miles across Colorado to the Nebraska border. The river, draining over 28,000 square miles, is Colorado's water workhorse. The South Platte and its mountain tributaries irrigate the state's fertile northeastern corner and yield tap water for over 60 percent of Colorado's population, including Denver, Boulder, and Fort Collins. From the air, this working river looks like a string of watery pearls, with numerous reservoirs that impound its tumbling waters. Still, despite the dams and irrigation projects, the river retains a wild character through much of its rugged mountain course.

Some of the river's best scenery remains in deep, wooded canyons in the low mountains southwest of Denver. The 72-mile South Platte River scenic drive,

South Platte River Roads

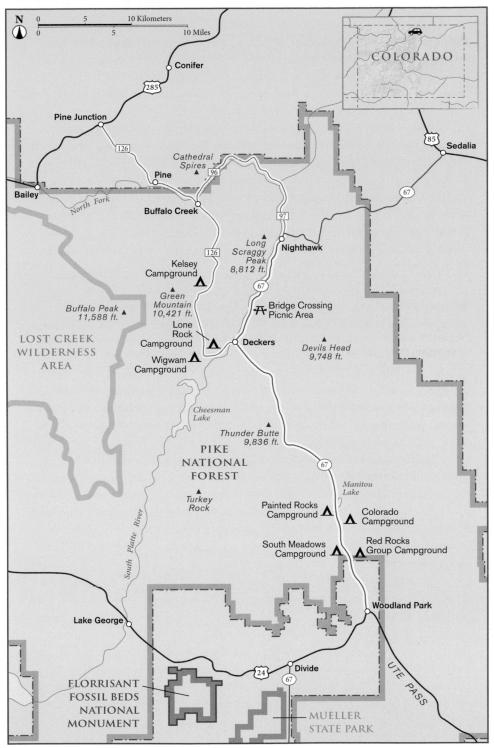

N

0   5   10 Kilometers
0   5   10 Miles

COLORADO

Conifer
285
Pine Junction
126
Sedalia
85
Cathedral Spires
96
Pine
Bailey
North Fork
67
Buffalo Creek
97
Long Scraggy Peak 8,812 ft.
Nighthawk
Kelsey Campground
126
Green Mountain 10,421 ft.
67
Buffalo Peak 11,588 ft.
Bridge Crossing Picnic Area
LOST CREEK WILDERNESS AREA
Lone Rock Campground
Deckers
Devils Head 9,748 ft.
Wigwam Campground
Cheesman Lake
Thunder Butte 9,836 ft.
PIKE NATIONAL FOREST
Manitou Lake
67
Turkey Rock
Painted Rocks Campground
Colorado Campground
South Platte River
South Meadows Campground
Red Rocks Group Campground
Woodland Park
Lake George
Divide
24
67
FLORRISANT FOSSIL BEDS NATIONAL MONUMENT
MUELLER STATE PARK
UTE PASS

following CO 67 and several county roads, explores these canyons and the surrounding piney mountains between Woodland Park and Pine Junction. The area, close to both Colorado Springs and Denver, is a popular destination for weekend campers, climbers, and anglers. Parts of the drive were severely burned in the 2002 Hayman Fire, one of the largest fires in Colorado's recorded history.

Weather along the drive is generally pleasant year-round, although spring, summer, and fall are the preferred travel seasons. Spring days are mild and windy, with highs reaching 60 degrees with occasional rain. Summer highs range between 60 and 80 degrees, with afternoon thunderstorms usually falling somewhere along the drive. Summer at the drive's higher elevations gives welcome relief from flatland heat. Fall brings cooler but dry days until the first snow falls in November. Winter days can be very mild, with highs reaching into the 50s. Snow generally clings to cold north-facing slopes, but the roads are usually dry, with ice only in shaded spots.

Woodland Park to Deckers

The scenic drive begins at the intersection of US 24 and CO 67 on the west side of **Woodland Park,** 20 miles northwest of Colorado Springs. Woodland Park, a mountain community at 8,500 feet, spreads across a broad, wooded valley west of the Rampart Range. The town offers all traveler services. The **Rocky Mountain Dinosaur Resource Center** is an interesting stop, especially for kids and dinosaur lovers, before heading out the drive. The center offers dinosaur skeletons, educational exhibits, and programs.

The drive's first 23 miles, following CO 67, traverse lovely countryside with rolling hills, forested mountains, grassy valleys, and shallow canyons to Deckers on the South Platte River. This slice of landscape is more representative of Colorado's Front Range than the usual image of immense snow-capped peaks. It's a land of intimate views—a sweep of wind-rippled grass, cloud reflections in a serene beaver pond, aspen groves strewn with sky-blue columbines, the dusty smell of dry ponderosa pine needles on the forest floor.

The drive heads north on CO 67, leaving most of Woodland Park's suburban development behind after 2 miles, and enters Pike National Forest at 4 miles. Pike National Forest sprawls across 1.1 million acres of central Colorado's mountains and includes not only the South Platte's canyons but also the historic landmark Pikes Peak, Lost Creek Wilderness Area, and the Mosquito Range. Sixty-four-site South Meadows Campground, the second in a succession of national forest campgrounds scattered along the highway, is reached at 5 miles. Past the campground the road leaves the pine forest and skirts the east side of willow-lined Trout Creek in a broad valley.

The highway passes Colorado Campground, with 80 sites, at almost 7 miles; crosses the creek; and reaches the turn to Painted Rocks Campground, a pleasant 18-site area just west of the drive. The Painted Rocks are small, eroded pinnacles nestled in the pine forest, the remains of downfaulted Paleozoic sandstone rocks that floor the valley north of Woodland Park. Both the highway and Trout Creek follow the Ute Pass Fault, a major Front Range fault that runs over 60 miles from south of Colorado Springs to north of Woodland Park.

Manitou Lake Picnic Area, with 42 sites and a historic picnic pavilion, sits alongside Manitou Lake, a 5-acre reservoir on Trout Creek. This popular recreation area offers fishing, canoeing, and hiking as well as picnicking. A fun, family-friendly hike follows trail #670 in a mile-long loop around the lake. The marsh at the southern end of the lake is rich wildlife habitat for waterfowl. Another hike is on a paved, 2-mile-long bike/hike trail, bordering the highway, which links the lake area with Colorado and South Meadows Campgrounds to the south.

The highway dips and rolls past Manitou Lake, running through open ponderosa pine forest and green meadows west of Trout Creek before turning away from the broad valley onto rounded ridges clad in spruce, fir, and aspen. At 13 miles the road crosses a divide, passes a pioneer cemetery, and drops down to West Creek's canyon. **Thunder Butte,** a ragged 9,836-foot mountain, dominates the horizon northwest of the drive, while domed Sheep's Nose, a premier rock-climbing crag, and Bell Rock sit to the west. The drive turns north and follows West Creek through a shallow, winding canyon, lined with pine, spruce, and fir, that alternately widens and narrows for 9 miles to **Deckers** on the South Platte River. Deckers, a small fishing resort with a restaurant and supplies, sits at a cross-road on the river. The townsite, founded about 1885 as Daffodil, was renamed in 1912 for Steve Decker, who operated a store and saloon here.

Deckers to Buffalo Creek

The scenic drive makes a loop from here, heading north on Jefferson CR 126 to Pine Junction on US 285 before backtracking to Buffalo Creek and following county roads along the North Fork and the South Platte River back to Deckers. The drive crosses the river at Deckers and heads west up CR 126 along the north bank. This river section offers excellent fishing with flies and lures only. Lone Rock Campground, with 19 sites, sits alongside the river upstream from Deckers. The drive continues above the river, crossing gravel slopes studded with ponderosa pines.

About 2.5 miles from Deckers the road turns away from the river up Wigwam Creek and shortly afterward swings northward up Sixmile Creek. The Wigwam Creek Road, which turns into Mutakat Road, turns south off the main drive, crosses Wigwam Creek, and heads southwest past Cheesman Lake and Lost Creek Wilderness Area toward Lake George and US 24. Wigwam Campground, with 10 walk-in sites, sits alongside the drive where it turns north. The paved road climbs steeply up Sixmile Creek's valley, widening to three lanes, and reaches a broad ridge crest after 3 miles. **Green Mountain,** its 10,421-foot summit wreathed in broken granite and forest green, looms to the west.

Kelsey Campground, with 17 sites nestled in pine and aspen woods, sits a mile farther up the drive. The road bends around 9,192-foot **Little Scraggy Peak** onto its east flank and reaches a scenic overlook. This viewpoint offers spectacular views eastward across the South Platte drainage: **Long Scraggy Peak** lifts its craggy ridge to the east, while the river canyon hides in a maze of forest below. The Rampart Range, dominated by **Devils Head,** rims the eastern horizon. The drive continues north along Little Scraggy's east slope onto a broad ridge. A roadside parking area here offers access to popular sections of the **Colorado Trail,** a 469-mile-long footpath that winds from Denver to Durango.

The road drops abruptly through pine forest and after 2 miles reaches the broad valley of the North Fork of the South Platte River and the picturesque community of **Buffalo Creek.** The town, mostly vacation cabins, is anchored by the **Green Mercantile,** an immense granite building perched on the riverbank alongside the drive. This old-fashioned country store, run by the same family since 1883, offers groceries and local chat. The two-story building, doubling as the local post office, was erected in 1898 by John W. Green Sr. after the original 1883 wooden structure burned down. Buffalo Creek began as a railroad stop for area mines and lumber in 1880 on the now-abandoned **Denver, South Park & Pacific Railway.**

Buffalo Creek to Pine Junction

The scenic drive forks at Buffalo Creek. For extra credit, drive a 10-mile spur which continues north up CR 126 to Pine Junction on US 285 west of Denver. This short road section, allowing drive access from Denver, is not to be missed. From Buffalo Creek the road twists through a granite-walled gorge. The river roars with mountain snowmelt alongside the drive in early summer. After a mile the road enters a wide, placid valley with the North Fork of the South Platte gently meandering between grassy banks. Grazing cattle and horses dot flower-strewn meadows and complete the pastoral scene.

Two miles later the road enters 6,738-foot-high **Pine** and the **North Fork National Historic District.** Pine, like its downstream neighbor, was established in the early 1880s as a railroad stop. This charming, historic community sits amid spectacular granite monoliths and bucolic meadows at Sphinx Park. Sphinx Rock, bearing a fanciful resemblance to its Egyptian namesake, looms east of town. Past Pine the highway twists up Pine Gulch through dry hills covered with ponderosa pine, mountain mahogany, and yucca and reaches **Pine Junction** and US 285 6 miles from Pine.

Along the South Platte River

To complete the scenic drive loop, backtrack to Buffalo Creek. The last leg of the scenic drive follows the South Platte's **North Fork** and the **South Platte River** for 24 miles back to Deckers. Much of this drive section is unpaved and is intensively managed by Pike National Forest as the South Platte River Corridor. This river segment, lying close to Colorado's major metropolitan areas, is both used and abused. The forest's management plan addresses and alleviates use problems to create a positive recreational experience for visitors. The 15-mile road section from Buffalo Creek to Nighthawk is a day-use-only area. Parking is permitted only in designated parking areas. Camping is allowed on the Nighthawk-to-Deckers section only in designated campgrounds.

The drive's first 10 miles, following Jefferson CR 96, heads northeast then southeast from Buffalo Creek to the confluence of the river's two forks at South Platte, following the abandoned rail bed of the Denver, South Park & Pacific Railroad, a narrow-gauge line that ran from Denver to the rich mining district of Fairplay and on to Buena Vista and Gunnison in the 1880s.

A couple miles from Buffalo Creek, the drive passes under the **Cathedral Spires,** a collection of soaring granite pinnacles and slabs perched high above the road. The spires, including Cynical Pinnacle and The Dome, offer some of Colorado's best granite rock climbing. The cliffs are accessed from a large parking area below the cliffs. *Rock Climbing Colorado* from FalconGuides has approach information and route descriptions of the best climbing routes. Downriver, the drive passes through Foxton, now a group of vacation cabins but once a railroad stop, and reaches Jefferson CR 97, South Foxton Road, after another mile. Just up the road to the north lies 2,122-acre **Reynolds Park,** part of Jefferson County's open space system, with 17 miles of hiking trails, camping at the tents-only Idylease Campground, and picnicking among the pines.

The drive winds southeast from here, bordering the North Fork and offering secluded fishing holes and picnic sites. A granite gravestone, inscribed "Tell my wife I died thinking of her," sits alongside the road among willows. After 10 snaking miles the road reaches the confluence of the North Fork and the South Platte River at the old railroad stop of South Platte.

This confluence, called **Two Forks,** was a battleground between the Denver Water Board and Coloradans concerned with losing some of the Front Range's

The Cathedral Spires, a popular rock climbing area, perches on a ridge above the North Fork of the South Platte River.

best recreational lands and one of the nation's prime trout fisheries. Denver proposed putting a large dam here that would bury these scenic canyons under 500 feet of lake water from the forks to Deckers, providing lawn and tap water to burgeoning Front Range cities. The EPA called the project an "environmental catastrophe" and denied a permit to build the dam, preserving the river and surrounding lands for wildlife and recreation.

Below Two Forks, the South Platte River tumbles down through wild Waterton Canyon before emptying into Chatfield Reservoir, a flood-control impoundment in the hills south of Denver.

At South Platte at the forks, the drive crosses a bridge over the river and bends southwest on Jefferson CR 97. This main river canyon is gentler than its North Fork cousin, with bulging granite domes and rounded hills veneered with fir and pine trees. The river itself is also calmer, riffling over cobbled shoals and gliding past immense boulders. Designated parking areas allow anglers access to the river, hikers and mountain bikers access to canyon trails, and cliffs like Java Dome, Murphys Dome and Atlantis for rock climbers. Five miles from Two Forks the road intersects Pine Creek Road, Douglas CR 40. This road climbs over the flattened northern end of the Rampart Range and ends at Sedalia 17 miles to the east.

Nighthawk spreads across the broad valley south of the road junction. Today it's a group of spread-out cabins, but in the 1890s it was a teeming gold-mining settlement and lumber camp. The town, platted in 1896, included a hotel, post office, general store, livery stable, blacksmith, and two newspapers, the *Mountain Echo* and the *West Creek Mining News.* A narrow-gauge railroad puffed through the canyon from 1904 to 1916.

The scenic drive parallels the South Platte for the next 10 miles to Deckers, passing a succession of picnic areas and campgrounds. Willow Bend and Scraggy View picnic grounds sit below the castellated ramparts of 8,812-foot Long Scraggy Peak that towers to the west. Fishing along this river section is by flies and lures only, with a two-trout limit and 16-inch minimum. The road then passes the Ouzel and Osprey campgrounds with walk-in sites. Past Bridge Crossing Picnic Area the canyon broadens with grassy meadows and open ponderosa pine forest. A couple of miles later the canyon again narrows and the road twists alongside the river to the scenic drive's end at Deckers and CO 67. Go left on highway 67 to return south to Woodland Park or right on 67 to Pine Junction and US 285.

Rampart Range Road Scenic Drive

Garden of the Gods to CO 67

General description: The 60-mile-long gravel Rampart Range Road travels the forested crest of the Rampart Range from the Garden of the Gods near Colorado Springs to CO 67, 10 miles west of Sedalia.

Special attractions: Garden of the Gods Park, Queens Canyon, Rampart Reservoir Recreation Area, Devils Head National Recreation Trail, Devils Head Lookout, scenic views, fishing, camping, hiking, picnicking, climbing, mountain bike trails, motorized vehicle trails, cross-country skiing.

Location: East-central Colorado. The drive runs along the Rampart Range between Colorado Springs and the mountains west of Sedalia. Access from the south is from Garden of the Gods Park and US 24. The drive's northern access is reached from south Denver and I-25 via US 85. Turn west on CO 67 at Sedalia.

Route name and number: Rampart Range Road, FR 300.

Travel season: Year-round. The lower section of the road, from Rampart Reservoir to Garden of the Gods, is unmaintained in winter and is usually gated. The northern section of the road, from 14 miles north of Mount Herman Road to north of Devils Head, is closed in winter, depending on snowfall and snowmelt. Travel at your own risk and carry chains and a shovel. Watch for icy spots in winter and slick sections after summer thunderstorms. Check with Pike National Forest for road closure information.

Camping: Seven national forest campgrounds lie along the drive. Two campgrounds at Rampart Reservoir Recreation Area are 21-site Thunder Ridge and 19-site Meadow Ridge. Campgrounds to the north are 13-site Springdale, 14-site Jackson Creek, 21-site Devils Head, 19-site Flat Rocks, and 11-site Indian Creek. Primitive dispersed camping is allowed on side roads off Rampart Range Road.

Services: No services are along the drive. Complete services are in Colorado Springs, Woodland Park, and south Denver. Limited services in Sedalia.

Nearby attractions: Pikes Peak Highway, Colorado Springs attractions, Cave of the Winds, Florissant Fossil Beds National Monument, Mueller State Park, Lost Creek Wilderness Area, South Platte River Scenic Drive (see Scenic Route 11), Roxborough State Park, Chatfield State Park, Colorado Trail.

The Route

Rampart Range Road, one of Colorado's best off-the-beaten-track drives, traverses the crest of the Rampart Range for 60 miles between Colorado Springs and the mountains west of Sedalia. The scenic gravel road yields spectacular views of Pikes Peak, the prairie, and the rugged Front Range and Tarryall Mountains, and offers

Rampart Range Road Scenic Drive

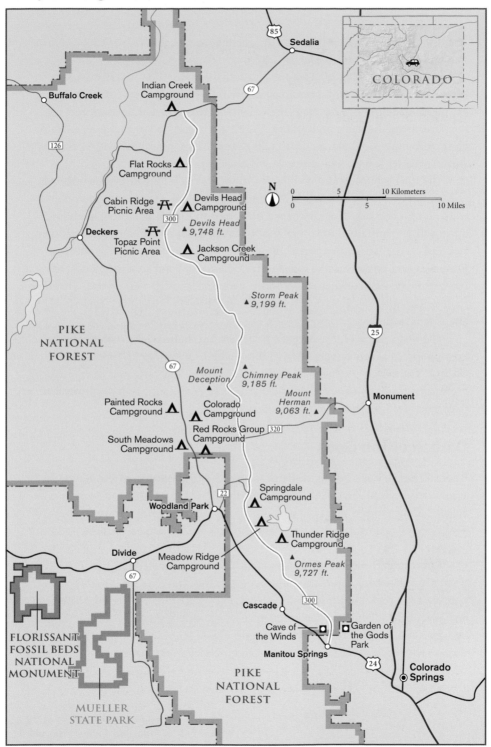

Sedalia

85

67

COLORADO

Buffalo Creek

Indian Creek
Campground

126

N

0   5   10 Kilometers
0   5   10 Miles

Flat Rocks
Campground

Cabin Ridge
Picnic Area

Devils Head
Campground

300

Devils Head
9,748 ft.

Deckers

Topaz Point
Picnic Area

Jackson Creek
Campground

Storm Peak
9,199 ft.

PIKE
NATIONAL
FOREST

25

67

Mount
Deception

Chimney Peak
9,185 ft.

Mount
Herman
9,063 ft.

Monument

Painted Rocks
Campground

Colorado
Campground

Red Rocks Group
Campground

320

South Meadows
Campground

22

Woodland Park

Springdale
Campground

Thunder Ridge
Campground

Divide

Meadow Ridge
Campground

Ormes Peak
9,727 ft.

67

Cascade

300

FLORISSANT
FOSSIL BEDS
NATIONAL
MONUMENT

Cave of
the Winds

Garden of
the Gods
Park

Manitou Springs

24

MUELLER
STATE PARK

PIKE
NATIONAL
FOREST

Colorado
Springs

quiet camping, diverse mountain biking, campgrounds, and one of Colorado's last manned fire lookouts, atop Devils Head.

Spring, summer, and fall are the best times to drive the road. Expect cool, breezy days in spring, with occasional showers and snowstorms. Summer days are pleasant and mild, with highs in the 70s and 80s. Severe thunderstorms occur regularly along the drive on July and August afternoons. Mornings are generally clear. Autumn offers colorful aspen foliage and bright, clear days with occasional storms. Winter brings cold temperatures and deep snows to the drive.

The road is plowed and maintained in winter from Rampart Reservoir Recreation Area to 14 miles north of Mount Herman Road. Drive with caution and watch for icy corners. The lower road section from the reservoir to Colorado Springs is unmaintained in winter and is usually gated closed. Drive at your own risk and carry chains and a shovel. By late March the lower road is passable to passenger cars. Inquire at the forest office for current road conditions. The lower road, running over corrugated sandstone bedrock, is rough year-round. The upper road section gets washboarded in summer after heavy rainstorms. Drive slowly to avoid vehicle damage.

The first section of the drive from the Garden of the Gods to Rampart Reservoir suffered severe damage during the Waldo Canyon Fire in June and July of 2012. The fire erupted west of the drive and spread quickly over several days, eventually burning down the east side of the Rampart Range into northwestern Colorado Springs, where over 350 homes burned.

Garden of the Gods

Rampart Range Road begins at the western end of the **Garden of the Gods,** a 1,367-acre Colorado Springs city park, north of US 24 and Manitou Springs. The Garden of the Gods is a dramatic landscape, a place of soaring sandstone hogbacks nestled against the Rampart Range's southern flank in an outdoor sculpture garden.

The strangely eroded rock formations have long attracted visitors. The Utes often camped among the rocks. Nineteenth-century travelers bestowed fanciful names on the rocks—Montezuma's Tower, The Three Graces, Kissing Camels, and Weeping Indian. After Colorado Springs was established in 1871, the Garden became a tourist attraction. Writer and poet Helen Hunt Jackson wrote, "You wind among rocks of every conceivable and inconceivable shape and size . . .

Uplifted sandstone formations scrape against the sky at the Garden of the Gods, a Colorado Springs city park.

all bright red, all motionless and silent, with a strange look of having been just stopped and held back in the very climax of some supernatural catastrophe."

Rampart Range Road begins on the west edge of the Garden at **Balanced Rock,** a tottering block perched on a sloping ledge of sandstone. The block, the most famous formation at the Garden of the Gods, appears in geology textbooks worldwide as one of the best examples of a balancing rock. The 35-foot-high rock, appearing to defy the laws of physics, weighs 700 tons or 1.4 million pounds. The precariously balanced rock is one of the most popular photo spots in Colorado Springs, with thousands of visitors stopping every summer day to get their photo snapped holding up the block or pretending that they're pushing it over.

Balanced Rock and the rest of the gently tilting strata on the west side of Garden of the Gods are composed of Fountain Formation sandstone. This maroon formation, comprising alternating layers of sandstone, mudstone, and conglomerate, was deposited almost 300 million years ago as an alluvial apron by rushing streams and rivers below Frontrangia, an ancestral mountain range.

The dirt Rampart Range Road begins just east of Balanced Rock near the junction of Garden Drive and Garden Lane and heads northwest. Another balanced rock sits below the road past Balanced Rock and after 0.3 mile the road swings north around Ship Rock, a prominent promontory, and bumps north above a shallow canyon. A pygmy forest of piñon pine, juniper, and scrub oak lines the roadside.

Queens Canyon & Williams Canyon

The road's first couple of miles travel up rounded ridges west of the Garden of the Gods, and after 4 miles you reach a good viewpoint above **Queens Canyon.** This canyon, draining southeast from the Rampart Range, is lined with sharp granite precipices and buttresses. **Glen Eyrie,** Scottish for "Valley of the Eagle's Nest," sits at the canyon's entrance below the overlook. This Tudor-style castle, built among soaring sandstone towers, was the home of General William Jackson Palmer, the founder of Colorado Springs. Queens Canyon is named for his wife, Queen Palmer. An abandoned gravel strip mine sits opposite the overlook atop the ridge above Queens Canyon.

The road begins corkscrewing upward here, passing scrub oak copses and scattered ponderosa pines. The first 8 miles of road, passing over sandstone bedrock, has a rough, corrugated surface. Magnificent views of Pikes Peak and Colorado Springs unfold from the road as it slowly climbs the southern flank of the Rampart Range. At 6 miles the road traverses a ridge west of **Williams Canyon** and passes a water tower.

A mile and a half later the drive reaches a lofty viewpoint above upper Queens Canyon and then swings west above Williams Canyon. Upper Williams Canyon is a shallow gorge studded with granite crags. The lower canyon to the south is lined with white limestone cliffs and numerous caves, including the **Cave of the Winds.** By 8 miles the road encounters its first aspen grove tucked into a moist side canyon.

The drive climbs onto another lofty ridge and after 12 miles reaches the range crest and a spectacular fenced overlook perched atop granite crags. **Pikes Peak,** the 14,115-foot pioneer landmark of the Rockies, towers to the west. Far below the overlook stretches **Ute Pass.** The pass is not really a pass at all but a deep canyon that follows the Ute Pass Fault, a major fault eroded by Fountain Creek that separates the Rampart Range from the Pikes Peak massif. The canyon, offering relatively easy passage from the Great Plains into the mountains, was first followed by the Utes and other Native Americans. Wagon roads and the Midland Railroad later used the valley to reach the Fairplay and Cripple Creek mining districts. US 24 now ascends Ute Pass from Manitou Springs to Woodland Park.

Another scenic viewpoint perches on the rim of Ute Pass another 0.3 mile farther north. A roadside monument here commemorates Rampart Range Road's dedication on June 19, 1938, and the USDA Forest Service and Civilian Conservation Corps workers who built the scenic drive.

The road twists north at an elevation of 9,000 feet along the western edge of the Rampart Range, dipping through shallow canyons densely lined with pine, fir, and spruce or areas burned bare in the 2013 Waldo Canyon Fire. FR 303 is reached after 15 miles. This road allows access to 9,727-foot **Ormes Peak,** the range's southern high point. To hike up Ormes Peak, go right on FR 303 to a right turn on rough FR 302. Park below a hill that requires 4-wheel drive and hike the road to the south side of the peak, and then scramble up rocky slopes to the summit.

Rampart Reservoir to Mount Herman Road

Past FR 303 Rampart Range Road improves dramatically, with a smooth gravel surface maintained by the city of Colorado Springs for access to several reservoirs that store drinking water. At almost 18 miles a turnoff leads east 3 miles to **Rampart Reservoir Recreation Area.** The 400-acre reservoir, part of the Colorado Springs watershed, is a popular recreation site managed by the Forest Service. Facilities include the Meadow Ridge and Thunder Ridge Campgrounds, Promontory Picnic Area with 34 sites, the barrier-free BPW Interpretive Trail, a boat ramp, and a boat dock in summer. Wading, swimming, and waterskiing are prohibited on the lake.

The recreation area offers plenty of fine trails for hikers and mountain bikers. Lake Shore Trail, a popular 12-mile-long mountain bike and hiking path, circles the reservoir. Another popular trail, 1.2-mile Rainbow Gulch Trail (#714), begins on Rampart Range Road 1.5 miles north of the reservoir turnoff. The trail drops down to the reservoir through a ponderosa pine forest broken by open meadows. Hike it in July for fields of wildflowers.

Past Rainbow Gulch, the road climbs onto rolling grassy ridges studded with pine groves. Great views unfold along this road section. The Sawatch Range and the Continental Divide peaks poke above the far western horizon, and the snow-capped summits of Mount Evans and Longs Peak are far to the north. Alert drivers can spot elk, mule deer, and wild turkey browsing in the meadows. Springdale Campground sits at 9,200 feet in an evergreen copse on the northern meadow edge. Past the grassland the drive intersects with Loy Creek Road, a short paved road that drops a couple of miles down to **Woodland Park** and US 24. Another spur road to Woodland Park sits 1.6 miles to the north. Woodland Park offers all services for travelers.

The road rolls north, hemmed in by thick forest. Occasional pullouts yield views across dark ridges to distant peaks and the tawny prairie. The Rampart Range, seen from the plains and surrounding high peaks, appears almost flat, with only occasional peaks rising above the level surface. Indeed, the range crest seldom climbs above 9,000 feet and only in eroded valleys does it drop below that elevation. The Rampart Range is what geologists call a pediment, or old erosional surface. Its granite hills are the worn-down stubs of what were once great mountains. The pediment, once continuous with the high plains and extending over much of the Front Range, was uplifted some 28 million years ago.

Mount Herman Road (FR 320) branches east 4 miles north of Loy Creek Road. This scenic dirt road edges around 9,063-foot **Mount Herman** to Monument and I-25. Rampart Range Road continues north, passing numerous side roads and Saylor Park, a popular cross-country skiing area. At the microwave towers, some 36 miles from the road's start, a gate is locked in winter, limiting access to the road.

Past the gate the drive drops down a shallow canyon. A stream lined with aspen groves and beaver ponds borders the road. Beyond the canyon the road swings around a boulder–studded mountainside and twists northward. FR 348, reached at 42 miles, heads west through Long Hollow to CO 67.

FR 507, reached at 44 miles, heads northeast down scenic Jackson Creek. Jackson Creek Campground sits 2 miles down the road. Farther down Jackson Creek are numerous domes that offer superb slab climbing routes, including Split Dome, Flathead Dome, The Taj Mahal, Mega Dome, and Jackson Creek Dome.

Check out *Rock Climbing Colorado* from FalconGuides for climbing information and route descriptions.

The scenic drive swings around the west side of Devils Head. Topaz Point Picnic Area and Viewpoint sit on a rocky knoll west of the road. A short hike to the overlook yields a full view of the South Platte River country to the west from a weathered granite shelf. A display identifies the surrounding mountains.

Devils Head

Devils Head, the 9,748-foot high point of the Rampart Range, dominates the northern section of the drive. The peak rears above the dusty road, its steep forested flanks broken by ragged granite crags and outcrops. The Forest Service's last Front Range fire lookout is stationed atop the peak. Since 1912 a spotter has been stationed here looking for forest fires. The current tower, built in 1951, was added to the National Register of Historic Places in 1991. The tower is usually staffed from mid-May until mid-September.

The 1.5-mile **Devils Head National Recreation Trail** (#611), beginning from a trailhead south of Devils Head Campground, threads up the Head's northern slopes to the fire lookout. The last trail section scales a series of staircases with 143 stairs to the rocky summit. The expansive view is astounding, taking in the entire Front Range from the Spanish Peaks almost 150 miles to the south to flat-topped

Pikes Peak dominates the evening sky above forests and meadows along the Rampart Range Road.

Longs Peak to the north. The Great Plains stretch eastward toward a Kansas horizon, while mountain ranges piled on ranges spread west. Denver's urban sprawl lies in the broad Denver Basin to the northwest, its glass buildings shimmering in the sun. Legend says that over $60,000 in gold coins was stashed somewhere on Devils Head's rough flanks after a train robbery in the 1870s. Treasure hunters still canvas the mountain in search of the hidden gold stash, while mineral collectors search for gem-quality topaz and arm-sized smoky quartz crystals. Devils Head also offers excellent climbing, with almost 500 established routes on its featured rock faces.

Rampart Range Road passes below the west slopes of Devils Head, and reaches a spur road that leads 0.5 mile south to Devils Head Campground and the trailhead for the Devils Head Trail. Cabin Ridge Picnic Area sits a mile farther north. The road begins losing elevation past Cabin Ridge, passing from spruce and fir forest to an open ponderosa pine woodland. Flat Rocks Campground and overlook sit another 4 miles up the road. The overlook offers views of wooded ridges and canyons, the flat-topped mesas around Castle Rock, and the distant plains. This upper road section crosses the **Rampart Range Recreation Area,** with 120 miles of all-terrain vehicle and motorcycle trails. The area is busy in the summer, especially on weekends.

The drive ends at a T-junction with CO 67 at a Pike National Forest work center. Indian Creek Campground lies just west of the highway junction. A right turn runs steeply down Jarre Canyon and reaches Sedalia and US 85 in 10 miles, while a left turn descends Douglas CR 67 to the South Platte River and Deckers.

South Park–Tarryall Loop Scenic Drive

Lake George through South Park & Back to Lake George

General description: This paved 121-mile loop drive follows Tarryall Creek along the Tarryall Mountains into South Park, traverses the park's western edge beneath the Park and Mosquito Ranges, then turns east and crosses the park and Wilkerson Pass back to Lake George.

Special attractions: Pike National Forest, Lost Creek Wilderness Area, Puma Hills, Tarryall Creek, Tarryall Reservoir State Wildlife Area, South Park National Heritage Area, Fairplay, Como, South Park City, Mosquito Range, Antero Reservoir State Wildlife Area, Buffalo Peaks, Spinney Mountain State Park, Wilkerson Pass, hiking, backpacking, fishing, climbing, scenic views, picnicking.

Location: Central Colorado.

Route numbers: US 24 and US 285; Park CR 77.

Travel season: Year-round. The highways are plowed in winter. Be prepared for blowing and drifting snow during blizzards, icy roads, and hazardous driving conditions. Park CR 77 can be temporarily closed in severe weather.

Camping: Several national forest campgrounds lie along the drive. North on Park CR 77 are Happy Meadows Campground (8 sites), Spruce Grove Campground (27 sites), and Twin Eagles Campground (9 sites). West of US 285 between Kenosha Pass and Antero Junction are Kenosha Pass (25 sites), Lodgepole (34 sites), Jefferson Creek (17 sites), Michigan Creek (12 sites), Selkirk (15 sites), Fourmile (14 sites), Horseshoe (19 sites), Weston Pass (14 sites), and Buffalo Springs (18 sites) campgrounds. Elevenmile State Park offers 335 campsites in 9 campgrounds. Elevenmile Canyon south of Lake George has 4 campgrounds—Riverside (18 sites), Springer Gulch (15 sites), Cove (4 sites), and Spillway (23 sites); Blue Mountain Campground (21 sites) is south of Lake George. Primitive dispersed camping is permitted on national forest land. Practice low-impact camping and put fires out.

Services: All services are in Fairplay. Limited services in Jefferson, Hartsel, and Lake George.

Nearby attractions: Breckenridge, Boreas Pass, Brown's Canyon, Arkansas Headwaters State Park, Sawatch Range, Elevenmile Canyon, Cripple Creek, Florissant Fossil Beds National Monument, Bristlecone Scenic Area, Mosquito Pass, Guanella Pass Scenic and Historic Byway (Scenic Drive 15), South Platte River Roads (Scenic Drive 11).

The Route

The 121-mile-long South Park–Tarryall drive makes a spectacular loop through some of Colorado's most spacious scenery. The drive traverses the granite-studded canyons and valleys of Tarryall Creek and crosses the open, sweeping grasslands of South Park, a high intermontane basin that sits in the state's middle. This land

South Park–Tarryall Loop Scenic Drive

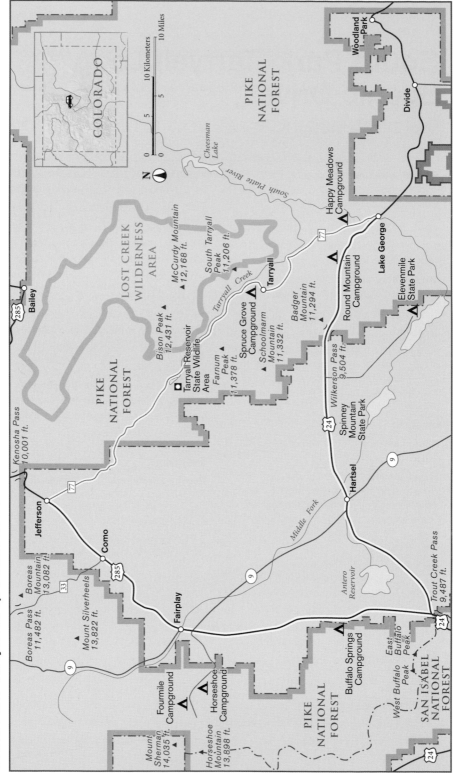

of wide views and historic sites boasts a long human history, from the Ute tribe who hunted buffalo on the park's broad expanse, to silver and gold prospectors who mined around Fairplay, to sheep and cattle ranchers. Today this is a land of peace and quiet. Wind ruffles the surrounding pine forests, thunderstorms spread a veil of rain and lightning over the mountains, and short grass broken by fence lines and roads carpets the park floor.

The **South Park National Heritage Area,** designated in 2009 by President Barack Obama and Congress, preserves the historic and natural resources found along this scenic drive. The well-preserved area is an excellent example of western America's colorful mining and ranching history, as well as a prehistory that dates back to paleo-Americans that left distinctive Clovis points over 12,000 years ago.

South Park, lying at 9,000 feet, and the higher surrounding mountains are cool in summer and cold in winter. Summer days are generally clear; thunderstorms build up in the afternoon over the high peaks to the west. Expect heavy localized rain and lightning. Avoid being in the open or under trees during lightning storms. Autumn brings clear, warm days and a frosting of snow to the higher ranges. Winters are cold and windy. Heavy snow blankets South Park and the Mosquito and Park Ranges. Ground blizzard conditions are common during snowstorms. Temperatures are frigid, often dropping below zero, in South Park because cold air sinks onto the valley floor from higher slopes. Spring days are cool and often windy. The snow cover slowly melts, leaving dry grass by April.

Tarryall

The drive begins 1 mile west of Lake George and 45 miles west of Colorado Springs along the South Platte River. Turn north off US 24 onto roughly paved Park CR 77. This first leg of the byway journey ends 42 miles ahead in Jefferson on US 285. The paved road turns north along the river and follows a broad, grassy valley through rolling, ponderosa pine–clad hills. After a mile the river leaves the road and bends into a deep canyon that twists northeastward through the Front Range to Denver. A spur forest road follows the river for a mile to 8-site Happy Meadows Campground, a popular summer site for anglers.

After leaving the river, the road follows broad Tappan Gulch northward past small ranches and grassy meadows grazed by horses and cattle. Low granite hills, sparsely covered with ponderosa pines, line the valley floor. After 4 miles the road crosses a divide below 8,954-foot Tappan Mountain and drops into Tarryall Creek's scenic drainage. Tarryall Creek slices through a wide canyon that separates the rugged Tarryall Mountains to the northeast from the Puma Hills to the west. The creek meanders through a verdant valley here, swinging past wide meadows, hay fields, and steel-gray granite crags.

A mile after reaching the creek, the drive intersects Matukat Road, FR 211. This scenic dirt road sweeps around the east flank of the Tarryalls and offers views into the South Platte River drainage. After another mile, the drive turns west away from the creek up Marksbury Gulch. The gulch is named for an early homesteader, buried in the Lake George cemetery, who was killed by Utes after stealing a pony. The China Wall, a long granite escarpment, parallels the dry arroyo on its north side. The road passes boulder-strewn hillsides, climbs into rounded grassy hills, crosses a divide, and drops into the historic town of **Tarryall** at 12 miles.

Tarryall, formerly called Puma City, got its start in 1859 when prospectors found gold nuggets "as big as watermelon seeds" in the creek below. The new town supposedly got its name when a miner remarked, "Let us tarry all." Those who came later, however, found the best placer sites claimed and derided the town as "Grab all" before starting the competing town of Hamilton on the opposite creek bank and heading across South Park and founding Fairplay. Hamilton quickly surpassed its neighbor and boasted a transient population of 6,000 by 1860. The town offered saloons, casinos, its own newspaper, and a theater.

Tarryall, officially laid out in 1861, was the Park County seat for a short while. In the summer of 1861, miner John Parsons began his own mint, stamping out $2.50, $5, and $20 gold coins that are worth more than $30,000 today. Slowly the placer claims were exhausted and miners deserted Tarryall and Hamilton for new strikes elsewhere. By 1875 the towns were mostly empty.

Tarryall now is a small community of rustic cabins. Still visible, however, is Whiskey Hole. This deep pit was set aside during the boom days for poor miners to pan enough gold to buy a shot of whiskey at local watering holes. The Tarryall School, listed on the National Register of Historic Places, sits on the roadside entering Tarryall. The elegant white clapboard building, with a steeple and bell, was built in 1922 and now serves as a town meeting hall. Nothing remains of Hamilton save a few mining scars.

The Tarryall Range

From Tarryall, the road descends through open grasslands to Tarryall Creek. The drive parallels the meandering creek through canyons and valleys for the next 12 miles to Tarryall Reservoir. The Puma Hills, a long ridge of timbered hills topped by 11,378-foot Farnum Peak, border this spectacular road section on the west, while the **Tarryall Range,** a 25-mile-long sierra studded with bold granite cliffs and deep forests of aspen and evergreen, lifts its serrated escarpment to the east.

The 119,790-acre **Lost Creek Wilderness Area** protects most of the Tarryall Range from encroaching civilization. Numerous hiking trails wind up ponderosa pine–covered slopes, passing trickling creeks lined with columbines and aspens,

Tarryall Peak rises beyond twisting Tarryall Creek and the historic Williams Ranch.

and switchbacking to the summit of 12,431-foot Bison Peak, the range high point. The Tarryalls are formed by Pikes Peak granite, a billion-year-old, pink, coarse-grained rock that formed after a massive underground reservoir of molten magma slowly cooled over millions of years. Eons of erosion chipped away at the granite, sculpting today's rocky wonderland of spires, flying buttresses, domes, castles, and rounded boulders. The Tarryall Range was designated a National Natural Landmark in 1966 for its superb wilderness and scenic qualities.

Besides being an excellent getaway for hiking and backpacking, the wilderness area offers rock climbing up granite cliffs, fly fishing in cold streams, and wildlife observation. The area is one of the best spots to spot Rocky Mountain bighorn sheep, the Colorado state mammal. Any hiker scrambling to the cobbled summit of the high peaks here has a good chance of seeing these elegant, sure-footed mammals. Other wildlife includes mule deer, black bear, mountain lion, golden eagle, elk, turkey, porcupine, and raccoon. The wilderness is easily accessed from the scenic drive at Spruce Grove Campground, Twin Eagles Campground, and at Ute Creek. The Pike National Forest office in Colorado Springs offers detailed maps and trail descriptions.

Spruce Grove Campground, with 27 sites at 8,600 feet, sits off the drive a mile north of Tarryall. This lovely campground, surrounded by jagged cliffs, nestles among tall pines along the swift creek. It makes a perfect base camp for exploring the Lost Creek Wilderness Area. Good hikes from the **Spruce Grove Trailhead** are Lizard Rock Trail (#658), a 5.8-mile, out-and-back hike to an overlook; Hankins Pass Trail (#630), which climbs over Hankins Pass and descends to the Goose Creek Trailhead; and Lake Park Trail (#639) which climbs from Hankins Pass to a lovely open park surrounded by granite cliffs.

Twin Eagles Campground and Trailhead, a favorite stop for anglers, lies 2 miles northward along a sharp bend of Tarryall Creek. The Brookside-McCurdy Trail (#607), a primary trail that bisects the wilderness area, heads north here, climbing to McCurdy Park below 12,168-foot McCurdy Mountain, one of the Tarryall Range's high points.

The drive bends northwest along the southern edge of Tarryall Creek's broad valley, carpeted with green hay fields and dotted with grazing cattle, which stretches away from the road to the rugged Tarryall Range. This valley is the historic Williams Ranch, which was initially settled in 1882 by Welsh immigrant John Williams and his wife, Mary. They raised seven children in the idyllic and picturesque valley.

Stop at a two-panel roadside kiosk that interprets the valley and range. It also offers Isabella Bird's description of the valley on a solo exploration along Tarryall Creek in 1873. Bird, the first woman to climb Longs Peak in today's Rocky Mountain National Park, described the scene in her book *A Lady's Life in the Rocky Mountains*:

> I rode up one great ascent where hills were tumbled about confusedly; and suddenly across the broad ravine rising above the sunny grass and deep green pines, rose in glowing and shaded red against the glittering blue heaven a magnificent and unearthly range of mountains as shapely could be seen, rising into colossal points, cleft by deep blue ravines, broken up into shark's teeth with gigantic knobs and pinnacles rising from their inaccessible sides, very fair to look upon a glowing, heavenly, unforgettable sight, and only four miles off.

The road follows twisting Tarryall Creek, passing grassy banks lined with dense willow thickets and dipping across dry drainages below timbered Farnum Peak. After almost 22 miles the drive reaches the **Ute Creek Trailhead,** a popular jumping-off point for backpackers trekking into Lost Creek Wilderness Area. The 12-mile round-trip hike up 12,431-foot **Bison Peak,** the highest mountain in the Tarryall Range, follows Ute Creek Trail (#629) to a junction with Brookside-McCurdy Trail, which it follows to a ridgeline and then to the summit. Expect spectacular views and a magical maze of granite pillars and buttresses on the final slope. A detailed Bison Peak hiking description is in *Climbing Colorado's Mountains* from FalconGuides.

The valley broadens beyond Ute Creek, but steep mountain slopes clad in pine and granite tower above the drive. Fishing along this section of Tarryall

*Horses graze in South Park below Mount Guyot and Boreas Mountain on the
Continental Divide.*

Creek is allowed with artificial flies and lures only. Watch for private river sections
that don't allow public fishing.

After driving 23 miles from US 24, views of the snow-capped Park Range
unfold to the west beyond tawny hills covered with short grass. A couple miles
later is 886-acre **Tarryall Reservoir State Wildlife Area.** Stop at a large parking
area below the concrete dam to view Tarryall Falls, a lovely waterfall that tumbles
30 feet from an excavated channel to the creek below. Above the waterfall, the
700-acre lake is a glistening jewel nestled among treeless, rolling hills studded
with brief rock outcrops. It's a popular destination for anglers who come to fish
for trout and picnic on its shores. Several stone levees jut into the water from
the north shore, allowing anglers to toss lines far out on the lake. Two campgrounds—Potato Gulch and Derbyshire—on the lake's northeast shore provide
quiet overnight stays.

South Park, Jefferson & Como

The scenery dramatically changes beyond the reservoir as the drive ventures onto
the hilly northeastern fringe of **South Park.** The road continues northwest along
Tarryall Creek, crossing dry Schoolhouse and Graveyard Gulches and passing
abandoned cabins, a cemetery, and picturesque ranches. Scrubby forests scatter

across the rolling hills, including 10,073-foot Observatory Rock, a prominent cliff-rimmed peak to the southwest.

Twelve miles from the reservoir, Michigan Creek and the drive enter northern South Park. A wide, lush grassland, watered by snowmelt from the peaks of the towering Park Range, stretches westward to the distant forest edge. The creek cuts through meadows enclosed by barbed-wire fences.

The drive's first leg ends 5 miles later in **Jefferson** at US 285. Jefferson was hastily erected in 1879 when the Denver, South Park & Pacific Railroad pushed across South Park in a race to reach Leadville and its productive mines before the rival Denver & Rio Grande Railroad, laying track north from Cañon City along the Arkansas River, grabbed the lucrative ore-transport business. The historic pale-blue **Denver, South Park & Pacific Railroad Depot,** built about 1880 and listed on the National Register of Historic Places, still stands alongside the highway. The depot, one of the last surviving structures of the railroad, served passengers and freight until 1937. By 1881 the town boasted a post office, a couple of butcher shops, lumber mill, saloon, blacksmith shop, hotel, and 300 residents. Jefferson became an important shipping and ranching center for area cattle and sheep outfits, a role it continues to play.

The drive's next leg runs 16 miles south on US 285 along the western edge of South Park from Jefferson to Fairplay and another 23 miles to Antero Junction at the park's southwestern corner. South Park is an intermontane basin 50 miles long and 35 miles wide with an area of more than 900 square miles, just slightly smaller than Rhode Island. Elevations range from 8,500 feet to higher than 10,000 feet. The park, covered with short grass, is broken by several long, forested hogbacks.

The South Platte River, arising on the Continental Divide near Hoosier Pass, drains South Park and the surrounding mountains. Mountains rim South Park—the Puma Hills, bisected by Wilkerson Pass on the east; the dark rounded peaks of the old Thirty-Nine-Mile Volcanic Field to the south; and the lofty snow-capped Mosquito and Park Ranges on the west and north. The Mosquito Range includes four peaks—Mounts Lincoln, Bross, Democrat, and Sherman—that top 14,000 feet. Mosquito Pass, Colorado's highest pass at 13,180 feet, crosses the range west of Fairplay before dropping west to Leadville. South Park, one of Colorado's four mountain basins (the other ones being North Park, Middle Park, and the San Luis Valley), was originally named Valle Salada (Salt Valley) for the white saline deposits left on flat, evaporated lake beds on the valley floor. One of the salts is sodium chloride, or common table salt.

From Jefferson, the drive crosses well-watered meadows covered with summer wildflowers, including sky-blue iris. West of the highway looms the snow-covered Park Range, an extension of the Front Range. The Continental Divide, separating the Pacific and Atlantic Ocean drainages, meanders along the range crest over high peaks including 13,370-foot Mount Guyot and 13,082-foot Boreas Mountain. Gravel roads climb west from the highway into Pike National Forest up Jefferson, Michigan, and Tarryall Creeks to alpine valleys, beaver ponds, and several forest campgrounds.

The **Boreas Pass Road,** ascending Tarryall Creek from Como to 11,482-foot Boreas Pass, offers an excellent backcountry route to Breckenridge. The well-maintained gravel road generally follows the old narrow-gauge Denver, South Park & Pacific Railroad grade. The railroad, in use from 1881 to 1937, climbed 4.5 percent grades and 435 curves on this stretch of mountainous track. Selkirk Campground, with 15 sites, sits along the road at 10,500 feet.

The drive reaches **Como,** an old railroad town, 7 miles from Jefferson. Como, like neighboring Jefferson, was a boom town during the heady days of railroad construction, with a population exceeding 6,000, who mostly lived in tents. The town also prospered with coal mining in the nearby hills. The danger-ous Como mines claimed numerous victims, including 35 Chinese miners in 1885 and 25 Italian immigrants in 1893. The mines closed in 1896 and Como began a quiet life as a railroad center. Stop in town to view the historic **Como Roundhouse,** a six-door roundhouse used for storing train engines that was built by Italian stonemasons in 1870. It was listed on the National Register of Historic Places in 1983.

There is also the **Como Depot,** which was built in 1879 and abandoned after the last Denver, South Park & Pacific Railroad train pulled out in April 1937. The depot, used for storage through the rest of the 20th century, slowly began falling apart, with parts of the roof and siding weathering off the building. In 2008, the Denver, South Park & Pacific Historical Society and Como resident David Tom-kins began renovating the crumbled site, by stabilizing the building, repairing the foundation, and restoring both the interior and exterior as close as possible to the original depot. The old depot now has new life as a Como history museum. A section of track was laid between the depot and the roundhouse by 2017 and an authentic 1912 Baldwin steam locomotive, nicknamed Klondike Kate #4, is now stored in the roundhouse and fired up on summer weekends and special occasions.

The highway climbs a low, forested ridge southwest of Como, drops across Trout Creek, and steeply ascends to the summit of 9,943-foot Red Hill Pass. Red Hill is a long hogback of tilted Dakota sandstone that runs southward across South Park from here. The road descends the summit's western slope, runs across grassy benches, and enters Fairplay 3 miles later. Here the drive intersects CO 9, which heads north to Hoosier Pass and Breckenridge.

Fairplay

Fairplay, South Park's largest town and the seat of Park County, sits at 9,953 feet on gravel benches above the Middle Fork of the South Platte River in the park's extreme northwestern corner. Once a brawling, boisterous mining camp, Fairplay retains a quaint historic charm, with log cabins, gingerbread-adorned Victorian homes, and a friendly atmosphere. The town sprang up in 1859 at the core of a rich placer mining district by miners incensed by claim-grabbing at Tarryall across the valley. The frontier town slowly grew not only as a mining center, but also as a freight, transportation, and supply hub. By the 1870s Fairplay boasted hotels, a post office, a brewery, a stone courthouse, a newspaper, and, of course, several churches to minister to the miners.

The **Sheldon Jackson Memorial Chapel,** named for the superintendent of the West's Presbyterian missions, was built in 1874 on the corner of 6th and Hathaway Streets. This elegant white church, now part of the South Park Community Church, is considered to be one of the nation's best examples of Timber Gothic architecture with its board and batten siding, pointed windows, and wheel window below an ornate steeple. It's listed on the National Register of Historic Places along with the nearby Fairplay Hotel, Park County Courthouse and Jail, and South Park City District. Sheldon Jackson (1834–1909), a Presbyterian minister and missionary, established over 100 churches in the western United States, including the Fairplay church. He also traveled to the mining camps above town on Mount Bross to preach to miners. In 1885 he was appointed education agent to the Alaska Territory, where he forbade the use of indigenous languages by students and for instruction.

Old Fairplay lives on today in the **South Park City Museum,** a living-history museum that preserves buildings and artifacts from the past. Real history is found in real people. Trod the dusty streets here, peer through shop windows, examine an old cabin, and study a miner's hand tools. South Park City gives the traveler a moment to experience history, to share in its making, to take a step backward in time to a place where every day is yesterday. The mining boom began in 1859 with the discovery of precious gold. Miners set up camps across the mountains, which became towns like Buckskin Joe, Leavick, and Eureka overnight. South Park City is a fictional town that's an amalgamation of all those mining communities. The museum preserves 44 buildings, including 7 on their original sites, and over 60,000 artifacts, tools, photographs, and memorabilia from Colorado's booming mining past. The museum, on the south side of Fairplay, is open daily from May 15 to October 15.

The historic Sheldon Jackson Memorial Chapel in Fairplay is one of the best examples of Timber Gothic architecture in the United States.

Plenty of gold nuggets and flakes came from the South Platte River by Fairplay. If you want to try your hand at gold panning, head to **Fairplay Beach** on the south side of town and start finding a fortune. All you need is a permit from the town clerk or website for $5 a week. The beach also has fishing, picnic tables, and hiking trails.

Fairplay, with a 2010 population of 679, is the fifth-highest incorporated town in Colorado. It's also the model for the town of South Park in the hit animated TV series *South Park*. It offers all services to visitors, including accommodations, dining, groceries, and gas. An exciting time to visit Fairplay is during its famed Burro Days on the last weekend of July. The culminating event is a 29-mile burro race from Fairplay to the summit of 13,185-foot Mosquito Pass that's esoterically dubbed the World Championship of Burro Racing.

Fairplay takes its burros seriously. A burro, simply a donkey used as a pack animal, was an important part of every 19th-century miner's kit and was often his best friend in the mountains. Prunes, Fairplay's most famous burro, was a special donkey and friend to his owner, Rupe Sherwood. Prunes and Rupe prospected and panned gold all over the Fairplay and Alma district for more than 50 years until Rupe retired part-time to Denver. Prunes spent his golden years roaming around Fairplay, a well-loved donkey who was fed pancakes by housewives in the morning.

In the winter of 1930, a blizzard descended on the town. Prunes holed up in a shed but the door blew shut, trapping him inside. By the time local children found him, Prunes was weak, starving, and near death. Townspeople nursed him to health and he managed to last until spring, when Rupe came up to spend the summer. Prunes died shortly afterward at age 63. He was buried in town and a monument was erected to his memory. Rupe cried at the ceremony dedicating the monument, and said, "Lord, I hate to see him go. I would trust him above any man." A year later Rupe also died and was cremated, with his remains buried beside his old partner. The shrine includes Prunes' harness under glass. Stop by and pay your respects to the famous shaggy burro and his human buddy on the south side of Front Street between 5th and 6th Streets.

The Mosquito Range

The drive continues south from Fairplay on US 285 for 23 miles to Antero Junction. This highway section crosses rolling hills and sloping plains of stream-deposited glacial gravels on South Park's western margin beneath the rounded **Mosquito Range,** a high range that twists south from Hoosier Pass to Trout Creek Pass. Most of the range crest soars above timberline and includes four 14,000-foot peaks. The high peaks west of the drive—14,035-foot Mount Sherman,

13,898-foot Horseshoe Mountain, and 13,739-foot Ptarmigan Peak—are rounded bumps on the range crest. Glaciers contoured and smoothed the range's ancient sedimentary rock layers into broad valleys and steep-walled cirques.

Most of the range names are of Civil War vintage, with miners naming Mount Lincoln for the Civil War president and Mounts Sherman and Sheridan for his generals. Myth has it that the Mosquito Range acquired its name in 1861 when a mosquito was found pressed on the blank spot of a legal document where the name of a proposed mining district was to be written, giving the name to the district, pass, mountain, and range.

Several gravel roads head west from the drive onto the eastern flank of the Mosquitos. Fourmile Creek Road (CR 18), a mile south of Fairplay, twists up Fourmile Creek past 19-site Horseshoe and 14-site Fourmile Campgrounds to the abandoned ghost townsite of Leavick. An easy trail climbs west from here to the summit of Mount Sherman, considered the easiest of Colorado's 54 "Fourteeners," or 14,000-foot mountains, to scale. The Weston Pass Road (CR 5 and 22), 4.5 miles south of Fairplay, heads west and ascends 15.5 miles to the summit of 11,921-foot Weston Pass on the crest of the Mosquito Range. *The west side of the pass is four-wheel-drive only, unmaintained, and open only in summer.*

The **Buffalo Peaks,** a twin-summited mountain of lava and volcanic ash, dominates the southern Mosquito Range and the scenic drive. The peaks, in a 43,410-acre wilderness area, are densely forested and teem with wildlife, including bighorn sheep and elk. Access is via several forest roads that head west from US 285. This drive section ends at Antero Junction at US 285's junction with US 24. US 285/24 continues west over Trout Creek Pass to Buena Vista. The drive, however, turns east on US 24 onto the treeless steppe of South Park.

Across South Park

The last segment of the scenic drive runs east 39 miles across South Park, over Wilkerson Pass, and then down to Lake George and the drive's starting point. The highway drops away from Antero Junction, crosses several dry arroyos, and reaches the old Colorado Midland Railway grade after a couple of miles. The grade parallels the highway from here to Hartsel before bending southeast to **Elevenmile Canyon.** The Colorado Midland, built by Colorado Springs mining magnate John J. Hagerman in the 1880s, was the first standard-gauge railroad into the Colorado Rockies. The line ran from Colorado Springs to Leadville, burrowed through the Continental Divide below Hagerman Pass, and then ran through Glenwood Springs to Grand Junction. The railroad often ran "Wildflower Excursion" trains from Colorado Springs to South Park for passengers to collect colorful bouquets of summer flowers. The rail line closed in 1918 and was torn up in 1921.

The highway, running northeast, passes prominent Twin Peaks, swings down a dry, shallow valley, and after 5.6 miles reaches the turnoff on CR 437 to Antero Reservoir. **Antero Reservoir,** a popular fishing lake, was built in 1909 on a dried lake bed as a water-storage lake for Denver. The lake dried up in 2002 but was refilled in 2007 and stocked with rainbow, cutthroat, brown, and brook trout. The lake's shallow, warm water lets the fish quickly grow to lunker size. Bag limit is 2 trout per day. A 38-site campground and boat ramp are on the lake's south shore; the north shore is day-use only.

Numerous Native American sites line this highway section, including a large campsite and battleground near Twin Peaks. South Park, with plentiful game, including buffalo and deer, was a popular summer hunting ground for the Ute, Comanche, Cheyenne, Kiowa, and Arapaho tribes. Legendary scout and trailblazer Kit Carson witnessed a three-day battle between the Comanches and Utes in eastern South Park in 1844. The Utes were defeated on the third day after 40 braves were killed and more than 100 Ute horses were taken as battle spoils.

Hartsel sits at the junction of the two forks of the South Platte River in the middle of the park, 13 miles from Antero Junction. The town once thrived as a mini-resort on the Colorado Midland railroad line. A small hot spring, with 134-degree water, attracted visitors who stayed overnight at a hotel. The now-abandoned hot spring lies south of town along the riverbank. The hot spring, on private property, has been called "Colorado's hottest hot spring"—the radon-laden water is radioactive. The area was homesteaded by rancher Sam Hartsel in 1862. His Hartsel Springs Ranch thrived with Texas longhorn and Hereford cattle grazing on the fertile grasslands along the river. Hartsel also pumped hot spring water to his nearby ranch house using a pipeline made of drilled-out logs.

US 24, after intersecting CO 9, which runs north to Fairplay and southeast to Cañon City, crosses the South Platte River. The drive continues east, skirting several barren mountains, and passes the turnoff on CR 447 for 7,662-acre **Eleven Mile State Park** and 6,080-acre **Spinney Mountain State Park** after 11 miles. Elevenmile's 3,405-acre reservoir, finished in 1932 as part of Denver's water supply, is one of Colorado's most popular mountain lakes. Trophy-size trout, kokanee salmon, and northern pike are regularly pulled from its chilly waters. The state park also has 335 campsites in 9 campgrounds, over 5 miles of trails for hiking and mountain biking, and boating for power boats, jet-skis, canoes, kayaks, and sailboats.

Neighboring **Spinney Mountain State Park,** a day-use area only open in warm weather, boasts a 2,450-acre lake that's part of Aurora's water supply. Spinney, one of three Gold Medal lakes in Colorado, is renowned for trophy-sized rainbow, brown, and cutthroat trout, and northern pike. Biologists say that closing the lake to winter fishing helps grow the big fish since 10- to 12-inch trout that are stocked in the fall can feed all winter. All water-contact sports like swimming, scuba diving, and waterskiing, are prohibited. Spinney does, however, allow boating during daylight hours, but watch for high winds and waves in the afternoon. It's also an excellent birdwatching spot for waterfowl and raptors.

The highway climbs into the Puma Hills, a scraggy mountain range bordering the eastern edge of South Park, beneath 11,294-foot Badger Mountain, and snakes up to the summit of 9,504-foot **Wilkerson Pass.** Imaginative eyes can spot a Native American head composed of metamorphic cliff bands on Badger Mountain's western slope to the north. The mountain, topped with antennas, was named for 19th-century rancher John Badger.

Wilkerson Pass, with picnic tables, short trails, restrooms, and a Forest Service visitor center, offers spectacular views west across barren South Park to the snow-capped Mosquito Range and beyond to the Sawatch Range from an overlook. To the east towers bulky 14,115-foot Pikes Peak, surrounded by a green forest mantle. After enjoying the view, take a hike on the 0.9-mile Puma Point Trail which loops through aspen groves and meadows on the pass. The visitor center, staffed by volunteers, is open in summer only but the restrooms are open most of the year.

The highway winds down the Puma Hills' gentle east flank, passes 16-site Round Mountain Campground, and twists down Pulver Gulch to the South Platte River, Lake George, and the end of the scenic drive. Elevenmile Canyon, offering 4 campgrounds, trout fishing, and excellent rock climbing, is south of Lake George, while **Florissant Fossil Beds National Monument,** protecting 30-million-year-old fossils, lies 7 miles to the southeast. Continue east another 45 miles on US 24 to Colorado Springs.

Mount Evans Scenic Drive

Idaho Springs to the Summit of Mount Evans

General description: The 28-mile Mount Evans Highway, the nation's highest automobile road and a National Forest Scenic Byway, climbs from Idaho Springs to the 12,271-foot summit of Mount Evans.

Special attractions: Pike National Forest, Arapaho National Forest, Mount Evans Wilderness Area, Echo Lake, Mount Goliath Natural Area, Summit Lake, camping, picnicking, fishing, rock climbing, wildlife observation, spring skiing, hiking, bristlecone pines, scenic views.

Location: Central Colorado. The drive is west of Denver in the Front Range.

Route name and numbers: Mount Evans Highway, CO 103 and 5.

Travel season: Summer only. The road (CO 5) usually opens to Summit Lake by Memorial Day and to the summit by late

June, depending on winter snowfall. The road closes on Labor Day weekend. The lower-elevation highway is open year-round. Expect severe conditions on the upper mountain in summer, with possible thunderstorms and even snow. The road can be slick and icy.

Camping: Two national forest campgrounds—West Chicago Creek (15 sites) and Echo Lake (17 sites)—lie along the drive. Three picnic areas are on the drive.

Services: All services are in Idaho Springs.

Nearby attractions: Guanella Pass Scenic and Historic Byway (Scenic Drive 15), Oh My God Road, Central City, Georgetown National Historic District, Georgetown Loop Railroad, Loveland Ski Area, Arapahoe Basin Ski Area, Golden Gate Canyon State Park, Clear Creek Canyon, Red Rocks Park, Denver area attractions.

The Route

Colorado's Front Range lifts its snow-flecked peaks high above the parched eastern plains. The sawtooth mountains cut across the horizon, their old, sturdy summits etched against an azure sky. While the procession of seasons alters the mountain garb—carpets of summer wildflowers, emerald green forests in spring, aspen leaves that flutter like newly minted gold coins in autumn, and winter's blanket of dazzling snow—the peaks seem unchanging, silent, and even aloof. The Front Range escarpment fronting the prairie is dominated by three massive peaks that lift above their neighbors: Pikes Peak, Longs Peak, and Mount Evans.

Mount Evans, rising to 12,271 feet, is Denver's mountain. It's always visible from the city streets—glistening in the sun like a distant alabaster castle or its ridges obscured by windswept clouds. Its conspicuous presence is a reminder that out there, beyond the urban gridlock, is a wild, wonderful world waiting to be explored.

Mount Evans Scenic Drive

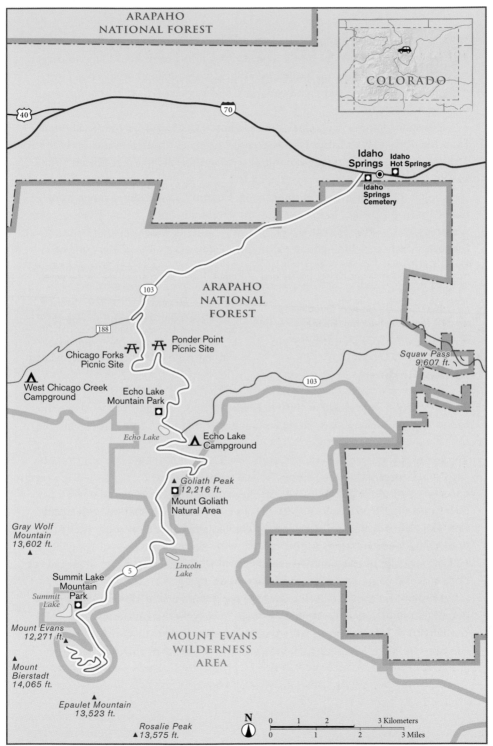

ARAPAHO
NATIONAL FOREST

COLORADO

40

70

Idaho
Springs
Idaho
Hot Springs

Idaho
Springs
Cemetery

103

ARAPAHO
NATIONAL
FOREST

188

Ponder Point
Picnic Site

Chicago Forks
Picnic Site

*Squaw Pass
9,607 ft.*

103

West Chicago Creek
Campground

Echo Lake
Mountain Park

Echo Lake

Echo Lake
Campground

▲ *Goliath Peak
12,216 ft.*
Mount Goliath
Natural Area

*Gray Wolf
Mountain
13,602 ft.*
▲

*Lincoln
Lake*

5

Summit Lake
Mountain
Park

*Summit
Lake*

*Mount Evans
12,271 ft.*
▲

MOUNT EVANS
WILDERNESS
AREA

▲ *Mount
Bierstadt
14,065 ft.*

▲
*Epaulet Mountain
13,523 ft.*

Rosalie Peak
▲*13,575 ft.*

N

0   1   2   3 Kilometers
0   1   2   3 Miles

The 28-mile-long Mount Evans scenic drive, a National Forest Scenic Byway, explores this lofty peak. The paved highway, beginning off I-70 in Idaho Springs, twists and winds up canyons and across ridges, passes ancient bristlecone pine forests and clear alpine lakes, and ends with spectacular views that encompass all of central Colorado.

The state highway to Mount Evans's summit, CO 5, is open only in summer from Memorial Day to Labor Day weekend. The lower drive section from Idaho Springs to Echo Lake is open year-round. The summer weather on Mount Evans, like any high Colorado peak, is fickle. Expect clear skies in the morning and clouds and thunderstorms in the afternoon. Summer temperatures range from the 80s at Idaho Springs to the 30s atop the mountain. Snow, below-freezing temperatures, and high winds can occur on any summer day. Be prepared by bringing warm clothes, including long pants and a raincoat. Beware of lingering on the summit or high ridges during lightning storms. The road surface may be slick with rain, snow, and ice during and after storms—drive cautiously. Many visitors will experience altitude sickness from the quick elevation gain. The rarefied air at the summit offers less oxygen than lower elevations. The best remedy is to descend from the upper heights.

Idaho Springs

The drive begins at exit 240 on I-70 in Idaho Springs, 30 miles west of Denver. **Idaho Springs,** at 7,540 feet, stretches along narrow Clear Creek Canyon among dry, steep-walled mountains.

Idaho Springs was the site of Colorado's first important gold strike. In January 1865, George Jackson, a prospector and cousin of scout Kit Carson, descended Chicago Creek alone on a hunting trip. He camped at the confluence of Chicago Creek and Clear Creek just south of today's exit 240 and kept warm with a campfire. The next morning he "removed the embers and panned out eight treaty cups of dirt, and found nothing but fine colors; with one cup I got a nugget of gold." Jackson marked his claim and returned later in the spring to pan out thousands of dollars' worth of gold, and the stampede was on.

Miner Street in Idaho Springs quickly became a wall-to-wall tent city, with a population of 12,000. Its less-populous eastern neighbor, Denver, had only 2,000 residents. The placer deposits were soon exhausted, but the discovery of rich ore veins in the surrounding metamorphic gneiss and schist rock kept the town

The Argo Gold Mine and Mill offers tours of a historic 19th-century mine in Idaho Springs.

Guanella Pass Scenic & Historic Byway

Georgetown to Grant

General description: This 22-mile paved road, a National Forest Scenic Byway, climbs from Georgetown over 11,669-foot Guanella Pass to Grant in the Front Range.

Special attractions: Pike National Forest, Arapaho National Forest, Georgetown National Historic District, Mount Evans Wilderness Area, Mount Bierstadt, hiking, backpacking, camping, fishing, scenic views, cross-country skiing, historic sites, aspen colors.

Location: Central Colorado. The drive begins in Georgetown off I-70 west of Denver and ends at Grant on US 285 east of Kenosha Pass.

Route numbers: Guanella Pass Road, Clear Creek CR 381, Geneva Road, Park CR 62.

Travel season: Year-round. The drive is regularly plowed in winter, although heavy

snow may temporarily close it. Carry chains, a shovel, and warm clothes in winter. The drive is not recommended for oversize RVs or trailers.

Camping: Four national forest campgrounds lie along the drive. North of Guanella Pass summit are Clear Lake (8 sites) and Guanella Pass (18 sites). Campgrounds South of pass summit are Geneva Park (26 sites) and Burning Bear (13 sites) Campgrounds.

Services: All services are in Georgetown.

Nearby attractions: Lost Creek Wilderness Area, Colorado Trail, Kenosha Pass, Fairplay, South Park-Tarryall Loop Scenic Drive (Scenic Drive 13), South Platte River Roads (Scenic Drive 11), Mount Evans Scenic Byway (Scenic Drive 14), Arapaho Basin Ski Area, Central City and Blackhawk National Historic District.

The Route

The Guanella Pass Scenic Byway traverses 22 miles of the Front Range mountains, passing abandoned silver mines, sweeping across swatches of alpine tundra littered with wildflowers and willow thickets, dropping down glaciated valleys and abrupt canyons, and exploring the range's geologic history.

The Front Range, the Rocky Mountains' easternmost range, forms a lofty escarpment that soars over the rolling Great Plains from Cañon City into Wyoming. This long, twisting spine, including part of the Continental Divide, is formed by ancient granite, gneiss, and schist rocks that are the roots of a billion-year-old ancestral mountain range. Repeated faulting, folding, heat, pressure, a final uplifting during the Laramide Orogeny some 60 million years ago, and a final excavation by recent glaciers sculpted the range into its present shape.

Guanella Pass Scenic & Historic Byway

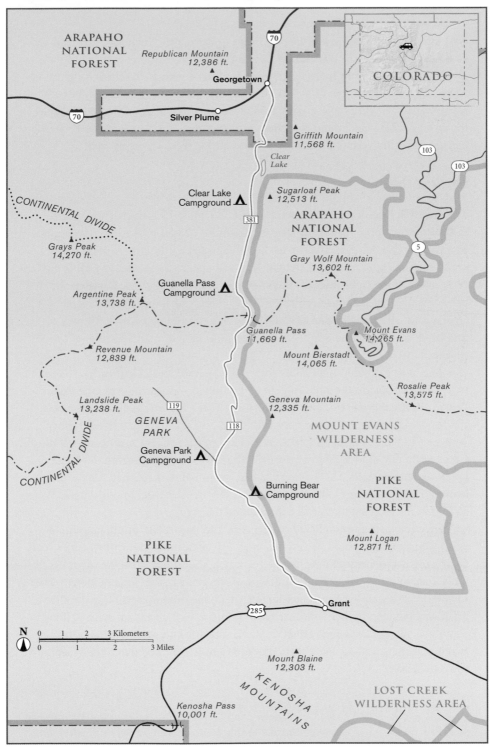

ARAPAHO
NATIONAL
FOREST

Republican Mountain
12,386 ft.

Georgetown

70

70

Silver Plume

COLORADO

Griffith Mountain
11,568 ft.

103

103

Clear
Lake

Clear Lake
Campground

Sugarloaf Peak
12,513 ft.

ARAPAHO
NATIONAL
FOREST

381

CONTINENTAL DIVIDE

Grays Peak
14,270 ft.

Gray Wolf Mountain
13,602 ft.

5

Guanella Pass
Campground

Argentine Peak
13,738 ft.

Mount Evans
14,265 ft.

Revenue Mountain
12,839 ft.

Guanella Pass
11,669 ft.

Mount Bierstadt
14,065 ft.

Rosalie Peak
13,575 ft.

Landslide Peak
13,238 ft.

119

GENEVA
PARK

118

Geneva Mountain
12,335 ft.

MOUNT EVANS
WILDERNESS
AREA

CONTINENTAL DIVIDE

Geneva Park
Campground

Burning Bear
Campground

PIKE
NATIONAL
FOREST

Mount Logan
12,871 ft.

PIKE
NATIONAL
FOREST

N

0   1   2   3 Kilometers
0   1   2   3 Miles

285

Grant

Mount Blaine
12,303 ft.

KENOSHA
MOUNTAINS

LOST CREEK
WILDERNESS AREA

Kenosha Pass
10,001 ft.

Summer and autumn are the best times to drive over Guanella Pass. Daily summer highs reach the 60s and 70s, while cooler temperatures prevail atop the timberline pass summit. Expect afternoon thunderstorms with rain and lightning. Autumn brings warm, clear days, chilled nights, and spectacular displays of golden aspen leaves. The first snow usually falls in October and lasts until late May, making an accessible wonderland for cross-country skiers. Spring comes slowly to the high country, but with warmer days the snowfields recede by early June.

Georgetown

The Guanella Pass drive, a National Forest and Colorado Scenic Byway, begins in **Georgetown** off I-70 west of Denver. Take exit 228 off I-70 and follow scenic byway signs through Georgetown to the drive's start on the town's south edge.

Georgetown, nestled in Clear Creek's wide upper valley at 8,519 feet, is the centerpiece of the **Georgetown–Silver Plume National Historic District,** which preserves the area's unique architectural and mining attributes. Picturesque Georgetown still remains one of Colorado's richest mining towns, with over $200 million of silver and gold dug from the surrounding mountains during its 19th-century heyday.

The town started in June 1859, when George and David Griffith, two Kentucky brothers, heard the siren of gold and plodded westward during the Pikes Peak or Bust gold rush to claim their fortune. These late arrivers found the best claims already taken at Central City and Idaho Springs, so they trekked farther west up Clear Creek Canyon to the confluence of Clear Creek and South Clear Creek at the site of today's downtown Georgetown. Here George's pan revealed specks of shining gold. The brothers staked a claim and established the Griffith Mining District. George Griffith was named District Recorder and his name affixed to the growing huddle of cabins along the creek.

George's town grew to 2,000 residents by the mid-1860s, but the best gold veins were soon exhausted. Silver, however, was plentiful and for the next 20 years Georgetown and Silver Plume, its upstream neighbor, thrived on the silver boom. Only Leadville, the "Silver King," outshone Georgetown, the "Silver Queen." The town quickly became the commercial hub of a huge mining district, with mills, a brick schoolhouse, numerous churches to minister to the heathen miners, luxurious hotels like the acclaimed Hotel de Paris, four fire companies, saloons, brothels, two newspapers, and, in 1877, the Colorado Central Railroad that linked Georgetown to Denver.

The famed Georgetown Loop Railroad crosses a high trestle on its run between the old mining towns of Georgetown and Silver Plume.

The drive's character changes abruptly past Burning Bear Campground. The road reaches a terminal moraine of boulders left by massive glaciers that formed Geneva Park and switchbacks steeply down Falls Hill into Geneva Creek's steep V-shaped canyon. The rushing creek tumbles in misty cascades over boulders and bedrock below the road. After a 1-mile descent the road again reaches the creek.

The drive's last 4 miles follow the canyon southward through lush aspen and willow woodlands along the creek. Primitive camping is found along the creek or stop for lunch at Whiteside Picnic Area. The drive ends on US 285 at Grant, a small hamlet named for former president and Civil War hero Ulysses S. Grant. Denver lies almost 60 miles to the east, and Fairplay, via Kenosha Pass, sits 28 miles to the southwest on US 285.

Peak to Peak Scenic & Historic Byway

Central City to Estes Park

General description: This 63-mile-long drive parallels the forested east flank of the Front Range between Central City and Estes Park.

Special attractions: Clear Creek Canyon, Central City–Black Hawk National Historic District, Golden Gate Canyon State Park, Ward, Brainard Lake Recreation Area, Indian Peaks Wilderness Area, Rocky Mountain National Park, Longs Peak, Enos Mills Cabin, Estes Park, hiking, camping, backpacking, rock climbing, historic sites, fishing, scenic views, autumn aspens.

Location: North-central Colorado. The drive begins at the junction of US 6 and CO 119 west of Golden and travels north on CO 72 and 7 to Estes Park.

Route name and numbers: Peak to Peak Highway; CO 119, 72, and 7.

Travel season: Year-round.

Camping: National forest campgrounds along the way, south to north, are Cold Springs (36 sites), Kelly Dahl (46 sites), Pawnee (47 sites), Peaceful Valley (17 sites), Camp Dick (41 sites), and Olive Ridge (56 sites). Golden Gate State Park east of the drive has two campgrounds—Reverend's Ridge (97 sites) and Aspen Meadows (35 tent sites). Longs Peak Campground (26 tent sites) is in Rocky Mountain National Park.

Services: All services are in Central City, Black Hawk, Nederland, and Estes Park. Limited services in Lone Pine, Rollinsville, and Ward.

Nearby attractions: Mount Evans Scenic Byway (Scenic Drive 14), Guanella Pass Scenic and Historic Byway (Scenic Drive 15), Georgetown, Golden, Rollins Pass, White Ranch Park, Eldorado Canyon State Park, Boulder, Estes Park, Rocky Mountain National Park, Trail Ridge Road (Scenic Drive 17).

The Route

The Peak to Peak Highway, a National Forest Scenic Byway, unfurls for 63 miles between Clear Creek Canyon and Estes Park. The drive offers calendar-caliber scenery, with gorgeous views of the Continental Divide, high wooded hills, exhilarating canyons and valleys, and the dun-colored prairie to the east. The drive, lying within Roosevelt National Forest, is bordered by the Indian Peaks Wilderness Area and Rocky Mountain National Park on the west.

The highway, although open year-round, is best driven in summer or autumn, when the fall colors peak. Summer temperatures vary according to elevation and range from the 40s to the upper 80s. Expect warm days, cool nights, and regular afternoon thunderstorms. September can bring almost perfect weather,

Peak to Peak Scenic & Historic Byway

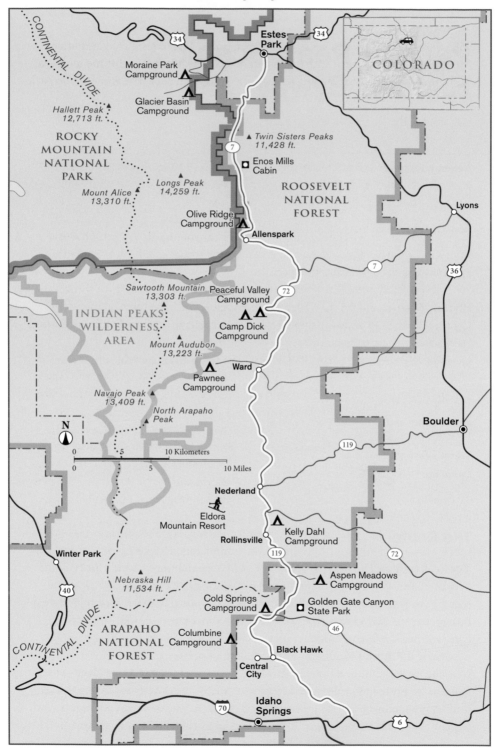

with warm, clear days and spectacular aspen golds. Winters are cold and often windy. Days can be warm with highs climbing to the 40s, but nighttime temperatures often fall to 0 degrees. Spring days are windy and cool. The winter snowpack melts below timberline in May and June.

Central City & Black Hawk

The drive begins at the junction of US 6 and CO 119 12 miles west of Golden. US 6 twists up Clear Creek Canyon, a precipitous gorge that slices through the lower Front Range escarpment. The same highway junction can be reached 2 miles east from I-70's exit 244. The drive, heading northeast up CO 119 alongside North Clear Creek, gently ascends the dry, cliff-lined canyon. Mine tailings, a reminder of the area's golden history, line the creek bank. Occasional placer mining claims are still worked by weekend prospectors.

After 6.5 miles the highway enters the **Central City–Black Hawk National Historic District** and 0.5 mile later enters **Black Hawk.** The town, along with Central City lying 1 mile west up Gregory Gulch, sits in what early miners dubbed "the richest square mile on earth."

The story began in early 1859, when John Gregory, a Georgia prospector working Cherry Creek's placer gravels in today's Denver, trod up a snowy canyon and found promising color. Gregory had stumbled onto a veritable treasure trove and took out more gold in his first week than all of Cherry Creek had yielded the previous summer. Word spread quickly and Colorado's first gold rush was on. More than 5,000 miners teemed into Gregory's Diggings over the next few months, and several camps scattered over the mountain slopes. Two of the camps grew into burgeoning mining towns—Black Hawk, named for the trademark of an early mining company, and Central City, dubbed for the town's central location among the mining camps.

By the mid-1860s **Central City**'s population surpassed 15,000 and the community boasted a diverse, cultured, and cosmopolitan air. The famed **Central City Opera House,** still active today, offered its first production, *Camille,* in 1861. A darker side existed as well. An 1861 election hosted "217 fistfights, 97 revolver fights, 11 Bowie knife fights, and 1 dog fight." Despite those frightening statistics, no one was killed that election. The Colorado Territory's first legal hanging occurred here in January 1864.

Central City and Black Hawk thrived on the riches extracted from the surrounding mountains and gulches. Numerous prospectors struck the mother lode and basked in wealth and power. Other millionaires, besides Gregory, included future US senator Henry Teller and Jeremiah Lee, a 29-year-old ex-slave of Robert E. Lee. The fabulous Argentine Lode was found in Lee's OK Mine. Teller built the

Central City's streets, lined with Victorian-era buildings, attract visitors to what was once "the richest square mile on earth."

stone **Teller House,** a town landmark, in 1872. When President Ulysses S. Grant stayed there in 1873, he found the path from his carriage to the Teller House bricked with silver bars.

With the rise of the silver towns in the 1880s, the area's fortunes sagged, and by 1900 the towns settled into retirement. The Opera House, refurbished and reopened in 1932, brought music lovers and tourists to the quaint towns. Writer Jack Kerouac penned his 1950s Central City experience in the classic novel *On the Road*:

> Central City is two miles high; at first you get drunk on the altitude, then you get tired, and there's a fever in your soul. We approached the lights around the opera house down the narrow dark street; then we took a sharp right and hit some old saloons with swinging doors.

Central City and Black Hawk, today preserved in a National Historic District, offer many attractions. The **Gilpin County Museum,** housed in an old stone school, displays community history, including a railroad diorama, 19th-century pharmacy collection, and other mining town displays and artifacts.

Tours are given at the Teller House and Central City Opera House, built in 1878. The Central City Opera, the nation's oldest summer opera company, offers excellent productions every summer. The **Teller House,** now a casino and restaurant, is worth a stop to view its famous painting *Face on a Barroom Floor,* an allusion to an 1887 poem by Hugh Antonine d'Arcy. The face of the beautiful woman with a sidelong glance has long both enchanted and baffled visitors. Some believe it was inspired by the poem, while another myth relates that a spurned artist painted a portrait of an unfaithful girlfriend so she would be stepped on. The truth, however, is that Herndon Davis, a Denver artist commissioned to paint some Old West scenes for the Opera House in 1936, did the deed late one night.

Davis told the *Denver Post* in 1954, "The whim struck me to paint a face on the floor of the old Teller House barroom. In its mining boom heyday, it was just such a floor as the ragged artist used in d'Arcy's famous old poem. But the hotel manager and the bartender would have none of such tomfoolery. They refused me permission to paint the face." Instead Davis recruited the bellboy to aid and abet the tomfoolery, sneaking in after midnight to paint the masterpiece by candlelight. The face, modeled after Davis's wife, quickly became part of Central City's lore.

Most folks come now for the gambling, which became legal in 1991. Since casino gambling was approved by voters for a handful of Colorado mountain towns, both Central City and Black Hawk have mined heaps of gold from the pockets of visitors. Black Hawk, straddling the highway, has particularly benefited from the new gold rush, with 18 casinos open in 2019, while Central City has 6. Be prepared in summer and on weekends for traffic congestion and parking problems, and watch your wallet around those one-armed bandits.

Golden Gate Canyon State Park

The drive continues up North Clear Creek Canyon past Black Hawk, the steep slopes coated in a mixed pine and fir forest and pockmarked with abandoned mine adits, tunnels, and tailings. After a couple of miles the highway leaves the drainage and climbs north onto high wooded ridges. The Roosevelt National Forest boundary lies at almost 12 miles. A look back reveals Mount Evans, its snowy 14,264-foot bulk outlined against the southern sky. Atop a ridge crest the drive intersects CO 46. This scenic back road drops east down Ralston Creek to **Golden Gate Canyon State Park** and meanders on to Golden.

The state park, also accessible from a turnoff on CO 119 at 16 miles, makes a good stopover. The 11,998-acre parkland is ideal for hiking, with 36 miles of trails threading the backcountry, including 19 miles shared with mountain bikers and equestrians. The 12 trails are named for different animals and each is marked with that animal's footprints. Good hikes include the 4.6-mile Mule Deer Trail and 2.1-mile Eagle Trail up City Lights Ridge. The evening view from the ridge is marvelous, with the Denver lights glimmering in the twilight. Panorama Point, accessible by car on Tremont Mountain's north flank, overlooks the Continental Divide and the Indian Peaks which stretch north to flat-topped Longs Peak. Thirty-five-site

Aspen Meadows (tents only) and 97-site Reverend's Ridge campgrounds sit on the park's north side east of the drive. Other overnight accommodations are group campsites, cabins, yurts, and a 4-bedroom guest house.

Rollinsville & Nederland

The road continues north from the state park, dipping through shallow valleys at South Beaver Creek and Lump Gulch before spiraling down Gamble Gulch to **Rollinsville.** This town, founded in 1873 by John Quincy Adams Rollins, allowed no casinos, dance halls, or saloons. Besides purchasing mines, Rollins built a toll road over 11,671-foot Rollins Pass on the Continental Divide to Middle Park. Later the Denver, Northwestern & Pacific Railroad acquired the right-of-way and built a temporary track with 33 tunnels along the route. A small settlement, called Corona by railroad workers since the site was the "crown of the world," was atop the high pass. Buildings once here included a hotel, railroad station, restaurant, and worker housing. All that remains are concrete foundations, as well as supports for cables strung over roofs to keep them from blowing away in hurricane-force winds. The line remains the highest altitude reached by an American railroad. The railroad operated until 1928 when railroad developer David Moffat's 6-mile-long tunnel under the Divide was completed.

After the tracks were removed in 1935, the abandoned rail bed was idle until it was converted into a jeep road in 1956. It's now one of Colorado's most popular back road 4x4 excursions. The rough road heads west from Rollinsville up South Boulder Creek and over Rollins Pass to Winter Park.

The drive ambles north from Rollinsville and passes the 46-site Kelly Dahl Campground. The road swings around 8,922-foot Tungsten Mountain and drops down to 8,236-foot-high Nederland and Middle Boulder Creek. **Nederland** spreads across a broad valley above Barker Reservoir and Boulder Canyon and below the Continental Divide. The town, established in 1877, once boomed with gold, silver, and tungsten mining and now serves as a gateway to the Indian Peaks Wilderness and a getaway for Boulder residents.

Author Helen Hunt Jackson described 1870s Nederland as a "dismal little mining town," but now it's a venerable, cozy village with an unpretentious charm. The town works hard at preserving its quiet atmosphere by not becoming a tourist trap or a Boulder bedroom community. It still functions as a regional supply center with a hardware store, auto parts shop, a printer, doctors, and veterinarians. It also offers numerous stores for visitors, including a marvelous rock shop, and over a dozen restaurants. For lunch or dinner, try The Deli at 8236, a hangout for Grateful Deadheads with band posters that's named for its elevation.

Eldora Mountain Resort, west of Nederland, is a perfect alternative to the busy Summit County ski areas. It's only 30 minutes from Boulder, has affordable lift tickets, and over 300 inches of annual snowfall. The area boasts a 1,240-foot vertical drop from the top of 10,600-foot Bryan Mountain, 53 runs on 680 skiable acres, and four terrain parks. Eldora, with both beginner terrain and black diamond trails, offers a popular learn-to-ski program for kids and adults.

CO 119, beginning in Nederland, heads northeast into Boulder Canyon, a popular rock climbing and hiking area, and descends 17 miles to Boulder, home of the University of Colorado.

Ward & Indian Peaks

The Peak to Peak Highway, now following CO 72, climbs north from Nederland. For 9 miles the road twists and curls over forested ridges and through shallow canyons before swinging onto the eastern flank of 11,471-foot Niwot Mountain. Vast views unfold from the road. Lower mountains recede east to the Great Plains and the flat horizon.

Ward sits below the drive above upper Lefthand Canyon. Established in 1865, Ward is another mining camp that settled into peaceful retirement after its gold heyday. Calvin Ward discovered the golden Ward Lode here in 1860. The "Switzerland Trail of America"—the now-defunct Denver, Boulder & Western Railroad—served the town after 1898. A fire in 1910 destroyed 53 buildings in Ward. Ward marks the northern boundary of the Colorado Mineral Belt, a 50-mile-wide swath of mountains that runs from here to southwestern Colorado and contains most of the state's mineral wealth.

For a spectacular side journey, drive 0.1 mile from the Ward turnoff and take a left turn on FR 112 toward Brainard Lake. The paved road climbs 5 miles past picturesque Red Rock Lake to popular **Brainard Lake Recreation Area,** the gateway to 76,711-acre **Indian Peaks Wilderness Area.**

The Indian Peaks, including Pawnee, Shoshoni, Navajo, and Arikaree Peaks, form a mountainous escarpment along the Continental Divide above 10,345-foot-high Brainard Lake. Snowfields and small glaciers cling to the serrated peaks through much of the summer. Glaciers excavated these spiked, weather-beaten mountains and their alpine cirques. The wilderness area, established in 1978, preserves some of Colorado's best mountain scenery. Unfortunately, its proximity to the state's major population centers along the northern Front Range has caused severe overuse. The USDA Forest Service imposes visitor restrictions to protect and rehabilitate the area's fragile alpine ecosystems. Permits are needed for overnight camping, and there are limitations on fires and pack animals. Bicycles and motorized vehicles are prohibited.

The stunning Indian Peaks tower above an angler casting a fishing line across Red Rock Lake in the Brainard Lake Recreation Area.

Brainard Lake Recreation Area, at road's end, makes a good jumping-off point for day hikers and mountain climbers. Mount Audubon, the round-shouldered 13,223-foot peak to the northwest, makes a good climb via a marked 3.8-mile trail (#913). The Pawnee Pass Trail (#907) offers an excellent 4.2-mile round-trip hike past Long Lake to scenic Lake Isabelle below Shoshoni, Apache, and Navajo peaks. The Mitchell Lake Trail (#912) offers a 5-mile round-trip hike through woods to Mitchell Lake and then up to Blue Lake nestled below 12,979-foot Mount Toll.

Numerous facilities are around Brainard Lake, including four picnic areas and 47-site Pawnee Campground. Night temperatures can be frigid at the campground during its May through September season. Snowdrifts often linger in the forest well into July. Both Brainard Lake and Red Rock Lake offer excellent trout fishing.

From Ward the drive continues north over wooded ridges before steeply dipping into Peaceful Valley along Middle St. Vrain Creek. The 17-site Peaceful Valley Campground sits west of the hairpin turn at the canyon bottom. The highway runs down the sharp canyon, its walls studded with towering granite cliffs, before climbing out to its junction with CO 7 from Lyons. CO 72 ends here. The drive turns west on CO 7.

The new highway crosses rolling hills seamed by shallow, grassy valleys. A ponderosa pine woodland covers the land. Aspen groves tuck into moist ravines, and willow thickets border trickling creeks. Ponderosa pine forests dominate Colorado's mid-elevation mountains. These open forests congregate on warm, south-facing slopes, where temperatures can be as much as 20 degrees warmer than on north-facing slopes. Acidic needles in the springy pine duff on the forest floor inhibit the growth of a shrub and grass understory, allowing the trees to retain precious moisture.

A scenic overlook 3 miles from the junction faces north to 13,911-foot Mount Meeker and the Wild Basin area of Rocky Mountain National Park. The turn to **Allenspark** is 0.5 mile farther. The town, named for 1859 homesteader Alonzo Allen, caters to visitors with several restaurants, shops, and motels. Olive Ridge Campground, a pleasant 56-site area a couple of miles up the road, sits west of the highway and makes a good base camp for forays into Wild Basin.

Rocky Mountain National Park & Longs Peak

From Olive Ridge Campground to Estes Park, the highway parallels the eastern boundary of **Rocky Mountain National Park.** This immense parkland spreads across 414 square miles of pristine high country, including the twisting Continental Divide. The park, Colorado's largest, boasts 104 peaks above 10,000 feet and 71 reaching above 12,000 feet. Flat-topped Longs Peak is the park's high point at 14,259 feet.

The road descends north from Olive Ridge and crosses North St. Vrain Creek. Past the creek, a turn west on CR 84 leads to **Wild Basin,** a rugged backcountry cirque in the park's remote southern reaches. Follow the dirt road west a few miles to the Wild Basin Ranger Station and Wild Basin Trailhead. Numerous trails lace the basin, threading along sparkling streams to tantalizing above-timberline lakes like Ouzel, Bluebird, Thunder, and Sandbeach Lakes, and waterfalls like gorgeous Ouzel Falls.

The highway runs north below bulky **Mount Meeker,** a towering pile of granite rubble, and through Meeker Park, a small hamlet with stables, the **Meeker Park Lodge,** and cabins. The family-run lodge started in 1921 when O.L. Dever and his wife Crete, both schoolteachers, made a rustic retreat. They built cabins and then a lodge in 1935, attracting tourists and locals to their dining room for meals and entertainment like gin rummy, canasta, and Chinese Checkers. Now the lodge is a low-key getaway run by the three Dever sisters—Laura, Bonny, and Patty.

Meeker Park Picnic Area with 8 picnic sites lies a mile beyond at mile marker 11 on the east side of the drive. On the opposite side of the highway is Meeker Park Overflow Campground with 29 first-come first-served sites. This is not a full-service campground and is best for tenters.

Another 0.4 mile up the drive is famed **Chapel on the Rock,** formally called Saint Catherine of Siena Chapel, a stone Catholic chapel built atop a massive block of granite. Monsignor Joseph Bosetti found the outcrop in 1916 and immediately thought of the Biblical allusion to building the church on a rock. The historic chapel, finished in 1936, has withstood fire and flood, including a flood of Biblical proportions in September 2013. Heavy rain on Mount Meeker swept a wall of water, rock, and debris a quarter-mile wide down the valley by the chapel, snapping trees, moving boulders, and destroying most of the nearby St. Malo Retreat, Conference, and Spiritual Center. The Chapel and its rock were spared from the flood. Pope John Paul II visited the Chapel on the Rock in 1993. He spent the day hiking area trails and praying at the Chapel. The site, open to the public, is popular with weddings and tourists.

As the drive passes Mount Meeker, the precipitous east face of **Longs Peak** monopolizes the view. Longs Peak, named for 1820 explorer Major Stephen Long, dominates the Front Range like no other mountain save Pikes Peak to the south. Its flat summit, long a pioneer landmark, gleams like an alabaster tower above the sere prairie. The Arapaho Indians called the peak, along with Mount Meeker, "The Two Guides," and early French trappers named them "The Two Ears." An awesome 2,000-foot-high granite wall chiseled by glaciers forms the sheer east face of Longs Peak. Mount Meeker and Mount Lady Washington flank the peak on the south and north respectively. **The Diamond,** the peak's bold upper face, offers some of North America's best alpine rock climbing, including the Casual Route and The Yellow Wall.

After traversing into Tahosa Valley between the Longs Peak massif and the Twin Sisters, the highway reaches the turnoff to the Longs Peak Trailhead. The Longs Peak Road leads a mile west to 26-site Longs Peak Campground, a tents-only area, and the trailhead. The trail climbs the peak via the **Keyhole Route,** the peak's standard nontechnical climbing route. The trail ascends 7.5 miles up the Longs Peak Trail and gains 4,850 feet of elevation to the summit. Allow at least 12 hours for the round-trip hike. The Park Service advises starting the hike by 3 a.m. to avoid the almost daily summer thunderstorms and to carry proper rain gear and extra clothes. For a detailed route description to the Keyhole Route and technical climbing routes on Longs Peak, pick up a copy of *Best Climbs Rocky Mountain National Park* (FalconGuides).

Enos Mills

A half-mile past the trailhead sits a monument to **Enos Mills,** Rocky Mountain National Park's founding father. A short hike up a closed dirt road up the highway from the monument bumps back to his one-room log cabin nestled among pines and wildflowers. Enos Mills came to Longs Peak in 1884, a sickly Kansas lad in search of better health among the clean mountains. He first climbed the peak the following year, homesteaded at its base, and began a life-long career as an alpine guide and nature writer. He dubbed Longs Peak "the king of the Rocky Mountains" and made 297 ascents. In 1889 19-year-old Mills met naturalist John Muir in San Francisco and began a friendship with the elder conservationist.

In 1902 Mills built rustic Longs Peak Inn in the meadows across today's highway from his cabin and began writing numerous classic books like *Spell of the Rockies* that detailed his wilderness experiences and the joy of outdoor adventure. Mills wrote: "He who feels the spell of the wild, the rhythmic melody of falling water, the echoes among the crags, the bird songs, the wind in the pines . . . is in tune with the universe."

Mills, a firm believer in the national park idea and in the preservation of America's wildlands, advocated the creation of a national park surrounding Longs Peak and lectured tirelessly across the country promoting the preserve. In 1915 his dedication bore fruit when Rocky Mountain National Park was created. Mills died in 1922.

The **Enos Mills Cabin,** run by the Mills family, keeps the memory and writings of this legendary Colorado naturalist alive. The cabin displays Mills's photographs, camera, climbing equipment, specimen collections, and original book editions and documents. The cabin, listed on the National Register of Historic Places in 1973, is open year-round by appointment only. Call (970) 586-4706 or write info@enosmills.com for more information and reservations.

Lily Lake to Estes Park

Twin Sisters Trailhead sits past the Enos Mills Cabin. The trail spirals upward to the top of 11,428-foot Twin Sisters. Excellent views of Longs Peak and the Tahosa Valley stretch to the west from the summit. The drive continues north, crosses a broad divide, and begins dropping toward Estes Park.

Popular **Lily Lake** tucks against Lily Mountain along the road. Park in lots on either side of the highway and take a hike around the lovely lake, which lies just inside the Rocky Mountain National Park boundary. The 17-acre lake, originally a mountain pond, was dammed in 1915. The 0.8-mile Lily Lake Trail, handicap accessible and family-friendly, follows the edge of the lake. Anglers cast lines for cutthroat trout in the catch-and-release lake. Restrooms, drinking water, and interpretive signs are at the trailhead and picnic tables scatter along the trail. Above the lake on the south side of Lily Mountain is **Jurassic Park,** a sport climbing area with routes up cliffs and fins and dramatic views of Longs Peak. Get access and climbing route information in the comprehensive guidebook *Rock Climbing Colorado* (FalconGuides).

The highway twists down Lily Mountain's steep eastern slope, dropping past rough rock outcrops and scattered ponderosa pines. The road levels out on a wide bench beside Mary's Lake before making its final plunge around Prospect Mountain and entering **Estes Park** and the drive's end at the highway's junction with US 36.

Estes Park forms the eastern gateway to Rocky Mountain National Park. The town, named for the area's first homesteader, Joel Estes, who settled here in 1859, fills the wooded valley with homes, shops, hotels, restaurants, and tourist traps. The setting is, despite unbridled growth, enchanting, with snow-capped peaks and wooded ridges surrounding the town and valley. English traveler Isabella Bird, the first woman to ascend Longs Peak, wrote in 1873: "Never, nowhere, have I seen anything to equal the view into Estes Park."

The Beaver Meadows and Fall Creek entrances to the national park lie just west of town. Three park campgrounds—Moraine Park, Glacier Basin, and Aspenglen—are close to Estes Park, and Trail Ridge Road, another magnificent scenic drive (see Scenic Route 17), begins at Deer Ridge Junction in the park. Lumpy Ridge, called by the Arapaho Indians *Thath-aa-ai-atah*, or "Mountain of little lumps," walls in Estes Park on the north. This high ridge, studded with superb granite crags, offers excellent rock climbing. At the drive's end, the junction of CO 7 and US 36, a turn east leads to Lyons, while a west turn eases through downtown Estes Park and on to the national park.

17

Trail Ridge Road All-American Byway

Estes Park to Grand Lake

General description: Trail Ridge Road, one of Colorado's most spectacular and popular scenic drives, traverses glaciated valleys and above-timberline Trail Ridge in Rocky Mountain National Park for 45 miles.

Special attractions: Rocky Mountain National Park, Horseshoe Park, Trail Ridge, Tundra Nature Trail, Alpine Visitor Center, Fall River Pass, Milner Pass, Kawuneeche Valley, camping, hiking, scenic views, overlooks, wildlife, fishing, photography, wildflowers.

Location: North-central Colorado. The drive connects Estes Park and Grand Lake.

Route name and number: Trail Ridge Road, US 34.

Travel season: May through October. The exact opening and closing dates vary every year due to snow removal in spring and the first winter snowstorms. Check with the park for current road information, conditions, and closures.

Camping: Five campgrounds are in Rocky Mountain National Park, including two along the drive. Aspenglen Campground (54 sites) near the Fall River entrance. Timber Creek Campground (98 sites) on the drive's western slope in the Kawuneeche Valley. Moraine Park (247 sites), and Glacier Basin (147 sites) are near the Beaver Meadows entrance. Longs Peak Campground (26 tent sites) is 11 miles south of Estes Park.

Services: All services are in Estes Park, Grand Lake, and Granby.

Nearby attractions: Estes Park, Peak to Peak Scenic and Historic Byway (Scenic Drive 16), Arapaho National Recreation Area, Cache la Poudre–North Park Scenic Byway (Scenic Drive 18), State Forest State Park, Never Summer Wilderness Area, Indian Peaks Wilderness Area, Wild Basin, Longs Peak, Bear Lake, Glacier Gorge.

The Route

Rocky Mountain National Park, one of Colorado's most spectacular natural areas, protects an immense swath of pristine high country along the Continental Divide. The divide, the literal roof of the Rockies, twists down North America's mountain backbone, splitting the Atlantic and Pacific watersheds. Jagged peaks march along the divide in the park, lifting glacier-carved ridges and summits into the sky. The 45-mile-long Trail Ridge Road, the highest continuous auto road in the US, traverses this superlative parkland—crossing broad valleys with meandering rivers; passing herds of elk, deer, and bighorn sheep; climbing forest-clad slopes; and winding along lofty Trail Ridge.

The 414-square-mile park encompasses 113 named peaks above 10,000 feet, 104 over 10,000 feet, and Longs Peak, the park's high point, which soars

Trail Ridge Road All–American Byway

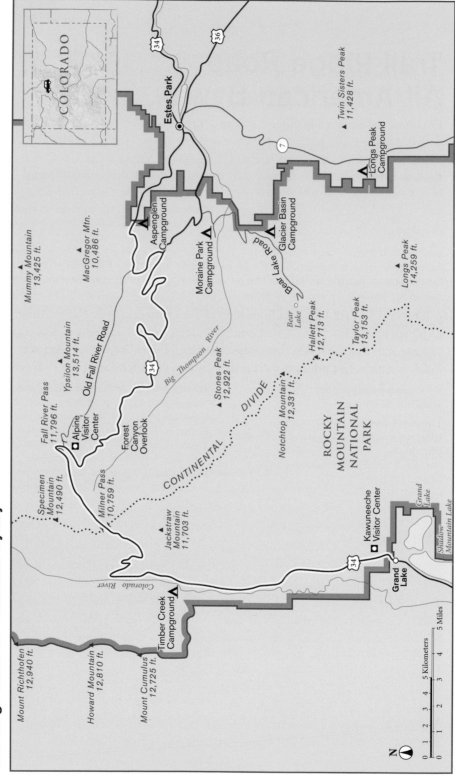

COLORADO

Estes Park

34
36
7

Twin Sisters Peak
11,428 ft.

Longs Peak
Campground

Mummy Mountain
13,425 ft.

MacGregor Mtn.
10,486 ft.

Aspenglen
Campground

Moraine Park
Campground

Glacier Basin
Campground

Bear Lake Road

Ypsilon Mountain
13,514 ft.

Old Fall River Road

Big Thompson River

Bear Lake

Hallett Peak
12,713 ft.

Taylor Peak
13,153 ft.

Longs Peak
14,259 ft.

Fall River Pass
11,796 ft.

Alpine Visitor
Center

Forest Canyon
Overlook

Stones Peak
12,922 ft.

CONTINENTAL DIVIDE

Notchtop Mountain
12,331 ft.

ROCKY
MOUNTAIN
NATIONAL
PARK

Specimen
Mountain
12,490 ft.

Milner Pass
10,759 ft.

Jackstraw
Mountain
11,703 ft.

Kawuneeche
Visitor Center

Grand
Lake

Shadow
Mountain Lake

34

Mount Richthofen
12,940 ft.

Colorado River

Howard Mountain
12,810 ft.

Timber Creek
Campground

Mount Cumulus
12,725 ft.

34

Grand
Lake

N

5 Kilometers
5 Miles
0 1 2 3 4 5

14,259 feet above sea level. Two small ranges—the Never Summer Mountains and Mummy Range—split from the divide and the Front Range in the park's northwest corner. Besides being a place of mountain splendor, Rocky Mountain National Park is a land of valleys, rivers, and lakes. The park holds more than 150 lakes, and almost 500 miles of streams thread its valleys and canyons. The park is a mother of rivers, with four major rivers arising on the Continental Divide: the Cache la Poudre, Big Thompson, and St. Vrain Rivers on the eastern slope and the Colorado River on the western side. Rocky Mountain National Park is also the land above the trees. One-third of the park lies in the alpine zone above timberline, a cold, windswept land where summer visits for a brief two months.

Trail Ridge Road is only the latest in a series of range crossings from the eastern plains to Middle Park's lush grasslands. Trail Ridge, with its gentle contours, forms a natural route over the otherwise rugged Continental Divide. Native American hunters used the Ute Trail as early as 12,000 years ago. A Clovis spear point found on Trail Ridge confirms their ancient presence. Later Native Americans built low rock walls to funnel game to hidden hunters. Eagle traps, low pits covered with an animal skin, also dotted the broad ridge. The Ute and Arapaho Indians, settlers, and prospectors regularly crossed the ridge during the 19th century. Trail Ridge Road, built in three years, opened in 1932 and bypassed the dangerous Fall River Road.

Trail Ridge Road, the pathway to the high tundra, is America's highest through highway. It runs above 12,000 feet for 4 miles and above 11,000 feet for 11 miles. The road, climbing almost 5,000 vertical feet from Estes Park to the ridge's high point, journeys through three life zones in 20 miles to an alpine climate similar to that in northern Alaska and Canada. Each 1,000 feet ascended is the equivalent of a 600-mile trip northward. No other road in the Colorado Rockies offers such a unique opportunity to study, explore, and appreciate the delicate but rigorous world above tree line.

Trail Ridge Road opens in late May, depending on snow removal, and usually closes by late October after the first major snowfall. Unpredictable weather rules during summer and autumn on the drive. Mornings are usually clear, calm, and warm. Temperatures vary from the 70s and 80s in the lower elevations to the 40s and 50s above timberline. Expect afternoon thunderstorms along the road, with localized heavy rain, hail, and snow. High winds usually accompany the storms. Winds exceeding 150 miles per hour have been clocked on Trail Ridge. Snow can fall during any month on the upper elevations. Be prepared by bringing warm clothes, rain gear, and sun protection. Lightning is a serious hazard along Trail Ridge. Keep off exposed ridges and trails before and during thunderstorms.

Estes Park to Horseshoe Park

The drive begins 5 miles northwest of **Estes Park,** where US 34 enters Rocky Mountain National Park at the Fall River Entrance Station. The park's other entrance at Beaver Meadows lies southwest of Estes Park via US 36 and leads to Moraine Park Museum, Glacier Basin and Moraine Park Campgrounds, and the Bear Lake area. US 36 also climbs from the Beaver Meadows entrance to a junction with US 34 and Trail Ridge Road at Deer Ridge Junction.

The highway runs west from the entrance station in an open ponderosa and limber pine forest. Aspenglen Campground, with 54 sites, sits at 8,230 feet near the Fall River just past the park boundary. All sites are reservable up to 6 months in advance at recreation.gov. The road heads up a granite-studded canyon between MacGregor Mountain on the north and Deer Mountain to the south and climbs into **Horseshoe Park.** A huge valley glacier, spilling down today's Fall River drainage from Trail Ridge, excavated this broad U-shaped valley during three ice advances. The glacier melted away about 12,000 years ago after the last glacial period—the Pinedale. Lateral moraines, piles of jumbled boulders, edge the valley, while a giant terminal moraine, marking the glacier's farthest advance, blocks the valley's eastern end. This terminal moraine also dammed the valley, forming a large, shallow lake. Mountain erosion eventually filled the lake with sediment, leaving a level, marshy valley floor with the Fall River looping across it.

The road continues west on the valley's north edge and soon reaches the Sheep Lakes Information Station on the road's south side. The Sheep Lakes, four small glacier-formed kettle lakes, are scattered across the valley floor.

A couple of pull-offs in Horseshoe Park make good stops to view wildlife. Mule deer, elk, and bighorn sheep regularly graze in the meadows and willow thickets along the Fall River. The mammals are best viewed during early morning or evening when feeding in the park. Elk herds, driven to lower elevations by deep snowpack, congregate in Horseshoe Park in spring, winter, and fall. The autumn rutting period is spectacular when the bull elk bugle their mating calls, vie for herd dominance, and gather harems of females. Mature elk weigh more than 1,000 pounds and are unpredictably aggressive during mating season. It's best to view them from the parking areas with binoculars or a long telephoto lens on your camera.

Two bighorn sheep flocks, totaling between 300 and 500 animals, inhabit Rocky Mountain National Park. While they usually keep to the high country, the Mummy Range flock occasionally descends Bighorn Mountain to natural salt licks in Horseshoe Park. The bighorn sheep road crossing in Horseshoe Park, just past

Longs Peak rises beyond a bull elk grazing alongside Trail Ridge Road.

the information station, is closely regulated to protect Colorado's state animal. Sheep, of course, have the right-of-way, and there is no roadside parking except in designated lots. Visitors are also advised not to approach any wild animals.

The bighorns usually move in small groups across the road between 9 a.m. and 3 p.m. After spending a couple hours in the valley, they recross the road and climb steep slopes to the north.

The 9-mile-long **Old Fall River Road** climbs from western Horseshoe Park up Fall River's glacier gorge to 11,796-foot Fall River Pass on Trail Ridge's northern end. The road, two-lane and paved to Endovalley Picnic Area and then dirt and one-way to its terminus, makes a spectacular side trip. It passes numerous glacial features, 25-foot-high Chasm Falls, and ancient subalpine spruce and fir forests. Old Fall River Road, a property on the National Register of Historic Places, follows an old Arapaho path called the "Dog's Trail." The road, the national park's first high drive, opened in 1920 but saw little use after Trail Ridge Road opened in 1932 because of landslides, avalanches, and 16 percent grades.

Trail Ridge Road loops south across Horseshoe Park; crosses a hilly moraine with aspens, willows, and Colorado blue spruce; and ascends the valley's southern flank. The **Horseshoe Park Overlook** offers views into the park below. The Mummy Range, a 20-mile-long Front Range spur, towers to the northwest. A row of jagged peaks, including 13,514-foot Ypsilon Mountain and 13,502-foot Fairchild Mountain, loom above Horseshoe Park.

The viewpoint also offers a look at one of the national park's newest geologic features. **Lawn Lake,** a small natural lake nestled in the heart of the Mummy Range, was enlarged in 1903 to provide irrigation water for farms near Loveland on the plains east of the mountains. In the early morning hours of July 15, 1982, the lake brimmed with snowmelt that slowly seeped around a damaged outlet valve. The water quickly eroded into the earthen dam and at 5:30 a.m. the levee gave way, plunging 674 acre-feet of water down Roaring River's narrow canyon. The 30-foot-deep deluge scoured the canyon floor, breached Horseshoe Park's north lateral moraine, and deposited a huge alluvial fan near the park's head with up to 44 feet of debris and boulders weighing more than 400 tons. The relentless water continued toward Estes Park. Horseshoe Park's wetlands, however, slowed the advance and allowed for the evacuation of downtown Estes Park. The flood buried the town's main street under 6 feet of mud. Three park campers, two in Aspenglen Campground, died in the flood.

The road climbs uphill and reaches **Deer Mountain Overlook** after 0.6 mile. This point gives great views of the Mummy Range, granite domes on MacGregor Mountain's flank, Little Horseshoe Park below, and 10,013-foot Deer Mountain to the east. Deer Ridge Junction—the intersection of US 34, US 36 from Moraine Park, and Trail Ridge Road—sits just ahead. A resort, Deer Ridge Chalet, once sat here, but the Park Service acquired the place in 1960, tore the buildings down, and restored the natural ecosystem.

Deer Ridge Junction can also be reached from the Beaver Meadows Entrance Station west of Estes Park by driving up US 36 for 3 miles. Trail Ridge Road officially begins at this highway junction.

Hidden Valley

The drive runs northwest and bends into **Hidden Valley.** The shallow valley, formed by the south lateral moraine of the Fall River glacier on its north side, is a lush, hidden oasis. Dense willow thickets and meadows of grasses and sedges line twisting Hidden Valley Creek. Silted-in beaver ponds form meadows in the east part of the valley. After a couple of miles the road reaches active beaver ponds. A wooden boardwalk offers a way to explore the ponds, traversing out among willows and fresh-cut aspen, a favorite beaver food. Look for these forest engineers swimming in their pools during morning and evening.

Hidden Valley Creek also harbors a reintroduced population of threatened greenback cutthroat trout, a Colorado native. This trout, surviving only in isolated lakes and rivers in Colorado's Rockies, almost became extinct due to habitat loss, interbreeding with other trout species, and competition from nonnative fish. The downstream moraine here blocks nonnative trout from living in Hidden Valley, allowing the greenback cutthroat trout to once again flourish. Fishing for greenback trout is on a strict catch-and-release program.

The drive continues up Hidden Valley and after 0.5 mile loops southeast. A short spur road goes right here and follows Hidden Valley Creek to a parking area at **Hidden Valley Picnic Area.** The site has 4 tables in a pavilion, picnic tables scattered on surrounding hillsides, and restrooms. Hidden Valley, open all winter, is ideal for winter sports, including snowshoeing, snowboarding, backcountry skiing, and sledding on former ski slopes above the parking. This is the site of the former Hidden Valley Ski Area which operated from 1949 to 1992. Hidden Valley is the only place in the national park that allows sledding. Bring a plastic sled, saucer, or tube (no metal runners allowed) and hike up to the top of the ski area's bunny slope and let 'er rip. Rent or buy a sled in Estes Park if you come unprepared. A good out-and-back, 2.5-mile snowshoe trek begins at the parking lot and climbs the old ski slopes to Rainbow Curve.

The road climbs southeast from Hidden Valley through a mixed forest of aspen, lodgepole pine, subalpine fir, and Engelmann spruce and reaches the **Many Parks Curve** viewpoint in 1.5 miles. The overlook yields dramatic views into several large grassy parks tucked into the Front Range, including Horseshoe Park, Moraine Park, Beaver Meadows, and Estes Park. Forested lateral moraines left by retreating glaciers border the open grasslands. Coarse alluvium, deposited by the Lawn Lake flood, blocks the river and forms a small lake in Horseshoe Park to the north.

The highway bends onto a steep mountainside above upper Hidden Valley, steadily climbing through old-growth spruce and subalpine fir woods. A parking area in the upper valley gives views of the abandoned ski area and of open slopes carpeted with summer wildflowers. Melting snow irrigates marsh marigolds, paintbrush, lousewort, chiming bells, delphinium, and a forest of spruce and white-barked subalpine fir.

The drive continues ascending and after another mile reaches 10,829-foot **Rainbow Curve Overlook,** a lofty viewpoint poised on a ridge over 2 miles high. Trail Ridge's humped shoulder looms to the south, verdant Horseshoe Park and the twisting highway in Hidden Valley lie far below, and the snowy Mummy Range stretches across the northern horizon. Early mountaineer William Hallett named the range for its fanciful resemblance to a reclining Egyptian mummy.

The road edges west across the north slope of the Knife's Edge, a narrow rocky ridgeline. A scattered forest of weathered lodgepole pine and spruce spreads over the hillside. As the road climbs toward timberline, the forest becomes stunted and dwarfed. Severe winds, gusting over Trail Ridge, force the trees to hug the ground or form tree islands. Distinctive "banner trees" form when the branches grow on the tree's eastern or leeward side, out of the wind. Timberline, the elevation that marks the forest boundary, occurs between 10,000 and 11,500 feet in Rocky Mountain National Park. Beyond the dwarfed trees stretches grassy alpine tundra—the land above the trees.

Trail Ridge

As the highway nears timberline, it passes a small glacier-carved cirque. This amphitheater, the headwaters of Sundance Creek, exhibits a cirque's distinctive features—a moraine of loose rubble, a rocky headwall dissected by the scraping glacier, and a semicircular shape. Past the cirque the drive crosses a low timberline gap onto **Trail Ridge** itself. This 11,440-foot pass, called Ute Crossing, marks the highway's junction with the old Ute Trail that traverses the ridge. The 15-mile-long trail, called *Taieonbaa,* or "Child's Trail," by Native Americans, begins in Beaver Meadows, threads along the ridgetop, and drops down to Kawuneeche Valley on the west.

The drive twists along Trail Ridge for the next 7 miles to Fall River Pass. Several excellent viewpoints and points of interest sit alongside the road. **Forest Canyon Overlook,** at 11,716 feet, perches high above Forest Canyon on the west side of the highway. Huge glaciers chiseled this deep U-shaped valley along a major fault line now followed by the Big Thompson River. Ragged peaks, including Mount Ida, Terra Tomah Mountain, and Sprague Mountain, line the Continental Divide's serrated ridge across the abyss. Three small glaciers, slowly melting away in the warming climate, still tuck under the divide's escarpment. Hanging valleys and cirques hide numerous lakes and tarns below soaring rock buttresses, cliffs, and snowfields. Keep on the paved trail to the overlook to avoid damaging fragile tundra plants.

Almost 2 miles later the road reaches **Rock Cut Overlook,** a spectacular 12,110-foot point past a road cut. The excellent 0.5-mile **Tundra Communities Trail** (1-mile round-trip hike) gently climbs eastward from the parking area to the rounded ridge crest and offers a great introduction to alpine ecology. The tundra inhabitants have superbly adapted to its rigorous climate and short growing season. A scant 6- to 10-week growing season, wind speeds as high as 170 miles per hour, intense ultraviolet radiation, desiccating air, low soil moisture, and intense sunlight all conspire against life. Yet despite the rigors, life not only survives but also flourishes atop Trail Ridge. Meadows with thick, wiry grasses spread over the ridge, and perennial flowers and herbs huddle against the ground. More than 185 flowering plants grow here, including alpine sunflower, alpine aven, bistort, moss campion, lousewort, marsh marigold, dwarf clover, and phlox.

A colorful riot of wildflowers, including alpine sunflowers, Indian paintbrush, alpine aven, bistort, and forget-me-nots, line the short wheelchair-accessible trail in July and early August. The trail begins at 12,100 feet at Rock Cut parking area and climbs to 12,304 feet at the **Toll Memorial** at trail's end. The memorial commemorates Roger Toll's service to the National Park Service with a plaque and a peak finder that locates other national parks and their distance from the memorial. Points of interest on the trail are the Mushroom Rocks, scenic views of Longs Peak, and mountain mammals like elk, marmots, and coneys.

Hikers need to stay on the paved walkway and other existing tundra trails. The fragile tundra has almost no carrying capacity, and any human use quickly affects the plants. The National Park Service established "tundra protection areas" along Trail Ridge Road to preserve the delicate alpine grassland from being loved to death by footsteps. Also, don't pick the flowers.

The highway drops north from Rock Cut Overlook to 11,827-foot Iceberg Pass and then swings up the Tundra Curves to a lookout above Lava Cliff cirque. Tall cliffs of welded volcanic tuff form the cirque's abrupt east-facing wall. The road continues climbing and in 0.8 mile passes Trail Ridge Road's 12,183-foot high point. Edging across broad grassy slopes, the drive gently descends to 12,048-foot **Gore Range Overlook.** This viewpoint, sitting above the head of Forest Canyon, offers expansive views of the **Never Summer Range** to the west and the Gore Range some 75 miles distant. Longs Peak, a pioneer landmark of the northern

Front Range, lifts steep slopes broken by granite cliffs to its flat-topped summit. The road swings northeast and steadily drops another mile to 11,796-foot Fall River Pass and the Alpine Visitor Center.

Fall River Pass to Grand Lake

Fall River Pass, the terminus of Old Fall River Road, divides the Cache la Poudre and Fall River drainages. At the pass is the popular **Alpine Visitor Center,** which dispenses park information, sells books and maps, and offers exhibits on tundra ecology and geology. A nearby store sells gifts, snacks, and lunches in the only restaurant in the national park. Outside the center are spectacular views into Forest Canyon.

From here Trail Ridge Road begins a serious descent from the pass, dropping steeply down to 11,640-foot **Medicine Bow Curve,** a sharp hairpin turn with an overlook. The road bends west, reaches timberline in another mile, and descends through spruce forest and lush flower-strewn meadows into the upper Cache la Poudre River valley. Poudre Lake, the headwaters of the 75-mile-long Cache la Poudre River, sits atop the Continental Divide on 10,759-foot **Milner Pass.** A nearby trail scrambles a mile up Specimen Mountain to the Crater, where bighorn sheep forage in summer. The trail is closed to hiking until after lambing season in mid-July, and the mountain is closed all year to protect a sheep mineral lick.

Lake Irene, a serene pond surrounded by spruce and fir, is nestled just down the highway. The 8-table Lake Irene Picnic Area with vault toilets is near the landslide-dammed lake. The road threads down Beaver Creek's steep canyon, passing Sheep Rock and Jackstraw Mountain to the south, and continues on down to 10,148-foot **Farview Curve Overlook.** This viewpoint, the last lofty overlook on Trail Ridge Road, gazes west into Kawuneeche Valley. During the ice ages the park's largest glacier stretched 20 miles down the valley to Grand Lake. The Colorado River, originating at the valley's head, meanders through dense willow thickets and beaver ponds in this flat-floored, glacier-carved valley. The Never Summer Range, called *Ni-chebe-chii,* or "Never No Summer" by the Arapaho, lifts its craggy crest to the west.

The switchbacking road drops steeply for the next 4 miles through thick spruce, fir, and pine woods to the valley's eastern edge. The **Colorado River Trailhead** sits west of the road. The trail heads north 7 miles to La Poudre Pass on the park's northern boundary. An easy shorter hike goes 3.6 miles up the river to the ghostly remains of Lulu City, an 1880s mining camp. Watch for moose along the wet bottomlands. On the opposite side of the highway is the **Timber Creek Trailhead.** Take a 4.8-mile hike up to breathtaking Timber Lake nestled in a cirque below Mount Ida.

Rocky outcrops frame flat-topped Longs Peak, the Rocky Mountain National Park high point, from Trail Ridge Road.

The highway runs south along the eastern edge of the valley. Beaver Ponds Picnic Area, the 98-site Timber Creek Campground, and several trailheads sit along the drive. **Holzwarth Trout Lodge Historic Site,** past the campground, makes a good stop. The historic site began as the Holzwarth Homestead in 1916 and later became a dude ranch after the Fall River Road was built. The site, reached by a 0.5-mile trail, is seen on a self-guided hike or tours led by volunteers in summer.

The highway continues south through lodgepole pine forest and open grasslands. Deer, elk, and moose frequently graze in the wide roadside meadows along the road. The **Kawuneeche Visitor Center,** sitting at 8,720 feet, is the drive's last point of interest. The center offers displays on the park's history, geology, and natural history; distributes free park information and permits; and sells books.

Trail Ridge Road scenic drive ends almost a mile past the visitor center on the park boundary. US 34 continues past 30,690-acre Arapaho National Recreation Area, a watery recreation land with five major reservoirs and **Grand Lake,** Colorado's largest natural lake and the end of the scenic drive.

18

Cache la Poudre–North Park Scenic Drive

Fort Collins to Walden

General description: This 101-mile-long scenic drive follows CO 14 from Fort Collins on the eastern edge of the Front Range to Walden in North Park. The road runs through Poudre Canyon and climbs over Cameron Pass to North Park.

Special attractions: Poudre Canyon, Cache la Poudre Wild and Scenic River, Roosevelt National Forest, Cache la Poudre Wilderness Area, Comanche Peak Wilderness Area, Cameron Pass, Rawah Wilderness Area, State Forest State Park, North Park, Arapaho National Wildlife Refuge, hiking, camping, backpacking, fishing, rock climbing, kayaking, cross-country skiing.

Location: North-central Colorado. The drive begins in Fort Collins off I-25 and ends in Walden.

Route name and number: Cache la Poudre–North Park Scenic Byway, CO 14.

Travel season: Year-round. Chains or adequate snow tires might be needed in winter.

Camping: Many national forest campgrounds line the drive, including Ansel Watrous (16 sites), Stove Prairie Landing (9 sites), Dutch George (21 sites), Upper and Lower Narrows (15 sites), Mountain Park (55 sites), Kelly Flats (29 sites), Big Bend (9 sites), Sleeping Elephant (15 sites), Big South (4 sites), Aspen Glen (9 sites), Chambers Lake (51 sites), Long Draw (24 sites), and Grandview (9 sites) east of Cameron Pass, and Pines (11 sites) and Aspen (7 sites) on the west. Colorado State Forest State Park has 5 campgrounds: The Crags (26 sites), Ranger Lakes (32 sites), North Michigan (13-sites), Bockman (52 sites), North Park (29 sites), and over 60 dispersed campsites.

Services: All services are in Fort Collins and Walden. Limited services along drive.

Nearby attractions: Rocky Mountain National Park, Trail Ridge Road (Scenic Drive 17), Lory State Park, Horsetooth Reservoir, Mount Zirkel Wilderness Area, Rabbit Ears Pass, Arapaho National Forest, Routt National Forest, Never Summer Wilderness Area.

The Route

The 101-mile-long Cache la Poudre–North Park Scenic and Historic Byway weaves through the Cache la Poudre River's deep canyon from Fort Collins to the 10,276-foot summit of Cameron Pass before plunging into North Park, a broad intermontane basin ringed by snow-capped mountains. The highway traverses a landscape seamed by canyons, excavated by glaciers, and studded with granite cliffs. It climbs over the Medicine Bow Mountains, a windswept gallery of towering peaks, and threads along the Cache la Poudre River, a designated Wild and Scenic River. Four wilderness areas—the Cache la Poudre, Comanche Peak,

Cache la Poudre–North Park Scenic Drive

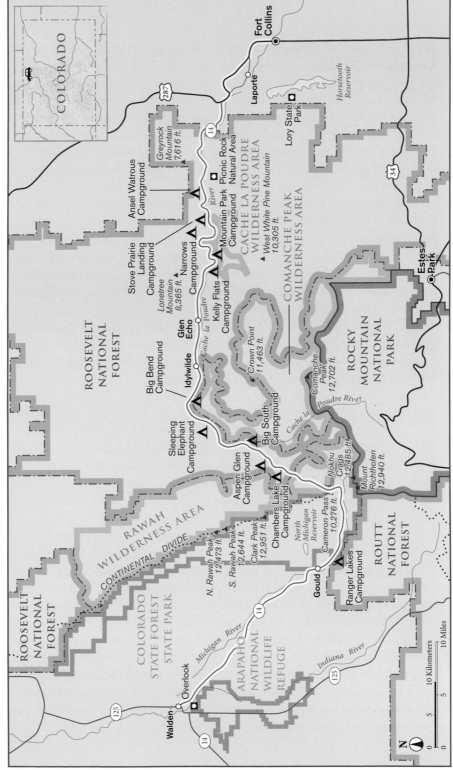

Neota, and Rawah wildernesses—in Roosevelt National Forest and State Forest State Park line the drive.

The lower part of the drive from Gateway Natural Area, as well as the rest of the Cache la Poudre River to its confluence with the South Platte River by Greeley, forms the **Cache la Poudre River National Heritage Area.** This 45-mile-long heritage corridor encompasses the river's floodplain and interprets the development of western water law, the evolution of water delivery systems to Front Range cities, and the river's significance for economic growth and recreation.

The drive, open year-round, is best in summer and fall. Elevations vary from 5,000 feet to over 10,000 feet, offering a diverse range of temperatures and climates. Summer high temperatures vary from the 90s at Fort Collins to the 50s atop the Cameron Pass. Nights in the higher elevations can be cold. Afternoon thunderstorms frequently build over the mountains, bringing localized heavy rain. Autumn yields brisk but mild weather, with colorful aspens lining the highway. Winter days are cold, with highs between 10 and 40 degrees. Heavy snow falls on the pass and the drive's western slope. Be prepared for icy roads, particularly on shaded corners, and carry chains or have adequate snow tires. Spring creeps up the drive from the prairie beginning in April. The roadside snowpack is melted by late May. Expect crisp, breezy days and cold nights.

Fort Collins

The drive begins at **Fort Collins** on CO 14/US 287. Sitting 2 miles west of I-25, Fort Collins sprawls along the Cache la Poudre River at the foot of the Front Range escarpment. The city, poised on the edge of the Great Plains and the Rocky Mountains, relies on an economic base of agriculture, high-tech industry, and Colorado State University.

Started in 1862 as an army fort by two companies of the Kansas Volunteer Cavalry, Camp Collins's mission was to protect travelers, settlers, and the US Mail on the Overland Trail. A flood erased the post in 1864 and a new camp, designated Fort Collins, was erected at today's townsite. After Native American attacks abated, the fort was taken over by the Larimer County Land Improvement Company, and streets were platted for a new town in 1873. The town thrived as a farming hub, and in 1879 the Agricultural College of Colorado, now Colorado State University, opened its doors.

Points of interest include the Fort Collins Museum of Discovery, the historic Avery House, and an Anheuser-Busch brewery. The city, a recreational haven, offers nearby hike and bike trails and fishing areas at Horsetooth Mountain Park and Reservoir and Lory State Park.

The drive heads northwest from Fort Collins on CO 14 across rolling farms and ranches. US 287 makes a quick bypass around **Laporte,** while CO 14 runs west through the town. Laporte, settled as a fur post by French trappers in 1858, was the area's first settlement. The name, French for "the gate," came from the natural gap in the hogbacks northwest of here, where today's highway runs. Antoine Janis, Colorado's first permanent white settler north of the Arkansas River, claimed the river bottom west of Laporte in 1844. Legend says that years earlier Janis, part of an American Fur Company supply train, stashed several hundred pounds of gunpowder and other supplies in a hole along the river one winter to lighten wagon loads, returning the next year to retrieve the goods. Afterward, trappers called the river Cache la Poudre, meaning "cache of the powder."

Lory State Park to Poudre Park

Past Laporte is the turn south to **Lory State Park.** This secluded 2,492-acre parkland is a marvelous, off-the-beaten-track natural area. The park preserves the diverse ecology of the Rockies foothills, with grasslands, upturned sandstone hogbacks, and ponderosa pine forests. Twenty-six miles of marked trails thread through the park, offering adventure to hikers, mountain bikers, and horseback riders. Climbers scale 6,780-foot Arthur's Rock, a granite crag perched above Horsetooth Reservoir. Prairie rattlesnakes are common in summer, especially around talus and on the lower grasslands.

The highway bends northwest, crossing and paralleling the hogbacks, high ridges tilted upward when the Rocky Mountains rose. Soft, easily eroded shale and mudstone layers form broad vales between the rocky hogbacks. Ten miles from Fort Collins, the drive reaches Ted's Place and the intersection of US 287 and CO 14. Turn west on CO 14. Ted, or Edward Irving Herring, established his place in 1922 at the scenic entrance to Poudre Canyon.

CO 14 heads west up a broad valley through low, tawny hills and after a mile and a half enters **Poudre Canyon** (pronounced POO-der by locals) and the Front Range mountains. The highway threads alongside the **Cache la Poudre River** in the depths of Poudre Canyon for the next 50 miles. The 126-mile-long river, beginning from Poudre Lake on 10,070-foot Milner Pass and the Continental Divide on Trail Ridge Road in Rocky Mountain National Park, dashes through the deep craggy canyon, empties onto the plains at Fort Collins, and ends in the South Platte River near Greeley.

Throughout its length the Cache la Poudre remains a wild stream, with only a few small dams blocking its upper forks. The river's marvelous scenery, excellent recreational opportunities, and wild character led to the designation of 76 river miles as Colorado's first National Wild and Scenic River in 1986. The Poudre

Canyon yields excellent fishing for brown and rainbow trout, offers serious white-water challenges to rafters and kayakers, provides surprisingly good climbing on its cliffs, and boasts numerous national forest campgrounds and picnic areas. The river corridor, close to the urban Front Range cities, is popular, especially on summer weekends.

The drive enters 813,799-acre Roosevelt National Forest just past the canyon entrance. The forest, originally part of the 1897 Medicine Bow Forest Reserve, became Colorado National Forest in 1910 and was renamed for conservationist President Theodore Roosevelt in 1932.

After driving 2.8 miles from the highway junction, the highway reaches **Picnic Rock Natural Area.** This scenic stretch of river, shaded by cottonwoods, offers both flat water and slight rapids, making it ideal for beginning kayakers and tubers once dangerous spring runoff lessens in mid-July. The 3-mile river section from Gateway Natural Area to Lower Picnic Rock at the natural area, sometimes called the **Filter Plant Run,** is the only whitewater stretch suitable for novice rafters. Make sure you take out if you're tubing or boating at Picnic Rock because you'll want to avoid a small diversion dam downstream. The area also offers picnicking, fishing, and hiking.

The right turn to **Gateway Natural Area** is 5.4 miles from the drive's start. This Fort Collins-owned site is a gorgeous stop for mountain adventures close to town. The site, located at the city's old water filtration plant (operated 1905 to 1987) at the confluence of the Cache la Poudre River and its North Fork, offers shaded picnic tables, a launch for rafters and kayakers, a kid's playground, interpretative signs, and three hiking trails. The 0.8-mile Black Powder Trail climbs to a wide view of Poudre Canyon; the 0.3-mile Overlook Trail scrambles to a ridgetop; and an easy 1-mile hike along a closed road leads to Seaman Reservoir on the North Fork. The fee area is open daily from dawn to dusk.

The scenic drive curves west, following the river up the twisting canyon. Steep, dry hillsides, covered with grass and low scrub, border the blacktop. Greyrock Trailhead sits 8 miles up-canyon on the left or south side of the highway. Carefully cross the highway and a footbridge over the river to the trailhead for a 7.3-mile hike on the **Greyrock National Recreation Trail,** one of the most popular hikes in the canyon. The hike follows 3.1-mile Greyrock Trail (#946) and 2.6 Greyrock Meadows Trail (#947) with extra mileage to climb up and back to the rounded granite summit of 7,616-foot **Greyrock Mountain** and expansive views across the Front Range. Greyrock is also an excellent backcountry rock climbing area with many traditional-style moderate routes. Consult *Rock Climbing Colorado* (FalconGuides) for beta and route descriptions on Greyrock.

Up Poudre Canyon

The drive continues west through the town of **Poudre Park** and passes 2-table Poudre Park, 6-table Diamond Rock, and 3-table Ouzel Picnic Areas. Ansel Watrous Campground, with 16 sites, sits among ponderosa pines in a broad canyon section. Nearby is the trailhead for Young Gulch Trail (#999). **The Palace,** one of the canyon's most popular rock climbing venues, is 15 miles from Teds Place and past a tunnel. Climbers wade the river when it's low to a couple of rocky ridges with cliffs and pinnacles laced with bolted sport routes. The Narrows canyon section from Stove Prairie Road to the Narrows Campground is also a popular climbing area with numerous cliffs like Eden Wall, Snake Eyes Wall, and Twilight Wall rising above the highway and river.

A couple of miles west of Ansel Watrous, the highway swings under granite cliffs, passes through a tunnel and enters the Little Narrows. The river, making a bend, slices through bedrock with the road perched alongside. The canyon again broadens at 9-site Stove Prairie Landing Campground. Upper Landing Picnic and Stevens Gulch Picnic Areas, both with river access for fishermen, lie another 0.5 mile west.

Past the picnic areas, the highway enters the **Big Narrows,** an impressive defile filled with soaring buttresses, cliffs, and arêtes. The frothy river churns over boulders in a mist of white spray and with a thunderous roar. Moist hanging canyons, filled with Douglas firs, clumps of grass, and ferns, climb above the river's cobbled south bank. Some of the canyon's best rock climbing is found on Ra's Buttress, Pee Wee's Playhouse, and Eve's Cave in the Big Narrows. The 15-site Narrows Campground, divided into Upper and Lower sections, sits beside the river past the confined canyon segment.

Winding Poudre Canyon, making an immense horseshoe bend, briefly opens at Dutch George Flats and pleasant 21-site Dutch George Campground. Farther west is 55-site Mountain Park Campground, a popular overnight spot with showers, river access, and hiking trails, including the 2-mile **Kreutzer Nature Trail.** The excellent 5-mile loop **Mount McConnell National Recreation Trail** (#992), beginning at the campground, winds through fir and pine forest to Mount McConnell's 8,020-foot summit on the northern edge of 9,258-acre **Cache la Poudre Wilderness Area.** This small wilderness, traversed by the river's South Fork, protects a sparsely visited region of rugged mountains and canyons to the south.

The Poudre Canyon constricts down to a rocky, confined gorge past Mountain Park. Kelly Flats Campground, with 29 campsites spread along the river bank, is in open forest along the river. As the drive heads west, cliffs above the road grow taller and the canyon's narrow floor alternately widens and narrows. Mountain mahogany and sagebrush cover dry south-facing slopes above the highway, while ponderosa pine and Douglas fir populate the moister north-facing slopes. Open grasslands blanket the valley floor at Indian Meadows, a popular fishing site. Check signs that mark fishing areas which are restricted to flies and low catch limits.

Rustic and **Glen Echo,** small resort villages with summer cabins, straddle the broad valley further west. Willows and tall cottonwoods shade the riverbanks. **Profile Rock,** the craggy silhouette of a rugged face, towers south of the river and road almost 3 miles past Glen Echo. A half-mile upriver from the rocky visage is a small national forest visitor center housed in the old Arrowhead Lodge, a summer resort that opened in 1935. Besides picking up maps and canyon info, the center is an ideal spot to see bighorn sheep on slopes to the north.

Poudre Canyon assumes a different complexion 3 miles past Profile Rock. The roadside **Home Moraine Geologic Site,** an interpretive pullout, marks the easternmost advance of a great valley glacier that excavated the broad U-shaped

The Cache la Poudre River, fed by mountain snowmelt, drops over boulders in Poudre Canyon.

valley to the west. Time and the flow of the river chiseled the confined, V-shaped canyon the drive has followed from its mouth by Teds Place. The pullout gives a view of the terminal moraine, a jumble of boulders and cobbles, which marked the glacier's farthest advance eastward.

The highway runs up the broad valley, its flanks stair-stepping up to forested summits. Before Kinikinik, the drive passes the Poudre Rearing Unit, state fish hatchery, a brooding facility that produces millions of rainbow and greenback cutthroat trout eggs and stocks over 50,000 trout in Front Range waters. Farther along is the 9-site Big Bend Campground and a bighorn sheep viewing area on the short road to the campground. Around the next highway bend, 40 miles from Teds Place, is Roaring Creek Trailhead on the right. Roaring Creek Trail (#952) climbs steeply into a high canyon filled with meadows where moose often graze.

At Kinikinik's summer cottages, the Poudre River and canyon make a big bend southwest. The canyon's southern rim forms the northern boundary of 66,791-acre **Comanche Peak Wilderness Area,** a large swath of high mountains topped by 12,702-foot Comanche Peak in the Mummy Range.

The highway heads southwest up the wide canyon. Sheer crags etched by glaciers perch on steep canyon slopes. Sleeping Elephant Campground, with 15 aspen-shaded sites, sits along the right side of the highway, and rocky 9,145-foot Sleeping Elephant Mountain looms overhead to the east. Tunnel Picnic Area, with 3 sites, sits alongside the river by Tunnel Creek. **Poudre Falls,** a spectacular whitewater cascade, gushes through a narrow chasm after the highway crosses from the river's west to east bank. The best view and photographs are from a pull-off on the right. At 4-site Big South Campground, the highway leaves the Cache la Poudre River and Poudre Canyon and begins steeply climbing up Joe Wright Creek's side canyon. Big South Trail (#944) begins near the campground and heads up the river canyon through wild and rugged Comanche Peak Wilderness Area. Backpackers find 19 designated sites along the trail's first 7 miles.

Rawah Wilderness Area & Cameron Pass

The road passes 9-site Aspen Glen Campground and a national forest information kiosk on the right. A string of popular fishing lakes and reservoirs scatter throughout a lodgepole pine forest off the highway. Barnes Meadow Reservoir sits south of the drive and **Chambers Lake,** named for early trapper Robert Chambers, spreads to the north. The Laramie River, running north to Wyoming and the North Platte River, begins here. Chambers Lake Campground, a 3-loop campground with 51 sites on the southern shore of Chambers Lake, is a popular base camp for anglers, hikers, and boaters. The busy campground offers a refreshing respite from summer with crisp nights and cool temperatures. The large lake has plenty of arms so it's easy to get away from people and cast a line for rainbow, brook, and cutthroat trout. Chambers Lake is wakeless, so bring a canoe or low-powered boat.

The 76,394-acre **Rawah Wilderness Area** stretches north from the highway, encompassing almost the entire eastern flank of the Rawah Range, a southern extension of Wyoming's Medicine Bow Mountains. The Arapaho Indians used their word for "wilderness," *rawah,* to describe this pristine sierra of high peaks and crystal lakes. A good day hike into the wilderness area is up Blue Lake Trail (#959) from a trailhead south of Chambers Lake. The 10-mile round-trip hike climbs to Blue Lake, a glistening timberline lake.

The drive continues climbing above the shallow creek valley, edges past Joe Wright Reservoir, and reaches the broad summit of 10,276-foot **Cameron Pass.** The high pass, named for pioneer railroad builder General Robert Cameron, is flanked by white fir forest that climbs to timberline on snow-capped 12,951-foot Clark Peak. The 9,924-acre **Neota Wilderness Area** protects an above-timberline region of flattened ridges fringed by fir and spruce. If you want to climb a mountain, head up 11,852-foot North Diamond Peak on the Continental Divide west of Cameron Pass. For a complete trail description, check out *Climbing Colorado's Mountains* (FalconGuides).

The drive heads down the pass's west slope and after a mile bends west above the Michigan River valley. The highway edges past a scenic overlook that offers a superlative view south of ragged 12,485-foot Nokhu Crags and 12,940-foot Mount Richthofen on Rocky Mountain National Park's northwest corner. The road continues to descend and passes a turnoff that leads south to the Lake Agnes Trailhead.

The 0.8-mile **Lake Agnes Trail,** the best hike along the scenic drive, climbs over glacial moraines to gorgeous Lake Agnes, a timberline lake cupped in a deep basin below the Nokhu Crags. Reach the trailhead by driving 1.8 miles up a rough road south of the highway. Nokhu is an abbreviated name derived from *Nea ha-no-Xhu,* or "Eagle's Nest" in Arapaho. Nearby 26-site Crags Campground, administered by the State Forest State Park, is scattered throughout spruce forest along the side road.

The byway drops into the Michigan River's broad, willow-covered valley, one of the best places in Colorado to see moose. This area, along with the western flank of the Rawah Range, is part of **State Forest State Park.** This 70,838-acre parkland, Colorado's largest state park, is administered by the Colorado Parks and Wildlife as a trust land, funding the state's public school system. Besides recreational uses, grazing, logging, and hunting are permitted. The park offers five campgrounds with 152 sites, over 60 dispersed primitive campsites, yurts and cabins, over 90 miles of hiking trails, 130 miles of mountain bike trails, and fishable lakes and streams. Kelly Lake, just below the range crest, is one of the few places

The Rawah Range rises sharply above grazing cattle on the eastern edge of North Park.

in Colorado that holds the rare golden trout, an introduced California species. The park's diverse habitat also shelters more than 125 bird species, as well as mammals including marmot, marten, beaver, red fox, coyote, mink, bighorn sheep, and moose. The park's moose population usually shelters among the willows along the upper Michigan River on the drive.

Past the campground at Ranger Lakes, the highway and river swing northwest around 10,390-foot Gould Mountain. A dense lodgepole pine forest, broken by scattered aspen groves, borders the asphalt. The small town of **Gould** offers gas and groceries. The state park headquarters and the turnoff to North Michigan Reservoir sits a couple miles farther.

The drive bends west and crosses the Michigan River valley. The ragged crest of the Rawah Range forms an immense wall to the east, while low-browed hills stretch along the valley's western rim. Wide grasslands, sprinkled with grazing cattle, spread out from the river. The highway, running northwest along rolling hills, passes open lodgepole pine and aspen woodlands before leaving the river valley and the mountains behind.

North Park

North Park, a huge glacial basin hemmed in by mountains, lies ahead. The basin, 35 miles wide and 45 miles long, is characterized by sagebrush rangelands and slow rivers. The Utes, who frequently hunted the park's bison in summer, called it "Cow Lodge" and "Bull Pen." Lieutenant John C. Fremont, one of its first Anglo explorers, noted in his 1844 journal, " . . . a beautiful circular valley of thirty miles in diameter, walled in all around with snowy mountains, rich with water and grass, fringed with pine on the mountain sides below the snow, and a paradise to all grazing animals."

The road crosses low, sagebrush-covered bluffs and dips across Owl Creek's shallow valley. Seven miles after leaving the Michigan River, the highway reaches Brocker Overlook above **Arapaho National Wildlife Refuge.** The 24,804-acre refuge, established in 1967, provides important nesting habitat for migratory waterfowl along the Illinois River. Water diverted from the river irrigates meadows and fills shallow ponds. After the ice melts in the refuge in late May, thousands of ducks, including pintail, mallard, gadwall, and American wigeon, as well as Canada geese, begin arriving to nest and raise their broods. Other shore- and waterbirds seen are Virginia rails, Wilson's phalaropes, avocets, sandpipers, great blue herons, bitterns, and grebes. Numerous raptors—eagles, hawks, and prairie falcons—wheel across the sky in search of prey. Moose, elk, and mule deer range across the refuge, particularly during winter. A 6-mile self-guided auto tour, beginning 3 miles south of Walden on CO 125, explores the wildlife area.

The byway continues northwest along a bluff above the river and 3 miles later enters **Walden** and the scenic drive's end. Walden, North Park's largest town and a ranching center, is named for Mark Walden, the former postmaster of the nearby ghost town of Sage Hen Springs. The town, founded in 1889, was originally called Sagebrush for the ubiquitous stands of gray *Artemisia tridentata* that blanket North Park. Walden offers all visitor services, including gas, restaurants, and lodging.

Independence Pass Scenic Drive

Twin Lakes to Aspen

General description: This 44-mile-long drive climbs over 12,095-foot Independence Pass, Colorado's highest paved pass, and the Continental Divide between the upper Arkansas River Valley and Aspen.

Special attractions: Twin Lakes, Mount Elbert, Colorado Trail, La Plata Peak, Independence Pass, Independence ghost town, Hunter-Fryingpan Wilderness Area, Collegiate Peaks Wilderness Area, Continental Divide, Braille Nature Trail, camping, mountaineering, rock climbing, fishing, hiking, backpacking, scenic views.

Location: Central Colorado. The drive runs from US 24, 20 miles north of Buena Vista, to Aspen.

Route name and number: Independence Pass Road, CO 82.

Travel season: Spring through fall. The highway opens sometime in May and closes after the first major snow, in late October or early November. Vehicles over 35 feet long are prohibited from crossing Independence Pass.

Camping: National forest campgrounds are on the drive. On the east side pass are Dexter (12 sites), Whitestar (49 sites), Lakeview (35 sites), Parry Peak (25 sites), and Twin Peaks (36 sites) Campgrounds. On the west side are Lost Man (10 sites), Lincoln Gulch (7 sites), Weller (11 sites), and Difficult Creek (47 sites) Campgrounds.

Services: All services are in Aspen, Buena Vista, and Leadville. Limited services at Granite and Twin Lakes.

Nearby attractions: Leadville National Historic District, National Mining Hall of Fame, Arkansas Headwaters Recreation Area, Turquoise Lake, Buena Vista, Mount Massive Wilderness Area, Maroon Bells–Snowmass Wilderness Area, Maroon Lake, Hunter-Frying Pan Wilderness Area.

The Route

This 44-mile scenic drive crosses 12,095-foot Independence Pass, Colorado's highest paved pass, perched atop the Sawatch Range in central Colorado. The Sawatch Range, crested by the twisting Continental Divide, is one of the state's main mountain ranges. It stretches more than 100 miles from the Eagle River and I-70 south to Marshall Pass and the Cochetopa Hills above the San Luis Valley. *Sawatch,* a Ute word meaning "water of the blue earth," describes an ancient lake that once filled the San Luis Valley. Later explorers, including Captain John Gunnison in 1853, applied the name to the mountain chain. The spelling of Sawatch was also changed from Saguache, which one wag said could only be pronounced by sneezing.

Independence Pass Scenic Drive

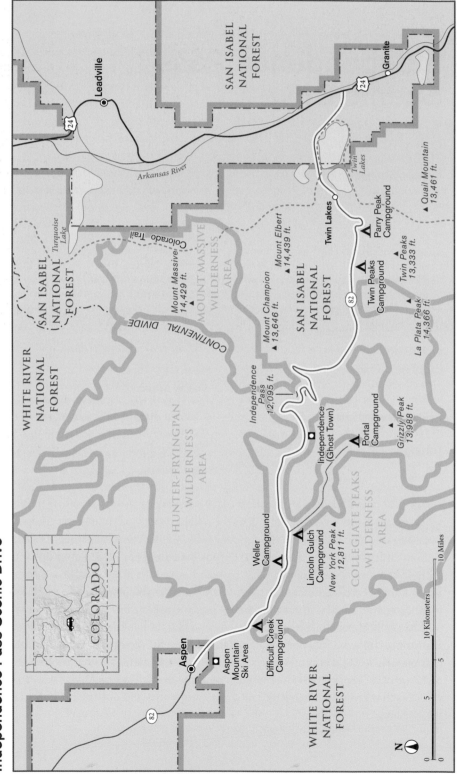

WHITE RIVER NATIONAL FOREST

SAN ISABEL NATIONAL FOREST

SAN ISABEL NATIONAL FOREST

SAN ISABEL NATIONAL FOREST

Leadville

Granite

Arkansas River

Turquoise Lake

Colorado Trail

HUNTER-FRYINGPAN WILDERNESS AREA

MOUNT MASSIVE WILDERNESS AREA

CONTINENTAL DIVIDE

Mount Massive ▲ 14,429 ft.

Mount Champion ▲ 13,646 ft.

Mount Elbert ▲ 14,439 ft.

Independence Pass 12,095 ft.

Independence (Ghost Town)

Portal Campground

Grizzly Peak ▲ 13,988 ft.

Twin Lakes

Twin Lakes

Twin Peaks Campground

Twin Peaks ▲ 13,333 ft.

Parry Peak Campground

Quail Mountain ▲ 13,461 ft.

La Plata Peak ▲ 14,366 ft.

COLLEGIATE PEAKS WILDERNESS AREA

Lincoln Gulch Campground

New York Peak ▲ 12,811 ft.

Weller Campground

Difficult Creek Campground

Aspen Mountain Ski Area

Aspen

WHITE RIVER NATIONAL FOREST

COLORADO

N

0   5   10 Kilometers

0   5   10 Miles

Independence Pass offers spectacular views of La Plata Peak, Colorado's fifth-highest mountain.

The Sawatch Range, lying within the San Isabel and White River National Forests, contains 14 of Colorado's 53 ranked 14,000-foot peaks, including four of the five highest. Mount Elbert, the state's highest point at 14,439 feet, tops the list, followed by 14,429-foot Mount Massive, 14,423-foot Mount Harvard, and 14,360-foot La Plata Peak.

Large tracts of wild lands—the Holy Cross, Mount Massive, and Collegiate Peaks Wilderness Areas—straddle the range and preserve large areas of pristine, roadless mountains. The range's snowy crest also gives birth to numerous rivers, including the Arkansas, Taylor, Roaring Fork, Fryingpan, and Eagle. On the east the Independence Pass scenic drive follows Lake Creek's deep, glaciated valley between Mount Elbert and La Plata Peak, while on the west the drive plunges down the Roaring Fork River corridor surrounded by the Hunter-Fryingpan and Collegiate Peaks Wilderness Areas.

Heavy snow closes the highway in winter. The road opens, usually in May, when deep drifts on the upper section melt enough for snowplows to scour the roadway. It closes again when snow flies, usually in late October. Expect cool temperatures atop the pass from May through October, with afternoon thunderstorms and even summer snow. Summer temperatures reach into the 70s. As a rule of thumb, air temperatures decrease 3 degrees for every 1,000 feet of elevation ascended. Consequently, the lower elevations, including Aspen and Twin Lakes, are warmer than the pass summit, with temperatures above 80 degrees in summer.

If you're hiking on ridges atop the pass, watch for lightning on summer afternoons. Also use caution when crossing snowfields—they are deceptively dangerous. Carry and know how to use an ice axe and wear proper footwear.

Twin Lakes

The drive begins at the intersection of US 24 and CO 82, 20 miles north of Buena Vista and 15 miles south of Leadville in the Arkansas River valley. Granite, almost 3 miles south of the intersection, was the site of the area's first gold discovery in 1859. The camp was short-lived, as richer deposits were found upstream at California Gulch near today's Leadville. Turn west on CO 82, the Independence Pass Road. Vehicles over 35 feet long are prohibited from crossing Independence Pass.

The highway runs east alongside turbulent Lake Creek as it rushes across a huge boulder-strewn moraine left by the ancient Lake Creek Glacier, an immense glacier that scoured out the deep valley to the west. The moraine forms **Twin Lakes,** two large lakes that have been enlarged for water storage as part of the Fryingpan-Arkansas Project. This huge water project, supplying water primarily to Colorado Springs and Aurora on the Front Range, pumps water from the western slope of the Continental Divide to Turquoise Lake west of Leadville. The water is piped south to Twin Lakes, where it is used to generate electrical power before being sent to thirsty Front Range cities.

The highway reaches the north side of Twin Lakes and Mountain View Overlook after 1.5 miles. The drive continues west across sagebrush-covered slopes above the lake. At 2.4 miles the road passes 12-site Dexter Campground and a boat ramp, both part of San Isabel National Forest's **Twin Lakes Recreation Area.** Farther west a side road leads north to 35-site Lakeview Campground and Mount Elbert Picnic Area. The Fryingpan-Arkansas Project Visitor Center is reached at 4.5 miles. The center explains the history and hydraulics of the project. The Twin Lakes, covering a combined 2,700 surface acres, offer excellent fishing, with lake trout exceeding 30 pounds and 40 inches in length as well as plump rainbow and cutthroat trout.

Beyond the visitor center, the highway bends southwest through piney hills, passes 49-site Whitestar Campground on the lakeshore, and enters the town of **Twin Lakes.** This picturesque community, set at 9,015 feet at the foot of **Mount Elbert,** was settled around 1880 after the initial silver rush to nearby Leadville.

Twin Lakes is filled with historic sites including the original schoolhouse built in 1895.

The valley yielded a few prosperous lodes, such as the Little Joe, Bartlett, and Fidelity mines, but it was the natural beauty that attracted newcomers then and now.

The town, offering few services, sits near a major avalanche chute that erased the western part of town on January 21, 1962. The slide, occurring at 5:30 in the morning, swept down Mount Elbert, erasing four houses and killing 7 people, including 5 in the Shelton family. Survivor Barbara Adamich later told the *Denver Post* that she woke up that morning "in an immense sandwich of splintered wood and snow." All that remains are overgrown cabin foundations in the meadows below 12,682-foot Parry Peak, a spur of Mount Elbert.

Starting in 1982, Twin Lakes hosted an infamous tomato war between Coloradoans and Texans every September until it ended in the early 1990s. Ammunition was thousands of pounds of overripe tomatoes launched by the opposing sides. While driving through, keep an eye out for a uniformed police officer mannequin in his roadside patrol car.

To learn more about the colorful history of Twin Lakes, stop at a parking area on the south side of the highway in the middle of town and take a short walking tour of the **Twin Lakes National Historic District.** The town was originally settled as Dayton in the 1860s, hoping to attract miners with rumors of gold. After 1879 the town changed its name to Twin Lakes and flourished as a center for silver mining. The buildings in the historic district date from this rambunctious era and include the Red Rooster Tavern, now a visitor center; the Clarion Hotel; a log cabin; an assay office; and a shed. The site also has picnic tables and restrooms.

Just east of Twin Lakes is the **Interlaken Resort District,** the abandoned site of the 1880s Interlaken Resort established by mining man James V. Dexter. The resort, sprawling over 100 acres, featured stables, a dance pavilion, and a hotel that catered to wealthy tourists who came to boat in summer and ski in winter. The resort closed in the 1950s when the lakes were enlarged for water storage. Reach the historic area by hiking or mountain biking on the easy 3-mile Interlaken Trail from a parking area at the Twin Lakes dam.

Lake Creek Valley

Past Twin Lakes the highway bends southeast for a mile, skirting marsh and willow thickets on the west edge of the lake before swinging into Lake Creek's narrowing valley. The creek rushes over worn cobbles and boulders in a shallow canyon below the road. Dense forests of lodgepole pine and aspen line the way and blanket steep mountainsides. Parry Peak Campground, with 25 sites, lies near the valley entrance and popular 36-site Twin Peaks Campground spreads alongside the highway a mile farther west.

Monitor Rock, a bold white cliff, looms over the drive on the southern flank of Mount Elbert. Glacial striations, scratched by boulders embedded in a deep glacier as it crept down the valley, scar the massive rock. A short walk to the cliff's rounded southern buttress reveals deep, parallel grooves in the smoothed rock surface. Over the last few million years, glaciers periodically excavated this valley and the rest of the Sawatch Range. The scenic drive travels through U-shaped valleys on both sides of the pass. The glaciers that once rested here were several thousand feet thick, with only the high peaks poking above the whiteness. The glaciers sculpted today's mountain scenery, leaving cirques, arêtes, hanging valleys, and moraines as evidence of their passage.

Besides being a remnant of Colorado's glacial past, Monitor Rock is also a fine rock climbing area with numerous routes ascending its steep West Face. Climbers park in a roadside pullout on the south side of the highway that's 5.2 miles from Twin Lakes and then hike a short trail to the Trailhead Wall sector. The *Trooper Traverse,* a classic route up Monitor's south ridge, was first climbed by Colorado climbing legend Harvey T. Carter in the late 1960s.

The valley broadens past Monitor Rock, and the creek swings between willow-lined banks. Thick stands of aspen border the drive and offer spectacular golden colors in late September. **La Plata Peak,** a prominent 14,360-foot mountain, dominates the valley. La Plata's high ridges, corniced with winter snow and studded with rock pinnacles and crags, sweep south to the peak's rounded summit. La Plata Peak, one of the range's most satisfying climbs, was named by pioneer surveyor Ferdinand Hayden in 1874 with the Spanish word for silver.

The La Plata Trail is the best route to the peak's summit. Park alongside the scenic drive at the turnoff for FR 391, the South Fork of Lake Creek Road, almost 15 miles from the drive's start at US 24. From the trailhead, hike down the road and cross Lake Creek on a bridge. Then follow a single-track path 0.25 mile to gorgeous **La Plata Falls,** a 45-foot plunge into a rock-walled slot canyon. Past the falls, the trail wanders through thick spruce forest into La Plata Gulch and then ascends east up a grassy, above-timberline spur to the summit ridge. *Hiking Waterfalls in Colorado* (FalconGuides) gives concise directions to the falls.

At 15 miles the highway heads northwest up Lake Creek's North Fork into a flat-bottomed valley. Dense willows carpet the moist valley floor and hem in the creek. Beaver ponds quiet the tumbling stream and make good fishing holes for trout. A few miles later the highway makes a sharp switchback in Lake Creek's upper valley and begins climbing steeply up a shelf road chiseled into the steep mountain slope. Watch for fallen boulders on this road section.

Just over 1 mile later the highway exits the shelf into **Mountain Boy Gulch,** a hanging glacial valley filled with verdant meadows and dense spruce and subalpine fir forest. An unnamed waterfall sweeps over a cliff band at timberline west

of the drive, and thick snow cornices line the Continental Divide's ridgeline above the cirque. The road switchbacks up the valley's northern slopes, twisting through stunted, windswept trees at timberline. Past tree line the drive bends sharply west and begins its final ascent to the broad pass summit.

Independence Pass

Americans have long been a pass-loving people. A sense of freedom is found in crossing a wild sierra. Out there, beyond the summits, stretches a whole new world, waiting patiently to be discovered and explored. After surmounting a pass, the first instinct is to continue, to plunge down into the unknown valleys below. But here, atop 12,095-foot **Independence Pass,** stop and linger. Breathe in this moment and the majestic mountain panorama.

A parking area and sign mark the lofty pass summit. A short trail winds south to a lookout point above Mountain Boy Gulch. Towering 14,000-foot mountains surround this overlook: La Plata Peak rises to the southeast; Mount Elbert and its high satellite peaks dominate the eastern skyline; and rows of mountains and ridges march westward to the Maroon Bells, Snowmass Mountain, and Capitol Peak.

The pass summit introduces the world above the trees, a world more similar in climate and flora to the lands beyond the Arctic Circle thousands of miles to the north than to the nearby lowland valleys along the Arkansas and Roaring Fork rivers. Mats of wiry grass sprinkled with delicate wildflowers brighten the broad crest. Deep snowdrifts and cornices, persisting well into August, cling to leeward edges and deep ravines. Frigid tarns of snowmelt fill shallow depressions and reflect sky and clouds. Beyond the pass, rounded ridges clad in tundra plants and alpine flowers sweep up to boulder fields, rocky buttresses, and windy summits.

Independence to Aspen

The highway falls abruptly west, edging north down a steep shelf road for over a mile. Watch for fallen boulders on the roadway. No guardrail or shoulder comforts the nervous driver here. After reaching the valley floor and timberline, the drive bends south above the Roaring Fork River below its headwaters at Independence Lake and heads downhill through subalpine fir forest and open meadows.

At this hairpin turn is a large parking area on the right and the trailhead for Linkins Lake Trail (#1979) and Lost Man Trail (#1996) in the Hunter-Fryingpan Wilderness Area. **Linkins Lake Trail** climbs 0.6 mile to a lovely alpine lake at 12,008 feet. The **Lost Man Trail** makes an open loop 8.8-mile hike to a lower

La Plata Falls plunges into a slot canyon.

trailhead at Lost Man Campground in the next valley to the west. The trail climbs over 12,815-foot Lost Man Pass to Lost Man Lake and then descends a glaciated valley to the lower trailhead. A fun 3.5-mile round-trip hike follows Lost Man Trail to Technicolor-blue Independence Lake tucked against the Continental Divide.

The ghost town of **Independence** sprawls across a hillside 2 miles below the pass summit. Gold was discovered on Independence Day 1879 in this alpine valley, bringing a stampede of prospectors to a new town dubbed Independence, the first mining camp in the Aspen area. By 1880 the path over what was then called Hunter's Pass and later Independence Pass became a horse trail operated by the Twin Lakes and Roaring Fork Toll Company. On November 6 the following year, the company opened a frightful wagon road that climbed the lofty pass between Leadville and the burgeoning silver town of Aspen. The road was an instant success, with freight traffic swarming over the divide. Hefty tolls ensured temporary prosperity. For five winters, an army of snow shovelers labored to keep the road open—a feat today's highway department will not undertake with the area's high avalanche danger. The stagecoach trek over the pass took 24 hours, five changes of horses, and three toll gates. In 1888 the railroad reached Aspen and the trail closed down until resurrected as an automobile road in the 1920s.

The town of Independence, at its peak in the early 1880s, boasted a population of 2,000 and 10 saloons. By the turn of the 20th century, the last prospector had pulled up stakes, leaving the town for the owls and mice. Weather-beaten cabins and a few crumbling buildings are all that remain of Independence today. The 17-acre townsite, one of the best preserved 19th-century mining towns, has 19 remaining log buildings and 9 foundations. Farther west is the old mill site with better-preserved ruins, including the stamp mill, mill office, boarding house, and ore storage bins. The ghost town, preserved through the efforts of the Aspen Historical Society, makes a good stop. Walk through the grassy streets that once bustled with dusty miners and burros laden with bedrolls and gold pans and imagine the daily rigors and trials faced by the 19th-century miners. To help preserve this bit of Colorado history, donate at the parking area. No dogs are allowed.

The highway drops west and passes Lost Man Trailhead, the jumping-off point for a favorite hike into the 82,026-acre **Hunter-Fryingpan Wilderness Area,** and 10-site Lost Man Campground 2 miles west of Independence. A dense forest of lodgepole pine, spruce, and fir shades this pleasant 10,700-foot-high campground. The Braille and Discovery trails, both 0.5 mile long, explore the forest farther down the road. The Braille Trail is designed for visually impaired people, while the Discovery Trail is wheelchair accessible. The Braille Trail was the first designated blind trail in the world when it opened in 1967.

The highway narrows past the trails and winds down a steep canyon above the Roaring Fork River. Numerous granite crags nestle in the woods between here and Aspen, offering a diverse selection of routes for rock climbers. Some of the best cliffs include the Grotto Walls, Whirlpool Rock, Olympic Crag, and Weller Slab. Find more information in *Rock Climbing Colorado* from FalconGuides.

Lincoln Creek Road, FR 106, starts 10 miles west of Lost Man. This road, passable to most vehicles, leads southeast for 6 miles up Lincoln Creek to Grizzly Reservoir and Portal Campground. The road, a rough 4x4 track past the lake, continues south to the ghost town of Ruby at the old Ruby Mine at 11,400 feet. A few crumpled cabins remain at the townsite. Towering above Ruby are 13,988-foot Grizzly Peak, one of Colorado's 100 highest mountains, and 13,780-foot Garfield Peak, named for 20th President James Garfield, who was assassinated in 1881.

Past the Lincoln Creek turnoff, the road narrows and twists underneath the looming **Grotto Walls,** a popular climbing site. Look for a left turn marked "Grottos Day Use Area" past the highway bends. A trail begins at a parking lot at the road's end, crosses the river on a footbridge, and heads east across glacier-polished granite 100 yards to **The Grottos.** The Grottos are a series of caverns, cascades, and pools chiseled by the Roaring Fork River before it cut its present channel. The water-polished caverns, roofed by a slit of light, are best accessed via their west end. They are generally dry, although snow and ice linger inside an ice cave at The Grottos through early summer. The Grottos are a kid-friendly area, but keep an eye on the little ones because there are fast river currents and drop-offs. After exploring The Grottos, hike north across bedrock until you hear the river roar. Drop down to see the Roaring Fork gush over **Cascades Waterfall,** a long cascade between deep pools.

Another 0.3 mile down the highway is a small parking area on the left or south side of the asphalt near mile marker 51. Below the road is **Devil's Punchbowl,** a favorite summer swimming hole. The river plunges through a narrow gap into the punchbowl, a deep pool surrounded by overhanging, 20-foot-high granite cliffs. Daredevil divers jump off the south-side cliff into the clear pool. Leap if you're brave enough but scout the landing first to avoid submerged boulders and remember that the water, even on the hottest day, is frigid. Cliff jumping is extremely dangerous. Serious injuries can occur to divers. Always check the area first for hazardous conditions, unpredictable currents, and understand the risks to life and limb before jumping.

The drive continues west another 0.6 mile to pleasant Weller Campground, its 11 sites surrounded by a lush aspen grove. Aspens sprinkle among fir and spruce forests along the road or form moist glades with a thick understory of grass, columbines, and ferns. In late September the aspens drape sheer mountainsides with their rippling gold color.

Past the campground the highway abruptly narrows to one and a half lanes and creeps shelflike above a granite slab. After 0.25 mile the highway widens and drops onto a broad glaciated valley. The road stair-steps down to a lower valley. Difficult Creek Campground, with 47 sites and a group area, hides along the river among dense willow thickets and beaver ponds.

Heading west the highway crosses meadows below steep aspen-covered hillsides. **North Star Nature Preserve,** threaded by a footpath, protects critical elk habitat along the valley floor. In the 1970s, developers planned to build 1,500 homes and commercial buildings here but lowered the density on the North Star Ranch and then The Nature Conservancy bought 175 acres in 1977 and donated them to Pitkin County the following year. The area was a wildlife area with hiking its primary use until about 2012 when the placid river stretch became a popular spot for standup paddling. Over 100 paddlers and boaters float the river on summer days, which has led to conflict between users and wildlife, including the area's great blue heron rookery.

The highway reaches 7,908-foot-high **Aspen** and the drive's end a mile farther downstream. Aspen, Colorado's most famous ski resort, began as a silver mining camp in 1879. Prosperity poured from its wealthy lodes, including the Smuggler, Montezuma, Midnight, and Molly Gibson mines, until the great silver crash of 1893. At that time, Aspen, with a population of 12,000, was the state's third-largest city. The town, one of the first to run on electricity, boasted six newspapers, two banks, the Wheeler Opera House, and the luxurious Hotel Jerome. Victorian homes and buildings from that prosperous era still line the streets. Skiers began sampling Aspen's deep powder snow in 1936, and by the late 1940s the town stood poised to become one of America's great ski resorts.

Now Aspen boasts four great ski areas—Aspen Mountain, Aspen Highlands, Buttermilk, and Aspen Snowmass. Aspen Mountain, sometimes called Ajax, covers the mountain's north flank above the town. Founded in 1946, the small 673-acre ski area is an intimate throwback to Colorado's early skiing days in the 1960s. Aspen offers all visitor services including excellent restaurants and accommodations, as well as numerous festivals and events, including the Aspen Music Festival & School with over 300 summer events and Theatre Aspen's summer repertory featuring Broadway stars in a town park.

A popular Aspen visitor attraction is the **John Denver Sanctuary,** a small, quiet park along the south bank of the Roaring Fork River near Rio Grande Park that attracts fans of the singer-songwriter who lived in Aspen. Scattered across the compact area on the town's north side are large white boulders etched with lyrics from Denver's famous songs. John Denver loved his adopted state of Colorado, writing its second official state song, "Rocky Mountain High," after a backpacking trip to Williams Lake below Mount Sopris in the early 1970s. John died in a plane crash off Monterey, California, in October 1997.

Cottonwood Pass Scenic Drive

Buena Vista to Almont

General description: This 60-mile-long paved and gravel road crosses 12,126-foot Cottonwood Pass on the Continental Divide and follows the Taylor River to Almont.

Special attractions: Cottonwood Hot Springs, Collegiate Peaks Wilderness Area, Mount Yale, Cottonwood Pass, Taylor Reservoir, Taylor Canyon, Continental Divide, Colorado Trail, camping, hiking, backpacking, rock climbing, fly fishing.

Location: Central Colorado. Drive runs from Buena Vista in the Arkansas River Valley to Almont, 11 miles north of Gunnison.

Route name and numbers: Cottonwood Pass Road; Chaffee CR 306; FR 306, 209, and 742.

Travel season: Late spring through autumn. The drive closes after the first big snowfall and opens in late spring after snowmelt. Check with the national forest offices for opening and closure dates.

Camping: Nine national forest campgrounds are along the drive: Cottonwood Lake (25 sites), Collegiate Peaks (56 sites), Lakeview (65 sites), Lottis Creek (45 sites), Cold Spring (6 sites), Lodgepole (16 sites), Rosy Lane (20 sites), One Mile (25 sites), and North Bank (17 sites).

Services: All services are in Buena Vista, Gunnison, and Crested Butte. Limited services in Almont.

Nearby attractions: Elk Mountains, Crested Butte, West Elk Scenic Byway, Gunnison, Curecanti National Recreation Area, West Elk Wilderness Area, Tincup, Cumberland Pass, St. Elmo, Mount Princeton Hot Springs, Arkansas Headwaters State Recreation Area, Buffalo Peaks Wilderness Area.

The Route

The Sawatch Range lines the west side of the Arkansas River Valley, its high peaks soaring to meet the clouds and sky. This long mountain range, stretching over 100 miles from the Eagle River to Marshall Pass, is studded by 15 14,000-foot peaks, including 14,439-foot Mount Elbert, Colorado's highest point. Only two highways—Independence and Monarch Passes—and a handful of gravel roads cross the range.

Cottonwood Pass Road, surmounting the Continental Divide at 12,126 feet, is the only one of the gravel roads passable in a standard two-wheel-drive vehicle. The road makes a spectacular backcountry tour that is easily accessible from the Front Range cities. It threads up Cottonwood Creek past beaver ponds and along the edge of the Collegiate Peaks Wilderness Area, loops above timberline to the pass summit, and drops down through broad Taylor Park and the Taylor River Canyon to Almont and the **Gunnison River.**

Cottonwood Pass Scenic Drive

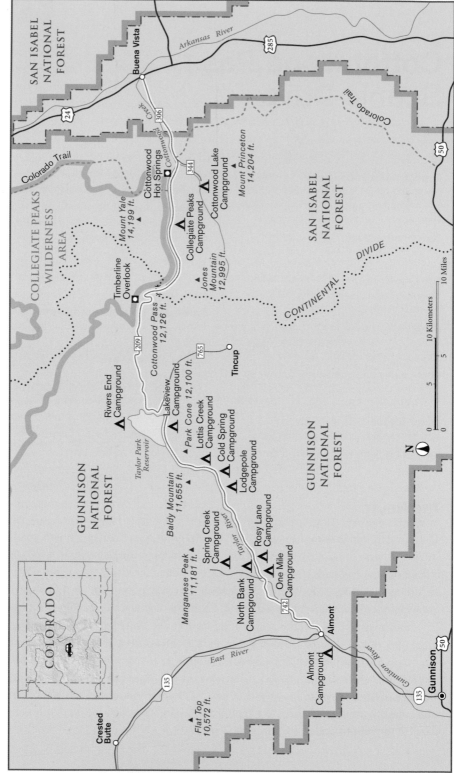

Cottonwood Pass opens in May or June, depending on snowfall amounts, and closes after the first major snow, usually in November. Check with the forest office for closure dates and road conditions. Temperatures vary greatly on the drive, depending on elevation. Summer days are pleasant, with highs ranging from 60 to 80 in the lower elevations and the 50s and 60s atop the pass. Expect afternoon thunderstorms. Watch for lightning if hiking on ridges. Temperatures begin declining in early September, with the difference between day and night temperatures differing as much as 40 degrees. September and October are generally dry, although cold fronts bring rain and snow to the high country. The drive offers one of Colorado's best foliage tours in late September.

Buena Vista

The Cottonwood Pass scenic drive begins at the traffic light marking the intersection of US 24 and Chaffee CR 306 in **Buena Vista.** The town, at an elevation of 7,954 feet, was settled by silver miners in 1879. The Denver & Rio Grande Railroad arrived in 1880 en route to the upstream Leadville mines. The town grew as a supply and transportation center for towns and mines in outlying canyons, including Clear Creek and Chalk Creek Canyons. A mill and smelter built in 1881 brought additional prosperity. Buena Vista quickly outgrew Granite, the county seat 20 miles upriver, and the town was voted the new county seat. When Granite refused to yield the county records, Buena Vista locals broke into the courthouse at night and claimed the papers and county business. Buena Vista was a rowdy town, and 36 bars did their best to fuel the brashness.

Today Buena Vista thrives on tourism and bills itself as the "Whitewater Capital of Colorado." The nickname is no lie—the Arkansas River offers some of the nation's best kayaking and rafting adventures. The Numbers rapid, upstream from town, offers a technical and treacherous run for kayakers. Brown's Canyon, the most popular river run in Colorado, lies a few miles downstream in **Browns Canyon National Monument.** The river plunges through a series of demanding rapids with names like Widowmaker, Big Drop, and Zoom Flume. Numerous outfitters offer guided river trips through the summer. The Arkansas River here is part of the 152-mile-long **Arkansas Headwaters Recreation Area,** a Colorado state parkland that stretches along the river from Leadville to Pueblo.

Buena Vista, meaning "good view" in Spanish and pronounced "BYOO-nah VIS-ta" by locals, sits in a superlative location at the confluence of Cottonwood Creek and the Arkansas River. The towering Sawatch Range, flanking the river valley to the west, forms a staggering presence. Low peaks, covered with brushy pines, rise eastward to the Buffalo Peaks at the southern end of the Mosquito Range. Westward looms the Collegiate Peaks section of the Sawatch, rising 6,000 feet from the valley. Bulky 14,201-foot Mount Princeton, with long, sweeping ridges, dominates the view. Another "Fourteener," 14,199-foot Mount Yale, lies half-hidden by lower mountains to the northwest.

Cottonwood Creek

The drive heads west from Buena Vista toward the deep cleft chiseled by Cottonwood Creek between the Mounts Princeton and Yale. The road leaves Buena Vista after a mile, running across a gravel bench dotted with scattered homes. **Cottonwood Creek** hides beneath tall cottonwoods north of the road, while Mount Princeton looms to the southwest.

After 4.5 miles the road enters **San Isabel National Forest,** a 1,120,233-acre forest that stretches across central and southern Colorado. The road enters the mountain rampart and Cottonwood Creek's canyon 0.25 mile farther up. The drive twists along the tumbling stream, its banks a tangle of cottonwoods and willows. Abrupt slopes climb north of the road, broken by white cliffs, scree, and ponderosa and piñon pines.

Cottonwood Hot Springs is on the north side of the creek as the drive enters the canyon. This no-frills hot spring resort is off-the-beaten-track and rarely visited compared to its famous neighbor Mount Princeton Hot Springs to the south. The area, once a sacred healing site for the Utes, bursts from the ground into five gravity-fed, thermal pools lined by stone walls that range between 94 and 100 degrees—perfect temperatures for a relaxing soak. The hideaway has an inn with both private and dorm rooms and creekside cabins with private soaking pools. The rustic accommodations are a far cry from 1878 when the resort had a hotel with a library, dining hall, and parlor. The area's first resident doctor said "restoration to health is assured" by soaking in "the life-giving waters." Learn more about Cottonwood Hot Springs in *Touring Colorado's Hot Springs* (FalconGuides).

A couple of miles past the hot springs, the road bends up the creek's main fork. A left turn on FR 344 runs southwest to Cottonwood Lake. This small lake nestled in woods offers good rainbow trout fishing from its banks. Cottonwood Lake Campground with 25 sites sits on the lake's south shore.

The paved road (CR 306) ascends the broad, glaciated valley for 8 miles before steeply switchbacking for 5 miles through spruce forest and open meadows to reach timberline and the cloud-scraping pass summit. The rugged country abutting the drive on the north lies within 167,584-acre **Collegiate Peaks Wilderness Area,** an untrampled swath of peaks and valleys spreading north to the highway over Independence Pass.

Mount Yale in the Collegiate Peaks Wilderness Area looms above changing aspens along the Cottonwood Pass road.

Several roadside trailheads offer access to the wilderness area. The Avalanche Trailhead, at 9 miles, twists up Avalanche Gulch on the Colorado Trail. The 56-site Collegiate Peaks Campground, a mile east of Denny Creek, is the jumping-off point for hikers to climb 14,199-foot **Mount Yale.** The 9.5-mile round-trip hike starts at the Denny Creek Trailhead, 12 miles from Buena Vista and west of the campground.

From the trailhead on the north side of the road, hike up Denny Creek Trail for 1.25 miles to the junction of the Hartenstein Lake and Mount Yale trails. Keep right on the Yale Trail and hike up Delaney Gulch. Switchback up steep grassy slopes to a shoulder at 13,900 feet on Yale's west ridge, and then scramble up Class 2 terrain to the cloud-scraping summit. An excellent 7.5-mile round-trip hike from the same trailhead is to Hartenstein Lake, a lovely alpine tarn tucked into an alpine cirque at 11,451 feet.

Jones Mountain, a round-shouldered 12,995-foot peak, dominates the upper valley. Good views of the mountain are found at **Holy Water Beaver Ponds** at mile 13. A paved parking lot allows travelers to stop and catch a glimpse of an elusive beaver swimming across a mirrored pond densely lined with willows, a favorite beaver food. The beaver, North America's largest rodent, builds numerous dams that stair-step up most of Colorado's high mountain valleys. The chains of lakes constructed by these busy conservationists combat erosion, provide flood control, and create habitat for birds and fish. Their ponds silt up over time, creating rich soil for mountain meadows. Forests of spruce, set off with glades of quaking aspen, blanket the mountain slopes above the beaver ponds.

Before the road passes Jones Mountain, the Ptarmigan Trailhead is on the left. The 3.4-mile Ptarmigan Lake Trail, a family-friendly hike, follows Ptarmigan Creek for a couple miles past two tarns and good backcountry campsites and then climbs above timberline to glassy 12,132-foot Ptarmigan Lake. Follow the trail along the east shore to the south end of the lake for the best views of Mount Yale.

Cottonwood Pass Summit

Just before the pass summit the road curves across an above-timberline cirque excavated by ancient glaciers. Low clumps of willows clot the roadside. The ascending road makes a last hairpin turn and edges along a shelf road for 0.5 mile to the 12,126-foot summit of **Cottonwood Pass.** This saddle lies astride the Continental Divide, the twisting mountain backbone that separates the Atlantic and Pacific watersheds.

Cottonwood Pass has long been an important mountain crossing. An early wagon track, roughly following today's pass road, served as the main route into Aspen until the Independence Pass trail opened in 1881. The road, although serving Tincup and Taylor Park, fell into relative disuse until the Forest Service reconstructed the road in 1960.

A spacious panoramic view enfolds from the pass summit. To the west is Taylor Park, The Three Apostles, and Castle Peak. Numerous unnamed 12,000-foot peaks in the Sawatch Range surround the pass. A short hike up the **Continental Divide Trail** scrambles south for 0.6 mile up the Divide ridge to a higher viewpoint atop unnamed Point 12,580. To climb 2 more ranked peaks, continue south on the trail for another 3.9 miles to Point 12,792 and 13,055-foot Chalk Rock Mountain. Return to Cottonwood Pass on the trail for a 9-mile hike.

Taylor Park

The pavement ends atop the pass. The west side is a gravel road for the 14 downhill miles to Taylor Park Reservoir. The drive, now FR 209, drops northwest above a high cirque and reaches Timberline Overlook, a roadside pullout, after a mile. Here the road begins descending toward the cirque floor and timberline. Spiraling down, the road parallels Pass Creek, running through spruce forest and below open slopes. Numerous beaver ponds step down the valley floor. As the road descends, the forest is mixed lodgepole pine and aspen.

After 8 miles the road reaches the edge of **Taylor Park,** a high intermontane basin covered with forest and sagebrush meadows. The park is named for James Taylor, leader of a group of 1860 prospectors. The drive gently descends over ridges and through shallow valleys. Taylor Park Ranger Station sits 12 miles from the pass summit at 9,524 feet. A mile and a half later the drive merges with paved FR 742 and turns southward. An overlook with picnic tables sits at the junction.

Taylor Park Reservoir, with 2,033 surface acres, spreads across the valley floor west of the road. The drive twists south on gravel benches above the lake. FR 765 heads east a couple of miles down the drive, leading to the picturesque mining town of Tincup. The road climbs over Cumberland Pass from Tincup and provides access to several excellent jeep trails.

The **Taylor Park Trading Post,** established in 1940, is at the junction with FR 765. The business, serving fishermen, campers, and scenic drivers, has a general store, Nugget Café, rustic cabins, and an RV park. Past the junction, the drive crosses Willow Creek and turns west above the lake. A viewpoint offers excellent views of the wind-tossed lake and a long row of peaks perched on the Continental Divide. Lakeview Campground, with 65 sites, sits south of the drive, while another road offers lake access at the Taylor Park Marina. The regularly stocked lake yields excellent fishing for trophy-sized lake trout, northern pike, kokanee salmon, and rainbow, brown, and Snake River cutthroat trout.

Taylor Canyon to Almont

The road continues along the lake's southern shore, winding through lodgepole pines and blue spruce. After 2 miles the drive reaches the large earthen dam that forms the reservoir and drops into **Taylor Canyon.** Taylor Dam Vista Point overlooks the dam. The 206-foot-high dam, finished in 1937, backs up 106,200 acre-feet of Sawatch snowmelt used for summer irrigation water.

The drive, paved FR 742, follows the **Taylor River** for 21 miles through Taylor Canyon to **Almont** and the Taylor River's confluence with the East River. Steep walls, blanketed with spruce, pine, and aspen and broken by ragged cliffs, climb above the river to 12,100-foot Park Cone and 11,655-foot Baldy Mountain in the upper gorge. The river rushes through cobbled rapids and pools in deep ponds by dark boulders. The Taylor River offers productive fly fishing for rainbow and brown trout. Be aware that private property borders much of the river. Look for public access areas.

A trio of forest campgrounds—45-site Lottis Creek (4 ADA sites and 38 electric sites), 6-site Cold Spring, and 16-site Lodgepole—scatter above the river in the central canyon. Farther west are 20-site Rosy Lane, 25-site One Mile, and 17-site North Bank campgrounds. Decent rock climbing is found on the towering granite cliffs near North Bank. More broken cliffs scatter along the canyon flank.

The canyon widens past the campgrounds and leaves Gunnison National Forest. Dry, rolling hills tinted gray with sagebrush surround the canyon, with groves of spruce and fir tucked into moist side ravines. Hay fields and cattle spread across the wide canyon floor, before the river again plunges into a cliff-lined gorge. **Gunnison Mountain Park,** with a campground, picnic facilities, pavilion, river access, and nature trail, lies below cliff bands in this lower canyon. The prominent cliffs, called Tombstone Wall and Decade Wall, have bolt-protected climbs up metamorphic rock. Cottonwoods and willows border the tumbling Taylor River.

At Almont, a small resort town, the road and drive dead-ends on CO 135. The East and Taylor Rivers join here in this shallow valley to form the Gunnison River, which runs 165 miles from here to its confluence with the Colorado River in Grand Junction. Almont, established in 1881 as a railroad stop, was named for a famed Kentucky racehorse. A turn north or right on CO 135 leads 17 miles to Crested Butte, a classic Colorado mountain town, while a south or left turn heads 11 miles to Gunnison and US 50.

West Elk Loop Scenic Byway

Gunnison to Crested Butte to Paonia to Blue Mesa Reservoir

General description: This 164-mile-long loop drive encircles the West Elk Mountains, passing numerous geologic features, aspen woodlands, and spacious valleys.

Special attractions: Curecanti National Recreation Area, Dillon Pinnacles, Blue Mesa Reservoir, Morrow Point Reservoir, West Elk Wilderness Area, Crawford State Park, Needle Rock, Lost Lake, Kebler Pass, Crested Butte National Historic District, Crested Butte Mountain Resort, hiking, camping, backpacking, sailboarding, skiing, scenic views, fall colors, fishing.

Location: West-central Colorado. The drive makes a loop around the West Elk Mountains between Gunnison, Paonia, and Crested Butte.

Route name and numbers: West Elk Loop Scenic Byway; US 50; CO 92, 133, and 135; Gunnison CR 12.

Travel season: The paved highway portions are open year-round, although snow may temporarily close the highways. Adequate snow tires or chains are advised. The gravel road over Kebler Pass closes in winter and opens in late spring when the snow melts away.

Camping: Numerous campgrounds lie along the drive. In Curecanti National Recreation Area are 6 on the highway: Stevens Creek (53 sites), Elk Creek (160 sites), East Elk Creek (1 site), Dry Gulch (9 sites), Red Creek (2 sites), and Lake Fork (90 sites). Crawford State Park has 2 campgrounds: Iron Creek (45 sites), Clear Fork (21 sites). Other campgrounds on the drive are Erickson Springs (18 sites), Lost Lake Campground (19 sites), and Lake Irwin Campground (25 sites), and Almont (10 sites).

Services: All services in Gunnison, Crawford, Hotchkiss, Paonia, and Crested Butte.

Nearby attractions: Black Canyon of the Gunnison National Park, Gunnison Gorge, Grand Mesa, Lake City, McClure Pass, Maroon Bells–Snowmass Wilderness Area, Glenwood Hot Springs, Marble, Cottonwood Pass, Tincup.

The Route

The 164-mile-long West Elk Loop Scenic Byway loops around the rugged **West Elk Mountains** in western Colorado. The drive explores a diverse landscape. Precipitous peaks lift snow-capped summits into the turquoise sky. Aspens spread golden tapestries across rolling hillsides. Granite cliffs stud sharp canyons, their walls chiseled by time and the river. It's a land of majestic grandeur, but it's also a land of details waiting to be discovered. It's in those close-up vignettes that the world comes more alive—the clarity of a jewel-like dewdrop on a shaft of grama grass; the rustle of scrub oak leaves from a rufous-sided towhee; the cold smoothness of a river-worn cobble; ridgeline trees silhouetted against an evening thunderstorm.

West Elk Loop Scenic Byway

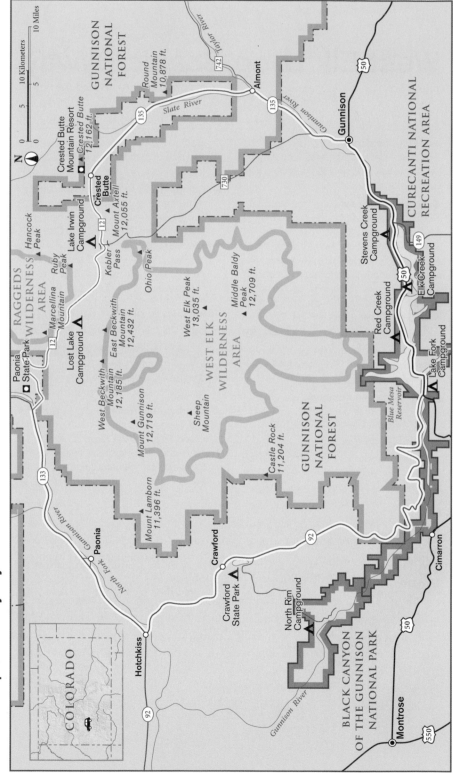

Traffic along the drive's 132 paved miles and 32 gravel miles is generally light, although the US 50 section west of Gunnison can be busy in summer. The mountain roads are winding and narrow, with occasional turnoffs. Watch for blind corners. The gravel segment is easily driven in summer and fall by passenger cars. Muddy and slick patches linger after heavy rain. Winter snow closes Kebler Pass, although the rest of the route remains open.

Summer and autumn are the best times to drive the roads, with pleasant daily high temperatures between 60 and 80 degrees, depending on the elevation. A range of elevations, from 5,351 feet at Hotchkiss to the 9,980-foot summit of Kebler Pass, and the diverse topography make for a variety of climates and ecosystems on the drive. Expect regular afternoon thunderstorms in summer, with localized heavy rain on the mountains. Occasional cool, rainy periods occur in September, and by late October snow falls on the high country. Winters are frigid. Every winter Gunnison, lying in a valley, records a number of national lows with below-zero temperatures. Daily highs climb into the 20s. Crested Butte tends to be a little warmer, but an annual average of 230 inches of snow falls on its ski slopes. Warmer winter weather and less snow are found in the North Fork Valley at Paonia and Hotchkiss. Spring begins in April at the lower elevations and creeps up the slopes until early June, when most of the snow is melted. Spring brings unpredictable weather with warm, breezy days and unsettled periods with rain and sleet.

Gunnison to Crawford

The drive begins in **Gunnison** on US 50. Gunnison, at 7,703 feet, sits in the broad Gunnison Valley at the confluence of the Gunnison River and Tomichi Creek. Gunnison has strong farming and ranching roots, although it was established in 1880 as a railroad stop and supply center for nearby mining areas. Originally called Richardson's Colony for local town organizer Dr. Sylvester Richardson, the community was renamed for ill-fated railroad surveyor Captain John Gunnison. Gunnison and his party, surveying a possible transcontinental railroad route, camped here on September 6, 1853. The group explored westward along today's US 50, before Gunnison and 7 of his party were killed by a band of Pahvant Utes in Utah's Sevier Valley in late October. Gunnison, home of Western Colorado University, thrives as a ranching and tourism hub.

The drive's 28-mile first segment goes west on US 50. The highway runs through the broad river valley lush with cattle paddocks and hay fields. Narrowleaf cottonwoods densely line the Gunnison River's banks. Just west of Gunnison, a left turn leads south to **Hartman Rocks Recreation Area,** with over 14,000 acres managed by the Bureau of Land Management and 160 acres managed by the City of Gunnison off Gold Basin Road. The recreation area's rolling hills, 4 miles southwest of town, are covered with sagebrush, laced with hiking and mountain biking trails, and studded with granite outcrops that offer lots of fun climbing adventures. Check *Rock Climbing Colorado* (FalconGuides) for info on climbing at Hartman Rocks. Hartman Rocks has 45 miles of singletrack trails, 45 miles of roads, and 50 designated campsites. In winter, 16 miles of roads are groomed for cross-country skiing and a few miles of singletrack trails are groomed for fat-tire biking.

After a few miles, the highway and river enter **Curecanti National Recreation Area,** a 43,095-acre site managed by the National Park Service. Blue Mesa, Morrow Point, and Crystal Lakes, part of the Bureau of Reclamation's Colorado River Storage Project, offer fishing, camping, and boating recreation and provide water for irrigation and hydroelectric power. The two lower reservoirs fill the narrow floor of the Gunnison River's upper Black Canyon, forming long, fjordlike lakes, while **Blue Mesa Reservoir,** the upper reservoir, drowns a wide valley.

The highway enters a shallow canyon and passes Neversink, Cooper Ranch, and Beaver Creek picnic areas. All three offer Gunnison River fishing access. Past Beaver Creek the highway winds alongside upper Blue Mesa Reservoir, a narrow lake amid granite bluffs and sagebrush-covered hillsides. At the Lake City Bridge and the junction with CO 149, the lake opens into broad Iola Basin.

The highway borders Blue Mesa Reservoir for the next 19 miles to its dam. Blue Mesa, Colorado's largest reservoir, stretches 20 miles from its dam to the inlet near Gunnison, covers 9,000 surface acres when full, boasts 96 miles of shoreline, and reaches 330 feet in depth near its dam. Blue Mesa is Curecanti's most accessible and most popular recreation site. The lake offers excellent fishing, particularly for big mackinaw lake trout. The largest "macs," preferring deep, cold water, reach weights exceeding 30 pounds. Kokanee salmon and brown and rainbow trout also flourish in Blue Mesa Reservoir. The reservoir also offers excellent winter ice fishing.

High, flat-topped mesas, capped with a layer of volcanic West Elk breccia, surround Blue Mesa Reservoir. The breccia, a mixture of ejected rock fragments and ash, exploded from immense volcanoes in today's West Elk and San Juan Mountains. Below the mesa rims, erosion chisels strange shapes from the volcanic palisades.

Several picnic areas and campgrounds scatter along the lake and highway. Stevens Creek Campground, 12 miles west of Gunnison, offers 53 lakeside sites in 3 loops. Elk Creek Campground spreads 160 sites across a dry vale. Some sites are handicap-accessible and a concessionaire offers showers. Nearby is the Curecanti visitor center with informative displays on area natural history, history, geology, and recreational opportunities. The Bay of Chickens, a mile past Elk Creek and the visitor center, is the lake's best sailboarding area. Nine-site Dry Gulch and

2-site Red Creek Campgrounds are located off the drive in their respective side canyons north of the highway.

The Dillon Pinnacles Trail begins at a trailhead with a picnic area and restrooms on the north side of the Middle Bridge between the lake's Sapinero and Cebolla basins. The **Dillon Pinnacles,** a bizarre collection of spires, buttresses, gargoyles, fins, and hoodoos, sits prominently above the drive near the lake's west end. The 2-mile trail climbs to a bench below the pinnacles. Sagebrush colors the rounded mesa slopes above the lake a dull gray, while green cottonwoods and scrub oak tint side canyons and ravines.

The drive crosses the bridge, passes a scenic overlook of the Dillon Pinnacles above the south shore, and loops around Sapinero Mesa's broad north flank to the Lake Fork Bridge over the Lake Fork Arm. The 65-mile-long Lake Fork of the Gunnison River drains south of its headwaters at Sloan Lake below Handies Peak south of Lake City. Lake Fork Campground, with 90 sites, is on the right past the bridge. US 50 climbs a hill and intersects CO 92, the second leg of the byway journey.

Turn north or right on CO 92. The drive's second segment travels 52 miles to Hotchkiss in the North Fork Valley. The two-lane highway drops past 90-site Lake Fork Campground, a pull-through RV camping area, and crosses Blue Mesa Lake's 342-foot-high earth and concrete dam. The dam, completed in 1965, plugs the narrow river channel with over three million cubic yards of fill. The highway creeps across the 800-foot-long dam and twists onto a bench above Morrow Point Lake and the precipitous upper **Black Canyon of the Gunnison River.**

The Black Canyon, one of Colorado's most startling earth features, stretches 50 miles through the Gunnison Uplift. The Gunnison River, the state's fourth-largest river, sliced into ancient two-billion-year-old bedrock over the last three million years to create this marvelous chasm. The river cuts downward about 1 inch per century. The lower canyon is protected in Black Canyon of the Gunnison National Park, while the upper canyon hides two fingering reservoirs beneath somber canyon walls.

The highway winds along a granite bench along the north edge of the canyon. Geologists say the bench is the erosional remnant of a gentle highland that rose here over two billion years ago. Above the bench stretch the Morrison Formations multicolored layers of siltstone, sandstone, and mudstone and Dakota sandstone, and rimming the mesas above is West Elk breccia.

The road passes several scenic viewpoints before reaching **Pioneer Point** in Curecanti National Recreation Area. Two spectacular overlooks, reached by a half-mile trail, view the inner gorge. Curecanti Needle, one of the canyon's prominent landmarks, juts into Morrow Point Lake far below. The 700-foot-high pyramid-shaped Needle once was the emblem of the Denver & Rio Grande Railroad, which

traversed the canyon in the 1880s. Trains often stopped for travelers to admire Curecanti Needle. The excellent **Curecanti Creek Trail,** beginning at the parking area, descends 2 miles and loses 900 feet of elevation in a side canyon to the lake.

The drive bends away from the gorge at Pioneer Point and runs north up Curecanti Creek's valley before crossing the creek and climbing southward through thick aspen forest. The road clings to steep slopes above Morrow Point Lake and bends through shallow valleys. The southern edge of Black Mesa forms a cliffed palisade above the road. Aspens and scrub oaks blanket roadside slopes.

Hermits Rest Overlook, the next stop, is a lofty 8,973-foot viewpoint poised almost 2,000 feet above the lake. Steep slopes loom above the green water, breaking to crags and forested ridges. Beyond tower the San Juan Mountains, including bulky 14,308-foot Uncompahgre Peak and pointed 14,016-foot Wetterhorn Peak. The overlook, part of the recreation area, has a large parking area, restrooms, picnic tables under a pavilion, and interpretive signs. The strenuous 3-mile-long Hermits Rest Trail descends 1,800 feet to the lake and a primitive campground.

The highway bends away from the canyon brink, doglegs through a couple of moist ravines filled with trickling creeks and aspen groves, and emerges on the rounded rim above **Crystal Lake.** The Crystal Creek Trail leads 2.5 miles west through scrub oak and aspen forest to a sweeping 8,900-foot overlook above the lake and distant mountain views. The road descends north through oak thickets into Crystal Creek's shallow valley. Past Big Hill, the highway skirts Crystal Valley and drops into Onion Valley. Low hills covered with piñon pine and juniper trees flank the valley.

The road swings past Gould Reservoir and numerous ranches before reaching 734-acre **Crawford State Park** and its 400-acre reservoir. This area offers excellent perch and crappie fishing, boating, waterskiing, swimming, and 45-site Iron Creek and 21-site Clear Fork Campgrounds. The park makes a perfect base camp for exploring the surrounding area, including the Black Canyon of the Gunnison National Park and West Elk Mountains. A turn at the lake leads 11 miles south to the North Rim of the Black Canyon of the Gunnison National Park. The wild and remote North Rim gives excellent views into the yawning granite abyss, a scenic rim drive, and a 13-site campground.

Crawford to Paonia

The highway crosses the Smith Fork River and enters **Crawford.** This pleasant ranching town, named for Native American scout and former Kansas governor

The view from Hermit's Rest Overlook includes Morrow Point Lake in the upper Black Canyon and the distant San Juan Mountains.

Captain George Crawford, began as a layover on the arduous Hartman Cattle Trail between Gunnison and the North Fork Valley. By 1881 ranchers had settled the area, bringing cattle herds to graze the upland meadows, and the town was established in 1883. The old cow town still has cattle drives on its main street, but also quaint bed-and-breakfast inns, cafes, and a few shops. If you're hankering for lunch, stop by Diamond Joe Café or Old Mad Dog Café, originally opened by rock-and-roller Joe Cocker.

Crawford sits in a spectacular setting. Grand Mesa rims the northern skyline and the spiked peaks of the West Elk Range fill the eastern horizon. Most of the West Elks are protected in the 176,412-acre **West Elk Wilderness Area,** one of Colorado's largest wildernesses. The range boasts numerous high peaks, including 13,035-foot West Elk Peak, the range high point.

Needle Rock, rising above the Smith Fork valley east of Crawford, is a Delta County landmark. The formation, towering 800 feet above the valley is the hardened throat or conduit of an extinct volcano. The rock, forming a volcanic plug, is solidified lava that remained after the volcano's softer outer layers eroded away. Drive a few miles out Needle Rock Road from Crawford to see the wonder upclose. A parking area on its southeast side is the trailhead for the quarter-mile Needle Rock Trail which climbs to the rock's north side. Rock climbers continue to the airy summit by ascending steep, rotten rock on a route first climbed by 15-year-old Ward Rube in 1921.

The drive turns northwest from Crawford onto fertile Crawford Mesa and drops 11 miles through barren shale hills to 5,351-foot-high **Hotchkiss** in the North Fork Valley. Hotchkiss, nicknamed "The Friendliest Town Around," was the first hamlet established in the fertile North Fork Valley along the North Fork of the Gunnison River. Enos T. Hotchkiss wandered into the valley, a popular Ute wintering site, in 1879 and returned with others in 1881 after the Utes were removed to reservations. Hotchkiss homesteaded the area and planted an orchard. A small community of homesteaders, ranchers, and farmers sprang up, and the town incorporated in 1901. The town's first commercial building, listed on the National Register of Historical Places, was an old hotel that now houses several shops. The railroad, en route to the up-valley coal mines, came through in 1902. Hotchkiss continues its rural tradition with an economy based, as it was more than a century ago, on cattle, sheep, fruit, logging, and the annual Delta County Fair each August.

CO 92 intersects CO 133 in Hotchkiss. Turn east on CO 133 for the drive's 24-mile third leg. The highway crosses cornfields and climbs onto a shale bluff

Anthracite Creek joins the North Fork of the Gunnison River on the edge of the West Elk Mountains.

north of the river. A couple of pullouts overlook the broad valley. The river riffles below over gravel bars. Thick cottonwoods broken by pastures cover its floodplain. The **West Elk Range,** including 11,396-foot Mount Lamborn and 10,806-foot Landsend Peak, dominate the valley view. The highway descends onto the valley's north edge and runs through a pastoral countryside with hay fields and grazing cattle and horses. **Paonia** is reached after 9 miles.

While the drive and highway bypass Paonia on its north side, it's worth a turn on CO 187 to visit the town. Paonia, situated on the south bank of the North Fork of the Gunnison, lies at the upper end of North Fork Valley, with mountains and mesas looming above. The town, established in 1881 by rancher Samuel Wade, was named Paonia, a misspelling of the Latin name for peonia, a common area flower. In 1882 Wade brought a trunk of young fruit saplings from Gunnison on a difficult, cold two-week trek, giving the town its main business for the next century. The orchards flourished in the valley's mild climate, with its more than 300 sunny days a year and cool nights. Paonia, with more than 3,000 residents, thrives with its orchards, nearby coal mining, sheep and cattle ranching, and its many artists and artisans. The town once made *Ripley's Believe It or Not* with its record 20 churches per capita. A chamber of commerce visitor center sits along the drive just north of Paonia.

Quaint Paonia is simply Colorado's coolest town, with quiet streets lined with shady cottonwoods and a diverse population of artists, hippies, mountain bikers, vintners, and farmers. Grand Avenue, the walkable 2-block downtown district, is where it all happens. Park and stroll down Grand and you'll find an eclectic mix of shops, galleries, and restaurants, including Blue Sage Center for the Arts, Paradise Theater, Ollie's Ice Cream Shop, Nelle's Café, and the Living Farm Café, which dishes out delicious locally grown food with vegan options. On the edge of town are produce stands, you-pick-it farms, and wineries.

Paonia and the North Fork Valley is considered the birthplace of Colorado's farm-to-table movement with farms, orchards, and gardens filled with fresh, organic food that's now appearing in swank restaurants from Telluride to Aspen. The town is also the epicenter of the **West Elk Viticultural Area,** with numerous vineyards and wineries surrounding the town, including the highest ones in North America. Most have tasting rooms open from Memorial Day through September.

Four wineries north of town are worth a taste. Black Bridge Winery near the river offers an earthy Pinot Noir. Drive back roads to the other ones on the high mesa north of Paonia and the North Fork. Azura Cellars has a delicious Pinot Gris that's sampled from a patio with spacious mountain views. Reach Stone Cottage Cellars on a steep dirt road and taste test berry-flavored Merlots in a stone cottage. Then head to Terror Creek Winery, supposedly the highest commercial vineyard in the world at 6,400 feet. If you prefer craft beers, stop at Revolution Brewing in Paonia for ales, porters, and IPAs made from locally grown hops.

Paonia to Kebler Pass

Past Paonia the North Fork Valley begins to narrow, with steep shale hillsides covered with piñon pine, juniper, and scrub oak climbing away from the river. Orchards, including apple, pear, peach, and cherry, line the highway and perch on river terraces. **Delta County,** with over 450,000 apple trees, produces two-thirds of Colorado's apples.

The narrow, 15-mile canyon between Paonia and Paonia Reservoir boasts a long history of coal mining. The highway runs past several mining towns, including Somerset. Coal, first discovered here in 1883, boomed during World War I when the town peaked with about 700 residents, and again in the 1970s. Even in 2000, 4 working mines—Somerset, Bear, West Elk, and Cyprus—produced over three million tons of coal annually. As America has moved away from coal to alternative sources of clean energy and natural gas, the coal industry declined along with Somerset's economy. While 950 miners worked at three coal mines in early 2010, by 2017 only 220 miners remained at the West Elk Mine east of town. Most of the coal silos along the highway, which allowed for rapid loading of railroad cars, have been demolished.

The canyon narrows past Somerset and the road winds above the river. Below Paonia Dam, the drive intersects Gunnison CR 12, the 32-mile fourth segment of the drive. CO 133 continues north past Paonia State Park, and over McClure Pass to Carbondale.

Turn right or east on CR 12 and head up Anthracite Creek's canyon. This gravel road section to Crested Butte offers some of Colorado's best back road scenery and spectacular aspen foliage in late September. The road runs up the canyon for 6 miles, its south-facing flank coated with scrub oak and mountain mahogany and its cross-river north-facing flank dense with aspen, spruce, and fir trees. Erickson Springs Campground, with 18 campsites, restrooms, tent pads, and a well, nestles below the Raggeds Wilderness Area. Past the campground is the trailhead for Dark Canyon Trail (#830), a scenic trail across the south part of the Raggeds Wilderness Area with a deep canyon, waterfalls, and spectacular views.

The road crosses the creek here and begins steeply switchbacking up the valley's south slope. After climbing for a couple of miles, the angle eases and the road bends across Watson Flats through oak thickets and open meadows. The drive bends east and heads toward 11,348-foot Marcellina Mountain, an immense rocky peak seamed with snow gullies and serrated rock ridges. The West Elk Range looms to the south across a broad aspen-filled valley, including 12,185-foot West Beckwith Mountain and 12,432-foot East Beckwith Mountain.

The road, following an old Ute trail, runs across a rolling bench below Marcellina Peak through lovely aspen groves. Two wilderness areas flank the drive.

Ruby Peak and The Dyke ridge anchor the southern end of the Ruby Range above Kebler Pass.

The 65,393-acre **Raggeds Wilderness Area** protects a magnificent swath of high peaks, including Marcellina Mountain, north of the byway. The **West Elk Wilderness** encompasses the volcanic West Elk Range to the south. Both Beckwith Mountains and the Anthracite Range south of Kebler Pass lie in the wilderness area.

The road scales a rounded ridge below Marcellina Mountain, passes the Ruby Anthracite Trail (#836), and 1.5 miles later reaches a right turn to **Lost Lake Slough.** This national forest road (FR 706) climbs 2 miles south to the lake, a tranquil pond cradled in a glacier-carved basin beneath East Beckwith Mountain. The peak soars above aspen and spruce forest and ridges lined with cliffs. This idyllic spot, with 19-site Lost Lake Campground and good fishing, makes a pleasant overnight stay. The campground has 5 sites for campers with horses. Nearby is an accessible picnic area and a fishing platform on the north side of the lake.

The 4.7-mile Lost Lake Loop Trail is an easy day hike that passes three lakes—Lost Lake Slough, Lost Lake, and Dollar Lake—and offers superb views, a waterfall, summer wildflowers, and gentle grades.

The drive continues over aspen-covered hills and twists down to Anthracite Creek and Horse Ranch Park, a spacious valley filled with low willows. The road bends east along the creek and skirts The Dyke, a sawtoothed wall of pinnacles that marks the southern end of the Ruby Range. The Ruby Range, a small sierra that connects the Elk Range on the north to the West Elk Range, is a long ridge decorated with numerous sharp peaks. Ruby Peak and Mount Owen, the 13,058-foot range high point, tower north of The Dyke.

The road gently climbs out of the valley through a thick spruce woodland and tops out on the wide 9,980-foot summit of **Kebler Pass.** A few lonely gravestones sit in the old Irwin Cemetery atop the pass. The silver mining town of Irwin once thrived near here, with over 5,000 residents in 1879 despite the town's location on Ute territory. The town once boasted a bank, the *Pilot* newspaper, hotels, 3 churches, 6 sawmills, 23 saloons, and the exclusive Irwin Club, which hosted ex-president Ulysses S. Grant in 1880. Irwin quietly faded away after the great silver crash of 1893. A side trip on FR 730 begins just east of the Kebler summit and heads south to 10,033-foot Ohio Pass and down Ohio Creek to Gunnison.

Kebler Pass to Gunnison

The scenic drive continues east on CR 12, swinging north from the pass and descending into Coal Creek's glaciated valley. The road bends east almost a mile from the pass. A left turn here on FR 826 bumps two miles north to **Lake Irwin,** a picturesque lake tucked into the east flank of the Ruby Range. A 25-site campground sits alongside the popular lake. From the turn, the drive drops down Coal Creek's narrow canyon 7 miles to Crested Butte along a wide road that follows the abandoned Crested Butte branch of the Denver & Rio Grande Railroad.

Crested Butte, a charming, unpretentious Victorian town, offers superb powder skiing in winter and is Colorado's mountain bike capital in summer. The picturesque town, hiding in the morning shadow of 12,162-foot Crested Butte, its namesake peak, sits at 8,885 feet in a basin surrounded by lofty peaks. Crested Butte began as a gold camp and supply center in the early 1880s. As the gold and silver boom abated, discoveries of nearby high-grade coal deposits turned Crested Butte into a Colorado Fuel & Iron company town until the mine closed in 1952. Snow measured in feet allowed Crested Butte to reinvent itself from a shuttered mining town to a recreational playground in the early 1960s when Mt. Crested Butte Ski Area opened its slopes.

Much of old Crested Butte, a National Historic District, retains its 19th-century ambiance with historic log cabins and Victorian-era buildings. The town, respecting its mining roots, is a place where locals have traded gold pans, picks, and hardhats for downhill skis, mountain bikes, and hiking boots. A walking tour explores historic Crested Butte, threading down Elk Avenue, the town's main drag, and exploring side streets lined with renovated miner's cabins and painted-lady Victorians.

Crested Butte and Mount Crested Butte, its ski resort neighbor three miles up the valley, is a year-round playground. While downhill and Nordic skiing rules the winter, a diversity of outdoor fun brings hikers, mountaineers, mountain bikers, wildflower-lovers, photographers, and fishermen to the Butte's streets. Besides walking down friendly Elk Avenue, Crested Butte offers world-class mountain scenery, superb restaurants and brewpubs, and festivals.

A popular summer pastime is stopping on Elk Avenue at the Eldo Brewery and Tap Room for a homemade brewski on their sunny second-floor deck. Another local pub is Irwin Brewing Company on Belleview Avenue. Just down Elk Avenue is the Mountain Bike Hall of Fame, which depicts the rise of the clunker bikes first used to cross Pearl Pass to Aspen in 1976, and the Crested Butte Western Heritage Museum with exhibits on the area's mining, ranching, and skiing heritage.

Crested Butte, billing itself as the "Last Great Colorado Ski Town," takes its snow seriously. Crested Butte Mountain Resort is built on snow, with an average of 300 inches or 25 feet of snow, blanketing the mountain every winter. Most of the snow is deep powder—perfect for skiing and snowboarding. Of course, sometimes there's too much white stuff, like the 90 inches that fell in 10 days in January 2017. So much snow fell that the ski area closed for a couple days for avalanche control. When the slopes finally opened, the local snow pirates were first in line for the season's best runs.

Crested Butte Mountain Resort offers some of Colorado's best skiing, with not only deep snow but also varied terrain, a long season, a ski school, three terrain parks, spectacular scenery, and, best of all, few crowds. The resort, at least a 5-hour drive from the Front Range cities in dry road conditions, is remote and off-the-beaten-ski-track. The mountain offers 1,547 skiable acres on the northern slopes of Crested Butte Mountain and 2,775 feet of vertical drop from the top of High Lift to the base. Expert skiers can trek to the summit for a 3,062-foot run down Peak and Treasury Trails. While the mountain is renowned for extreme skiing, with 542 acres of double-black diamond terrain, over 80% of its trails are for beginner and intermediate skiers.

Don't forget to stop for lunch on the mountain at Colorado's coolest après ski bar. **The Ice Bar,** a ski-in bar and restaurant in front of Uley's Cabin mid-mountain, is made of blocks of ice so keep your hats and gloves on while imbibing. After a Colorado craft beer or a cocktail like a Breath of God, a local favorite made with rum, beer, cassis, and bitters, order a gourmet lunch like Alamosa Striped Bass Filet or Elk Bourguignon. Bon appétit!

Crested Butte, lying below its namesake mountain, offers high-country ambiance, Victorian storefronts, and great skiing.

Surrounding Crested Butte are over 50 kilometers of groomed cross-country ski trails. **The Nordic Center** by downtown Crested Butte offers ski rentals, clinics, lessons, and backcountry tours. There is plenty more x-country skiing in the Slate River Valley and up to the classic mining town of Gothic to the north.

Besides fabulous skiing, Crested Butte offers winter festivals and events for your amusement. **Big Air on Elk** is one of the best. Elk Street shuts down for a few days while skiers pulled by snowmobiles fly off a 50-foot jump while hundreds of partying spectators cheer. The Extremes competition in March brings the world's best skiers who plunge down runs like The Big Hourglass, which is so dangerous it's not open to skiers. Later in March is the Al Johnson Memorial Uphill-Downhill Race, a crazy event that features wild costumes.

Crested Butte is also ground-zero for Colorado mountain biking. This is one of the places where mountain biking was invented in the United States in the late 1970s when locals pedaled clunkers over Pearl Pass. They refined their bikes, created a new sport, and Crested Butte became the capital of American mountain biking. The area offers over 750 miles of singletrack trails, old mining tracks, and 4x4 roads from easy cruiser rides to bone-jarring descents. Beginner rides include trails at the ski resort, Lupine Trail, Cement Creek Trail, and Wagon Trail. Experts hit the famed **Trail 401** with a 1,500-foot descent down Mount Belleview, Dyke Trail, Strand Hill Trail, Teocalli Trail, and Doctor Park Trail.

After entering Crested Butte, follow Whiterock Avenue for 0.5 mile to 6th Street and CO 135. Turn south on CO 135. This last part of the scenic drive travels 28 miles south to Gunnison and the drive's endpoint. The highway runs along the Slate River in a broad, grassy valley. Whetstone and Red Mountains, their lower slopes cloaked in aspens and evergreens, loom to the west. After a few miles the Slate joins the East River. The road continues along the East River and passes through a narrow canyon below humpbacked 10,878-foot Round Mountain. Low sagebrush-covered hills border the valley and highway. At Almont the East and Taylor Rivers combine to form the Gunnison River. The highway runs through low bluffs along the Gunnison, passes 10-site Almont Campground, and emerges into a broad valley. The last 11 miles traverse the Gunnison River's cottonwood-lined banks. Small ranches and fields full of grazing cattle and horses line the asphalt. The highway passes the Ohio Pass turnoff and bends south to downtown Gunnison and US 50 at the drive's end.

Silver Thread Scenic Byway

South Fork to Blue Mesa Reservoir

General description: This 117-mile route follows the Rio Grande and climbs over Spring Creek Pass and the Continental Divide to historic Lake City in the heart of the San Juan Mountains. It finishes by heading north across sagebrush-covered hills to Blue Mesa Reservoir.

Special attractions: Wagon Wheel Gap, Creede National Historic District, Rio Grande, Clear Creek Falls, Spring Creek Pass, Slumgullion Earthflow, Colorado Trail, La Garita Wilderness Area, Weminuche Wilderness Area, Lake San Cristobal, Lake City National Historic District, hiking, camping, fishing, backpacking, scenic views.

Location: South-central Colorado. The highway runs between South Fork on the west edge of the San Luis Valley to Lake City, 55 miles southwest of Gunnison. It ends at US 50 and Blue Mesa Reservoir.

Route name and number: Silver Thread Scenic Byway, CO 149.

Travel season: Year-round. The highway may occasionally close due to heavy snow. Carry chains and be prepared for bad weather in winter.

Camping: Seven national forest campgrounds—Palisade (12 sites), Marshall Park (16 sites), Rio Grande (7 sites), Bristol Head (15 sites), Silver Thread (11 sites), North Clear Creek (21 sites), and Slumgullion Pass (21 sites)—are along the drive. The BLM's Gate Campground (8 sites) is north of Lake City.

Services: All services are in South Fork, Creede, and Lake City.

Nearby attractions: San Luis Valley, Los Caminos Antiguos Scenic Byway (Scenic Drive 6), Wheeler Geologic Area, San Luis Peak, San Juan National Forest, Alpine Loop Back Country Byway, Handies Peak, Big Blue Wilderness Area, Uncompahgre Peak, Curecanti National Recreation Area.

The Route

The Silver Thread Scenic Byway, following CO 149 between South Fork and Blue Mesa Reservoir, traverses a spectacular, off-the-beaten-track part of Colorado. The drive parallels the Rio Grande below a palisade of towering cliffs, passes through historic Creede, climbs over lofty Spring Creek and Slumgullion Passes, crosses an active earthflow, passes through historic Lake City in the rugged San Juan Mountains, and ends at Blue Mesa Reservoir west of Gunnison.

The San Juans, Colorado's largest mountain range, are a tumble of peaks and canyons that spread across 10,000 square miles, an area the size of Vermont. The range encompasses almost all of southwestern Colorado south of the Gunnison River and west of the San Luis Valley and includes nine subranges: Sneffels Range, San Miguel Range, La Plata Mountains, La Garita Mountains, Needles Range, West Needles Range, Rico Mountains, Grenadier Range, and Piedra Mountains. The San Juans boast 10 14,000-foot peaks and over a million acres preserved in

Silver Thread Scenic Byway

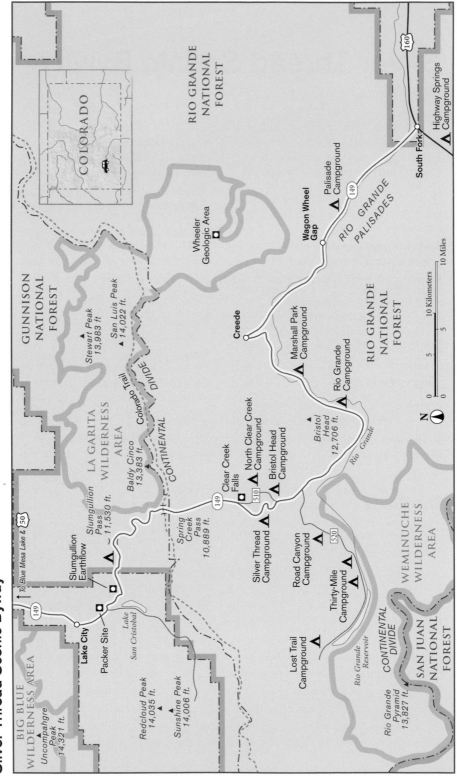

wilderness areas. The mountains are also the headwaters of numerous rivers, including the Rio Grande and the Dolores, Animas, San Miguel, Lake Fork, San Juan, Piedra, and Uncompahgre Rivers.

Climate changes dramatically along the byway because of a wide range of elevations, from 8,180 feet at South Fork to 11,530 feet atop Slumgullion Pass, the drive's high point. Summer days along the Rio Grande range into the 80s, but are usually cooler at the upper elevations. Expect afternoon thunderstorms, particularly in July and August, with locally heavy rain. Nights at the campgrounds are cool. Autumn offers warm weather, with generally clear skies and golden aspens. Cold fronts sweeping out of the north often bring snow in October. Winter arrives by late October and locks the land in a blanket of white until April. The road occasionally closes with heavy snow. Carry chains, a shovel, and extra clothes in winter. Snow lingers on the higher elevations well into early summer. The San Juan Mountains, the wettest part of Colorado, receive as much as 50 inches of annual precipitation and 350 inches of snow. Spring weather is unpredictable, with rain, snow, sleet, sun, and wind possible—all on the same day.

South Fork to Creede

The 117-mile Silver Thread Scenic Byway, a designated National Forest Byway, begins at the junction of US 160 and CO 149 in **South Fork,** 48 miles west of Alamosa on the western edge of the San Luis Valley. South Fork, a small resort and lumber town at the foot of Wolf Creek Pass, straddles the confluence of the Rio Grande and the South Fork of the Rio Grande. Head northwest up the Rio Grande's canyon on CO 149.

The road leaves South Fork and crosses the Rio Grande after 0.5 mile and enters 1.86-million-acre **Rio Grande National Forest** almost 5 miles up. **Collier State Wildlife Area,** providing crucial winter habitat for deer and elk, spreads along the river bottomlands here. Besides wildlife watching, the area offers fly fishing in the Rio and provides excellent birdwatching. The highway parallels the river in the bottom of a deep, broad canyon.

Long cliff bands, composed of welded volcanic tuff deposited from ancient volcanic eruptions, stair-step up the canyon sides, forming the **Rio Grande Palisades.** Open ponderosa pine forest scatters across the warm south-facing slopes, while glades of aspen mix with spruce and fir woodlands cover the cooler north-facing mountainsides. Tall mature cottonwoods and dense willow thickets, perfect habitat for yellow warblers, line the rushing Rio Grande. At 6 miles the wildlife area offers picnic tables and restrooms for picnickers, birders, and anglers.

Farther up, the canyon narrows and its cliffs steepen. Palisade Campground, with 12 pine-shaded sites, sits alongside the river at 10 miles. The campground, lying in the shadow of the looming Palisades, is a popular put-in point for river rafters. The river section from here to South Fork offers an easy and scenic half-day run. The Rio Grande from South Fork to Wagon Wheel Gap is also designated Gold Medal fishing waters, with anglers catching rainbow and brown trout.

After 11 miles the highway swings under an abrupt escarpment of tall cliffs broken into flying buttresses, arêtes, gargoyles, and castles. Immense talus slopes cascade down to the highway. These volcanic cliffs form **Wagon Wheel Gap,** a narrow gorge named for an abandoned wagon wheel found here in 1873. The wheel was supposedly left by the 1861 Baker prospecting party after being ordered by Utes to vacate their upstream camp. The party left so quickly that equipment and supplies were scattered along their retreating trail.

An interesting side-trip begins right of the Gap. Turn right or north on dirt Pool Table Road, FR 600, and drive 12 miles north to Hanson's Mill, the site of a former lumber mill. Road's end, in a high grassy park below Pool Table Mountain, is the jumping-off point for visitors who either walk or mountain bike 7 miles on East Bellows Trail (#790) or follow a 4x4 road (Forest Service says the "road is extremely rough with deep ruts") for 14 miles to **Wheeler Geologic Area,** one of Colorado's best unknown wonders. The area, tucked into a shallow canyon below Halfmoon Pass and the crest of the La Garita Mountains in 129,626-acre **La Garita Wilderness Area,** is a corrugated landscape of fantastic rock formations. Erosion sculpted the soft volcanic ash into a fairyland of spires, minarets, goblins, fluted cliffs, and jumbled badlands.

The ash was deposited 28 million years ago when a super-volcano collapsed, forming the La Garita Caldera, a huge 22-by-47-mile hole. This event is considered one of the largest volcanic eruptions in the earth's history and the biggest in the last 500 million years. Debris ejected from the explosion covered Colorado with ash and rock fragments up to 300 feet deep. The ash volume is estimated to be 1,200 cubic miles, enough to fill Lake Michigan.

Wheeler, named for Captain George Wheeler with the US Army's 1874 Wheeler Survey, was designated the nation's first national monument in 1908 by President Theodore Roosevelt since its "volcanic formations . . . are of unusual scientific interest as illustrating erratic erosion." The monument's isolation and low volume of visitors, about 50 a year, prompted the national park to remove the tract from the national park system in 1950.

The scenery changes dramatically past Wagon Wheel Gap. The canyon opens into a broad, grassy valley, flanked by sagebrush slopes on the north and spruce and fir forest on the rounded ridges to the south. The drive runs up the south side of the widening valley for 5 miles, crosses the Rio Grande at the abandoned site of Wason, now the Wason Ranch, and bends northwest up Willow Creek to Creede.

Martin Van Buren Wason originally settled at the mouth of Willow Creek before the Creede mining boom and built a toll road to Antelope Park before the railroad came. When silver was discovered in Willow Creek Canyon in 1889, Wason built another toll road up Willow Creek to Creede. The toll was unpopular with miners since it was the only way to the growing town. After a lengthy court battle, Wason ended up selling his road to the State of Colorado for $10,000. The town of Wason was the Mineral County seat in 1893 before being moved to Creede.

Creede

This historic mining town of **Creede,** nestled at the foot of a rocky canyon, got its start in 1889 after prospector Nicholas Creede stumbled onto a rich silver lode at a lunch stop. He supposedly exclaimed, "Holy Moses, I've struck it rich!" His wealthy Holy Moses Mine attracted thousands of fortune seekers.

Almost overnight the camp erupted into a tent city. The boom town grew by 300 people a day in the frenzied summer of 1890. By 1892 more than 10,000 people lived in Creede. The town just as quickly developed a boisterous, hell-raising reputation. Writer Cy Warman, who founded the town's first newspaper, immortalized Creede in a popular poem that read, "It's day all day in the daytime, And there is no night in Creede." Another writer noted, "At night there are no policemen to interfere with the vested right of each citizen to raise as much Cain as he sees fit and . . . three-fourths of the population are of the kind that does see fit."

The infamous town attracted numerous outlaws, gamblers, gunslingers, madams, murderers, and preachers. Its cast of characters included con man Soapy Smith, quick-draw artist Calamity Jane Canary, cigar-smoking card shark Poker Alice, lawman Bat Masterson, and Bob Ford, killer of Jesse James. Saloon-keeper Ford got his due when Ed O'Kelly, a Missouri friend of James, murdered him with a double-barreled shotgun in 1892.

Creede, nicknamed "Colorado's Silver Ribbed Treasure Trove," yielded a million dollars of silver ore every month in 1892. The following year, however, Congress enacted the Silver Act and the price of silver plummeted from $1.29 an ounce to 50 cents; Creede almost shut down overnight. Catastrophic fires and floods destroyed the town several times, but townspeople, overcoming adversity, rebuilt. The mines, far from exhausted, continued to work well into the 20th century. In 1939 some 500,000 ounces of silver were shipped every week, and in 1966 Mineral County produced almost 150,000 ounces of silver.

Creede, now a National Historic District, makes a delightful stop on the scenic drive. The picturesque town boasts numerous visitor attractions, including an underground fire station and the renowned **Creede Repertory Theater,** which rotates plays, musicals, and dramas nightly through summer in the old Creede Opera House. Don't forget to check out the famed **Creede Fork,** also called the "World's Biggest Fork," although it's just the largest in the United States. The 40-foot-long aluminum fork was built in 2002 by local artists Chev and Ted Yund.

The town makes a good base camp for exploring the surrounding high country and enjoying fishing in the Rio Grande, hiking into the La Garita Range, and mountain biking on trails like the fast Deep Creek Trail (#806). A 17-mile-long self-guided auto tour, the **Bachelor Loop Interpretive Site,** begins on Creede's south side and climbs up FR 503 to the Equity Mine before returning on Bachelor Road (FR 504). The tour offers 14 interpretive stops, including ghost towns, old mines, and the Sunnyside Cemetery, as well as several scenic overlooks.

Creede to Slumgullion Pass

The highway runs south from Creede and after a mile bends into the Rio Grande valley. The road heads southwest across terraced benches deposited on old river floodplains. Marshall Park Campground, with 16 sites, spreads along the river west of Seven-Mile Bridge. FR 528 and FR 528 head south from here to Spar City, a ghost town that was contemporary with Creede. Rio Grande Campground with 7 sites sits a few miles farther upstream along the river and provides good fishing access.

At mile 35 the highway and Rio Grande swing northwest up a broad valley flanked by rounded mountains. The river, its headwaters on the north flank of 13,478-foot Canby Mountain atop the Continental Divide west of here, uncoils in long, lazy loops across the flat valley meadows. The valley here was not actually carved by the river, but is a down-dropped block with faults on either side. A roadside overlook near the valley head offers views west toward the Rio Grande headwaters and the remote backcountry of the 488,210-acre **Weminuche Wilderness Area.**

Rocky 12,706-foot Bristol Head's high volcanic cliffs hem in the eastern skyline and form, along with its long northern ridge, the uplifted border of the valley. Jim Stewart's hidden treasure still resides somewhere on Bristol Head's western flank. In 1852 Stewart, an army mail courier, detoured through these mountains to avoid Native American trouble. While crossing a creek, he accidentally dropped his mailbag into the water. While drying out the mail, he panned the stream and found gold nuggets. Noting the location, Stewart later returned but was never able to find his placer gold stash.

FR 520 leaves the drive at the valley's northern end and heads west 9 miles up a narrow canyon to Rio Grande Reservoir, a long fingerlike lake that offers excellent fishing and camping opportunities. Road Canyon Reservoir, off FR 520, yields rainbow trout up to 6 pounds, while numerous backcountry lakes and streams in the Weminuche Wilderness south of Rio Grande Reservoir offer excellent fishing. The road, continuing west from the reservoir as a four-wheel-drive track, climbs another 20 miles to the 12,594-foot summit of Stony Pass along a historic wagon route before dropping steeply to Silverton.

The scenic drive, leaving the Rio Grande's valley, heads north up Spring Creek's shallow valley and passes Spring Creek Reservoir Picnic Site. This national forest area offers fishing in a small lake and picnicking at 2 tables. The highway twists up rolling ridges coated with stands of spruce, fir, and quaking aspen and grassy meadows. Bristol Head, Silver Thread, and North Clear Creek campgrounds lie on the drive or just off, on FR 510, North Clear Creek Road. Silver Thread Campground, with 11 sites, lies on a highway hairpin turn. A short trail leads east to South Clear Creek Falls from the campground. A couple of miles higher is a scenic overlook on the edge of an aspen-fringed meadow. The marvelous view west looks up the glaciated valley of South Clear Creek. Brown and Hermit Lakes glimmer on the valley floor, while 13,827-foot Rio Grande Pyramid, one of Colorado's 100 highest peaks, dominates the Continental Divide above. The 1874 Wheeler Survey called the pyramid "one of the handsomest and most symmetrical cones in Colorado."

The drive crosses a low divide and drops northeast into North Clear Creek's broad drainage. FR 510 heads east for 0.5 mile from the drive to **North Clear Creek Falls,** one of Colorado's most spectacular waterfalls. North Clear Creek meanders across a broad valley, through willow-lined banks, before plunging almost 100 feet over a cliff of hard basalt into a craggy chasm. The frothy creek continues down the steep, rocky canyon to the Rio Grande. The North Clear Creek Falls Observation Site offers a spacious parking lot, fenced overlooks, picnic tables, and restrooms.

From the falls the highway runs north up Spring Creek's brushy valley, past aspen groves and grasslands. After 7 miles the drive reaches the crest of 10,889-foot Spring Creek Pass atop the Continental Divide. East of here towers craggy Baldy Cinco, a 13,383-foot peak in the La Garita Wilderness Area. The **Colorado Trail,** a 469-mile-long footpath from Denver to Durango, crosses the highway here while following the divide westward toward its terminus in Durango. A kiosk on the pass summit gives information on local geology, recreation, and hiking.

Slumgullion Pass to Lake City

The byway drops down across the headwaters of Cebolla Creek and winds west through moist spruce forest for 6 miles to 11,530-foot **Slumgullion Pass.** This high point, not a true pass, divides Cebolla Creek from the Lake Fork of the

The Slumgullion Earthflow, beginning 850 years ago, continues slumping up to 20 feet downhill every year.

Gunnison River. Slumgullion Campground, with 21 sites, sits north of the highway on the west side of the pass. The drive begins steeply descending on 7 percent grades through dense spruce and aspen woodlands.

Windy Point Overlook yields great views west into the San Juans. To the southwest towers the Continental Divide ridgeline and 14,006-foot Sunshine Peak, 14,035-foot Redcloud Peak, and 14,058-foot Handies Peak; to the northeast looms pointed 14,016-foot Wetterhorn Peak and bulky 14,321-foot Uncompahgre Peak, the San Juans' highest mountain. Steep hillsides fall away below to the Lake Fork's deep canyon. A sign identifies the peaks and other notable features.

Below the overlook the highway passes the **Slumgullion Earthflow,** one of Colorado's most unique natural wonders. The first earthflow, or mudslide, occurred some 850 years ago on the southern flank of Mesa Seco to the north, when weak volcanic tuff and breccia, lubricated by heavy rains, slumped 5 miles down the steep mountainside to the valley floor. The 2,700-foot-high flow blocked the river and formed narrow Lake San Cristobal, Colorado's second-largest natural lake. A second flow began some 350 years ago and overlies the upper part of the flow. This active new slide sporadically lurches as much as 20 feet downhill every year. The trees studding the active flow are readily apparent by their drunken angles. The pass and earthflow were named for slumgullion, a yellowish stew concocted by hungry miners who tossed whatever ingredients they had on hand into a single pot, usually some combination of meat, potatoes, bacon, and beans. Slumgullion is also the muddy clay found in the bottom of a miner's sluice box.

Lake San Cristobal Overlook, with views of the lake and glaciated valley, sits on the slide's south side. The highway runs a mile across the slide and bends northwest down steep slopes to the valley floor.

A historic marker commemorating Alferd Packer and his grisly deeds lies north of the highway before crossing the Lake Fork. Packer, guiding a group of prospectors into the San Juans in the winter of 1873, murdered and ate his five clients. Packer escaped the clutches of the law for nine years before being apprehended in Wyoming under the assumed name of John Schwartze. The cannibal, sentenced to hang in 1883 until he was "dead, dead, dead," ended up spending 17 years in the state prison for his deed before being paroled. Legend says presiding judge Melville Gerry cursed, "Packer, you man-eating son-of-a-bitch, there were seven Democrats in Hinsdale County and you ate five of them." The salty story, made up by local Irish barkeep Larry Dolan to entertain his customers, was embellished over the years to its current mythological status.

The Alpine Loop Back Country Byway, a Bureau of Land Management drive that climbs over Cinnamon and Engineer passes via jeep roads, begins 0.5 mile past the Lake Fork crossing. The highway continues north above the river, winding through aspen and pine forests to 8,663-foot **Lake City.**

Lake City, a National Historic District, is a picturesque resort and mining community nestled in the valley bottom. The small town is the seat of Hinsdale County, a county of peaks and valleys as big as Rhode Island. Locals boast that if the land were flattened out, the county would be as large as west Texas. Hinsdale County, with 0.75 residents per square mile, is considered the most sparsely populated county in the US, with Lake City as its only town. The county had a booming population of 843 in the 2010 census, far more than the 202 residents in the 1970 census.

Lake City started, like most Colorado mountain towns, as a mining settlement, after Enos Hotchkiss found gold in 1874. The town, a stage and freight hub for surrounding towns, flourished through the 1880s with two banks, seven saloons, two breweries, and the first newspaper and first church on Colorado's western slope. After the boom, Lake City carried on as a mining and ranching center, but today relies on gorgeous scenery to attract tourist dollars.

While Lake City is quintessential Colorado, summer visitors sometimes call it "North Texas" and proudly fly Lone Star flags in their front yards. The Texas invasion began in the 1920s when a Texan family named Wupperman moved to town. They noted in their diaries that Lake City was a "town full of widows" since the mines had long closed and the miners dead of black lung or by accident. The

Wuppermans invited their friends up from the south lands for summer fish fries and picnics and soon folks returned every year, although not without upsetting locals. In the mid-1950s the town game warden was concerned that Texan fishermen were decimating the trout population.

The town is a great base to explore the San Juan Mountains and the area's rich historical legacy. Numerous ghost towns scatter across the mountains, with trails that climb the peaks and traverse nearby wilderness areas. Lake City is the launch site to climb 5 Fourteeners—Uncompahgre, Wetterhorn, Handies, Sunshine, and Redcloud. Handies Peak, south of town, is perhaps the easiest with a 5.5-mile hike through wildflower-strewn meadows and rocky talus slopes to forever summit views. The area offers productive fly fishing in the Lake Fork of the Gunnison or farther north in Big Blue Creek, a freestone river. There are also hundreds of miles of both singletrack trails and old mining tracks for mountain bikers to find excitement. Kids and beginner bikers ride an easy trail at Pete's Lake Nature Area while experienced pedalheads ride the 13-mile Thompson-Crystal Lakes Loop, which starts on the north side of the town cemetery.

Lake City to Blue Mesa Reservoir

The last scenic drive section rolls north for 55 miles from Lake City to Blue Mesa Reservoir and the drive's end at US 50 west of Gunnison. The highway follows slopes above the Lake Fork of the Gunnison River, which meanders through a sharp canyon lined with pale volcanic cliffs. It's difficult to reach the river for fishing since most of the adjoining land is privately owned and posted No Trespassing.

Farther north the highway crosses the river and trends along the west bank in a wide open valley, passing pastures dotted with grazing cattle. After 16 miles, the drive passes through The Gate, a portal of towering basalt cliffs. The Gate Campground, a BLM area with 8 campsites, is on the west side of the highway. Besides camping, it's a scenic spot for fishing access and picnicking beside the river.

The drive bends away from the Lake Fork, passing the dirt Blue Mesa Road cutoff, and twists through hills blanketed with sagebrush and pine woodlands before dropping down across Cebolla Creek and the remote hamlet of Powderhorn, a tiny post office community founded in 1880. Continue following the highway northeast through barren hills before descending a broad valley to **Blue Mesa Lake,** a reservoir on the Gunnison River that forms Colorado's largest lake. The drive skirts the southern coastline of the lake, passing a few spots with fishing access and picnic tables, before ending after crossing a bridge over the Gunnison River and reaching a T-bone junction with US 50. Gunnison is a dozen miles east on US 50.

San Juan Skyway All-American Byway

Durango to Ouray to Cortez Loop

General description: This 236-mile scenic drive makes a spectacular loop drive through the San Juan Mountains, crossing several high passes, twisting through canyons and valleys, and passing through historic towns.

Special attractions: Durango & Silverton Narrow Gauge Railroad, Durango National Historic District, Purgatory Resort, Animas River Canyon, Weminuche Wilderness Area, Molas Pass, Molas Lake, Silverton National Historic District, Red Mountain Pass, Box Canyon Falls, Ouray National Historic District, Dallas Divide, Telluride, Telluride Ski Resort, Lizard Head Pass, Lizard Head Wilderness Area, Ophir, Dolores River Canyon, Escalante Ruins and Canyon of the Ancients Visitor Center and Museum, Mancos State Park, scenic views, camping, backpacking, mountaineering, fishing, hiking, mountain biking, historic sites, fall colors.

Location: Southwestern Colorado. The loop drive follows US 550 from Durango to Ridgway, then goes west to Placerville, south to Telluride, and over Lizard Head Pass to Dolores. The drive finishes by heading east on US 160 back to Durango.

Route name and numbers: San Juan Skyway; US 550 and 160; CO 62 and 145.

Travel season: Year-round. Drive segments close occasionally in winter due to snow and avalanche danger. Chains often are required to drive in winter.

Camping: Many national forest campgrounds lie along the drive. Camping also available at Mesa Verde National Park's Morefield Campground (267 sites), Mancos State Park's Main and West Campgrounds (32 sites), and Ridgway State Park (258 sites and 25 walk-in sites). Dispersed, primitive camping is permitted on both Bureau of Land Management and national forest lands along the drive.

Services: All services are in Durango, Silverton, Ouray, Ridgway, Telluride, Dolores, Cortez, and Mancos. Limited services in small towns along the drive.

Nearby attractions: Alpine Loop Back Country Byway, Mount Sneffels Wilderness Area, Unaweep-Tabeguache Scenic and Historic Byway (Scenic Drive 27), Uncompahgre Plateau, Owl Creek Pass, Lake City, Mesa Verde National Park (Scenic Drive 28), Black Canyon of the Gunnison National Park (Scenic Drive 26), Hovenweep National Monument, Canyon of the Ancients National Monument, and Ute Tribal Park.

The Route

The San Juan Mountains, a 12,000-square-mile block of high country, encompasses almost all of southwestern Colorado. The San Juan Range, with a mean elevation of 10,000 feet, boasts more than 100 peaks topping 13,000 feet and 14 of Colorado's 53 ranked 14,000-foot peaks or "Fourteeners." This huge range,

San Juan Skyway All–American Byway

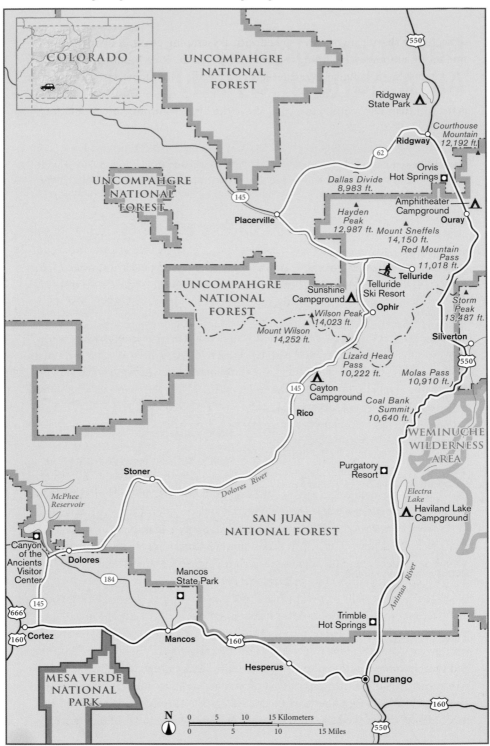

dissected by sharp canyons and spiked with skyscraping peaks, is divided into numerous subranges, including the San Miguel Range, Rico Mountains, La Plata Mountains, Sneffels Range, West Needle and Needle Mountains, Grenadier Range, La Garita Mountains, and Cochetopa Hills. The heart of the San Juans, however, is the San Juan Range itself, towering above the historic mining towns of Ouray, Silverton, and Telluride.

The San Juans formed some 35 million years ago, when immense volcanic eruptions spewed some 8,000 cubic miles of lava and thousands of feet of ash across the region. Precious minerals, including gold, silver, lead, copper, and zinc, percolated in underground fissures inside volcanic calderas. At today's prices the San Juans yielded billions of dollars of riches, and prospectors believe more lies buried beneath the mountain flanks in the region's 50 mining districts. Periodic glaciation over the last two million years sculpted the mountains with precipitous gorges, wide valleys, and serrated peaks and ridges. The range is also the headwaters of numerous rivers, including the Rio Grande and the San Juan, Mancos, Uncompahgre, San Miguel, Dolores, Animas, and La Plata Rivers.

The San Juan Skyway, a designated National Forest All-American Byway, traverses this rugged mountain heartland for 236 miles. The drive, making a huge loop, is one of America's most beautiful and most spectacular scenic drives. The drive described here begins and ends in Durango, although it can easily be started in Cortez, Ridgway, and other points. Allow at least eight hours to drive the route, but remember it could easily take eight days to explore the wealth of scenery and points of interest along the Skyway.

The highway, open year-round, is best in summer and fall. The wide variation in elevation along the drive, from 6,512 feet at Durango to 11,018 feet atop Red Mountain Pass, gives a wide diversity of both temperature and precipitation. Summer temperatures in the lower elevations at both ends of the road are typically warm, with highs ranging from 70 to 90 degrees. The mountain heights are as much as 20 degrees cooler. Afternoon thunderstorms are an almost daily occurrence somewhere along the highway; watch for slippery roads. Autumn is delightful, with cool, crisp days and spectacular aspen colors.

The first snow falls sometime in October on the high peaks, and winter begins in November with heavy snowfall. As much as 4 feet of snow can fall in a day, leading to extreme avalanche danger. Parts of the highway regularly close due to avalanches. The steep Uncompahgre Gorge highway section between Ironton Park and Ouray is the most dangerous, with the Riverside and Mother Cline Slides. The Riverside Slide, dropping 3,200 vertical feet down abrupt chutes, makes this highway Colorado's deadliest avalanche crossing. A snowshed now protects the road from the slide's wrath, but not before five highway travelers perished in

Golden aspens reflect in a pond near Sunshine Campground above Telluride.

avalanches. Chains often are required to drive the highway in winter. Watch for snowplows clearing the highway, and bring extra clothes and sleeping bags in case of a breakdown. Spring comes slowly to the high country, with the snow cover slowly retreating in April and May. Expect cool, breezy days with occasional snow and rainstorms.

Durango

The drive begins in **Durango** at the junction of US 160 and US 550. Turn north on US 550, nicknamed the Million Dollar Highway, on the town's south side. The road bypasses downtown Durango and heads up Main Avenue. Durango, straddling the Animas Valley, was established in 1880 as a Denver & Rio Grande Railroad town. Animas City, the area's first town, started just north of Durango in 1861 as a supply center for San Juan miners. The railroad, wanting to capitalize on the San Juan's rich mines, pushed its narrow-gauge tracks west from Alamosa to the Animas River valley. Animas City seemed the logical choice for the new railroad center, but the town and the railroad couldn't come to terms. Investors then set up the Durango Land and Coal Company and surveyed a new townsite 2 miles south of Animas City, calling it Durango because of the area's similarity to Durango, Mexico. The town thrived as a railroad hub, hauling valuable ore from mountain mines to Durango's smelter.

Long after the San Juan mines shut down, Durango is still a railroad town. The **Durango & Silverton Narrow Gauge Railroad,** a National Historic and National Engineering Landmark, begins at the train station on the town's south side and runs north up the old Denver & Rio Grande rail bed 45 miles to Silverton. This scenic train ride, threading through the steep Animas River gorge on 3-foot-wide tracks, is a living-history exhibit that takes travelers back in time to mining's heyday. Reservations and advance ticket purchases are advised, particularly during the busy summer months.

Durango also is a wonderful outdoor sports town, with nearby mountain bike trails, excellent fly-fishing streams, numerous four-wheel-drive tracks, kayaking and rafting on the Animas River, rock climbing on cliffs like the Watch Crystal, and a wealth of hiking paths. Durango is the terminus of the 486-mile **Colorado Trail,** a long-distance path that runs from Durango to Denver. Durango also offers all visitor services, including hotels, dining, groceries, and service stations.

The Animas Valley

The highway leaves Durango after 3 miles and runs north on the western edge of the **Animas Valley** for 15 miles. The Animas River, a 110-mile-long river originally called *Rio de las Animas Perdidas,* or "River of Lost Souls," by early Spanish explorers, meanders in long, graceful loops across the wide-bottomed valley past green pastures grazed by horses and cattle. Dense willows and tall narrow-leafed cottonwoods hug the river's rocky banks. The river did little to excavate this deep valley. Thick glaciers, spilling down from the high mountains, scoured the valley floor, chiseled its steep sidewalls, and left a characteristic U-shaped glacial valley behind. Sandstone cliffs abruptly lift from the valley, striping the slopes with diagonal bands.

Durango straddles the edge of the San Juan Mountains and the Colorado Plateau, a vast geographic province that spreads across the Four Corners region. As the highway runs north, it slowly leaves the plateau by traversing across upturned sedimentary rock formations: gray Mancos shale; Dakota sandstone; the dinosaur-bearing Morrison Formation; Entrada, Navajo, and Wingate sandstones; and finally old Permian redbeds at Hermosa. Still older formations, including the 300-million-year-old Hermosa Formation, lie farther north. The 2,000-foot-thick Hermosa Formation, laid down as marine sediments in basins offshore from the Ancestral Rockies, forms lofty gray ramparts above the highway north from Hermosa to Engineer Mountain.

As the highway runs north from Durango, it passes **Trimble Springs** at 6 miles. These hot springs, located just west of the road, were named for 1874 settler Frank Trimble. He developed two springs, spewing water as hot as 126 degrees, and built a hotel for visitors wanting to sample the springs' "curative value." A 40-room brick hotel, the Hermosa House, was erected in the late 1890s and offered stables, a gym, a bowling alley, a golf course, and a saloon. After fire destroyed the hotel in 1938, it was replaced by another hotel that burned in 1957. The springs now offers a bathhouse, an Olympic-size outdoor pool, and a smaller hot pool. **Hermosa,** an old stage and railroad stop, is just north of Trimble. The town, settled in 1873 as a ranching center for the Animas Valley, now serves as a Durango bedroom community.

The highway continues north, skirting the valley's steep wall, and reaches another historic site near the valley head. **Baker's Bridge,** designated by a State Historical Society bronze marker, crossed the Animas River here. Charles Baker and several men prospected through the San Juans in 1860 and, after working their way down from Baker's Park at today's Silverton, resolved to spend the winter in the northern Animas Valley. The party laid out a townsite, built rustic log cabins, and suffered through the cold winter. With news of the Civil War, they abandoned the site and returned east. Baker fought in the Confederate Army, then returned west and was killed by Native Americans while prospecting in 1868.

The flat valley abruptly ends, replaced by forested hills. The Animas River leaves the valley and bends northeast into a steep, cliff-lined gorge. The drive also exits the valley, bumping across the narrow-gauge railroad tracks and climbing onto wooded slopes below the Hermosa Cliffs. A turnoff that sits past the tracks makes a good stop to watch the antique train rumble by. A side road, La Plata CR 75, drops east to a secluded glen and the remains of the old town of **Rockwood.** This town served as the jumping-off point for miners and freighters heading north to Silverton and Rico. An old wagon toll road, now a National Historic Landmark, twisted north from here, with one branch following today's highway up to Purgatory and over Scotch Creek Pass to Rico and the other branch to Silverton.

The highway runs north below a rock-walled escarpment and enters 1,878,846-acre **San Juan National Forest.** Dense scrub oak thickets line the asphalt, and beyond tower ponderosa pines and Douglas firs. Tamarron, a year-round resort, offers golf on an 18-hole course and other activities. The road swings past Haviland Lake, a small lake tucked among forested hills. It has barrier-free accessible fishing piers and is wakeless with only electric troll motored boats or hand-paddled craft. Haviland Lake Campground, with 43 shady sites for both RVs and tents, sits on its east shore. A mile-long trail heads southeast from Haviland Lake to small Forebay Lake.

Electra Lake, a 3-mile-long reservoir created for electric power, lies to the north. Water from the lake is channeled through an open wooden flume, one of only two still used for hydropower in the United States, to the Tacoma Hydro Generating Station 18 miles away. The private lake, owned by Xcel Energy but run by the exclusive Electra Sporting Club, is open for fishing and boating for a fee. All boats, however, must be clean, drained, and dry to keep the lake from being contaminated by invasive species. The highway sweeps across a high bench through dense aspen groves. **Engineer Mountain,** its talus flanks broken by cliff bands, looms to the north, and the West Needle Mountains rise to the northeast. At 25 miles from Durango, Castle Rock, a castellated 10,441-foot promontory, juts from the Hermosa Cliffs.

The highway becomes four lanes and reaches **Purgatory Resort,** Durango's hometown ski area. This popular destination ski resort, called "Best Value Ski Spot in North America" on TripAdvisor, is ski and snowboard nirvana. The area offers 1,505 skiable acres, a 2,029-foot vertical drop from summit to base, 11 lifts serving 92 trails, 5 terrain parks, an average of 260 inches or 21 feet of dry champagne powder, and kids ski free. The **Purgatory Nordic Center,** on the east side of the highway, offers 20 kilometers of groomed trails for cross country and skate skiing and 6 kilometers of snowshoe trails that thread across the surrounding woodlands. Rent skis and snowshoes or take private or group XC lessons at the center.

Coal Bank Summit & Molas Pass

The highway squeezes back to two lanes at the Cascade Village Hotel and crosses Cascade Creek at a hairpin turn below 12,968-foot **Engineer Mountain,** the 655th highest mountain in Colorado. The elegant peak is an area landmark with its double summits protected by gray cliffs that tower above the San Juan Skyway. First climbed in 1873 by H.G. Proust with a US Army Corp of Engineers survey crew mapping the area, the mountain was named for those geographical engineers. A steep hike up the 3.2-mile Engineer Mountain Trail, gaining 2,308 feet, passes through meadows filled with opulent wildflowers, subalpine forests, alpine tundra, and a final exciting scramble up the narrow Northeast Ridge, which requires some exposed climbing. Some folks might feel comfortable on a rope. The summit offers forever views east to the West Needles and beyond to the rugged Needle and Grenadier ranges. The trailhead is on the left just past the summit of Coal Bank Pass.

Past Cascade Creek the highway begins steeply ascending above Mill Creek. The blacktop switchbacks through a spruce forest sprinkled with aspen. Potato Hill rises to the east and beyond towers 13,158-foot Twilight Peak in the West Needle Mountains, its rocky flanks chiseled by glaciers into deep cirques, sharp arêtes, and flying buttresses. After a few miles, the highway heads up Coal Bank Hill and emerges on **Coal Bank Summit,** a 10,640-foot saddle between Engineer Mountain and Potato Hill.

The drive winds down from the pass summit, crosses Deer Creek, and swings up aspen-covered slopes. Most of the rolling countryside adjoining the highway was consumed in the 26,000-acre Lime Creek Burn fire in 1879. Civic groups later replanted much of the burn scar. After bending over West Lime Creek, the highway turns east and climbs alongside East Lime Creek. The creek trickles in a shallow valley, with aspens coating the warm south-facing slopes and dense spruce woods blanketing the cooler north-facing hillsides.

At 6.3 miles from Coal Bank Pass or 1.4 miles before the top of Molas Pass, take a right or south turn on the Andrews Lake Road (FR 590) and drive 0.6 mile up to a day-use parking area at 10,744-foot **Andrews Lake.** The small, lovely lake is popular with fishermen angling for trout. A short paved trail on the west side of the lake leads to a couple of wheelchair-accessible fishing piers. An excellent hike begins at the end of the paved trail. Hike south on moderate **Crater Lake Trail** (#623) for 5.5 miles to Crater Lake, a gorgeous forest-fringed lake tucked in a high cirque below 13,075-foot North Twilight Peak and 13,158-foot Twilight Peak, the high point of the West Needle Mountains. The placid lake perfectly reflects the mountains and delights photographers. Intrepid peakbaggers climb North Twilight from the lake by climbing south to a saddle and then scrambling up the peak's exposed and narrow east ridge (Class III).

The road continues up East Lime Creek from the Andrews Lake turn and 1.4 miles later reaches 10,910-foot **Molas Pass,** a spacious overlook which offers one of Colorado's most stunning mountain panoramas. Sharp peaks spike the horizon in a wide circle from the summit. The Needle and Grenadier Mountains tower to the east, their ragged flanks strewn with glacier-carved buttresses and cirques. The Animas River gorge, an abrupt forested chasm, hides between the pass and the peaks. Molas Lake, its placid waters reflecting the sky, tucks into a hollow on a broad bench above the canyon. Spruce forest and open willow meadows surround the lake. Snowdon Peak, the 13,077-foot northern outpost of the West Needles, looms to the south. Rounded ridges, green with above-timberline tundra grass and broken by rocky crags on the skyline, stair-step up west from the pass.

The summit of Molas Pass has a large parking area, restrooms, and a short trail to the viewpoint. The **Colorado Trail,** running from Denver to Durango, crosses the pass 0.1 mile north of the parking lot. While the final 74 miles of the trail from Molas Pass to Durango is considered one of the most beautiful treks in Colorado, it's easy to do a shorter out-and-back day hike on the trail to experience its beauty.

The trail's segment 25, running 23 miles from Molas Pass to Bolam Pass, is perfect for hiking. A moderate 10-mile round-trip hike that gives a taste of the Colorado Trail starts at Little Molas Lake above the pass and then traverses broad meadows above the West Lime Creek Valley to Lime Creek's headwaters. Expect unforgettable views and gorgeous wildflower displays in July and August. The trail gains 775 feet from the 10,950-foot trailhead to Lime Creek. Find the trailhead by driving 0.4 mile north from Molas Pass and turning left or west on FR 584, which climbs a mile to a parking lot at road's end above **Little Molas Lake.** The small Little Molas Lake Campground, with both tent and RV sites, sits above the small lake, which is stocked with trout.

A few miles north of the pass summit is **Molas Lake** and campground, called the "most scenic campground in Colorado" by AAA. The area, given to the Town of Silverton by the Bureau of Land Management in 1925, offers over 50 campsites spread over 137 acres for tents, trailers, and RVs, the stocked 25-acre Molas Lake, and gorgeous views of the jagged Needle Mountains to the east. The campground is open from June 1 to September 30.

Silverton

The highway descends sharply for 5 miles from Molas Lake to **Silverton,** clinging to steep mountainsides above the Animas River. Thick spruce forest hems in the road, with open slopes offering glimpses north into Baker's Park. Finally the road makes a couple of hairpin turns, reaches the valley floor, and bends west up Mineral Creek. A right turn here leads to Silverton. A visitor center, housed in an ornate building, sits on the south edge of town.

Silverton, at an elevation of 9,320 feet, lies along the Animas River in Baker's Park, a flat, 2,000-acre glacial valley encircled by a wall of mountains. Winter blankets the town, one of Colorado's most isolated settlements, with over 300 inches of annual snowfall. Before modern snow-removal equipment, Silverton often was cut off from the outside world for weeks at a time; even now the highway shuts down for a few days each winter. The town is undeniably a tough place to live—the year-round average temperature is about 35 degrees and summer's growing season is but 12 days. Towering peaks ring Baker's Park, with 13,370-foot Sultan Mountain to the south, 13,068-foot Kendall Mountain on the east, and 13,487-foot Storm Peak to the north.

These mountains, fringed with forest, capped by snow, and filled with mineral riches, attracted the remote valley's first visitors in 1860. Charles Baker and six fellow prospectors trekked over Cinnamon Pass and wandered south down the Animas River to the broad park. These early miners panned the streams for the next couple of years, but found little placer gold to hold their interest. Not until 1870 did miners find promising color and stake their claims on the steep mountainsides. The Little Giant Lode up Arrastra Creek was the first producing mine in the area. The San Juans, however, still remained under Ute control. The Utes protested the miner incursions, and federal troops were dispatched to keep the

Victorian-style false fronts adorn shops and cafes in the historic mining town of Silverton.

Anglos off native lands. The Brunot Treaty in 1873, however, removed the Utes from their mountain homeland and opened the San Juans for prospecting.

Miners flocked into the area, and by 1873 more than 1,500 mining claims were filed. Silverton, established in June 1874, was deemed the county seat. The new town was supposedly dubbed Silverton after a miner remarked, "We may not have gold here, but we have silver by the ton." Wagon routes over Stony and Cinnamon Passes connected Silverton to the outside world until July 8, 1882, when the Denver & Rio Grande Railroad completed its narrow-gauge track from Durango to Silverton. The town boomed through the 1880s, with millions of dollars worth of gold and silver mined from the hills, but the 1893 silver crash slowed the growth. At its peak Silverton boasted more than 30 mills, 2 smelters, 37 saloons, and numerous card houses, opium dens, and "pleasure palaces" on its infamous Blair Street.

Silverton today wears its colorful history well. Most of the town, preserved as a National Historic District, still reflects the mining heyday of 150 years ago. The town appears at first glance like a movie set, with false-fronted buildings, opulent Victorian homes, the gold-domed county courthouse, the 1903 brick jail that houses the **San Juan County Historical Society Mining Heritage Center,** and rustic miner's cabins. The 3-story, 14,000-square-foot Mining Heritage Center interprets Silverton's colorful mining history with artifacts, historic photographs, mining machinery, and replica underground tunnels. Silverton boasts 3 of Colorado's 25 designated National Historic Landmarks—Silverton Historic District, **Mayflower Mill,** and **Durango & Silverton Narrow Gauge Railroad.**

The town is the northern terminus of the historic railroad, the last vestige of Silverton's railway glories. The steam-powered train, built by General William Jackson Palmer's Denver & Rio Grande Railway, runs 45.2 miles on 3-foot-wide tracks from Durango to Silverton (Palmer founded Colorado Springs). The railroad opened in 1882, hauling rich ores from the San Juan Mountains to mills, and has operated continuously but now hauls railroad buffs and tourists instead of gold and silver.

Silverton, remaining true to its rough-and-tumble mining past, is an authentic mountain town with an independent spirit. It's easy to walk Greene Street, the town's main drag, or Blair Street, once a notorious den of inequity with over 40 brothels and saloons, and feel that you're stepping back in time to the glory days when gold and silver ruled. Good places to explore the area's rich heritage are **Hillside Cemetery; Christ of the Mine Statue** for an eagle's eye view of town; the self-guided **Mayflower Mill** historic site; **One Hundred Mine,** a gold mine in Galena Mountain; and **Animas Forks,** a well-preserved ghost town 15 miles up CR 2. Hillside Cemetery, perched northeast of town, makes an interesting stop. Grave markers of young men that read "Killed in Mine Accident" testify to the dangers found underground, while other graves remember victims of diseases like typhoid fever, pneumonia, and the 1918 flu epidemic. If you want a historic overnight stay, book a room at the 1883 **Grand Imperial Hotel.**

Silverton is now the jumping-off place for rugged adventures in the surrounding mountains and valleys, including waist-deep backcountry powder, plunging waterfalls, cliffs for climbing, trails that switchback up to alpine cirques and airy summits, and stony 4x4 tracks over high passes including Cinnamon and Ophir Passes.

Skiers love Silverton in winter where snow is measured in feet on **Silverton Mountain ski area.** The area offers big-mountain skiing with 2,000 vertical feet of chutes and gullies from the 13,487-foot summit, over 400 inches of annual snowfall, a single chairlift, and a lodge in a Quonset hut. It's an experts-only area that requires all skiers carry avalanche beacons, shovels, and probes. The area also offers over 22,000 skiable acres reached by helicopter.

Mineral Creek to Red Mountain Pass

The drive bends west from Silverton on US 550 and heads up the **Mineral Creek** valley. The North Star Mine and Mill, surrounded by quaking aspens, sits across the creek west of town. FR 585 turns off the highway and heads west up Mineral

Creek's South Fork in a broad, glaciated valley for 5 miles to the 26-site South Mineral Campground. This 9,800-foot campground makes a good base camp for exploring the surrounding peaks and basins.

Ice Lake Basin, 3 miles to the west, sits amid sheer-cliffed peaks including 13,894-foot Vermillion Peak, Colorado's 74th highest mountain, U.S. Grant Peak, Golden Horn, and Pilot Knob. The **Ice Lake Trail** (#505), simply one of the state's most beautiful hikes, begins at South Mineral Campground and steeply climbs past waterfalls and wildflower-filled meadows to Ice Lake Basin and several turquoise lakes. The moderately difficult trail gains 2,430 feet in 3.5 miles from the trailhead to 12,270-foot **Ice Lake,** the bluest lake imaginable. The lake's fluorescent blue comes from fine powder suspended in the water that was ground from bedrock by an ancient glacier. Another unique alpine tarn is **Island Lake** in the next cirque north of Ice Lake Basin. Follow an easy trail across a mountainside to the lovely lake tucked beneath U.S. Grant Peak. A small rocky island rises from the middle of the lake.

The highway bends north and heads up Mineral Creek's broad valleys carved by glaciers. Numerous avalanche chutes slice through the forest on the steep valley sides. Halfway up the valley or 4.2 miles west of Silverton is a left turn onto the **Ophir Pass Road** (FR 679). The road crosses Burro Bridge and climbs 4 miles to the 11,789-foot pass summit. The track, one of the area's easier 4-wheel-drive routes, continues down an old stage and wagon road 6 miles to Ophir, an old mining town, and CO 145 west of Telluride. The road is rated moderate because a narrow half-mile road section on the west side of the pass makes it difficult for vehicles to pass each other. If you drive the road, remember that downhill traffic should yield to uphill traffic on this dangerous road segment.

US 550 heads up the valley to the foot of Red Mountain Pass and the old 1883 townsite of **Chattanooga.** While almost nothing remains now, the town once held 300 residents and 75 buildings. A fire and disastrous snowslides wiped out the town. Reverend J. Gibbons noted in 1898 that "the ruins of roofs and houses were strewn for half a mile over the valley and the population of this once-flourishing hamlet dwindled down to two."

The Million Dollar Highway, traversing the old Silverton Railway's right-of-way, turns west onto the Chattanooga Loop and begins the final 3-mile ascent to the summit of **Red Mountain Pass.** The blacktop, with no guardrail, edges along precipitous slopes. Look down the valley for great views of Bear Mountain. Note the forest shape on its flank; it appears to be a giant bear licking a honeycomb. The highway bends into a steep gorge, passes the remains of the Silver Ledge Mine, and climbs up to 11,018-foot Red Mountain Pass. Abandoned buildings of the Longfellow Mine and a small, willow-lined tarn sit on the summit.

The dangerous one-way **Black Bear Road** (FR 648), one of Colorado's toughest jeep tracks, climbs west from here for 3.2 miles to the summit of 12,840-foot Black Bear Pass. The road then descends into Ingram Basin, a high-elevation cirque, and passes Ingram Lake and Black Bear Mine. After 5.6 miles the rough road begins descending The Steps, a series of rock steps that require technical driving skills and a short-wheel-base, high-clearance, 4-wheel-drive vehicle. The mile-long section from the top of The Steps to the Bridal Veil Powerplant is a one-way, downhill-only road. Past The Steps, the road makes 11 tight, narrow switchbacks down a steep slope before dropping into Telluride.

The Uncompahgre Gorge to Ouray

The Million Dollar Highway between Silverton and Ouray follows an old toll road that was started in 1880 and finished in 1884 by road builder and transportation magnate Otto Mears. The road operated as a mail, stage, and freight line until Mears opened his Rainbow Route railway from Silverton to the rich mines at the summit of Red Mountain Pass. The Million Dollar Highway, traversing the old rail and wagon route, was completed in 1924. The road section from Ouray to Red Mountain Pass cost about $1 million and gave the highway its name, although some say it was named for its million-dollar views.

The highway descends 12 miles from the pass summit to Ouray. The first section, a maze of switchbacks and hairpin turns, twists down steep slopes to Ironton Park. North of the pass summit the highway swings around the mostly abandoned Idarado Mine, one of the 20th century's largest ore producers. The mine, nicknamed "Treasury Tunnel," yielded gold, silver, copper, lead, and zinc. Its tunnels bore through the mountains to the Smuggler Mine above Telluride. The surrounding mineralized peaks, including Red Mountain on the cast, are tinted yellow and orange with iron oxides and are pockmarked by old mines, weathered buildings, and ore dumps. Several towns once scattered across the slopes here, including Red Mountain and Guston. Millions of dollars' worth of gold and silver streamed from the area mines. Wealthy producers included the Guston, Yankee Girl, and Robinson Mines.

Red Mountain Creek runs through Ironton Park. Aspens blanket the mountainsides above, creating a stunning display of color in late September. The old mining town of Ironton sat near the valley head. After a couple of miles, the highway leaves the valley and drops into the **Uncompahgre Gorge,** a deep canyon sliced by the Uncompahgre River. The road angles across steeply tilted cliffs of quartzite, slate, and schist, and scree slopes.

Below some switchbacks by mile marker 88 are 3 crosses and a roadside memorial on the east side of the highway that honor 6 avalanche victims—Reverend Marvin Hudson and his daughters Amelia and Pauline, and snowplow drivers Bob Miller in 1970, Terry Kishbaugh in 1978, and Eddie Imel in 1992. The deadly East Riverside Slide, an avalanche chute now covered with a snowshed, killed the six victims in separate winter accidents. The Hudsons died on March 3, 1963, after stopping to put on tire chains. Previous victims include 2 men and a team of mules in 1883. The avalanches begin with extreme snow loading at the top of Curran Gulch below the summit of 12,801-foot Abrams Mountain.

The **Million Dollar Highway** features 70 named avalanche paths along the 23 highway miles between Silverton and Ouray and guardrails are almost non-existent since snowplow drivers have to push the winter's 350+ inches of snow off the highway edge. Highway 550, the most avalanche-prone highway in the United States, also has 50 slides zones on Molas Pass and 20 on Coal Bank Pass. The Lizard Head Pass section of the San Juan Skyway has another 48 avalanche paths.

The highway edges north along the east slope of Red Mountain Creek and the Uncompahgre Gorge and passes FR 878, the start of the four-wheel-drive **Alpine Loop Back Country Byway.** This excellent 75-mile tour, requiring a 4-wheel-drive vehicle, makes a loop drive through the San Juans, crossing Engineer and Cinnamon Passes between Silverton, Lake City, and this point near Ouray.

Farther north the highway, clinging to cliffs, crosses **Bear Creek Falls.** The creek cascades 227 feet down to the river below. Park at a turnoff on the west side of the road to view the falls. The tollgate for Otto Mears's road sat at this narrow site so wagon trains couldn't avoid paying the $3.75 toll for a vehicle with two animals. A nearby monument remembers Mears and his contribution to Colorado history.

The drive runs through a short tunnel and emerges at Lookout Point above Ouray. A vast amphitheater of cliffs, formed by volcanic San Juan Tuff, soars above the town to lofty peaks and sharp ridges. Amphitheater Campground, with 35 sites, is reached from a side road past the viewpoint. The highway snakes down into Ouray.

Mountains dominate 7,760-foot-high **Ouray,** one of Colorado's historic mountain towns. Ouray, named for a famed 19th-century Ute chief, sits cupped in a wide amphitheater lined with towering cliffs and mountains. Three big waterfalls thunder within shouting distance of Ouray, and five creeks dash through town to the Uncompahgre River. Box Canyon, on the southwest edge, is most impressive, with Canyon Creek roaring through a narrow gorge. Geothermal hot springs dot Ouray, filling pools and bathhouses. The springs, named Uncompahgre, or "hot water springs," by the Utes, still attract visitors to the town.

Ouray, pronounced "YOU-ray," began with rich gold and silver strikes in late 1875. The following year the town was surveyed and quickly boomed. The first building was supposedly a saloon, but by the end of 1876, a school, 214 cabins, 2 hotels, and a post office also lined the streets. The 1893 silver crash brought Ouray to its financial knees, but Tom Walsh's rich Camp Bird Mine in Yankee Boy Basin west of town brought new prosperity in 1895. The fabulous lode yielded over $20 million in gold before Walsh sold the mine in 1902 to an English consortium. Through the 20th century Ouray relied on an economy based on mining and tourism.

Now Ouray makes a fabulous base camp to explore what locals call the "Switzerland of America." A legacy of old mining roads lace the mountains and canyons, making Ouray the jeep capital of America. Some of the best back roads are the Corkscrew Road, Poughkeepsie Gulch, Engineer Pass, Yankee Boy Basin, and Imogene Pass. Jeep rentals are available in town. Numerous trails also thread the backcountry, climbing to waterfalls, alpine basins, and sheer peaks like 14,150-foot **Mount Sneffels** and 13,819-foot Teakettle Mountain,

The 9-block-long town, a National Historic District, offers neat streets lined with restored Victorian homes, brick buildings, the haunted Beaumont Hotel, the **Ouray County Museum,** and a designated walking tour.

Ouray is Colorado's hot springs heaven with 4 developed hot springs—Ouray Hot Springs Pool, Wiesbaden Hot Springs Spa, Twin Peaks Lodge and Hot Springs, and Box Canyon Lodge and Hot Springs (hotel guests only). The **Ouray Hot Springs Pool,** on the north end of town, gives a relaxing soak at day's end in several pools and soaking areas. There are waterslides and an obstacle course for kids. For a more intimate experience, head up the hill to **Wiesbaden Hot Springs,** with an outdoor pool, a private soaking pond called The Lorelei, and an underground vapor cave filled with hot steam. The Wiesbaden, open for day soakers, offers a 17-room lodge for overnight guests. For more information about all of Ouray's hot springs, consult *Touring Colorado Hot Springs* (FalconGuides).

On the southwest side of town is the **Ouray Ice Park,** which opened in 1995 as the world's first park devoted exclusively to ice climbing. The Ice Park is the best and most accessible place to go ice climbing in the United States, with over 200 manmade ice and mixed climbs scattered in 14 different climbing sectors in a mile-long stretch of the Uncompahgre Gorge. Besides the world-class ice routes, the park has a practice wall where climbers can brush up on technical skills or learn the slippery sport. Every January ice climbers take over Ouray when the town hosts the **Ouray Ice Festival,** attracting climbers from across the US and Canada for camaraderie, fun, and competition.

Ridgway

The drive's next 10 miles on US 550 connect Ouray to Ridgway, an old railroad hub. The highway runs through a narrow gap lined with towering sandstone walls and takes leave of the San Juan Mountains. The valley ahead, flanked by forested slopes, is lush with green pastures, grazing cattle, and narrow-leaf cottonwoods. Herds of elk and deer graze in roadside meadows, particularly from late fall to spring. The drive yields spectacular vistas of the ragged Sneffels Range to the west, low-browed Grand Mesa far to the north, and Chimney and Courthouse Peaks to the east. This drive segment ends in Ridgway at the intersection of US 550 and CO 62.

Orvis Hot Springs, halfway between Ouray and Ridgway, offers a relaxing stop after climbing a tough peak. This popular hotspot has 7 soaking areas with temperatures ranging between 65 and 112 degrees. Four of the pools are outdoors so soakers can enjoy warm sunshine and starlit evenings. Orvis is clothing-optional so don't be surprised if you see au naturale people relaxing in the natural lithium water.

Ridgway, called "the coolest town you've never heard of" by *Forbes Magazine*, straddles the Uncompahgre River below the Sneffels Range. Ridgway started as a railroad junction and transportation hub in 1890 by road builder Otto Mears for his Rio Grande Southern Railroad. The railroad, which ran 172 miles from Ridgway to Durango via Dolores, linked the rich, isolated mines at Telluride, Ophir, and Rico with the Denver & Rio Grande Railroad's main line in Montrose. The town, earlier known as Dallasville, was renamed by the railroaders for R. M. Ridgway, the superintendent of the Denver & Rio Grande's mountain division. During its heyday, the town boasted a railroad yard, stockyards, the 55-room Mentone Hotel, and a depot that still stands.

Now Ridgway is a quiet crossroads with an eclectic population of artists, adventurers, retirees, and ranchers and a laid-back, friendly atmosphere. Sherman Street, the town's main street, heads west from US 550 toward Telluride. North of Sherman are plenty of shops, restaurants, and Hartwell Park, a big green square shaded by tall cottonwoods—perfect for picnics and summer festivals like the Ridgway Rendezvous in August. Ridgway is a designated Creative District for its artists, galleries, and public art, including murals and sculptures. If you stop for lunch in Ridgway, try Kate's Place, Provisions Café, Colorado Boy Brewery, or Eatery 66.

For a taste of Ridgway's railroad heritage, stop at the free **Ridgway Railroad Museum** and a Chamber of Commerce visitor center on the south side of Sherman Street west of the junction of US 550 and CO 62. The museum preserves and interprets the area's rich railroad history through exhibits, photographs, and artifacts. The museum also has a 16-acre site at 200 North Railroad Street with a half-mile of track. A train shed and the museum's rolling stock is at that site, including the unique #4 **Galloping Goose** railcar that once ran on the Rio Grande Railroad tracks through the San Juan Mountains between 1931 and 1951. The unusual

Ouray, named for a famed Ute Indian chief, offers hot springs, waterfalls, historic buildings, and a towering mountain backdrop to travelers.

Galloping Goose, a hybrid of a school bus and truck, carried mail, freight, and a few passengers to cut operating costs. Nearby is the **Ouray County Ranch History Museum** which preserves the area's rich ranching history.

Ridgway serves as a gateway to the San Juan Mountains to the south and 3,201-acre **Ridgway State Park** 4 miles to the north on US 550. The park, dominated by Ridgway Reservoir, is the area's premier lake for water sports with a boat ramp, marina, and lots of cold water for boaters, water-skiers, paddleboarders, boardsailors, and anglers. Fishermen cast lines for rainbow trout up to 20 inches long, perch, smallmouth bass, splake, kokanee salmon, and state-record brown trout that exceed 30 pounds. The park's 3 campgrounds—Dakota Terraces, Elk Ridge, and Pa-Co-Chu-Puk—offer 258 sites for RVs and trailers, 25 walk-in tent sites, and 3 yurts. There are also 14 miles of hiking trails, picnic areas, a swim beach, and visitor center at the 5-mile-long, 1,030-acre reservoir.

The Dallas Divide

From US 550 on the east side of Ridgway, turn west on CO 62. The road crosses the Uncompahgre River and passes through town as Sherman Street. Hartwell Park makes a good picnic site with its shaded tables. The highway bends north out of Ridgway, climbing a scrubby slope of gray shale into Dallas Creek's broad, lush valley, aptly named Pleasant Valley. Bales of fresh hay, drying in the sun, and cattle scatter across green, fenced paddocks. Loghill Mesa walls the valley on the north, while Miller Mesa hems it in on the south. Round Top, a 7,386-foot shale knob, guards the valley's eastern entrance north of the highway. The drive rushes southwest past neat ranch homes, crosses cottonwood-lined Dallas Creek, and stumbles onto a magnificent panorama. **Mount Sneffels** and a long ridge of ragged peaks pierce the southern horizon, forming one of Colorado's most scenic mountain escarpments.

Pastoral ranchland, mostly part of fashion designer Ralph Lauren's 17,000-acre Double RL Ranch, spreads across Dallas Creek's broad valley south of the highway. Humped ridges, thick with scrub oak and aspen, climb to spruce-coated hills, rounded by ancient glaciers, along the foot of the Sneffels Range. The wall of mountains is marked by sheer cliffs, snowfields tucked under north-facing cliffs, ice-filled gullies, sharp summits, and aiguille-studded ridges. A series of high peaks—13,686-foot Cirque Mountain, 13,786-foot Potosi Peak, and 13,819-foot Teakettle Mountain—punctuate the ridge east of Mount Sneffels, an imposing 14,150-foot peak barricaded by immense cliffs. The long ridge to the west is topped by 13,809-foot Dallas Peak, 13,496-foot Mears Peak, and anchored on the west by pointed 12,987-foot Hayden Peak. The Sneffels Range, protected in the 16,587-acre **Mount Sneffels Wilderness Area,** is mostly composed of volcanic rocks.

Mount Sneffels was named in 1874 by the Hayden Survey for a mountain in Jules Verne's novel *Journey to the Center of the Earth.* Dallas Peak was named for George Dallas, US Vice President from 1845 to 1849 and mayor of Philadelphia. Mears Peak commemorates road and railroad builder Otto Mears, while Hayden Peak honors Ferdinand Hayden, leader of the Hayden Geological Survey of 1871 which documented much of the northern Rocky Mountains including Yellowstone. Hayden's indefatigable survey team, including pioneer photographer William Henry Jackson and painter Thomas Moran, later studied western Colorado from 1873 through 1876. The survey climbed, measured, and named the major mountains and ranges; followed the rivers and traversed the high passes; and gathered data on climate, plants, animals, and future mining and agricultural possibilities.

The East Dallas and West Dallas Roads head south from the drive to high valleys below the range crest. An excellent hike in the Mount Sneffels Wilderness Area begins at the end of East Dallas Creek Road (CR 7) at the Blue Lakes Trailhead. The 8.6-mile, round-trip hike up **Blue Lakes Trail** (#201) is gorgeous, especially in summer when wildflowers carpet above-timberline meadows. The trail climbs past the 2 lower Blue Lakes to Upper Blue Lake, a glistening alpine lake tucked in an alpine cirque below Mount Sneffels at 11,720 feet. The views of Sneffels, Gilpin Peak, Dallas Peak, and S-4 are astounding.

The rugged Sneffels Range, dashed with early snow, rises above autumn's last golden cottonwood trees below Dallas Divide.

Past the Double RL Ranch, the highway ascends the broad flank of a plateau, gaining 1,500 feet in 4 miles to the 8,983-foot summit of **Dallas Divide** and one of Colorado's classic mountain vistas. A couple of overlooks, one below the top of the pass and the other at the summit, yield wide views of the mountainous escarpment to the south. To the east towers Uncompahgre and Wetterhorn Peaks, both over 14,000 feet, and blocky Chimney Peak and Courthouse Mountain. The divide's summit, surrounded by aspen-covered hills, was once the site of a railroad station, post office, and stock-loading chutes for cattle being shipped to market. The dense aspen forests atop Dallas Divide are spectacular in late September, when the flush of gold leaves brightens the hillsides. The overlooks provide superb opportunities for scenic photographs of snowy mountains looming above aspen woodlands.

The San Miguel River

The highway runs west from Dallas Divide down a shallow draw. Stands of aspen flutter on rolling hills among meadows of sagebrush and grass and low willows huddle along Leopard Creek. The Last Dollar Road, a scenic dirt road connecting Dallas Divide and Telluride, heads southwest across Hastings Mesa a mile west of the divide summit. The road offers scenic views of Mount Wilson and Wilson Peak in the San Miguel Range.

The highway, following the old railroad bed, drops west down Leopard Canyon toward the **San Miguel River,** a tributary of the Dolores River. The canyon deepens as it descends, with steep slopes broken by cliff bands above the drive. The timbered remains of a carnotite claim, the Omega Mine, perch high on the south mountainside near the canyon mouth.

The drive reaches the junction of CO 62 and 145 at **Placerville** in the San Miguel River Canyon, 24 miles from Ridgway. Turn south on Colorado 145 toward Telluride. The 133-mile-long Unaweep-Tabeguache Scenic Byway (Scenic Drive 27), heading north on CO 62, begins here.

Placerville, at 7,321 feet, spreads along the highway on the narrow floor of the San Miguel River Canyon. Although its origins are uncertain, the town sprang up sometime in the 1870s after prospectors discovered color in gravel deposits along the river floodplain. By 1878 a post office was established, and large placer operations lent the name Placerville to the new community. In autumn of 1890, about the time the placer deposits played out, the Rio Grande Southern Railway reached Placerville. The town formed a good railroad junction, with the main line steaming upriver to Telluride and another line heading down-canyon to other towns. Placerville quickly became a major shipping center for thousands of cattle in western Colorado. Even as late as 1949, more than 1,000 carloads of sheep embarked to market from here.

The drive heads south through Placerville on CO 145 and up the canyon. The San Miguel River, beginning in the mountains above Telluride, riffles over cobbles and worn boulders below the highway. Tall narrow-leaf cottonwoods and thick willows line its banks. The river, a favorite of fly fishermen and kayakers, offers excellent trout fishing. Red sandstone layers form cliff bands on the steep canyon walls.

The highway, following an old railroad grade, winds through a series of small towns that once served as mining centers and railroad stops. At Fall Creek, Fall Creek Road (CR 57P) climbs south to Woods Lake, a pretty lake nestled in a high cirque below Dolores Peak. The town of **Sawpit** boomed as a 1890s mining town after the Champion Belle Mine yielded $1,800 in silver with its first three carloads. The mill foundations are all that remain of **Vanadium,** another mining town that dug and milled vanadium, an alloy used in hardening steel. Uranium, used in World War II, also was extracted here. Silver Pick Road (CR 60M) heads south from Vanadium up Big Bear Creek to Silver Pick Basin, the base camp for climbers that scale the three "Fourteeners"—Wilson Peak, Mount Wilson, and El Diente Peak—in the San Miguel Range.

The drive begins climbing Keystone Hill 10 miles from Placerville. South Fork Road (CR 53L), leading to Ilium and Ames, turns south from the drive up the San Miguel's South Fork just after the ascent begins. The highway clings to the steep mountainside under a palisade of sandstone bluffs. Good views of Sunshine Peak and the South Fork valley lie south of the highway. After 3 miles the drive emerges in a flat-bottomed glaciated valley ringed by towering mountains. Telluride, a picturesque ski community, straddles the valley's eastern head. The scenic drive reaches a roundabout and goes right on highway 145 across the valley, but a spur road heads 3 miles east to Telluride.

Telluride

Telluride boasts perhaps the most spectacular setting of any American town. Mountains rise almost a vertical mile out of Telluride's broad valley. Cliff bands, seamed by frothy waterfalls, punctuate the mountain flanks, and spruce and fir forests, broken by glades of quaking aspen, spill down steep slopes. Snowfields whiten the upper alpine cirques and rocky ridges, and arêtes form bold outlines against the azure sky. Telluride is a place to savor, to stop and stretch, and to gaze in awe at nature's stunning artistry. It also offers some of North America's most magnificent skiing terrain.

The town, like most San Juan communities, began as a supply center for local mines. Gold was first discovered here in 1875, and the following year J. B. Ingram located the fabulously wealthy Smuggler Mine. The strike produced 18 ounces of gold and 800 ounces of silver per ton. The town, established in 1878, was named for tellurium, a rare element found in association with gold and silver. Colorful locals, however, said the name derived from "To hell you ride," a reference to the town's winter isolation and rowdy reputation.

Telluride thrived on its earth riches, eventually yielding almost $400 million from its mines, including the Black Bear, Liberty Bell, Cimarron, Japan, Champion, and Snow Drift Mines. Almost 300 miles of tunnels puncture the surrounding mountains. With the 1890 arrival of the railroad, Telluride boomed and reached a population of 5,000.

All the excitement also brought ruffians and outlaws. On June 24, 1889, a small-time robber and two of his gang helped themselves to $10,000 at the San Miguel Valley Bank and fled north to Brown's Park near Wyoming. Butch Cassidy had pulled off his first holdup and set off down history's path of infamy. The 1893 silver panic closed Telluride's silver mines and almost bankrupted the new railway, but valuable gold strikes brought new prosperity to the town in the late 1890s. With them came trouble between newly formed miners' unions and mine owners. By 1930 Telluride's population had dwindled to only 512 residents, even though over $60 million of precious metals had been dug from the district.

Deep snow, however, saved Telluride and created new fortunes based on feet of powder snow. The first rope tow opened in 1945 and hauled skiers up slopes for a couple seasons before closing. In 1958 the area reopened for skiing with a new tow powered by an auto engine and $5 lift tickets. The **Telluride ski area** grew from those humble beginnings and became a busy resort in the 1980s after the town airport was completed.

Telluride is now one of Colorado's best winter playgrounds with downhill and cross-country skiing, snowboarding, dog sledding, ice skating on the town rink, and world-class ice climbing on Bridal Veil Falls. While many skiers think steep expert plunges when **Telluride Ski Resort** is mentioned, the fact is that the **Telluride Mountain Village** area offers plenty of groomed terrain for both beginner and intermediate skiers. The area boasts over 2,000 skiable acres, 127 runs, a 3,845-foot vertical drop served by lifts and a 4,425-foot vertical drop reached by hiking, an astonishing 330 inches of snow every winter, 3 terrain parks, and stunning scenery. The longest run is 4.6-mile Galloping Goose. A free gondola carries skiers between Telluride and Mountain Village, climbing 1,790 feet in 3 miles.

Telluride, proclaimed a National Historic District in 1961, preserves its rich past. The New Sheridan Hotel, built in 1895, still beds visitors, and next door stands the 200-seat Sheridan Opera House, now a movie theater. The town, despite soaring land prices and encroaching condominium developments, maintains a quaint Victorian charm. A parade of festivals brings visitors to Telluride, including the premier **Telluride Bluegrass Festival** in June and September's renowned **Telluride Film Festival.**

After the snow melts, Telluride gears up for summer fun. The surrounding mountains are ground zero for alpine recreation with hiking trails, peaks to climb, bouldering and rock climbing areas, lakes and streams for fishing, mountain bike trails, scenic drives, waterfalls, hot springs, historic sites, ghost towns, 4x4 road adventures, camping, via ferrata, and festivals that celebrate Colorado.

The town makes a super base camp for backcountry explorers after the snow melts. Outdoor adventurers find plenty of recreation with hiking trails, mountains to climb, climbing areas, a via ferrata, fly fishing in streams and lakes, mountain bike trails, spectacular waterfalls, ghosts towns, and 4x4 tracks. Over 100 trails lace nearby valleys and peaks. Hike the Deep Creek and Sneffels High Line Trails north of town, explore a maze of trails in the Mountain Village, or hike Bear Creek Trail to Bear Creek Falls.

Off-road drivers find some of Colorado's best 4-wheel-drive trails for ATVs and lifted jeeps in the Telluride area. Drive over Black Bear Pass from US 550 and descend into Telluride on a steep, switchbacking nightmare, cross 12,840-foot Imogene Pass to Ouray, or drive Ophir Pass, one of the easier 4x4 tracks. It's easy to hire a guide and leave the driving to an experienced hand.

Other Telluride adventures are hiking to beautiful lakes like **Hope Lake** and **Navajo Lake;** fly fishing in the **San Miguel River;** taking a 9-mile raft trip down the lower San Miguel; knocking golf balls around **Telluride Golf Course;** and visiting waterfalls, including Bridal Veil Falls, the highest in Colorado, and Cornet Creek Falls. An airy adventure is edging across the **Telluride Via Ferrata,** a horizontal climbing route with cables, foot pegs, ladders, and beefy bolts. Hire a local guide if you don't have gear or experience.

Ophir & Lizard Head Pass

Back on the drive, CO 145 crosses the valley west of Telluride and swings up a mountain flank. The highway quickly reaches a rolling bench high above the San Miguel River's South Fork valley. The road rolls across this high plateau over open grasslands and through aspen groves. Marvelous views unfold from every highway bend. Wilson Peak, a sharp 14,023-foot mountain, and 12,930-foot Sunshine Mountain tower to the southwest, while peaks loom across the northern and eastern skylines. The Ophir Needles lift a ridge of pinnacles and buttresses above the asphalt.

Past Cushman Lake and 15-site Sunshine Campground, a side road climbs to the ghost town of Alta and Alta Lakes. Follow the spiraling dirt road to the 3 glistening lakes in a cirque below 13,470-foot Silver Mountain. The area has camping, hiking, fly fishing, mountain biking, and views of the serrated Ophir Needles. Also visit the ghost town of Alta, a deserted mining camp founded in 1877.

Past the Alta turn, the highway steeply drops toward the narrow canyon mouth of the Howard Fork and **Ophir.** Ophir began as an 1870s silver camp and flourished as a railroad stop in the 1890s. One of the first roads to Telluride came over 11,750-foot Ophir Pass from Silverton; today that road is a relatively easy but scenic four-wheel-drive tour from Red Mountain Pass on US 550. Old Ophir, a collection of rustic cabins, sits east of the drive in a U-shaped hanging valley. The railroad's famed Ophir Loop traversed the canyon entrance, where today's highway runs. The great loop twisted up wooden trestles to gain elevation to put the train into the upper valley below the final pull up Lizard Head Pass. The Ophir Wall, popular with local rock climbers, is the huge cliff on the left side of the valley left of the scenic drive. Consult *Rock Climbing Colorado* (FalconGuides) for climbing beta on the cliff.

The drive steadily ascends through spruce forest, wide meadows, and willow thickets to the summit of 10,222-foot **Lizard Head Pass,** the drive's high point. A small picnic area, parking lot, and overlook lie on the summit. Interpretative displays explain the area's history, geology, and natural history. The old Rio Grande Southern Railway climbed over the pass here, its bed sitting south of the highway in the meadow. The railroad, built by Otto Mears for $9 million, ran from Ridgway to Durango from 1890 until 1951. Native Americans used the pass for 7,000 years

before that. The first known white men in the area were 60 St. Louis Fur Company trappers who spent a summer trapping beaver around **Trout Lake** in 1833.

The pass is named for **Lizard Head,** a 13,113-foot tower with a reputation as Colorado's most difficult mountain summit to reach. The crumbling 400-foot-high volcanic peak was first ascended by pioneer climbers Albert Ellingwood and Barton Hoag in 1920. It was probably the most difficult rock climb in America at the time. Colorado Springs climber Ellingwood, who learned climbing skills as a Rhodes Scholar in England between 1910 and 1913, led Lizard Head with only 3 soft iron pitons and a short hemp rope for protection. The dangerous peak, considered Colorado's most difficult mountain summit to reach, is covered with loose rock and is rarely ascended.

Lizard Head sits, along with neighboring Wilson Peak, Mount Wilson, and El Diente Peak, in the 41,309-acre Lizard Head Wilderness Area north of the highway. The wilderness can be accessed by the Lizard Head Trail (#505) from a trailhead on the pass summit. Sheep Mountain, a 13,188-foot peak, looms south of the drive. Silverton hides a mere 9 miles as the crow flies from the pass over Vermilion Peak to the east.

The Dolores River Valley

The highway heads southwest from the pass summit, gently descending along Snow Spur Creek. As the road and creek drop, the valley narrows into a short, steep canyon. The Rico Mountains stud the western horizon, and 14,252-foot Mount Wilson and Lizard Head lift above rounded, spruce-covered ridges to the north. After a couple of miles the drive reaches the **Dolores River** in a glaciated valley. Beaver ponds block the meandering river. Thick spruce forest blankets the southern hillsides, while aspen groves broken by wide meadows coat the steep northern slopes. Cayton Campground, with 27 sites (including 18 electric sites), lines the riverbank a couple of miles down. FR 535 climbs out of the valley here and leads to Dunton, Dunton Hot Springs, and the West Dolores River. As the highway descends the river valley, it passes through a succession of tilted sandstone formations, including Dakota and Entrada sandstones and Triassic and Permian redbeds deposited on floodplains over 200 million years ago.

After almost 10 miles the glaciated valley squeezes into a river-cut canyon. The drive passes a **San Juan National Forest Information Station** just before Rico. This restored log building has a natural history museum, restrooms, free wifi, and dispenses guidebooks, maps, and advice on outdoor fun in the area.

Ponderosa pine branches frame changing aspens and ragged Ophir Ridge near Lizard Head Pass.

The highway continues west, passing **Rico Hot Springs,** several hot pots on private land, and then crosses the Dolores River to the old mining town of **Rico.** This charming town, at 8,827 feet, spreads along a hillside above the river. The road is lined with old stone and brick buildings and Victorian homes. Gold was discovered here as early as 1866, but Native Americans drove away the intruding prospectors. Mining, however, began in earnest after the Utes ceded the San Juans in 1873. Rico boomed after 1879 when silver was found on Telescope and Dolores Mountains. Later mines extracted lead, zinc, and gold from the area's volcanic rocks. The town boomed after the Rio Grande Southern Railroad connected Rico with Ridgway and Durango in 1891, with a population of about 5,000 in 1892. The busy town flourished with a 3-block red light district called "The Houses of Ill Fame," 23 saloons, 2 churches, 2 newspapers, a bank, mercantile store, court-house, and theater.

Now Rico, with a population of 265, is a quiet, laid-back town that serves as a jumping-off point for outdoor adventures. The historic town boasts the Artists of Rico (ARC), a thriving community of local artists and craftspeople. Stop by work-shops, studios, and galleries to talk with artists and enjoy their creations. East of town is **Rico Hot Springs,** with a couple of soaking pools along the Dolores River.

An interesting stop is the **Rico Historical Museum** in the historic 2-story firehouse. The museum interprets Rico's colorful mining and railroad history, displays photos of cowboys and miners, and offers fascinating exhibits about long-time area rancher Olive Truelson and Betty Pellett, a Broadway star who became a Rico mineowner and later was the first woman House speaker in the Colorado Legislature.

The highway exits Rico and follows the Dolores River for the next 37 miles. As the road heads west, the canyon widens and its slopes step back to rocky rims. Bands of sandstone cliffs, first a wave of salmon-colored Entrada sandstone and then blocky Dakota sandstone, form the canyon sides. The climate dries as the river and highway run west, with scrub oak and ponderosa pine covering the lower canyon slopes.

The 230-mile-long Dolores River originates south of Lizard Head Pass, runs southwest to Dolores, pools in McPhee Reservoir, and twists through sandstone canyons before emptying into the Colorado River above Moab, Utah. The river's name, given by 17th-century Spanish explorers, was shortened from the original *El Rio de Nuestra Señora de los Dolores,* or "The River of Our Lady of Sorrows," to simply the Dolores River. Franciscan priests Silvestre Escalante and Atanasio Dominguez crossed the Dolores River during their epic 1776 exploration of the American Southwest.

Stoner sits at the confluence of the Dolores and West Dolores Rivers partway down-canyon. The unincorporated town, named for nearby Stoner Creek, had a post office from 1917 to 1954. The Stoner Ski Area, which operated from 1951 to 1985, had a 1,250-foot drop, a few wide trails, a lodge and restaurant at the base, a ski school with 4 instructors, and $9 lift tickets. The biggest excitement after the ski area closed was in 2015 when stoners wanted the town to host the annual Colorado Invitational Bong-a-Thon, attracting cannabis lovers for pot-smoking contests, music, and camping. The weedfest, however, also attracted the ire of area residents and the Montezuma County commissioners, who filed a court injunction and stopped the event.

Dolores & the Canyon of the Ancients Visitor Center and Museum

Dolores, a pleasant town spread across the shallow valley at 6,936 feet, sits at the big bend of the Dolores River just upstream from McPhee Reservoir. Established in 1891 along the Rio Grande Southern Railroad, Dolores serves as the southwestern gateway to the San Juan Mountains.

The **Galloping Goose #5,** displayed at the Galloping Goose Historical Society Museum in Dolores, makes an interesting stop. As rail traffic decreased on the railroad, train mechanics devised this ingenious gasoline-powered railcar to continue mail and passenger service. Seven of these silver "railroad buses," made by grafting the bodies of 1927 Pierce Arrow touring autos to railcars, traversed narrow gauge tracks between Ridgway and Durango from 1931 until the railroad closed down in 1952. The Goose, without breakdowns or snowslides, could travel the route's 175 miles in nine hours. They could carry 7 or 8 passengers, mail, and small amounts of freight. Another Goose is displayed at the Ridgway Railroad Museum. The Dolores Goose occasionally makes runs on the Cumbres & Toltec Scenic Railroad in southern Colorado in the summer. Call (888) 286-2737 for information and to reserve a ride.

McPhee Reservoir, formed by the only dam on the otherwise free-flowing Dolores River, supplies irrigation water to the nearby Montezuma Valley for crops, including pinto beans. The 4,470-acre lake, Colorado's second-largest when full, is stocked with rainbow trout, bass, bluegill, and crappie. The 10-mile-long lake, with 50 miles of shoreline, is popular with anglers who catch trout, crappie, large- and small-mouth bass, northern pike, perch, and kokanee salmon. **McPhee Recreation Complex,** on the southwest shore, and **Horse Creek Recreation Complex** on the east shore are popular for boating, water skiing, fishing, hiking, and camping. McPhee Campground offers 71 sites, while the campground at Horse Creek has 65 sites.

Past Dolores, the drive climbs out of the Dolores River Canyon and heads south toward Cortez. A right turn on CO 184 leads to **Escalante Ruin** and the

Seven Galloping Goose railcars, carrying passengers and freight, operated in the San Juan Mountains between 1931 and 1952.

Canyon of the Ancients Visitor Center and Museum. The ruin, a 25-room pueblo occupied by the Ancestral Puebloans from the late 1000s to about 1300, perches atop a bluff overlooking the Montezuma Valley and McPhee Reservoir. The site, excavated in the 1970s as part of the Dolores Archeological Project, is named for its discoverer, Padre Escalante. He wrote in his 1776 journal, "Upon an elevation of the river's south side, there was in ancient times a small settlement of the same type as those of the Native Americans of New Mexico." Dominguez Ruin, named for Escalante's friar partner, sits nearby. The center, run by the Bureau of Land Management, houses artifacts from the ruin and focuses on the Ancestral Puebloans and historic Native Americans, and acquaints visitors with the 176,056-acre **Canyon of the Ancients National Monument,** a vast parkland west of Cortez filled with ancient ruins, rock art, recreation sites, and 3 wilderness study areas.

Cortez to Durango

The drive heads south on CO 145 for 10 miles, running past small ranches and farms shaded by tall cottonwoods. The highway ends at its junction with US 160 on the east side of **Cortez.** Turn left onto US 160 for the last 46 miles of the San Juan Skyway. Mesa Verde stretches its high escarpment to the south. Its entrance and a scenic park road begin 10 miles east of here on US 160.

Cortez, the seat of Montezuma County, still thrives as an agricultural and ranching town and offers all traveler amenities. Considered to be the archaeological center of the US, Cortez was originally called Tséyaa Tó, or "Rock water," by the Navajos for its nearby springs. Since its founding in 1886, Cortez has been the ranching and agricultural center for the Montezuma Valley.

Navajos live on the sprawling Navajo Nation to the southwest of Cortez in New Mexico, Arizona, and southern Utah, and Utes on the Ute Mountain Reservation south of Cortez. Ute arts and crafts are displayed at many Cortez galleries, and dances and cultural programs are held at the **Cortez Cultural Center** through the summer.

The **Ute Mountain Tribe,** one of 3 recognized tribes in the Ute Nation, are descendants of the Weeminuche Band, who once lived throughout the San Juan Mountains. They were relocated from their homeland to the reservation in 1897. Ute Mountain Reservation, covering 553,008 acres in southwest Colorado, includes lowland desert, mountains, and the southern part of Mesa Verde.

The tribe's **Ute Mountain Tribal Park** along the Mancos River in Mesa Verde is one of the most astounding archeological treasures in the United States with hundreds of cliff dwellings, surface sites, and rock art panels from the Ancestral Puebloan peoples and the historic Utes. Visitation to the 125,000-acre park is strictly regulated and all visitors must explore the area accompanied by a Ute guide. The park is a great outdoor museum with numerous ruins like Morris 3, She House, Porcupine House, Eagle Nest House, and Lion House, the largest in the park, that were inhabited between 1100 and the late 1200s before being abandoned. The sites remain the same as when the ancient ones left, with corncobs, potsherds, colored flint used to chip arrowheads, and yucca twine. The tribe offers a variety of tours, including full-day, half-day, and private trips that require driving on rough roads or taking a tribal shuttle, hiking several miles, and climbing ladders. For more information and reservations, visit utemountaintribalpark.info or call (970) 565-9653.

The San Juan Skyway runs east from Cortez, passing the entrance to **Mesa Verde National Park.** This marvelous parkland, one of America's premier archaeological areas and a United Nations World Heritage Site, is explored by the Mesa Verde drive (see Scenic Drive 28). It's worth at least a day to visit the park and its best sites. *National Geographic* calls it one of the world's 50 must-see attractions.

The drive continues east from the park's entrance on US 160 and drops into the broad valley of the Mancos River. The town of **Mancos,** at 7,035 feet, is a ranching and agricultural center nestled in the valley below the rugged La Plata Range, the westernmost extension of the Rocky Mountains in Colorado. The river was named *Rio de los Mancos* (River of the Cripple) by Escalante and Dominguez on their 1776 expedition, for one of their injured members. The town was laid out in 1881. One of the first families to settle here were the Wetherills at their Alamo Ranch. The Wetherill brothers were among the first Anglos to discover the cliff dwellings in nearby Mesa Verde, including Cliff Palace in 1888.

Mancos, named by *Smithsonian Magazine* in 2016 as one of "America's best small towns to visit," offers a quiet ambiance, good restaurants, a distillery, coffee house, a thriving arts community, and the **Columbine Bar,** one of Colorado's oldest continuously operating saloons. A plaque on the bar's brick exterior dates its establishment to 1910, but a painted sign hanging from the rafters says 1903. The plaque states that a newspaper article in 1948 called it "an old bar run by old timers." Local legend recalls that Mancos children were told to walk on the opposite side of Grand Avenue to avoid passing the notorious bar.

A turn north on CO 184 in Mancos leads a few miles north to **Mancos State Park.** The centerpiece of this 553-acre park is Jackson Gulch Reservoir, a 216-acre lake that supplies drinking water to Mancos and Mesa Verde National Park. This pretty recreation area, attracting Arizona and New Mexico visitors escaping the summer heat, offers dramatic views of the La Plata Range, 32 campsites in two campgrounds that are shaded by ponderosa pines, wakeless boating, trout fishing, birdwatching, and educational programs. The park also has 5.5 miles of trails including a 3.5-mile-long trail that circles the lake.

Route 160, the Navajo Trail, climbs eastward from Mancos to the crest of a divide between the Mancos River and Animas River watersheds before descending along the East Fork of the La Plata River. The La Plata Mountains tower to the north. **Hesperus Ski Area,** an intimate local slope, is on the south side of the highway before the small village of Hesperus. The 160-acre area has a 600-foot vertical drop, 26 trails, and 150 inches of annual snowfall. It's best known for night skiing, staying open until 9 p.m. most evenings, but also has a ski school, rentals, tubing, and base lodge.

Forest Road 124 heads north from **Hesperus,** following the La Plata River into the heart of the La Plata Mountains. The scenic road offers backcountry camping, fly fishing, hiking, and climbing the high peaks. The highway continues to descend eastward through Lightner Creek's steep canyon, and, 11 miles from Hesperus, completes the San Juan Skyway loop drive at the junction of US 160 and US 550 in Durango.

Flat Tops Trail Scenic Byway

Meeker to Yampa

General description: The 82-mile-long Flat Tops Trail, a National Forest Scenic Byway, traverses the upper White River valley and crosses Ripple Creek and Dunckley Passes on the White River Plateau.

Special attractions: Meeker, White River, Flat Tops Wilderness Area, Trappers Lake, Ripple Creek Pass, autumn colors, fly fishing, hiking, camping, backpacking, scenic views.

Location: Northwestern Colorado. The drive begins in Meeker, 41 miles north of I-70 and Rifle, and ends in Yampa, 31 miles south of Steamboat Springs.

Route name and numbers: Flat Tops Trail Scenic Byway, Rio Blanco CR 8, FR 16, Routt CR 17.

Travel season: Only the lower road outside Meeker is open year-round; otherwise, the

drive closes after the first snow and opens after the spring thaw. Check with the forest office for road conditions and closures.

Camping: Campgrounds along the drive are North Fork (28 sites) and Vaughan Lake (6 sites). Himes Peak (11 sites) is on FR 205 to Trappers Lake, and Trapline (13 sites), Bucks (10 sites), Horsethief (5 sites), Cutthroat (14 sites), and Shepherds Rim (15 sites) cluster near Trappers Lake. Other forest campgrounds are on side roads.

Services: All services are in Meeker and Yampa. Limited services in Buford.

Nearby attractions: Rifle Falls State Park, Rifle Mountain Park, Grand Hogback, Stagecoach State Park, Steamboat Lake State Park, Pearl Lake State Park, Steamboat Springs, Gore Pass, Finger Rock, Upper Yampa River, Dinosaur National Monument.

The Route

The White River Plateau, part of Colorado's plateau geographic province, lies west of the main bulk of the Rocky Mountains between the Yampa and Colorado Rivers. Deep canyons and valleys excavated by rivers and streams dissect this upland of raised sandstone layers. Ancient lava flows top the plateau's central section, forming the magnificent 235,214-acre **Flat Tops Wilderness Area.**

The 82-mile-long Flat Tops Trail Scenic Byway begins in Meeker west of the plateau and follows the White River's deep gash eastward almost to the heart of the Flat Tops before swerving northeast over Ripple Creek and Dunckley Passes to the Yampa River's upper valley. The road crosses the ancestral homeland of the Ute tribe, the second-oldest national forest in the US, and some of Colorado's best aspen colors and most dramatic scenic views.

Temperatures along the drive, open spring through fall, vary according to elevation. Summer highs in the lowlands near Meeker climb into the low 90s, while 4,000 feet higher atop the passes the temperatures range in the 60s or 70s.

Flat Tops Trail Scenic Byway

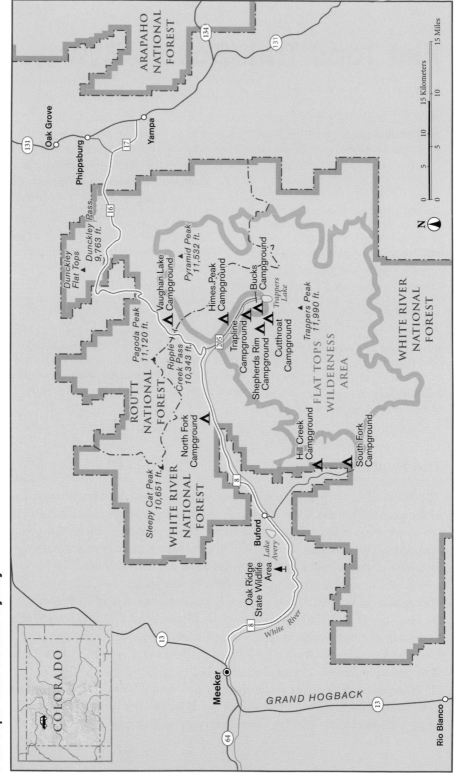

Expect chilly nights at the higher elevations, including Trappers Lake, with lows dipping to the 30s and 40s. Insect repellent checks mosquitoes along the drive's moist creeks, beaver ponds, and lakes. Expect afternoon thunderstorms, some locally heavy. Drive carefully during and after rain—the gravel roads can be slippery. September and early October brings cool, crisp days. The first snow falls on the higher mountains by late October, and the road closes in early November until spring thaw. Check with the forest offices in Meeker and Yampa for road closing and opening dates. The drive's upper reaches accumulate as much as 10 feet of snow, allowing for excellent snowmobiling and cross-country skiing.

Meeker

Meeker, a pleasant off-the-beaten-track town, nestles in the White River Valley. The fertile bottomland along the river has long attracted settlers. The earliest residents were Utes, who camped among cottonwoods along the river and grazed their horses in lush pastures. The Utes, Colorado's mountain tribe, ranged across the Rocky Mountains, gathering edible plants and hunting plentiful game. Summer camps in the mountains offered superb hunting, while winter camps were made in mild valleys.

After gold was discovered in Colorado's high country in the 1860s, a collision between the Utes and incoming prospectors and settlers was inevitable. A series of treaties drove the Utes from their ancestral mountain homeland. An 1868 treaty ceded central Colorado from the San Luis Valley to North Park to incoming Anglo settlers and miners. Western Colorado remained reserved for the Utes. Rich mineral discoveries in the San Juan Mountains, however, precipitated another pact, and the Utes were relocated to southwestern and northwestern Colorado. Settlers still chafed that almost a third of Colorado remained in Ute hands, and by 1876 the state legislature asked Congress to relocate the Utes to an Oklahoma reservation. In 1879 Colorado Governor Frederick Pitkin wrote, "If this reservation could be extinguished, and the land thrown open to settlers, it will furnish homes to thousands of the people of our State who desire homes." The beginning of the end of the Ute presence in western Colorado came near Meeker in 1879.

The fertile river bottom west of Meeker, originally known as Powell Park for Major John Wesley Powell, who explored here in 1868, was the site of the White River Indian Agency. The agency, established in 1869, had a succession of agents until Nathaniel C. Meeker came in 1878. Meeker, who established the town of Greeley as an agricultural utopia in the early 1870s, arrived with the idea of domesticating the Utes, changing them from a nomadic people to sedentary Christian agriculturists. Conflict became inevitable after Meeker forbade hunting, fishing, gambling, and other traditional activities. Meeker angered the Utes further

by digging an irrigation trench across their racetrack and plowing under a prime winter horse pasture. On September 29, 1879, the Utes rebelled by killing Meeker and 11 men at the agency, taking Meeker's wife and daughter and three others as captives. A military force led by Captain Thomas Thorburgh was also defeated by the Utes. After the hostages were released, a new agreement was signed in 1880 that pushed the White River Utes onto today's reservation in Utah. The Meeker Massacre site lies 4 miles west of Meeker on CO 64.

Today Meeker, the 6,180-foot-high seat of Rio Blanco County, serves as a supply center for area sheep and cattle ranches. The town, established in 1883, bills itself as the "Gateway to the Flat Tops." The town thrives on hunters who flock here in October and November and recreationists who come for the surrounding wilderness and spectacular mountain scenery. Meeker's **White River Museum,** housed in 2 original 1880 log cabins built by US cavalry troops that served as officers' quarters, offers displays of pioneer and Native American artifacts and historical photos. Annual events include the Wagon Wheel OHV Rendezvous, Meeker Classic Sheepdog Championship Trials, and the annual **Range Call Festival and Rodeo.** This community event, held every 4th of July since 1938, is Colorado's oldest continuously operating rodeo, although Meeker's first rodeo was in 1885. Besides bucking broncos and barrel racing, the event has a big parade, pancake breakfast, 5k run, root beer floats, and a concert with artists like Clint Black.

Meeker to Ripple Creek Pass

The drive heads east from Meeker along Rio Blanco CR 8 on the northern edge of Agency Park. The White River meanders gracefully across the grassy valley, past hay fields and grazing cattle. Low hills, coated with juniper and sagebrush, flank the flat-bottomed valley. After 6 miles the road passes 9,498-acre **Oak Ridge State Wildlife Area,** a large tract north of the byway with high eroded bluffs, rolling hills, and Lake Avery. The area offers bow hunting and trout fishing. Past the wildlife area, the broad valley narrows into a canyon.

The **White River Agency Monument,** marking the original agency site, sits alongside the road 7 miles from Meeker. Nathaniel Meeker floated the buildings downstream to Powell Park in 1878, thinking it a better farming area. Ranches spread across the canyon floor, with thick stands of cottonwoods and willows lining the river bank. Spruce and fir darken the moist north-facing slopes above the river, while junipers stud the dry south-facing hillsides.

The drive passes the **Lake Avery Unit of Oak Ridge State Wildlife Area** at 20 miles. This large reservoir offers great fishing year-round, as well as camping

Meeker, dubbed "Gateway to the Flat Tops," is a remote town where the Old West lives on.

and picnicking facilities. The drive enters 7,009-foot **Buford** a mile later. A store offers supplies and gasoline, the last services until Yampa. The settlement was named for Civil War Brigadier General John Buford, who commanded a cavalry division on the first day of the Battle of Gettysburg in 1863 that kept the Rebels at bay until reinforcements arrived. Buford died of typhoid fever at age 37 later that year. The New Castle–Buford Road, FR 244, begins here and twists south up the South Fork of the White River and across the White River Plateau's western edge to New Castle on the Colorado River.

The drive continues northeast, following the north bank of the White River. Large aspen groves spill down the south canyon slopes, and dense scrub oak thickets blanket the north hillside. The paved road ends at 31 miles and becomes gravel for the next 47 miles. The 2,285,970-acre **White River National Forest** borders the river north of the road. The drive enters the forest 11 miles east of Buford and becomes FR 8. North Fork Campground, with 28 sites at 7,750 feet on the left side of the road, spreads across grassy meadows among towering aspens 0.5 mile into the forest. The canyon narrows as the road runs east. After a few miles the road climbs away from the river up a shallow valley, swings across wooded slopes to Ripple Creek, and reaches a junction with FR 205 40 miles from Meeker.

FR 205 leads south above the North Fork of the White River 8 miles to **Trappers Lake Recreation Area,** passing 11-site Himes Peak Campground on the way. Trappers Lake, the headwaters of the White River, glistens like a shiny jewel cupped in a high basin surrounded by flat-topped mountain peaks. Sometimes called the "Cradle of Wilderness," Trappers Lake figured prominently in the preservation of public lands as wilderness. The area was first protected by President Benjamin Harrison in 1891 as the 1.2-million-acre White River Plateau Timberland Reserve, the nation's second national forest. In 1919 the USDA Forest Service decided to develop the recreational potential of Trappers Lake by building summer cabins, lodges, guest ranches, a loop road around the lake, and other amenities. A 27-year-old landscape architect, Arthur Carhart, was hired to study the plan.

After viewing the scenic site, Carhart made the radical assertion that the area should be preserved as untrammeled wilderness and any development should be made at least a half mile from the lakeshore. Carhart wrote in his report: "There are a number of places with scenic values of such great worth that they are rightfully the property of all people. They should be preserved for all time for the people of the Nation and the world. Trappers Lake is unquestionably a candidate for that classification."

The Forest Service, with Carhart's recommendation, dropped plans for the lakeside road and refused private home sites. Carhart went on, with famed naturalist Aldo Leopold from the Forest Service's Albuquerque office, to establish the nation's first wilderness area in New Mexico's Gila National Forest. In 1929 the Trappers Lake area became the Flat Tops Primitive Area, which, after the establishment of the national wilderness system in 1964, became the 235,214-acre Flat Tops Wilderness Area in 1979.

Trappers Lake serves as a popular starting point for hikers and horseback riders venturing into the wilderness area. The wilderness includes more than 30 fishable lakes and 160 miles of trails that lace its remote backcountry. Five forest campgrounds—Shepherds Rim, Cutthroat, Bucks, Horsethief, and Trapline—perch on ridges north of the lake. Several trails drop down to Trappers Lake, offering scenic views and fishing access. The lake houses native cutthroat trout that reproduce naturally in its clear, cold water. Fishing is allowed only with flies or one-hook lures; native trout between 11 and 16 inches must be released; and fishing is not permitted in the lake's inlets and outlet from January 1 through July 31 to allow trout to spawn.

An excellent hike climbs east from Trappers Lake on Trail #1814 to the lofty Chinese Wall, an above-timberline cliffed escarpment. A scenic 10.5-mile loop hike follows trails to Devil's Causeway, Chinese Wall, and Bear River. The **Devil's Causeway** segment is jaw-dropping, with the trail threading along a 3-foot-wide ridge with vertical drops on each side. For a 2- or 3-day backpacking excursion, start at Trappers Lake and make a 23-mile loop out to Wall Lake.

Ripple Creek Pass to Yampa

The drive, continuing east on CR 8, begins switchbacking up a broad ridge through lush aspen stands and open meadows. After 5 miles of climbing, the road, now in spruce and lodgepole pine forest, reaches **Ripple Creek Overlook.** This high viewpoint yields expansive views west down the White River Valley and south into the heart of the Flat Tops. Interpretive signs discuss the wilderness concept, watchable wildlife, and the area's geology.

The drive crosses 10,343-foot **Ripple Creek Pass** and enters 1,125,438-acre Routt National Forest 1.5 miles later. The road descends east down spruce-clad slopes above Poose Creek and reaches Vaughan Lake almost 3 miles later. A six-site forest campground at 9,720 feet nestles under trees along the edge of the small reservoir. Reach the lake by driving through the campground and following a short road to a parking area on the lake's east shore. The drive spirals down through thick aspen and conifer forest into the upper valley of the East Fork of the Williams Fork River. **Pyramid Guard Station,** built by the Civilian Conservation Corps in 1934 to 1936 near the valley head, continues to serve as a busy Forest Service center in summer. The buildings, including an office, barn, wood shed, and blacksmith shop, are built in the Rustic Style with log walls, exposed log eaves, and small windows. The station was placed on the National Register of Historic Places in 2007.

The aspen-lined lane runs north from the station in the Williams Fork River Valley. Tall cottonwoods and green meadows clot the river's banks, and gray sagebrush colors the dry hillsides above. The road crosses the river at the old townsite of Pyramid, now a collection of summer cabins, and begins ascending steep slopes above the valley.

After twisting up for 3 miles, the drive swings under the **Dunckley Flat Tops,** a long ridge broken into flat-topped 10,000-foot summits. The road threads across steep slopes, passing through thick aspen forest, and reaches the summit of 9,763-foot **Dunckley Pass.** An overlook yields superb views southward to 11,532-foot Pyramid Peak, the Little Flat Tops, and 12,133-foot Orno Peak in the Flat Tops Wilderness Area. Midsummer wildflowers, including columbines, carpet the lush meadows on the pass summit.

The drive drops east from the pass, dipping through several drainages before bending northeast down Oak Creek's valley. A side road, FR 959, leads 3 miles south to Sheriff Reservoir, 6-site Sheriff Reservoir Campground, and trails that lead south into the Flat Tops Wilderness. The road bumps through the shallow valley for a couple of miles past beaver ponds and a thick fir and spruce woodland, before turning up a grassy side canyon. A half mile later it crosses a low divide and the turnoff on FR 940 which leads 1.4 miles to Chapman Reservoir, popular 12-site Chapman Reservoir Campground. The area offers fishing, hiking, and ATV riding.

The last leg of the scenic drive drops east above Spronks Creek into a valley. The climate and vegetation change as the road descends, with sagebrush coating the drier slopes and aspens clinging to the moist north-facing hillsides. Rolling hills and scattered cattle ranches border the road after it leaves the creek. Keep right at the intersection with FR 925 and head south on Route CR 17. The now-paved road dips and rolls beneath towering 8,020-foot Rattlesnake Butte and Devils Grave Mesa. Sharp volcanic outcrops and pinnacles mingle with sagebrush on the steep mesa slopes. After a couple of miles the road bends east through hay fields and cattle pastures; passes the Byrd Homestead, the first recorded homestead in the Yampa Valley; and enters the small hamlet of **Yampa** perched on the banks of the Yampa River.

The 170-mile-long **Yampa River,** Colorado's longest free-flowing river, begins in the Flat Tops, heads north to Steamboat Springs, and flows west through valleys and canyons to its confluence with the Green River in the heart of Dinosaur National Monument near the Utah border. The Utes called an edible potato-like root that grew on the river's banks *yampa,* and the name was applied to the river and town. The town offers all visitor services.

Hills, banded with layers of sandstone, tower over grazing cattle near Yampa.

In early January 2015, flames burned down Yampa's historic **Royal Hotel.** The longtime landmark and prominent watering hole overlooked unpaved Moffat Avenue from its covered boardwalk and balcony. Locals sat outside the Royal or on the tailgates of pickup trucks to watch the annual 4th of July broom polo competition. The hotel was built in 1903 for the Moffat Railroad, which linked Denver to northwestern Colorado. Hotel history recounts that Old West author Zane Grey stayed there while writing *The Mysterious Rider*. It also served as a hospital ward in the 1919 flu epidemic and as a boarding house for ranch children attending school during the long winters. Hotel guests and employees said the Royal was haunted by a ghost named Rufus who was either a flu patient or a gambler killed while cheating at a poker table.

The drive ends at CO 131 in Yampa. Steamboat Springs sits 31 miles to the north and I-70 lies 39 miles to the south.

Grand Mesa Scenic Byway

Delta to I-70

General description: The 75-mile Grand Mesa Scenic Byway climbs from desert canyons and ranches to the subalpine summit of 10,000-foot-high Grand Mesa, the world's largest flat-topped mountain.

Special attractions: Cedaredge, Pioneer Town, Crag Crest National Recreation Trail, Land's End, Powderhorn Mountain Resort, lakes, fishing, camping, hiking, mountain biking, fall colors, cross-country skiing, snowmobiling.

Location: Western Colorado. The drive begins 4 miles east of Delta at the intersection of CO 92 and 65 and ends at the junction of CO 65 and I-70 east of Grand Junction.

Route names and numbers: Grand Mesa Scenic Byway, Land's End Road, CO 65, FR 100.

Travel season: Year-round. The paved section is open all winter and plowed and sanded after snowstorms. Land's End Road closes in winter.

Camping: Seven National Forest campgrounds—Jumbo (26 sites), Spruce Grove (16 sites), Island Lake (36 sites), Little Bear (36 sites), Cobbett (20 sites), Ward Lake (27 sites), and Crag Crest (11 sites)—are on the mesa top.

Services: All services are in Grand Junction, Delta, and Cedaredge. Limited services at Mesa.

Nearby attractions: Colorado National Monument, Uncompahgre Plateau, Unaweep Canyon, Black Canyon of the Gunnison National Park, West Elk Loop Scenic Byway (Scenic Route 21), West Elk Wilderness Area, Grand Junction attractions, Vega State Park.

The Route

Grand Mesa, lying between the Gunnison and Colorado Rivers in western Colorado, hides a remote, off-the-beaten-track landscape. It's a place studded with shining lakes nestled among spruce woodlands, meadows carpeted with summer wildflowers, creeks lined with willows, and a basalt rim formed by ancient lava flows. The 75-mile-long **Grand Mesa Scenic Byway** traverses this massive island in the sky.

The mesa, with its high point, 11,237-foot Leon Peak, boasts an average elevation of 10,000 feet. The rolling mesa top, called the world's highest flat-topped mountain, is a summer oasis of cool temperatures and plentiful rainfall that towers over surrounding desert valleys. More than 300 lakes stud the upland, and thick woodlands and broad meadows carpet the mesa's hillocks and swales. The drive yields stunning views: golden aspens that cascade over the mesa rim, the broad Grand Valley flanked by upturned plateaus, and snow-capped peaks that gleam in the summer sun.

Grand Mesa Scenic Byway

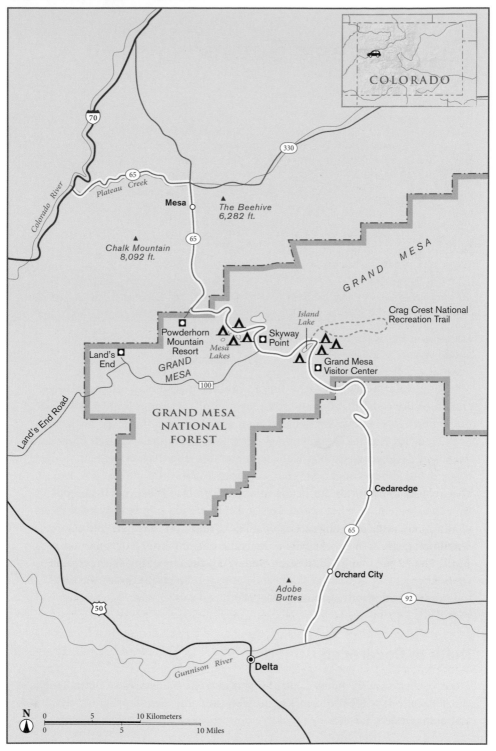

Dense aspen forests blunket the northern slopes of the Grand Mesa, the largest flat-topped mountain in the world.

Temperatures along the drive vary from the semiarid river valleys at either end of the drive and the road's 10,839-foot summit, an almost 6,000-foot elevation difference. Precipitation ranges from 8 or so inches in the desert lowlands to over 30 inches atop the mesa. Summer daytime temperatures regularly climb into the 90s in the lower elevations, while temperatures atop the mesa remain in the 60s and 70s. Summer nights are cool, and occasionally drop into the 30s. Expect afternoon thunderstorms during the summer, with locally heavy rain and possible hail. September brings warm days and cold nights, with infrequent showers. October begins the cool down, with dustings of snow on the higher elevations. The upper mesa road is locked under a mantle of snow from November through April. The Land's End Road closes in winter, but the rest of the drive remains open. Excellent cross-country skiing and snowmobiling trails thread the mesa top, while **Powderhorn Mountain Resort** offers downhill runs. Most of the snowdrifts melt by late May.

Delta to Cedaredge

The drive begins at the intersection of CO 92 and 65, 4 miles east of **Delta.** Delta, at 4,980 feet, sits at the confluence of the Gunnison and Uncompahgre Rivers. It's a pleasant western town, with a walkable downtown and plenty of restaurants.

Points of interest include the **Delta County Museum,** with displays of ranch and farm tools and a butterfly collection; 265-acre **Confluence Park** with 5 miles of hiking trails and a lake for fishing and boating; and **Fort Uncompahgre Living History Museum,** a replica of trapper Antoine Roubidoux's 1820s trading post. The famed **Ute Council Tree,** a spreading 215-year-old cottonwood on the town's north side, was used by Utes, including Chief Ouray, as a meeting place. The ailing tree, with broken limbs, was cut down after Ute prayers and blessings in August 2017. Grand Mesa National Forest's office sits on US 50 on Delta's south side and offers visitor information and maps.

From the junction of US 50 and CO 92 in Delta, drive east on Route 92 for 3.8 miles to the intersection of CO 92 and 65. Turn left or north onto CO 65 near the end of the four-lane highway stretch. The drive's first 11 miles run north to **Cedaredge.** The road goes over cornfields on the valley floor and after 0.8 mile crosses the Gunnison River. Tall cottonwoods and Russian olives line the riverbanks. The highway climbs north into scrubby hills of gray Mancos shale, a deposit laid down on an ancient seabed some 70 million years ago. The Mancos shale stretches along the foot of Grand Mesa, forming a wide, brightly colored band of dissected badlands, broad valleys, and humpbacked ridges. The **Adobe Buttes,** a shale area west of the highway beyond Tongue Creek's lush valley, offer excellent backcountry hiking through austere, barren hills.

The highway ascends a low shale hill onto a broad, gently tilted mesa seamed by Surface Creek's shallow valley. **Orchard City** lies along the creek at 5,800 feet. Orchard City is not actually a town at all but rather a collection of three separate towns—Cory, Austin, and Eckert—each with its own post office. The trio incorporated in 1912 to obtain bonds to build a water system so residents could tap into Grand Mesa's spring runoff for irrigation and home water. The road runs through Orchard City, passing the small towns, old stone buildings, and grassy paddocks with grazing horses and cattle. Surface Creek parallels the blacktop, with cottonwoods, willows, and Russian olives lining its banks.

After crossing the creek a couple of miles north of Eckert, the highway follows the Surface Creek valley and reaches 6,100-foot-high Cedaredge. Cedaredge, the valley's commercial center, is a lovely back roads town. It began as the headquarters for the Bar-I Ranch in the 1890s. Sophie Kohler, the foreman's wife, called the place Cedar Edge, and when the post office was established, the name became Cedaredge.

All that remains of the ranch are three wooden multisided silos. These sit in **Pioneer Town Museum,** a picturesque outdoor museum operated by the Surface Creek Valley Historical Society. The site is open during the summer, and there is no charge. Visitors enjoy a look back at western Colorado's frontier past. Take a stroll along the boardwalk on Pioneer Town's Main Street and imagine life in the 1880s. Visit historic buildings and houses, including the Lizard Head Saloon, Wells-Fargo Express, Coalby Store, barbershop, livery stable, the 1906 Cedaredge Town Jail, a Native American museum, blacksmith shop, schoolhouse, Chapel of the Cross, and three silos from the old Bar-1 Ranch. All are painstakingly furnished and outfitted with period artifacts and antiques. Cedaredge also offers numerous craft shops and hosts the Little Britches Rodeo each July. The town's annual **AppleFest** occurs the first Saturday in October each year.

Cedaredge marks the official beginning of the Grand Mesa Scenic and Historic Byway. The highway passes downtown Cedaredge and climbs north past scattered homes and apple orchards. The Surface Creek valley, along with the North Fork Valley at Paonia, is one of Colorado's renowned fruit-growing areas. Orchards were first planted in 1882 near Cory, and by the 1920s fruit farming became a major industry. Thousands of acres in the Surface Creek valley yield cherries, apricots, plums, peaches, nectarines, pears, and apples between July and October. Roadside stands sell fresh in-season fruit and vegetables at bargain prices.

Delta County is a Colorado agricultural heritage area, boasting over 1,250 farms, orchards, wineries, and ranches. The county's prosperous farms, mostly family owned and operated, grow high-quality fruits, vegetables, wines, and meats, including the legendary Olathe sweet corn. Delta County's booming agritourism business bring visitors to farms and orchards open for tours, 2 distilleries, 12 wineries, farm and ranch stays, you-pick fruits and veggies, farmer's markets, and agricultural workshops.

Grand Mesa

The drive passes apple orchards, drops over Young's Creek, and climbs onto a rolling benchland blanketed with sagebrush and a piñon pine and juniper woodland. **Grand Mesa** towers overhead with steep aspen-covered slopes spilling over basalt cliffs on its rim and down abrupt ravines. The drive climbs through four distinct biological life zones that represent a telescoped journey from Mexico to northern Canada's boreal forest.

The highway bends northwest and skirts the edge of a long ridge. After a few miles the road turns east, climbs onto the ridge, and begins sharply ascending hills thick with Gambel oak copses. Magnificent views unfold as the road climbs. The long snow-capped escarpment of the San Juan Mountains parades across the southern horizon, with several 14,000-foot peaks—Uncompahgre and Wetterhorn Peaks, Mount Sneffels, Mount Wilson, and Wilson Peak—bumping against the turquoise sky. The humped Uncompahgre Plateau spreads to the southwest above the Gunnison River valley. To the southeast towers the West Elk Mountains and the dark rim of the Black Canyon of the Gunnison River.

Aspens, among the most widespread trees in North America, attract leaf peepers for late September's color change on the Grand Mesa.

The highway finally leaves the oak woods behind and enters immense aspen groves. A paved overlook offers spectacular views just before the road enters 346,555-acre **Grand Mesa National Forest.** After entering the forest the drive turns away from the aspen-clad rim and climbs Ward Creek's shallow vale. Spruce dominates the forest atop the mesa, with only scattered patches of aspen, and dense mats of willows cling to the creek's banks.

The road swings past Ward Creek Reservoir, a roadside lake for fishing, boating, and hiking, and bends northeast to **Grand Mesa Recreation Area.** A series of shimmering lakes hide among the spruce forest on the mesa top, including Eggleston Lake, Ward Lake, Carp Lake, Baron Lake, and Island Lake, the largest on the Mesa. All offer excellent fishing for native cutthroat, rainbow, and brook trout. This popular scenic area, lying above 10,000 feet, offers plenty of campgrounds and miles of hiking trails, backcountry routes for jeeps and ATVs, and lakes for canoeing and stand-up paddling. Grand Mesa National Forest operates the **Grand Mesa Visitor Center** at Cobbett Lake, open daily from Memorial Day weekend until late September. The center provides information, books, maps, discovery hikes, presentations, and activities like Moose on the Mesa, a celebration of moose on the last Saturday in July every year.

The drive bends west above spruce-fringed Island Lake and runs along a bench below a cliffed ridge. **Crag Crest National Recreation Trail** (#711), a

10.3-mile circular trail, begins from the West Trailhead on the north side of Island Lake and climbs onto narrow, rocky Crag Crest, passing the 11,189-foot high point, and then descending into quiet forests and wildflower-sprinkled meadows. The trail yields breathtaking views of the glistening lakes scattered across the mesa top as well as vistas of the distant San Juan and West Elk ranges. The loop hike also has an East Trailhead by Eggleston Lake. Plenty of easier day hikes are on Grand Mesa, including the family-friendly, 1.25-mile Ward Lake Trail. Stop by the visitor center at Cobbett Lake for maps and ranger suggestions.

Grand Mesa offers some of Colorado's best cross-country ski terrain with as much as 400 inches of snow blanketing spruce forest and open meadows. The **Grand Mesa Nordic Council** maintains 54 kilometers or 32 miles of trails at 3 different trail systems—Ward, County Line, and Skyway. Warming huts are near the trailheads. The trails have both classic and skate skiing on flat and rolling terrain. Other trailheads lead to XC-ski and snowshoe adventures on ungroomed terrain. Mesa Lakes Resort offers ski rentals and lessons.

The Mesa is also a snowmobiling playground with designated snowmobile trails, off-trail riding, and plenty of chilly fun. Trails include the Land's End Loop, Bonham, Cold Sore, Bull Creek, and Vega, as well as the longest snowmobile trail in the lower 48 states. The **Sunlight to Powderhorn Trail** runs 123 miles from Powderhorn Mountain Resort to Sunlight Ski Area near Glenwood Springs. Snow machine tours, rentals, and lodging are available at Grand Mesa Lodge, Mesa Lakes Lodge, and Thunder Mountain Resort.

Grand Mesa is a massive layer-cake of horizontal rock layers. Late Cretaceous rocks—the Mancos shale and Mesa Verde sandstone—form the bottom layers at Cedaredge, while more recent sandstones and shales called the Green River and Wahsatch Formations form the upper mesa slopes. A thick layer of erosion-resistant basalt, deposited as lava flows in ancient river valleys over 10 million years ago, caps the mesa top. The lava spewed from vents on the mesa's east side, forming 25 separate flows between 10 and 70 feet thick. Grand Mesa's lava cap varies between 200 and 600 feet thick. Later erosion swept away the softer hills that surrounded the lava-filled valleys, leaving them as a high, isolated plateau. Glaciers also blanketed the mesa top and its northern slopes, leaving piles of boulders and gouging out depressions that later formed lakes.

Past the Crag Crest West Trailhead, the drive passes Grand Mesa Lodge, the turn for Island Lake Campground, and the Land-O-Lakes Trailhead. The easy 0.5-mile-long Land-O-Lakes Trail is a short interpretive hike with exceptional views. The highway runs west below broken cliffs and boulder fields before climbing higher on the flat mesa. A rest area sits at the 10,839-foot drive high point on the Mesa-Delta County line. The road continues through open meadows with willow-lined tarns tucked amid boulders and Engelmann spruce woods.

Land's End

At 32 miles the highway intersects Land's End Road, FR 100. This 12-mile-long gravel road travels west to **Land's End,** one of western Colorado's most dramatic viewpoints. The road heads southwest across the mesa, traversing the west rim of Kanah Creek's canyon for a few miles before bending west along the edge of a gigantic amphitheater. Wide meadows broken by sparse spruce woodlands and small aspen groves characterize the mesa top. A dense aspen forest spills down steep slopes below the cliffs along the rim and road.

As Land's End Road runs west, the mesa's climate becomes more temperate, moderated by warm winds that sweep up from the Grand Valley to the west. Sagebrush replaces the thick grasses, and the forest disappears altogether. After 10 miles the road bends northwest, dipping through shallow ravines and crossing hillocks. A short spur leads to Coal Creek Overlook, a spectacular point perched atop black basalt cliffs. Small waterfalls drop over nearby cliffs. A couple of miles later the road reaches Land's End.

A magnificent panorama stretches away from the overlook. Steep slopes, colored brilliant yellow with changing aspens in September, cascade down to barren hills. The Grand Valley, seamed by the Colorado River and divided into green fields surrounding Grand Junction, reaches west to Utah. The Book Cliffs and broken ridges march north from the valley, while the Uncompahgre Plateau, its northern edge eroded into Colorado National Monument's red rock canyons, looms to the southwest. The La Sal Mountains in Utah pierce the sky above the plateau. The views from Land's End are especially spectacular at sunset when red light shafts across mesas and mountains below the viewpoint.

The historic **Land's End Observatory,** a log and stone building erected in 1936 and 1937, sits at the overlook. The road, once called Veteran's Road, was built by World War I vets in 1933. To continue the scenic byway route, return 12 miles back to the road's junction with CO 65 and turn left. Land's End Road, however, continues west and twists downward for more than 5,000 feet to US 50.

Skyway Point to the Colorado River

The scenic drive continues north from Land's End Road across the rolling mesa top. After a mile, the highway reaches **Skyway Point** and the northern edge of

Grand Mesa. Stop and enjoy spacious views across the mesa's northern slopes and the rugged plateau country to the northwest. The highway descends in the shadow of tall basalt cliffs and boulder fields to a broad bench before making a U-turn westward. A thick spruce forest borders the asphalt.

The road passes Spruce Grove Campground and drops down to **Mesa Lakes Recreation Area.** The Mesa Lakes, scattered through the forest, are a popular overnight, hiking, and fishing destination. Popular sites are Jumbo Campground, Glacier Springs Picnic Site, and Mesa Lakes Resort.

The highway descends past a small reservoir and turns onto the northern flank of Grand Mesa. A couple of paved turnoffs give great views north down aspen-covered slopes to the Colorado River's salmon-colored Debeque Canyon. The road descends steeply for the next 4 miles, running through a spectacular aspen forest. Drive this road section in late September, when the colors run from orange and rust to gold and yellow.

At the bottom of the steepest slopes, the highway leaves Grand Mesa National Forest. The turn to **Powderhorn Mountain Resort** sits north of the boundary. Powderhorn has 1,600 skiable acres, a 1,650-foot vertical drop, 2 terrain parks, 42 trails, 250 inches of dry powder every winter, and spacious views across desert canyons. Powderhorn is Grand Junction's local ski mountain, offering fun skiing in the morning and wine tasting in Palisade in the afternoon. The area, perfect for beginners, families, and intermediate skiers, has short lift lines and no crowds. Take the West End Lift for glade runs, open terrain, and few skiers. At the base is affordable lodging and food and drink at the Sunset Bar & Grill.

The highway swings into a broad tilted basin, flanked by high ridges on the east and west and the lofty rim of Grand Mesa on the south. The road curves through a scrub oak woodland and after a few miles reaches pastures, ranchettes, and sagebrush hills. The Breaks form a high ragged ridge to the east, eroded into a red rock badlands. Chalk Mountain lifts a twin-summited peak with bare white cliffs to the west.

The drive descends shallow Coon Creek and runs down sloping pastures to the small ranching town of **Mesa.** The Beehive, a 6,282-foot butte, is a prominent landmark east of Mesa. Past Mesa the highway plunges into Mesa Creek's narrow canyon and reaches a junction with CO 330 at Plateau Creek. A right turn on CO 330 leads to Collbran and **Vega State Park.** The 1,823-acre state park, a busy recreation area for locals, offers fishing and boating in 2-mile-long Vega Reservoir, 109 campsites in 4 campgrounds, picnic areas, excellent birding and wildlife study, boating, ice fishing, and snowmobiling. The scenic byway bends left on CO 330 in Plateau Valley, crosses Plateau Creek, and heads west toward I-70 and Grand Junction.

The drive's last 10 miles twist down Plateau Creek's deepening canyon to its confluence with the **Colorado River.** This is dry, dusty country. Cliff bands of Mesa Verde sandstone tower above the highway, broken by erosion into bulging buttresses and tumbled boulders. Sagebrush, saltbush, dry grass clumps, and occasional piñon pines and junipers scatter over the canyon walls. The creek, lined by scraggly cottonwoods and tamarisks, riffles through cobbled rapids. The highway follows the canyon's immense curves and finally the road divides. The right branch continues on the creek's north bank to eastbound I-70, while the left branch crosses to the opposite shore and heads to the westbound interstate and Grand Junction.

26

Black Canyon South Rim Scenic Drive

Black Canyon of the Gunnison National Park

General description: A 13-mile road on the south rim of the Black Canyon of the Gunnison National Park.

Special attractions: Black Canyon of the Gunnison, Tomichi Point, Pulpit Rock Overlook, Chasm View, Painted Wall View, High Point, Visitor Center, East Portal, camping, picnicking, hiking, wildlife, rock climbing, scenic views.

Location: West-central Colorado. The drive begins 6 miles east of Montrose off US 50.

Route name and number: South Rim Road, CO 347.

Travel season: Spring, summer, and fall. Heavy snow occasionally blocks the drive from Gunnison Point Overlook to High Point during winter months. Check with park headquarters in Montrose for road closure and opening dates.

Camping: The South Rim Campground (88 sites) operates on a first-come, first-served basis (Loop C) and by reservation at recreation.gov (Loops A and B). Loop B has electrical sites.

Services: No services are along the drive. Montrose offers all services.

Nearby attractions: Curecanti National Recreation Area, Gunnison Gorge National Conservation Area, Montrose Historical Museum, Ute Indian Museum, Shavano Valley Rock Art Site, Owl Creek Pass, San Juan Scenic Skyway All-American Byway (Scenic Route 23), Ouray National Historic District, Black Canyon North Rim.

The Route

The 13-mile-long South Rim Drive explores the southern edge of the Black Canyon, a deep, precipitous gorge hacked out of ancient bedrock by the Gunnison River in the Black Canyon of the Gunnison National Park. The park protects 12 miles of the 50-mile-long canyon. The drive offers not only geologic lessons but also 12 scenic viewpoints, hiking trails, and wildlife study. Trails lead to overlooks perched along the canyon rim. Soaring cliffs provide adventure for rock climbers and homes for raptors, swallows, and swifts. The forested canyon rim yields glimpses of life: a porcupine-gnawed piñon pine, the rustlings of rufous-sided towhees in underbrush, the hoof beats of an alarmed mule deer, and the howl of a distant coyote.

The Black Canyon slices through an uplift that reaches elevations above 8,000 feet, over 2,000 feet higher than nearby Montrose in the Uncompahgre Valley. The canyon rim, with its higher elevation, consequently receives more precipitation than adjoining valleys, with an average of 20 inches annually. Each canyon

Black Canyon South Rim Scenic Drive

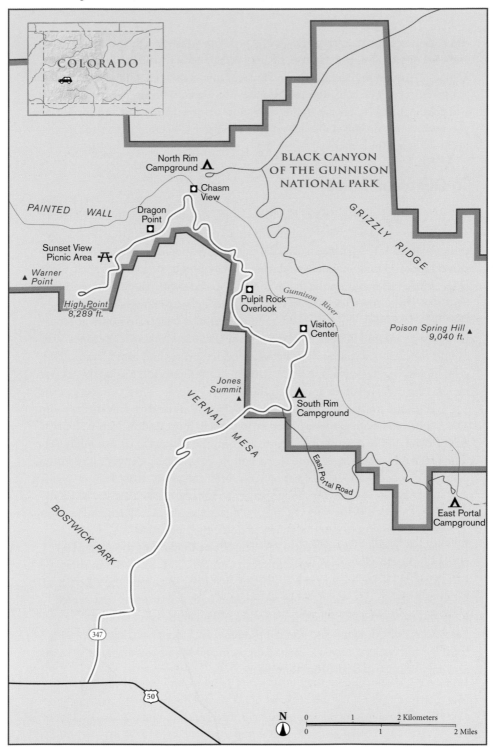

COLORADO

BLACK CANYON
OF THE GUNNISON
NATIONAL PARK

GRIZZLY RIDGE

North Rim
Campground

Chasm
View

PAINTED WALL

Dragon
Point

Sunset View
Picnic Area

Warner
Point

High Point
8,289 ft.

Pulpit Rock
Overlook

Gunnison River

Visitor
Center

Poison Spring Hill
9,040 ft.

Jones
Summit

South Rim
Campground

VERNAL MESA

East Portal Road

East Portal
Campground

BOSTWICK PARK

347

50

N

0   1   2 Kilometers
0   1   2 Miles

rim season is distinct. Spring arrives in April with windy weather, rain showers, and cool nights. Summer days can be hot, occasionally reaching 90 degrees, but regular afternoon thunderstorms and breezes moderate the temperatures. Night temperatures can be cool, dipping into the 40s. Autumn brings clear, glorious days and cold nights. Winters are frigid, with snow blanketing the rim and shaded canyon walls from late November into April. The drive is open in winter to Gunnison Point at the visitor center.

To Gunnison Point

The drive begins 6 miles east of Montrose at the junction of US 50 and CO 347. Turn north on CO 347. The road climbs up dry Piñon Springs Draw, a shallow canyon carved into Mancos shale, a dark gray formation deposited in a quiet seaway some 75 million years ago during the Cretaceous period. The shale forms sharp, barren badlands on the flanks of the Uncompahgre Valley around Montrose and Delta. After 1.5 miles of climbing, the highway emerges onto a wide, level bench covered with farm fields, and then climbs steeply up slopes covered with piñon pine and juniper. Five miles from US 50 the road reaches Jones Summit on the crest of a rolling ridge between Piñon Springs and Jones Draws. The state highway ends here at the Black Canyon of the Gunnison National Park border and the drive becomes South Rim Road.

East Portal Road, a spectacular side trip, begins at the park entrance station. The 5-mile road, with grades as steep as 16 percent, uncoils down steep slopes to **East Portal** on the canyon floor upstream from the national park boundary. The road is the vehicular access route to the bottom of the Black Canyon. East Portal, part of Curecanti National Recreation Area, offers camping, trout fishing, picnicking, and a feel for the canyon's inner gorge. The shady 15-site East Portal Campground is a first-come first-served area. Vehicles with an overall length exceeding 22 feet, including trailers, are not allowed down the steep road.

Past the entrance station to 30,750-acre **Black Canyon of the Gunnison National Park** is the three-loop South Rim Campground, with 88 campsites spread among a dense scrub oak woodland, that lies just beyond the entrance at 8,320 feet. The scenic campground operates on both a first-come, first-served basis and by reservation. Black bears are a problem at the campground. Use bear lockers to store food and scented products, including beverages, toiletries, tobacco, and cooking utensils; clean your picnic table and cooking area after use; and deposit trash at bear-proof dumpsters.

Dragon Point offers a spectacular view of the Gunnison River descending the steep-walled Black Canyon past the Painted Wall and Serpent Point.

The drive heads north from the campground and after a mile reaches **Tomichi Point** and the first view of the Gunnison's stupendous chasm. Nothing prepares the first-time visitor for the inaccessibility, sheerness, and depth of the canyon. The road to this point has climbed and traversed rolling ridges, with distant peaks and low-slung mesas poking above the landscape. But here the land falls away into abrupt, sudden space. Broken side canyons, sweeping rock buttresses, and gullies and ledges mantled with fir trees fill the gorge below.

Gunnison Point Overlook and the park's visitor center are 0.3 mile down the road from Tomichi Point. The visitor center displays exhibits about the canyon's geology, natural history, and human history, and provides information, maps, books, and daily ranger-led programs. The center has a large parking area, restrooms, and drinking water. The South Rim Road is closed beyond the visitor center in winter. The 0.5-mile **Rim Rock Trail** leads from the campground to the visitor center, following the rim. The 2-mile round-trip **Oak Flat Loop Trail** explores a scrub oak, fir, and aspen woodland, rock outcrops, and a shallow canyon on the rim west of the visitor center.

Gunnison Point, sitting atop an erosion-resistant pegmatite dike behind the visitor center, offers scenic views into the canyon's somber interior. A 500-foot trail leads to the overlook from the visitor center. Other pink pegmatite bands slice through the North Rim canyon walls across from Gunnison Point. Gneiss and schist, the softer metamorphic rocks that surround the pegmatite, weather more quickly and leave the resistant rock jutting into the canyon.

Descending into the Black Canyon is an ultimate adventure for climbers, anglers, and hikers. Seven established routes enter the canyon but all are steep, rocky, dangerous, strenuous, and unmaintained. The best descent is down the **Gunnison Route,** which begins at the visitor center. The rough trail descends a mile and 1,800 feet to the river and three backcountry campsites. A fixed chain lets you climb up and down a steep section. Ask at the visitor center for a free backcountry permit and updated trail information before descending. All hikers should be in excellent physical condition. Remember that the descent is the easy part—the uphill slog is tough.

Black Canyon Geology

The Black Canyon's geologic story is divided into two chapters: the existing rocks and their history, and the Gunnison River's erosion of the canyon. Much of the exposed rock is gneiss and schist, metamorphic rocks originally deposited as layers of sand, silt, and mud on the floor of a primordial sea some two billion years ago. Intense heat and pressure later "metamorphosed," or transformed, the rock to its present contorted state. Molten magma, later injected into cracks and fissures in the gneiss and schist, slowly cooled into pegmatite, a coarse-grained igneous rock. Pegmatite forms the striking dikes and bands that crisscross the canyon walls, particularly the Painted Wall. Other large magma bodies intruded into the metamorphic bedrock and form quartz monzonite, a hard, granitelike rock found on the sheer walls at Chasm View.

Time and the flowing Gunnison River created the Black Canyon. The canyon, a recent topographic feature, is between two and three million years old. Its story, however, began 60 million years ago with the uplift of the Rocky Mountains. As the mountains slowly rose, erosion attacked them with glaciers chiseling the high peaks and snowmelt-laden rivers, including the ancestral Gunnison, carving into the uplift in western Colorado. Volcanism in the West Elk Mountains to the north and the San Juan Mountains to the south also affected the course of the Gunnison River by channeling it between narrow highlands. The river, cutting through layers of volcanic ash and sedimentary rock, established a course atop the buried metamorphic basement rock. By the time volcanism ceased, the Gunnison was firmly entrenched in its bedrock canyon.

The Gunnison River, Colorado's fourth-largest river, originates on the Continental Divide far to the east of the Black Canyon. West of the town of Gunnison it drops into the 50-mile-long Black Canyon before emerging in the Uncompahgre Valley near Delta. Three dams—Blue Mesa, Morrow Point, and Crystal—impound the river in the upper canyon for flood control, water storage, recreation, and electric power. Below Crystal Lake the Gunnison plunges 12 miles through its narrow canyon in the national park before entering Gunnison Gorge, its lower canyon.

The Gunnison River boasts one of the nation's steepest river gradients, dropping 2,150 feet from the canyon head at Sapinero (now under Blue Mesa Reservoir) to its North Fork junction—an average fall of 43 feet per mile. By contrast, the Green River descends only 12 feet a mile in Dinosaur National Monument. In the national park below the scenic drive, the Gunnison's average gradient is 95 feet a mile. But in the 2 miles from Pulpit Rock to Chasm View, it descends an astounding 480 feet. That steep gradient, combined with the abrasion of tumbling boulders on its riverbed, gives the Gunnison a sharp cutting edge. Geologists estimate the river deepens the canyon about 1 inch every century.

Pulpit Rock, Chasm View, & the Painted Wall

Past the visitor center the drive heads northeast, following the rim's contours. Dense thickets of Gambel or scrub oak line the road, with occasional open meadows. Other shrubs mix in the pygmy woodland, including serviceberry and mountain mahogany, a favorite deer food. Mule deer flourish along the canyon rim. Keen eyes can sight them in roadside meadows and near the campground. Other mammals include porcupines, marmots, rock and ground squirrels, coyotes, gray foxes, black bears, and bobcats. Mountain lions, bighorn sheep, and elk occasionally wander through the park.

The road reaches **Pulpit Rock Overlook** 1.7 miles from the visitor center. The viewpoint offers a spacious view of the V-shaped upper canyon and Pulpit Rock, a semi-detached pinnacle. A 300-foot-long trail leads from the parking lot to an overlook on the right. At a junction before the viewpoint, go left and walk 225 feet to another overlook.

The canyon narrows past Pulpit Rock, and a series of overlooks scattered along the drive yield excellent views. Drive the looping road for 0.6 mile to **Cross Fissures View.** A 0.3-mile trail heads north on a rock peninsula with 3 overlooks into the canyon. Deep gullies flank the trail on either side and at trail's end is the Big Island, a massive block of rock separated from the South Rim by deep crevices or fissures.

Rock Point, the next overlook, is 0.15 mile from Cross Fissures. A fun 0.4-mile round-trip hike follows a good trail out to a fenced overlook on a rock point poised between two deep side canyons. Echo Canyon is the deep defile on the right.

The roadside parking for **Devils Lookout** is 600 feet from Rock Point's parking area. The 0.6-mile round-trip hike to the fenced overlook threads across a narrowing promontory that ends at Devils Lookout. This point, less visited than other South Rim viewpoints, offers an airy view directly down to the Gunnison River almost 1,800 feet below. It also looks north across the canyon to the cliffed North Rim and Mount Lamborn in the West Elk Mountains.

Chasm View, the South Rim's most spectacular and airy overlook, sits a mile past Devils Lookout. The cliffs fall abruptly away from the overlook railings to the river 1,840 feet below. North Chasm View Wall dominates the canyon here, its gray bulk seamed with cracks and fissures. The vertical cliff offers some of the best climbing routes in the Black Canyon, including The Cruise, Stoned Oven, and The Eighth Voyage. The opposite North Rim stands only 1,100 feet across the gaping abyss from the viewpoint, yet by car, it's 82 miles away via Montrose and Delta. Upstream from Chasm View is The Narrows, with towering cliffs hemming the river into a 40-foot-wide cleft, forming the most forbidding section of the canyon. A path leads 275 feet to the fenced overlook from roadside parking. Don't toss rocks off since climbers may be on the wall below or fishermen by the river.

At Chasm View the road swings south and begins climbing toward High Point. The roadside parking area for **Painted Wall View,** another dramatic overlook, is 525 feet past Chasm View. It's easy to leave your vehicle at the Chasm View parking lot and follow a trail along the side of the road to the trailhead. This point, reached by a 625-foot-long trail, offers spectacular views of the **Painted Wall,**

The 2,250-foot-high Painted Wall, rising out of the Gunnison River, is the highest cliff in Colorado.

Colorado's highest cliff, with a 2,250-foot vertical rise from base to rim. Numerous pink pegmatite bands slash across the wall.

Drive 0.4 mile to **Cedar Point,** the next overlook. The 0.2-mile **Cedar Point Trail** crosses the rimrock to 2 fenced overlooks that peer into the depths at towering rock islands and the roaring river far below. Across the canyon rises the Painted Wall and a series of buttresses divided by deep gullies weathered from joints in the rock. Interpretive posts along the trail identify common trees and plants on the South Rim, including piñon pine, juniper, scrub oak, sagebrush, mountain mahogany, and various wildflowers. Stay safe at the exposed overlooks by keeping behind the sturdy fencing.

Drive 0.25 mile from Cedar Point to the next overlook, a 0.17-mile trail follows the edge of a deep side canyon to **Dragon Point,** an airy fenced viewpoint poised above a vertical cliff directly opposite the Painted Wall. The wall is named for the painted pegmatite stripes that run diagonal across the towering cliff. The two widest bands are called the Dragons. Pegmatite, composed primarily of feldspar, quartz, and mica, is a coarse, pink igneous rock that was intruded as molten rock into cracks in the gneiss that composes the wall, and then slowly cooled. Some feldspar crystals in the Black Canyon exceed 6 feet in diameter.

The Southern Arête forms the far left side of the Painted Wall. This long, blunt prow is the longest rock climbing route in Colorado. Layton Kor, one of the world's best climbers in the 1960s, established the route with Wayne Goss and Larry Dalke in 1962. While not technically challenging, the route is rarely climbed due to its length, loose rock sections, and route-finding challenges. Consult the comprehensive guidebook *Rock Climbing Colorado* (FalconGuides) for information on climbing the Painted Wall, North Chasm View Wall, and other Black Canyon cliffs.

The Black Canyon's rims once offered the nomadic Utes cool summer campsites and plentiful game and edible plants. The Utes, however, rarely entered the precipitous canyon and called the depths *Tomichi*, or "Land of cliffs and water." Captain John Gunnison first explored the canyon region and river now bearing his name on a government survey to find a possible railroad route to California and the Pacific in 1853. After exploring the Black Canyon region, Gunnison and his party headed across Utah to Siever Lake. On October 26, Gunnison and 7 men were killed and mutilated by Pahvants or Utes. Gunnison's name lingers on in Colorado with a town, river, and national forest named after him.

The Black Canyon was first traversed in 1901 by William Torrance and A. L. Fellows on a water survey expedition. The duo endured nine days and 72 river crossings before climbing out of the canyon. Fellows described the trek: "Our surroundings were of the wildest possible description. The roar of the water falls was constantly in our ears, and the walls of the canyon, towering half mile in height above us, were seemingly vertical. Occasionally a rock would fall from one side or the other, with a roar and crash, exploding like a ton of dynamite when it struck bottom, making us think our last day had come."

Warner Point & High Point

The scenic drive continues ascending gentle slopes along the canyon rim from **Dragon Point** and reaches **Sunset View** after 0.7 mile. This viewpoint, the best place on the drive to view the sun setting behind the western canyon rim, looks down the Black Canyon to Gunnison Gorge. This lower canyon, composed of softer rock formations than the upper canyon, is broader and lower than the monument's narrow abyss. More side erosion has widened the gorge, and the Gunnison River's gradient drops to 35 feet per mile. The overlook has a parking lot, restrooms, picnic tables, and a short trail to a stunning canyon viewpoint.

The **Gunnison Gorge,** outside the national park boundary, is protected in a 62,844-acre National Conservation Area that includes 14 miles of the Gunnison River. This scenic canyon includes a narrow inner gorge walled by dark cliffs. Gunnison Gorge, accessed by trails on the east side of the Uncompahgre Valley, is a rugged playground for outdoor adventurers, including fishermen, rafters, kayakers, and hikers. The single-track **Sidewinder Trail** above the gorge's western rim is one of Colorado's best mountain bike rides.

A 40-mile stretch of the Gunnison River in the national park and National Conservation Area is a designated Gold Medal trout fishery. It's difficult to access the river in the Black Canyon with its steep, unmaintained trails, but the 14-mile section through Gunnison Gorge is considered one of Colorado's most prolific fisheries with as many as 10,000 trout over 6 inches per river mile. Anglers regularly catch trophy-size brown and rainbow trout from 12 to 20 inches long and occasional 24-inch monsters. The best trout season is June through September when the river is a bug factory with multiple insect hatches. The epic stonefly hatch in early June turns the river into an all-you-can-eat buffet for trout.

A mile farther is the end of the drive at 8,289-foot **High Point.** Douglas fir, mixed with piñon pine and juniper, blanket this lofty ridge and spill down the canyon's steep southern slope. High Point doesn't offer good views since thick vegetation obscures a clear line of sight. A large parking area and restrooms are at the short one-way road loop here.

The excellent 0.6-mile **Warner Point Trail** heads west from here to **Warner Point.** The moderate hike is easy to follow, has benches for contemplation, and interpretive markers with information about dead tree snags, wildfires, wildflowers, junipers, piñon pines, porcupines, birds, and the trail's namesake, Mark Warner.

The 8,302-foot point, the South Rim's highest place, is named for Reverend Mark Warner, who pushed for the canyon's preservation as a national monument in 1933. President Bill Clinton expanded the reserve's boundaries and signed legislation designating it as a national park. Warner Point yields wide vistas of the surrounding landscape. The snow-capped San Juan Mountains and Mount Sneffels stretch across the southern horizon; Grand Mesa's forested bulk lingers to the northwest; and pointed peaks in the West Elk Mountains form a jagged horizon to the northeast. This privileged view, reserved for those who walk out here, forms a fitting end to this spectacular scenic drive.

Unaweep–Tabeguache Scenic & Historic Byway

Whitewater to Placerville

General description: A 133-mile-long drive through western Colorado's lonely plateau country, including Unaweep Canyon and canyons along the Dolores and San Miguel Rivers.

Special attractions: Unaweep Canyon, Taylor Quarry Overlook, Driggs Mansion, Thimble Rock, Palisade Wilderness Study Area, Dolores Canyon, Sewemup Wilderness Study Area, The Hanging Flume, Norwood, San Miguel Canyon, rock climbing, camping, hiking, fishing, scenic views, rock art, rafting.

Location: Western Colorado. The drive begins at Whitewater on US 50 south of Grand Junction and ends in Placerville 25 miles west of Ridgway.

Route name and numbers: Unaweep–Tabeguache Scenic and Historic Byway, CO 141 and 145.

Travel season: Year-round.

Camping: Few established campgrounds along the drive. Primitive camping is allowed on BLM public lands. Big Dominguez Campground (9 sites), is 5 miles south of CO 141 off Divide Road. Primitive camping is 1 mile up Divide Road from the byway. Caddis Flat (3 sites) and Lower Beaver (3 sites) Campgrounds are northwest of Placerville.

Services: All services are in Grand Junction, Naturita, Nucla, Norwood, and Placerville. Limited services in Gateway.

Nearby attractions: Colorado National Monument, Grand Mesa, La Sal Mountains, Dominguez-Escalante National Conservation Area, Uncompahgre Plateau, Divide Road, Mount Sneffels Wilderness Area, Telluride National Historic District, Dallas Divide, San Juan Skyway All-American Byway (Scenic Route 23).

The Route

The 133-mile-long Unaweep–Tabeguache Scenic and Historic Byway threads across the splendid Colorado Plateau country along the western fringe of the Uncompahgre Plateau. It unveils a remote, hidden landscape along a couple of off-the-beaten-track state highways, exploring wondrous Unaweep Canyon and the harshly eroded canyons of the Dolores and San Miguel Rivers. The drive passes precipitous granite cliffs and sandstone battlements, twists along dusky red rivers, and crosses a land rich in prehistoric geology.

Mild weather dominates the drive year-round. The highways run over high desert country, characterized by sparse precipitation, hot summers, and short, chilly winters. Occasional thunderstorms rumble through in summer, with most of the rain dousing the drive's higher elevations in Unaweep Canyon and near

Unaweep–Tabeguache Scenic & Historic Byway

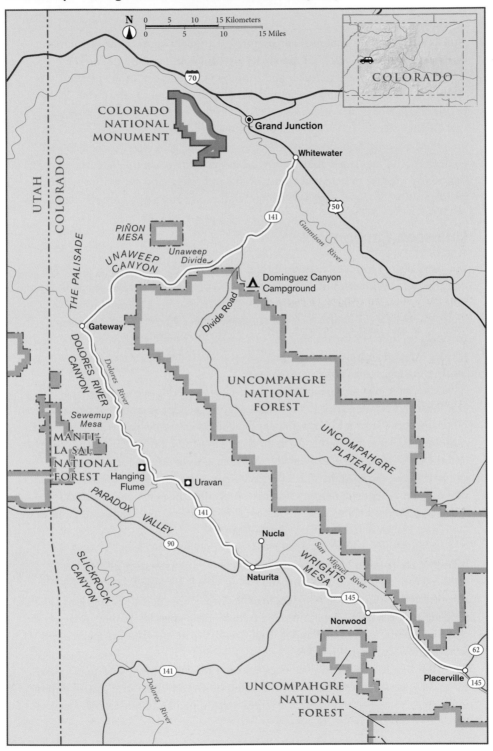

Norwood. Expect hot summer temperatures, with daily highs in the 90s along the rivers. Higher-elevation temperatures are cooler, but still reach the 80s. Autumn, beginning in September and running to November, offers pleasant driving weather. Days are usually clear and warm with occasional rainstorms. Winter begins in late November and ends by March in the lower elevations. Snow blankets Unaweep Canyon, Wrights Mesa, and shady slopes in the San Miguel Canyon but otherwise quickly melts. Days are cool with highs generally between 30 and 50 degrees, and nights are cold. Spring creeps onto the plateau in late March, with dry, windy weather punctuated by occasional rain, sleet, and snowstorms. The weather warms in April, and May brings wildflowers and grass to the lowlands.

Unaweep Canyon

The drive begins 15 miles south of Grand Junction at the intersection of US 50 and CO 141 at **Whitewater.** Turn west on CO 141. The drive's first leg runs 44 miles west through **Unaweep Canyon** to Gateway and the Dolores River Canyon. The paved road swings over the Gunnison River after 0.25 mile, crosses a cornfield on the river floodplain, and turns west up a shallow canyon. East Creek trickles through cottonwoods on the canyon floor. Piñon pines and junipers scatter over the dry, rocky slopes above.

East Creek, beginning on the Unaweep Divide in Unaweep Canyon, cuts east through upturned rock layers on the edge of the Uncompahgre Plateau. The Uncompahgre Plateau, a broad, flattened highland crested with dense forests and meadows, stretches northwest from the San Juan Mountains to the Grand Valley and the Colorado River. The plateau reaches heights of 10,000 feet. Numerous canyons crease the 25-mile-wide uplift, slicing deeply through sandstone layers that drape over its Precambrian basement rocks. The plateau's most dramatic canyons lie in Colorado National Monument's northern end and Unaweep, Dominguez, and Escalante Canyons in its midsection.

Lower Unaweep Canyon slowly widens as the highway climbs west. After 3 miles the road swings away from the creek and begins ascending a tilted bench on the south canyon slope. Dakota sandstone, forming a long tawny cliff band, rims the canyon. Immense boulders tumble down slopes above the highway. The sandstone blocks offer over a thousand boulder problems for climbers with a wide range of grades. As the road climbs, East Creek cuts deeply into soft shale layers, forming an abrupt canyon below.

After 8 miles the highway reaches **Grand Valley Overlook,** a dramatic viewpoint that peers north to the Book Cliffs and the Grand Valley and east to imposing basalt-rimmed Grand Mesa, the largest flat-topped mountain in the world.

Unaweep Canyon, lined with granite cliffs, is the abandoned channel of the ancestral Colorado River.

Portions of the first stage and wagon route to Gateway thread along the boulder-covered slopes north of East Creek below the overlook.

The 6-mile highway section from the canyon's lower gate to Grand Valley Overlook ascends **Ninemile Hill.** The highway roughly follows an old Ute trail that later became "Uranium Road," the only route that connected Grand Junction's processing mill with uranium mines along the Dolores River. In the early 1900s teamsters used the trail up Ninemile Hill to carry mail and supplies to Gateway and several now-abandoned mining camps in Unaweep Canyon. This long hill offered vicious 18 percent grades that required doubled horse teams. When autos began using the winding shelf road, passengers usually walked ahead to lighten the load and warn the driver of oncoming traffic, as the track was too narrow for two vehicles. The road was widened and improved in the 1930s for trucks hauling uranium. It finally was paved in 1958.

The canyon widens and flattens past the overlook, with tall cottonwoods and willow thickets lining the creek. Low sandstone cliffs and slopes covered with piñon pine and juniper stair-step back to a high rim. A mile past the overlook a dirt road heads south to **Cactus Park.** This dry, open valley, flanked by low hogbacks, was the channel of the ancestral Gunnison River between one and five million years ago. The 5-acre Gunnison Gravels Natural Research Area, 0.5 mile south of the drive, protects these ancient river deposits.

As the drive runs west, the low sandstone walls are replaced by cliffs of Precambrian metamorphic rock, the basement rock layer of the Uncompahgre Plateau. Unaweep Canyon's granite and metamorphic rocks, dated between 1.4 and 1.7 billion years old, are among Colorado's oldest exposed rocks. Some 300 million years ago the plateau was the site of "Uncompahgria," an ancestral Rocky Mountain range that rose above a shallow sea. Over ensuing millennia the range weathered down to its bedrock roots, and its eroded cobbles, gravels, and sands were deposited to the west, forming today's canyon country layers. Later sandstone was deposited on the old bedrock, forming the "Great Unconformity," with some 500 million years of geologic history missing.

Two abandoned towns sit near the drive at Nancy Hanks Gulch. **Copper City** and **Pearl City** both began in 1897 with the discovery of copper, gold, and silver in Unaweep Canyon. Both quickly flourished, with populations of about 100 each. Copper City took the lead, building two schools, stores, and cabins. Pearl City, however, kept the rustic look, and remained a community of tents during its 17-year existence. The Pearl City Hotel offered the town's deluxe accommodations, with three tents joined together. No permanent structures were ever erected. Area fortunes sagged after a 1901 mining downturn, but the pair lingered on. Pearl City folded up its tents in 1912 and Copper City followed suit in 1914. Nothing remains of either today, save a few old photographs.

As the drive heads west, the canyon deepens. Rosy sandstone caps the dark gray bedrock along the sidewalls. The creek becomes entrenched in a deep arroyo filled with reeds, cattails, tall grass, and cottonwoods. Broad ranches dotted with grazing cattle and wide hay fields grace the flat valley floor, offering a pastoral counterpoint to the rugged walls.

Divide Road begins just past a ranch. This gravel road twists more than 100 miles down the spine of the Uncompahgre Plateau, giving access to a vast swath of remote backcountry. Take a left turn here for a short drive up Divide Road to a stunning viewpoint above Unaweep Canyon. The gravel road climbs a couple of miles to the site of abandoned Taylor Granite Quarry, a rock quarry that operated in 1928. Park before a cattle guard and walk down to the cliff edge for one of western Colorado's most spectacular overlooks. Unaweep Canyon stretches westward. The highway below uncoils like a long snake up the sagebrush valley floor. Gentle slopes, forested with scrub oak, piñon pine, and juniper, slant upward to abrupt, towering granite cliffs. Above, steep slopes lean back to the valley's sandstone rim high above the floor. Near the overlook atop the Quarry Wall are several primitive campsites. Remember to pack out everything you pack in if you camp here.

Unaweep Canyon, slashing across the entire Uncompahgre Plateau, is a unique canyon. The U-shaped canyon is supposedly the only canyon in the world drained by two creeks. A divide in mid-canyon separates the East Creek and West Creek drainages. (The Ute name *Unaweep* means "Canyon with Two Mouths.") This deep canyon's formation has long been a geological enigma. Geologists agree the two small streams in today's canyon could not have chiseled the deep chasm, leading to several theories that explain its origin. Some say it was carved along a massive fault line, while others argue that glaciation alone excavated the gorge. The most credible explanation concludes that the canyon was the ancestral river bed of the Gunnison and Colorado Rivers. The Colorado River drained southward from Debeque Canyon through Unaweep Canyon and the Uncompahgre Plateau before an eroding tributary breached a divide northwest of the plateau and diverted the river flow into today's Grand Valley. This action, called stream piracy, left Unaweep Canyon high and dry.

From Divide Road, the drive continues west up Unaweep Canyon past steel gray cliffs seamed by black water streaks. The cliffs, ranging up to 500 feet high, offer excellent rock climbing on steep faces and cracks. Most of the best cliffs for climbing are owned by the Western Colorado Climber's Coalition (WCCC) or on Bureau of Land Management (BLM) land. The WCCC owns the Hidden Valley, Fortress, Sunday Wall, Upper and Lower Mothers Buttresses, and Television Wall, which are all accessed by legal approach trails. Otherwise, almost the entire canyon floor is privately owned.

Unaweep Divide to Gateway

Unaweep Divide, a broad 7,048-foot saddle in mid-canyon, separates East and West Creeks. Past the divide the highway begins gently dipping west, running through fields of grass and sagebrush. Several shallow lakes dot the canyon floor. Look for Fall Creek Waterfall plunging off a cliff 3 miles west of the divide. The seasonal falls is on private land.

The highway descends past **Thimble Rock,** a prominent stone pyramid towering south of the blacktop. Ledges studded with tall trees interrupt the formation's steep cliffs. The stone ruin of the Italian-style **Driggs Mansion** sits south of the highway in the morning shadow of Thimble Rock. Colonel Lawrence LaThourette Driggs, a wealthy New York lawyer, constructed this huge mansion between 1914 and 1918 on 320 acres of land. Nunzio Grasso, a mason from Grand Junction, used sandstone blocks quarried in nearby Mayflower Canyon to build the eight-room house, including a stone arch that mirrors an arch on Thimble Rock. The mansion, with two bedrooms, a common area, and a kitchen, boasted chandeliers and hand-carved stone mantles above the fireplaces. Despite its expensive construction, the Driggs family lived in the house for only a few months before leaving. After abandoning the mansion in Unaweep, Driggs became an aviation expert, lecturing and writing books about flying, and investing in Colonial Western Airways which became American Airlines.

The Driggs Mansion later became a hunting lodge named Chateau Thimblerock, but was again abandoned. It slowly deteriorated, becoming a haunt for lizards and owls with only stone walls and an archway remaining from its former glory. The house, on private property, remained a weathered outpost of graceful opulence until a grant from the Colorado Historical Society stabilized the site in 2012 and erected interpretative signs at a roadside viewpoint just past mile marker 129. Stay behind the fenced overlook and don't trespass to the mansion ruins.

The scenic drive continues down the valley across Gill Meadows and bends through a rock portal. The canyon widens as it descends, with broken granite crags scattered on the steep mountainsides above. The southern canyon walls and the Uncompahgre Plateau beyond lies in a wilderness of canyons and mesas blanketed with piñon pine, juniper, aspen, fir, and spruce forest. The northern canyon walls from here west to Gateway and the Dolores River are part of the remote 26,766-acre **Palisade Wilderness Study Area.** The northern slopes step almost 4,000 feet above the canyon floor to high mesa tops.

After 40 miles the canyon begins to narrow, its walls steepen, and the drive reaches **Unaweep Seep,** a collection of springs percolating from hillsides northwest of West Creek. A large parking area on the south side of the highway allows access to a viewing platform with interpretative plaques explaining the seep. Unaweep Seep offers an astounding diversity of plant and animal life. This unusual ecosystem, preserved as a registered Colorado Natural Area, displays numerous wildflowers as well as box elder, alder, smooth sumac, blackberry, and ground cherry. The 55-acre site also protects the rare Nokomis fritillary butterfly. This endangered butterfly, with 4-inch orange wings, is gorgeous as it flutters across the wet meadow. The Unaweep colony is seen from mid-July to early September. Other fauna inhabiting the canyon and surrounding mesas include mountain lion, black bear, elk, mule deer, and small mammals.

Past the seep the canyon pinches down. The creek dashes over worn cobbles and boulders below rocky ridges and granite buttresses. The highway twists through the canyon and passes West Creek Picnic Area at mile marker 117. This site, sitting in West Creek Narrows, offers picnic tables shaded by cottonwoods. A sign displays area riparian habitats. The road sharply curves through the canyon and at mile marker 115.6 crosses the **Uncompahgre Fault.** The scenery abruptly changes after crossing the fault. The fault vertically displaces some 8,000 feet of rock, and the drive passes from the ancient bedrock to easily eroded sandstones in the Paradox Basin.

Unaweep Canyon ends at the fault, and the highway runs west down a broad, shallow valley. Soft mudstone slopes climb upward to high, vertical cliffs of

The Palisade, a high sandstone fin, towers above the Dolores River at Gateway.

Wingate sandstone. The La Sal Mountains, a laccolithic mountain range in Utah, towers to the west above carved canyons and mesas. Immense old cottonwood trees spread gnarly branches over the creek along the road.

The blacktop gently drops and enters 4,595-foot-high **Gateway,** the lowest town by altitude on Colorado's Western Slope. Gateway, established in 1890, sits at the canyon gateway on an old Ute trail. Settlers built cabins, irrigated fields with ditches full of Dolores River water, planted orchards, and ran cattle over the dry mesas. The first road reached Gateway in 1906, and the first bridge spanned the river in 1912. Electricity finally came to town in 1952, but long-distance telephone service wasn't available until 1965. Gateway boomed with uranium mining in the 1940s and 1950s.

Today Gateway is a quiet garden spot on the edge of the red rock wilderness. The town offers a few services, including a store, gasoline, and a town park with shaded picnic tables and restrooms. The **Gateway Canyons Resort,** on the west side of the Dolores River opposite the town, is a four-season resort with guest rooms, two restaurants, a pool, spa, the Gateway Canyons Auto Museum with vehicles once owned by Howard Hughes and Clark Gable, and an adventure center that gets guests out hiking, rafting, mountain biking, riding ATVs, fishing, stargazing, and almost any other outdoor activity. The resort is owned by John Hendricks, founder of the Discovery Channel network. For more info, visit their website gatewaycanyons.com.

The Palisade, an immense 7,045-foot fin of salmon-colored Wingate sand-stone capped with Kayenta sandstone, looms above scree and boulder-covered slopes north of Gateway. The Palisade, part of a proposed wilderness area, is a long, narrow mesa ringed by tall cliffs. A classic scrambling route, first established by uranium miners, climbs a crack, traverses an amazing sidewalk ledge, and finishes up slabs to The Palisade's summit and the remains of an old cabin with a rusty spring bed.

Gateway to Naturita

The next drive segment runs 52 miles from Gateway to Naturita along the Dolores and San Miguel Rivers. The highway crosses the **Dolores River** and bends south in the river canyon. The 230-mile-long Dolores River begins high in the San Miguel Range near Lizard Head Pass, runs southwest to Dolores, and arcs north through a series of deep canyons along the western edge of the Uncompahgre Plateau to Gateway. Here it bends northwest, enters Utah, and empties into the Colorado River above Moab.

The highway runs south along the western edge of the wide canyon floor. The river loops in broad, chocolate-colored meanders and riffles over gravel bars. Tamarisk trees, an invasive Asian import, and occasional cottonwoods line the sandy riverbank. The canyon slopes rise above in step-like benches to a castellated rampart of ruddy Wingate sandstone that forms an unbroken wall of vertical cliffs.

Ten miles south of Gateway at mile marker 101.5 the road passes a dirt track that bumps west up Salt Creek to Sinbad Valley, a salt basin that reminded early miners of Sinbad the Sailor's sparkling Valley of Diamonds from *A Thousand and One Nights.* Past the turn the canyon narrows, with the river and highway making great horseshoe loops beneath immense red and black cliffs.

Sewemup Mesa, a proposed wilderness area, hems in the canyon on the west. This huge mesa, isolated by towering cliff bands, preserves a pristine high desert ecosystem on its broad upland with tall ponderosa pines and nesting sites for falcons and eagles. The mesa acquired its unusual name from the McCarty Gang's cattle-rustling operation. The outlaws brought stolen cattle up to isolated parts of the mesa, cut off the old brands with a knife, sewed up the wounded hide with wire, and remarked the cattle with their branding iron after the wound healed. Most of the gang later died in a shootout in Delta after a bank robbery.

As the canyon narrows, the Wingate cliffs dip into the river. The highway makes graceful loops along the glassy river through this spectacular canyon section. Past Roc Creek, the southern end of Sewemup Mesa, and its fertile hay fields and cottonwoods, the road makes one more grand horseshoe bend and exits the narrow gorge.

Early miners named Roc Creek for the legendary Roc, a huge bird that carried Sinbad the Sailor to the Valley of Diamonds. A few prospect holes and mines, including the Rajah Mine, are in upper Roc Creek where miners found uranium-bearing carnotite in 1881. The excellent **Roc Creek Petroglyphs Trail** climbs to a rock art panel with both pictographs and petroglyphs on a high cliff band near the mouth of Roc Creek. Park at mile marker 89.2 and hike 1.1 miles up an old road and trail to the site. The first part crosses fenced private property but the West End Trail Alliance and the BLM received permission from the landowner for hikers to access the site.

The canyon widens and the drive passes Mesa Creek and the **Lone Tree Placer Gravels** at mile marker 85.6. The gravels, washed from ore-bearing deposits high in the San Juan Mountains, attracted prospectors with their glittering gold in 1887. These placer miners hauled the gravels by wheelbarrows, chutes, and wagons down to the river's edge, where they could be washed in machines. The highest bench held the most riches, said knowledgeable miners, but it was too far from the river to be profitable and the technology to pump water uphill did not yet exist. Engineers designed and built a 6-mile ditch and 7-mile hanging flume to carry upstream water to the placer site. The highway climbs south on a broad bench, passes a dome-shaped coke oven used by blacksmiths during the flume's construction, edges under a sweeping band of rosy Entrada sandstone, and reaches the **Hanging Flume Overlook** on the west side of the highway.

The **Hanging Flume,** a National Engineering Landmark, clings to Wingate sandstone walls in the Dolores River Canyon below the viewpoint. The flume, constructed from 1889 to 1891, snakes along the cliffs 100 to 150 feet above the river. The 6-foot-wide and 4-foot-deep flume used 1.8 million feet of lumber, cost over $100,000, carried 80 million gallons of water a day to the mine, and turned out to be an engineering marvel. The mine, however, turned out to be a total bust. Most of the gold was unrecoverable leaf gold, and the St. Louis–based mining company closed the mine in 1893 after turning an $80,000 profit on a $1 million investment. Area ranches stripped some of the flume, reusing the lumber for fences, cabins, and ranch buildings.

The highway continues south on a broad bench above the river canyon and after a mile swings east. A short dirt track bumps south a couple hundred yards to a rocky overlook above the confluence of the Dolores and San Miguel Rivers. The rivers merge far below in a crimson-colored gorge flanked by towering sandstone cliffs. The drive bends southeast and follows the edge of the San Miguel Canyon. A wave of tawny Entrada sandstone overhangs the asphalt.

The canyon broadens and the road reaches the now-abandoned townsite of **Uravan.** The town, its name a contraction of uranium and vanadium, sprang up in 1936 as a company town for US Vanadium Corporation, part of Union Carbide.

The wooden remains of the Hanging Flume, used for an 1890s placer mine, cling to a sandstone face above the Dolores River.

Area mines yielded rich deposits of yellow carnotite, with radium, vanadium, and uranium ores. Vanadium, used to harden steel, was mined during both world wars, while uranium, recovered from mill tailings, went to the Manhattan Project in World War II to develop the world's first nuclear weapons. Only the mill ruins remain today on the old Club Ranch property, stair-stepping up the hillside above settling ponds. The town, its houses, stores, post office, and school have vanished. Everything was removed during environmental reclamation because of radioactive contamination.

The drive runs southeast along the San Miguel River in a broad, picturesque canyon. Steep slopes are broken by stepped benches dark with piñon pine and juniper trees, each rimmed with sandstone strata. Dakota sandstone forms a prominent battlement atop the canyon rim, its cliffs creased with cracks. Huge boulders cascade down steep slopes above the road. Fourteen miles from Uravan the highway intersects CO 90, which heads west up the Paradox Valley to Utah. A roadside monument here commemorates the passage of Franciscan priests Francisco Dominguez and Silvestre Escalante, who explored this area in 1776 in search of an easy route from Santa Fe in New Mexico to the distant California missions.

Naturita, with a population of 546, perches on terraced benches a couple of miles up the highway. Naturita Creek and this small 5,431-foot-high town, established in 1882 as a ranching and mining supply center, were named by pioneer

Evening light reddens a sandstone bluff on the edge of the Paradox Valley.

settler "Grandma" Rockwood Blake with a Spanish word meaning "close to nature." Five miles north is **Nucla,** a utopian agricultural community founded in 1896 as a communal experiment by the Colorado Cooperative Company.

Norwood & Placerville

The highway leaves the San Miguel River west of Naturita and bends up Naturita Creek's shallow canyon. CO 141 intersects CO 145 in the canyon. The drive continues southeast on CO 145. Past the junction the highway climbs onto **Wrights Mesa,** a long, flattened tableland between Naturita Creek and the San Miguel River Canyon.

Majestic views of the snow-capped San Juan Mountains spread away from the highway. The San Miguel Range looms to the south; Mount Sneffels studs the southeastern horizon; the Uncompahgre Plateau lifts its whiskered flanks to the east; and Utah's La Sal Mountains pierce the northwestern sky. The highway runs across the fertile mesa top, passing lush paddocks filled with grazing cattle and horses and green hay fields. The road passes Redvale, a small town founded in 1910 by an orchard company. Its high elevation coupled with a short growing season doomed the orchards.

Norwood lies 9 miles up the highway. This genuine Western community, named for a Missouri town by founder I. M. Copp for his hometown in 1885, serves as a supply hub for area ranchers and farmers. After Copp built a post office, way station, and store, Norwood grew and quickly added 2 saloons, several livery stables, 3 pool halls, 3 blacksmith shops, a school, and a bank. John Davis built the Western Hotel, now the **Norwood Hotel,** and rented rooms to local cowboys, travelers, and famed folks like Butch Cassidy and Marie Curie. Poltergeists that mess up beds, leave handprints, and walk down halls supposedly haunted the old hotel. Some guests report having blankets pulled off their bed during the night or seeing apparitions in their room. The town celebrates its history with Pioneer Days every September, featuring games, a feast, and parade.

The notorious outlaw **Butch Cassidy,** actually named Robert Leroy Parker, worked on a cattle ranch south of Norwood before his robber days. His first job was the San Miguel Bank in Telluride when he and accomplice Matt Warner entered the bank on June 24, 1889, threatened to kill the teller, and stole $20,750 or about half-a-million dollars today. Butch later hooked up with Tom McCarty of the McCarty Gang, racing horses, robbing banks, and spending their hard-stolen cash in Telluride saloons and brothels.

Past Norwood the highway crosses fields, enters a piñon pine woodland, and drops onto the lip of the San Miguel River's deep canyon. The road twists 2 miles down Norwood Hill to the canyon floor, passing a couple of scenic overlooks. The drive's last 12 miles wind along the river to Placerville. Much of the canyon's diverse riparian habitat is preserved in the **San Miguel River Canyon Preserve,** one of three local preserves owned and managed by the Nature Conservancy. This lush riverside environment, one of Colorado's last undisturbed, mid-elevation riparian areas, is rich in plant and animal life. The 2-mile stretch of river offers excellent birdwatching and wildlife observation. It's one of the best places in Colorado to spot a secretive river otter.

The San Miguel River, falling over 8,000 feet in 80 miles from its mountain headwaters to the Dolores River, tumbles over cobbles and boulders. Tall cottonwoods and willow thickets clot its grassy banks. Cliff bands, punctuated by steep slopes dense with Gambel oak, piñon pine, fir, spruce, and pine, stretch along the canyon walls. This river section offers good fly fishing, rafting, and kayaking. The drive quietly ends at **Placerville,** an old placer mining town, at the junction of CO 145 and 62. CO 145, part of the San Juan Skyway (see Drive 23), continues up the canyon 15 miles to Telluride, while CO 62 climbs east over scenic Dallas Divide to Ridgway.

28

Mesa Verde National Park Scenic Drive

Mesa Verde National Park

General description: The drive runs 21 miles across mesa tops and canyons in Mesa Verde National Park to the park museum. Ruins Road, formed by two additional 6-mile-long self-guiding loops, explores the cliff-bound cities and remains of the Ancestral Puebloan culture on Chapin Mesa.

Special attractions: Mesa Verde National Park, Far View Visitor Center, Mesa Verde Museum, Far View Ruin, Cedar Tree Tower, Spruce Tree House, Cliff Palace, Balcony House, Long House, Step House, Badger House, pit house and pueblo ruins, Spruce Canyon and Petroglyph Point Trails, panoramic overlooks, hiking, camping, interpretive programs, guided tours.

Location: Southwestern Colorado. The drive begins 10 miles east of Cortez on US 160. Durango is 30 miles east on US 160.

Route name: Ruins Road.

Travel season: Year-round. The park and drive are open all year. Services are curtailed from November to the end of April. The Ruins Road loop drive is open 8 a.m. to sunset and the museum is open 8 a.m. to 5 p.m. daily in winter. Check for times of off-season tours of Spruce Tree House and Cliff Palace. Expect hazardous road conditions in winter.

Camping: Morfield Campground, operated by a private concessionaire, is open April through October. The campground (267 sites) is 4 miles south of the park entrance. The campground offers tables, comfort stations, trailer dumping stations, and summer evening programs. For information and reservations call (800) 449-2288 or visit visitmesaverde.com/lodging-camping/morefield-campground/.

Services: Services, including supplies, groceries, gasoline, Laundromat, and showers, are at Morfield Village between May and October. Far View has a gas station, restaurant, cafeteria, gift shop, and lodge. Complete visitor services are in Cortez and Mancos.

Nearby attractions: Cortez, Mancos, Four Corners Monument, Ute Mountain Tribal Park, Hovenweep National Monument, Canyons of the Ancients National Monument, Escalante Ruins, Mancos State Park, La Plata Mountains, Durango, San Juan Scenic Skyway All-American Byway (Scenic Route 23), Durango and Silverton Narrow Gauge Railroad.

The Route

The **Ancestral Puebloans,** sometimes called the Anasazi, a Navajo word meaning "the ancient ones" or "enemy ancestors," describes a loose aggregate of Native American cultures that once inhabited the Colorado Plateau province in northern New Mexico and Arizona, southern Utah, and southwestern Colorado. Sharp, unfinished edges fill the plateau's distinctive landscapes. It's a harsh land of sandstone layers sliced by deep canyons and arroyos, lorded over by towering mesas

Mesa Verde National Park Scenic Drive

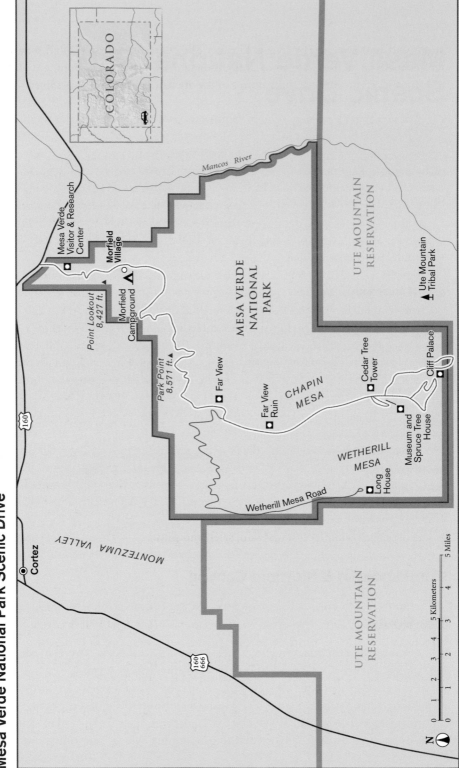

and buttes, and traversed by rivers of history and character. Sparse rainfall, a fierce temperature range, and a storm of sunlight dictate the plateau's environment and, in turn, shaped the destiny and cultures of the ancient peoples who have lived here over the last 10,000 years.

The Ancestral Puebloans, one of southwest America's three main cultural groups, developed, flourished, and vanished before Columbus set foot in the New World in 1492. The hallmark trait of their culture is the great stone cities built during their "classic" era almost 1,000 years ago. The Ancestral Puebloans erected massive, above-ground pueblos like those seen today at their descendants' villages in Taos, Acoma, and Hopiland. They also built pueblos nestled under the protective eaves of immense caves. Archeologists now call these ancient peoples the Ancestral Pueblos rather than Anasazi since they are the ancestors of today's Pueblo, Hopi, and Zuni tribes.

Mesa Verde National Park preserves these startling cliff towns, and the 33-mile-long Mesa Verde scenic drive explores and interprets this lost world of the Ancestral Pueblo people. The 52,485-acre national park, established in 1906, protects more than 4,000 prehistoric sites, including almost 600 cliff dwellings.

Mesa Verde made an ideal place for human habitation. More rain falls on this highland than in surrounding lowland valleys, and its gentle tilt to the south moderates winter temperatures. Precipitation on the semiarid mesa averages 18 inches a year, with the bulk of that coming in the 80 to 100 inches of annual winter snow. A long, 171-day frost-free growing season ensured good summer crops for the ancient farmers.

Expect cold, snowy winters and warm, dry summers when visiting the national park. Daily highs during the busy season, June through September, reach into the 80s and 90s. Thunderstorms often occur on July and August afternoons. Winters at Mesa Verde have low visitation and cold days. The road's upper elevations can be snowpacked and icy, particularly in shaded areas. Spring brings warm, breezy days and occasional rain, sleet, and snow.

Point Lookout & Morfield Canyon

The drive begins 10 miles east of Cortez on US 160. Exit south to Mesa Verde National Park and drive 400 feet to a left turn to the **Mesa Verde Visitor and Research Center.** The environmentally-friendly center, opened in December 2012, orients visitors to the national park, its archeological resources, how to explore the park, and nearby archeological sites. The building also houses park archives, its collection of 3-million artifacts, and serves as a state-of-the-art research facility. Stop at the center to purchase tickets if you wish to visit Cliff Palace, Balcony House, or Long House. The center also has a store that sells maps, books, trail guides, and other items and restrooms. Park fees are collected here from early January to early March.

Past the visitor center turnoff, the paved road runs south up a shallow draw bordered by shale hills studded with piñon pines and junipers. A trailer parking area sits alongside the road before the entrance station. Because the park road is narrow and winding, no trailers are permitted past Morfield Campground. Visitors not camping are required to leave their rigs here. The park entrance station is reached after a mile.

The road continues south and begins switchbacking upward under 8,427-foot **Point Lookout,** an abrupt, cliff-lined promontory. This airy lookout, reached via a 2.3-mile trail from Morfield Campground, marks Mesa Verde's northernmost point. Mesa Verde, Spanish for "Green Table," lifts sharply from the Montezuma Valley in southwestern Colorado. The high plateau, bordered by sheer cliffs and precipitous shale slopes, forms a natural fortress. Only the Mancos River, following a sinuous canyon, penetrates the lofty sandstone barrier. Mesa Verde is a textbook example of what geologists call a cuesta—a tilted mesa with a steep escarpment on one side and a gently dipping slope on the other. Deep canyons, draining southward to the Mancos River, dissect Mesa Verde between long fingerlike mesas laden with fertile, windblown soil deposits.

Past Point Lookout the road swings onto the mesa's east flank, edging south high above the Mancos Valley. This road section crosses gray Mancos shale, a 2,000-foot-thick layer of consolidated mud deposited 65 million years ago in a quiet, shallow sea. The shale weathers into the towering badlands that dominate Mesa Verde's steep edges. The formation, which swells and contracts with moisture, is prone to landslides and subsidence. The road here has been damaged and closed several times by landslides. The area above the road has since been reworked and anchored to avoid future problems.

Above the Mancos shale lies the Mesa Verde Group. Three distinct formations—Point Lookout sandstone, the Menefee Formation, and Cliff House sandstone—compose this group of rock layers. Both the Point Lookout and Cliff House sandstones are cliff-forming units laid down as shoreline sand deposits as the Mancos Sea alternately retreated and advanced. Point Lookout sandstone forms the massive ramparts above the drive's first miles, while the Cliff House sandstone caps the mesa's interior canyons and provides the open alcoves used by the ancient ones. The easily eroded Menefee Formation, squeezed between the two sandstones, formed from silt and sand deposited in swampy marshes and lagoons along an ancient shoreline.

The **Mancos Valley Overlook** sits near the end of the shelf road. Below the viewpoint spreads the broad Mancos Valley, divided by ranches and green pastures. At its head sits the town of Mancos and beyond loom the La Plata Mountains, a small, ragged range topped by 13,232-foot Hesperus Mountain.

Past the overlook the drive bends through a saddle and enters **Morfield Canyon** 4 miles from the park entrance. This wide canyon, rimmed by low cliffs and fringed by scrub oak–covered slopes, houses most of the park's visitor services. **Morfield Village** offers a laundry, gas station, store with supplies and souvenirs, restaurant, and showers. Morfield Campground has 267 campsites, including 15 full-hookup RV sites. Evening campfire programs are presented nightly June through Labor Day at the Morfield Amphitheater.

The campground area offers excellent hiking trails. Hiking is limited to only a few areas in Mesa Verde National Park to protect the park's archaeological treasures. Visitors hiking away from developed areas and off designated trails are subject to stiff penalties. Three trails roam the Morfield area. The 2-mile round-trip **Knife Edge Trail** follows the old shelf road from the campground to the Montezuma Valley Overlook. The 2.3-mile round-trip **Point Lookout Trail** treks to the point's precipitous edge and yields spectacular views. The 7.8-mile round-trip **Prater Ridge Trail** climbs west from the campground onto lofty Prater Ridge.

The North Rim & Park Point

The drive heads across Morfield Canyon and enters a 0.25-mile-long tunnel through Prater Ridge. After exiting the tunnel the road climbs upper Prater Canyon to 7,820-foot-high **Montezuma Valley Overlook.** Look for mule deer grazing on the canyon floor, particularly in early evening. The viewpoint, with picnic tables and ramadas, looks west across the Montezuma Valley. Numerous farms and ranches dot the valley around Cortez, one of southwest Colorado's largest towns. Beyond tower 9,977-foot Ute Peak and Sleeping Ute Mountain, a small laccolithic range that formed when intrusive volcanic rock blistered up through the surrounding sedimentary strata.

The road winds south from the overlook, ascending steep slopes covered with scrub oaks, piñon pines, and occasional Douglas firs. For the next 9 miles the road follows the **North Rim of Mesa Verde,** climbing over high ridges, dipping across shallow canyon heads, and edging along steep slopes that plunge down to the Montezuma Valley.

These upper elevations are heavily forested. Gambel or scrub oak heavily coats the hillsides, and Douglas fir, ponderosa pine, and even quaking aspen tuck into cool, moist ravines. Abundant wildlife populates Mesa Verde's diverse, wild habitats. Mule deer are abundant, while transient elk occasionally wander onto the escarpment. Mountain lion, black bear, coyote, bobcat, and gray fox roam this upland plateau, and scattered bighorn sheep inhabit the rocky canyons. Over 160 bird species are seen, including turkeys, golden eagles, hawks, owls, turkey vultures, ravens, Steller's jays, chickadees, nuthatches, and hummingbirds.

After 4 miles the road reaches 8,571-foot **Park Point,** the park's highest elevation. This lookout yields an overview of the surrounding Colorado Plateau. To the northeast lie forested plateaus topped by the snow-capped San Miguel and La Plata Ranges. Utah's canyon country stretches westward beyond Ute Peak to the Abajo and La Sal Mountains. The Chuska and Lukachukai Ranges, straddling the Arizona–New Mexico border, recede to the southwestern horizon, while the immense San Juan Basin, punctuated by the volcanic peak of Shiprock, basks south of Mesa Verde in New Mexico.

Far View

The drive winds another 5 miles along the North Rim to **Far View.** Here, perched on a flattened ridge, sits the former **Far View Visitor Center.** The center, which closed after the new visitor center opened at the park entrance in 2013, was still closed at the time of this book's publication. The round building, erected in 1966 in the National Park Service's Mission 66 architectural style, may one day become a natural history museum focused on biological research done by the University of Colorado Boulder and would be administered by the CU's Natural History Museum. The building is also being nominated for inclusion on the National Register of Historic Places. Also at Far View is Far View Lodge with 150 rooms and stunning views, and Far View Terrace Café, a restaurant with a food-court atmosphere.

An excellent summer side trip begins at Far View and travels 12 miles southwest to **Wetherill Mesa** on a narrow, winding road with sharp curves, steep grades, several overlooks, and a picnic area. Wetherill Mesa offers an uncrowded alternative to the busy Chapin Mesa ruins. At road's end are an orientation center, snack bar, and restrooms. The 5-mile Long House Loop Trail, a self-guided bike and hike loop, leads to Kodak House, Long House, and Nordenskiold Site No. 16 Overlooks, the trailhead for Long House, and a trail to 4 mesa-top sites in the Badger House Community. Visitors also follow a self-guided tour through Step House or take a 2-hour, ranger-led excursion into **Long House,** the park's second-largest ruin. The Long House tour, called "Mesa Verde's Most In-Depth Tour" by the Park Service, requires a 2.25-mile hike, an elevation gain of 130 feet, and climbing two 15-foot ladders at the site. Purchase tickets for Long House at the Visitor and Research Center at the park entrance.

The drive bends onto upper Chapin Mesa at Far View Visitor Center, begins descending southward, and a mile later reaches **Far View Ruin.** This large mesa-top village, located east of the road, is best visited on the return trip. Far View House, a rectangular pueblo with about 50 rooms, was a possible trading center inhabited from AD 1100 to 1200. A large population lived in the area surrounding Far View, with over 50 dwelling sites within the pueblo's immediate area.

While this area is colder in winter than farther south on the mesa, it receives more annual rainfall—an important consideration for these early farmers.

Water became the blood of the Ancestral Puebloan way of life when they became agriculturists. By controlling water, they controlled their destiny. Without water they would remain locked into a basic hunting-and-gathering economy, following game and harvesting seasonal plants. The miracle of water, however, grew nutritious crops like corn, beans, and squash that in turn made social and religious growth possible. Water, in a sense, created Mesa Verde's vibrant cities and gave their inhabitants the leisure time to develop crafts like basketry, pottery, and weaving. The ancient ones became masters of water exploitation in this semiarid land by utilizing floodwater and subsurface irrigation, planting crops near seepage springs, and building ditches and reservoirs to transport and store water.

Mummy Lake, sitting alongside the drive north of Far View Ruin, testifies to their reliance on water. A fan of uphill channels could have diverted runoff from rain and snow into a main ditch that drained into Mummy Lake. The stone-lined lake is possibly a reservoir 90 feet in diameter and 12 feet deep with a 500,000-gallon storage capacity. A distribution channel ran south from the reservoir to nearby fields for irrigation. The Far View Ditch, another canal, ran 5 miles down Chapin Mesa to the head of Spruce Tree Canyon. That water was probably used for irrigation, although no clear evidence indicates water ever flowed that far down the ditch. Some archaeologists also dispute that Mummy Lake was a reservoir or was used for water collection. Mummy Lake is reached on a short trail from Far View Ruin.

Chapin Mesa Archeological Museum & Spruce Tree House

The road continues south on Chapin Mesa and reaches Cedar Tree Tower after 3 miles. This small ruin, composed of a tower connected to a "kiva," or underground ceremonial chamber, lies east of the road. Prehistoric farming terraces scatter along a short trail south of the site. A major road intersection is 0.5 mile farther south.

A mile-long loop road continues south to the Chapin Mesa Archeological Museum, park headquarters, and Spruce Tree House. The **Chapin Mesa Archeological Museum** offers an excellent introduction to the evolution of the Ancestral Pueblo culture through a series of dramatic dioramas, numerous artifacts, including pottery, basketry, jewelry, and weaving, and a 25-minute film. A bookstore, restrooms, snack bar, and post office are located near the museum. A picnic area spreads along the rim of Spruce Canyon on the west side of the loop opposite the museum.

A self-guided paved trail begins at the museum and drops east into Spruce Tree Canyon to **Spruce Tree House,** the park's third-largest cliff dwelling. This well-preserved ruin, protected from weathering by an immense alcove, boasts 114 rooms and eight kivas and housed as many as 150 people. The site was named by its discoverers, Richard Wetherill and Charlie Mason, after a large Douglas fir that grew in front of the village. The tree was cut down in 1891. A booklet, available at the trailhead and museum, explains Spruce Tree House's important features.

Two other trails explore the Spruce Tree House area. The 2.4-mile **Petroglyph Point Trail** follows Spruce Tree Canyon's eastern edge to Petroglyph Point, passing several rock art panels, before climbing onto the rim for the return walk. The 2.4-mile **Spruce Canyon Trail** winds into Spruce Canyon before climbing onto Chapin Mesa near the picnic area.

Ruins Road

Ruins Road, consisting of two 6-mile-long loops, begins at the intersection with the headquarters road. The drive heads down Ruins Road and goes straight on the 6-mile-long **Mesa Top Loop.** This road explores the architectural development of the Ancestral Pueblo people by stopping at a succession of sites. Few places are found in the Southwest where their long march to civilization can be seen so clearly as along this loop drive.

The first stop is a pit house, a roofed semi-subterranean pit, built about AD 575 during an era archaeologists call the Modified Basketmaker period. The next viewpoint, **Navajo Canyon View,** overlooks deep Navajo Canyon, which contains over 60 cliff dwellings, including Echo House across the chasm. **Square Tower House,** one of Mesa Verde's most elegant ruins, nestles in a shallow cavern below the next stop. The 70-room pueblo boasts Mesa Verde's tallest structure, with one wall measuring 33 feet high.

The next three stops include pit houses erected before AD 700 and several above-ground villages dating from the Developmental Pueblo period between AD 800 and 1100. Sun Point Pueblo, at the next turnoff, dates from 1200 during the Classic Pueblo period, a time when the Puebloan culture reached its zenith. The people began leaving the mesa tops shortly after the pueblo's construction to build their villages in caves tucked under the canyon rims. Why they retreated into the cliffs is an enduring mystery. Defense reigns as the common explanation. A village built in a protective alcove was undoubtedly easily defended, particularly with bows and arrows, spears, and stockpiles of food and water. Little evidence exists, however, that these were people at war. But whatever the reasons, the move to their aeries in the high cliffs was the first step toward the total abandonment of the Mesa Verde by AD 1300.

Square Tower House, tucked beneath an arching cliff, is Mesa Verde's tallest structure.

Cliff Palace

Sun Point View yields cross-canyon views of numerous ruins built during the 13th century. The next two viewpoints look into Fewkes Canyon and several impressive sites, including Oak Tree House, Fire Temple, and New Fire House. **Sun Temple,** the last stop, sits on a narrow promontory above Fewkes Canyon. This large D-shaped building, while never completed, is thought to have been a ceremonial structure. Another overlook north of Sun Temple yields marvelous views of **Cliff Palace,** North America's largest cliff dwelling.

It was near this spot that two cowboys from the Mancos Valley stumbled upon this "magnificent city" on a cold snowy December day in 1888. Richard Wetherill and his brother-in-law, Charlie Mason, were searching this rough country for stray cattle when they happened upon the grandest cliff dwelling of all and transformed Mesa Verde from a remote plateau to America's greatest archaeological wonder. After their initial astonishment, they lashed several trees together, descended to the canyon bottom, and clambered up to the silent chamber. The ruin appeared almost undisturbed from the passage of centuries. Pots and stone tools remained hanging from the walls, awaiting the return of their owners. Parts of human skeletons scattered across the ground. The men dubbed their amazing discovery Cliff Palace.

Why the Ancestral Puebloans abandoned their homeland at Mesa Verde and the Four Corners region is an enduring mystery. While they left a rich legacy of crumbling ruins from their golden years, a time of growth, trade, and frenzied construction, they left few clues as to their disappearance. The 13th-century Mesa Verdeans had built a sophisticated society with all the tools for success in this arid country, including water-control projects, solar calendars that marked the solstices and equinoxes, multistoried apartment houses, and a flourishing trade network with the rest of the Southwest and Mexico.

But something happened, and between AD 1270 and 1300 the Puebloan homeland of a millennium was emptied of people. Archaeologists speculate a combination of factors forced the perplexing migration from the Four Corners area to New Mexico's Rio Grande Valley and Arizona's Hopi Mesas. A prolonged drought stunted crops by shifting moisture from spring and summer to autumn. The mesa's large population depleted ground cover and trees for construction and firewood, and centuries of farming robbed mesa soils of their productivity. Disease, internal bickering, social fragmentation, and raids by outside enemies also made compelling reasons to abandon the mesa for greener pastures elsewhere.

The drive continues back to the intersection with the other Ruins Road loop. Turn east or right on 6-mile-long **Cliff Palace Loop.** The road drops southeast

Over 200 people lived in Cliff Palace, the park's largest cliff dwelling, during the 1200s.

through a dense piñon pine and juniper woodland and reaches Cliff Palace after turning into a one-lane road past a junction with the return loop road. Parking is along the road as well as restrooms and picnic tables.

View Cliff Palace from a fenced overlook poised on the canyon edge above the cliff city. The ranger-led Cliff Palace tour is the best way to see the site, but visitation is limited to protect Cliff Palace from human damage. Purchase tickets up to 2 days in advance for the tour at the Mesa Verde Visitor and Research Center at the park entrance, Chapin Mesa Archeological Museum, and the Durango Welcome Center. Get the largest selection of available tours by registering at the visitor center or in Durango. Cliff Palace is usually open to tours from mid-April to mid-October, but dates may change due to preservation work at the site. Check with the park ahead of time to confirm when Cliff Palace is open.

The ranger-guided 0.25-mile loop trail descends into the ruin from the north and climbs out on the south side of the ruin. Hikers must navigate 120 stone stairs and five 8- to 10-foot ladders on the 100-foot climb out of the site. The tour is strenuous with uneven footing and physical exertion. The park recommends those with heart or respiratory problems not do the tour.

Cliff Palace, the park's largest cliff dwelling, housed more than 200 people in its 217 rooms and 23 kivas. The village, built between AD 1209 and 1273, exhibits superb construction and masonry skills. Cliff Palace was built by accretion rather than from a grand plan—rooms were added on as they were needed. Stones, often pecked with harder hammer stones into usable shapes, were laid with a mud mortar before being carefully plastered over. Painted designs often brightened the walls.

Willa Cather aptly described Cliff Palace in her 1925 novel *The Professor's House* as "a little city of stone, asleep. It was as still as sculpture. . . . It all hung together, seemed to have a kind of composition: pale little houses of stone nestling close to one another, perched on top of each other, with flat roofs, narrow windows, straight walls, and in the middle of the group, a round tower. . . . I had come upon the city of some extinct civilization, hidden away in this inaccessible mesa for centuries, preserved in the dry air and almost perpetual sunlight like a fly in amber, guarded by the cliffs and the river and the desert."

Balcony House

The road continues south, skirting the sandstone rim of Cliff Canyon. Several roadside overlooks view ruins, including the House of Many Windows, tucked into shallow caves across the canyon. The road bends east across the mesa, briefly dipping into **Ute Mountain Tribal Park,** a 125,000-acre park preserving the remote canyons to the south and numerous Ancestral Puebloan ruins and rock art sites on the Ute Mountain Reservation.

The next stop on the Soda Canyon rim offers **Balcony House,** one of the park's most popular ruin tours. This medium-sized, 45-room pueblo sits under an arching cave beneath the parking area. Balcony House, perched above abrupt cliffs, is the park's most defensible large ruin, with only one entry and exit path. An excellent year-round spring undoubtedly made this aerie attractive to its inhabitants. Like Cliff Palace, advance tickets are required to visit Balcony House. The site is open for visitors from mid-April to mid-October, although dates may change.

The hour-long, ranger-led tour descends a paved trail and climbs a 32-foot-high ladder into Balcony House. The exit back to the rim is through a crawl tunnel, and then up several wooden ladders and steps chopped into the cliff face. Visitors with health problems or fear of heights should bypass this tour.

Balcony House, a defensible aerie in a high cliff, is one of the park's most popular ruin towers.

The Soda Canyon Overlook Trailhead, the drive's last stop, sits a little farther up the road. This quiet 0.75-mile trail winds through piñon pine and juniper to a jutting promontory that yields a fine view of Balcony House and Soda Canyon. The loop road continues northwest back to the main intersection. Turn north or right for the 21-mile journey back to the park entrance and US 160.

29

Rim Rock Drive

Colorado National Monument

General description: This 22-mile drive explores the sandstone rim and canyons of Colorado National Monument on the northern edge of the Uncompahgre Plateau.

Special attractions: Monument Canyon, Independence Monument, Window Rock Nature Trail, Saddlehorn Visitor Center, John Otto's Trail, Coke Ovens, Ute Canyon, Cold Shivers Point, Devils Kitchen, hiking, camping, rock climbing, wildlife, interpretive programs.

Location: West-central Colorado. The drive is southwest of Grand Junction.

Route name: Rim Rock Drive.

Travel season: Year-round. Although the road is regularly plowed in winter, snow and ice may persist on shaded road sections.

Camping: Saddlehorn Campground offers 80 sites in 3 loops near the visitor center on the drive's west end. Campground is open year-round, although the restrooms and water are shut off in winter. A-Loop is open year-round on a first-come first-served basis. B-Loop sites are reservable at recreation.gov or by calling (877) 444-6777. The James M. Robb sector of Colorado River State Park south of Fruita has 63-site Fruita Campground which is ideal for RVs and trailers.

Services: All services are in Fruita and Grand Junction, including lodging, private campgrounds, gas, food, and medical facilities.

Nearby attractions: Grand Junction, Museum of Western Colorado, Highline Lake State Park, Colorado River State Park, Grand Mesa Scenic Byway (Scenic Drive 25), Land's End Road, Rattlesnake Canyon, Ruby and Horsethief Canyons, Kokopelli's Trail, Rabbit Valley Paleontology Area, Grand Mesa National Forest, Uncompahgre National Forest, Unaweep–Tabeguache Scenic and Historic Byway (Scenic Drive 27).

The Route

Thick sandstone layers drape across the Uncompahgre Plateau, a long hump-backed highland that stretches across western Colorado from the San Juan Mountains to the Colorado River on the eastern edge of the Colorado Plateau. Colorado National Monument, on the plateau's northern edge, protects a 20,533-acre wonderland of dipping sandstone strata chiseled by erosion into precipitous canyons, abrupt buttresses, sharp spires and buttes, and soaring cliffs.

This rugged national monument relates a spectacular lesson in geology. The monument's 1.5-billion-year-old basement rocks once floored a primeval ocean. The horizontal rock strata above—the Chinle, Wingate, Kayenta, Entrada, and Morrison Formations—tell more recent tales of immense dune fields, meandering rivers, and swamps alive with dinosaurs. The 22-mile Rim Rock Drive traverses the monument's canyons and airy rims, explores its geologic history, offers

Rim Rock Drive

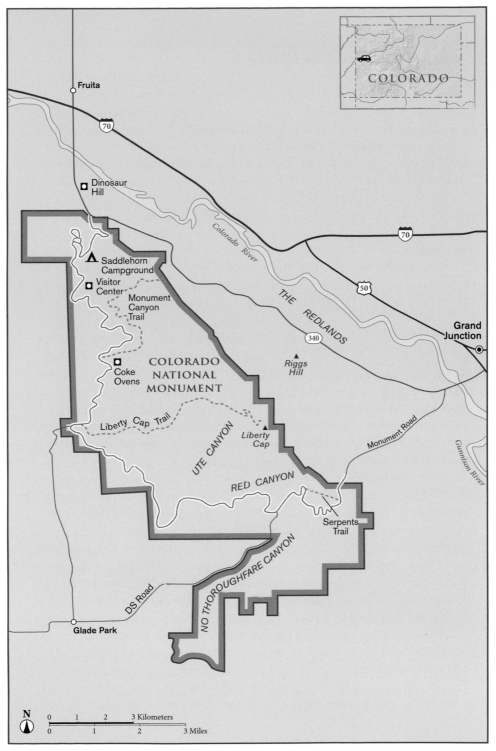

Fruita

70

Dinosaur
Hill

Colorado River

THE REDLANDS

COLORADO

70

50

Grand
Junction

Saddlehorn
Campground

Visitor
Center

Monument
Canyon
Trail

340

Riggs
Hill

COLORADO
NATIONAL
MONUMENT

Coke
Ovens

Liberty Cap Trail

UTE CANYON

Liberty
Cap

RED CANYON

Monument Road

Gunnison River

Serpents
Trail

DS Road

NO THOROUGHFARE CANYON

Glade Park

N

0   1   2   3 Kilometers
0   1   2   3 Miles

19 scenic overlooks, and passes trails that descend into the canyons, leading to spring-fed oases of grass, birdsong, and solitude.

Colorado National Monument offers a generally pleasant year-round climate. Temperatures, however, range from below zero in winter to 100 degrees in summer. Most summer days are sunny and warm with highs in the 80s and 90s. Hikers should carry a gallon of water per day and wear a hat. Temperatures in the canyons, with heat radiating off bare rock surfaces, can be extreme. Occasional afternoon thunderstorms douse the monument's rim and canyons in July and August. Autumn brings warm days and clear nights. Expect highs in the 70s and 80s with cool evenings. Winter days are cold and crisp, but highs often reach into the 40s. Snow occasionally blankets the monument under a mantle of white. Spring offers warm weather, windy afternoons, light rain showers, and wildflowers.

Rim Rock Drive is accessed at two points—at Grand Junction on the east and at Fruita on the west. The drive description begins at Colorado National Monument's west entrance on CO 340/Redlands Road almost 3 miles south of Fruita and I-70's exit 19 on the southern edge of the Grand Valley west of Grand Junction. The Colorado River, formerly called the Grand River, drifts lazily across the valley, meandering past cottonwood-lined banks, fruit orchards, and a series of towns, including Palisade, Grand Junction, and Fruita. Grand Junction, western Colorado's largest city, was named because the Gunnison River joins the Colorado River here. Mountains and cliffs hem in Grand Valley: Grand Mesa dominates the eastern horizon, the bare cliffs and eroded badlands of the Book Cliffs march across the northern edge, and the national monument's ragged cliffs and canyons mark the southern skyline.

Before the beginning of this drive, CO 340 swings south from Fruita north of I-70. **Fruita,** once a sleepy agricultural town, has transformed from its farm roots to a busy headquarters for outdoor lovers, especially mountain bikers. In the 1990s, two-wheelers discovered the diverse terrain surrounding Fruita and mapped out hundreds of miles of singletrack trails, creating a world-class fat-tire venue. Now mountain bikers call Fruita the best pedal destination in Colorado with its variety of trails from cruisers for kids and families to technical challenges for expert bikers. The 18 Roads sector in the BLM's **North Fruita Desert Area** offers flowing trails on hills, humps, and ridges. A killer ride is Chutes and Ladders Trail with steep ladders and fast downhill chutes. Also check out Zippity Do Da, Frontside, Edge Loop, and Kessel Run, an easy beginner trail. Other Fruita bike areas include Rabbit Valley Trails, trails at Horsethief Canyon, Highline Lake Trail, and the famous 142-mile Kokopelli Trail which runs west to Moab. Visit in April for the annual Fruita Fat Tire Festival to celebrate the cult of the bike.

From Fruita and I-70, the highway heads south past a Colorado Welcome Center and crosses the Colorado River's muddy channel. The road climbs away from the river through the multicolored siltstones and mudstones of the Morrison Formation. This 150-million-year-old formation preserves the skeletons of great dinosaurs that roamed the region's dense forests and swamplands, as well as some of the oldest mammal fossils found in the Western Hemisphere.

Numerous dinosaur bones are found in the Morrison rocks below the uplifted Uncompahgre Plateau between Fruita and Grand Junction. Barren **Dinosaur Hill** east of the highway and above the river is the site of paleontologist Elmer Riggs's 1901 discovery of an Apatosaurus skeleton. A bronze plaque honors the event. To explore this unique paleontology area, turn left or east from the highway and drive a short distance to the Dinosaur Hill Trailhead. The site has a shaded picnic area, restrooms, and interpretative signs. The 1.5-mile Dinosaur Hill Trail loops through the area, exploring this famed dinosaur locale. It's best to hike the trail clockwise from the trailhead. Partway up the hill, follow a short path left to a large boulder with a mold of the rear upper leg bone of a giant dinosaur on its face. The trail continues to a shaded overlook on top of the 4,726-foot hill and then descends the east side to the site of Riggs's discovery and a gated tunnel that leads into the hill where the bones were excavated.

West of this site in McKinnis Canyons National Conservation Area is the **Fruita Paleontological Area** where the unique fossil of a 6-inch-long, 1-ounce mammal was found in 1998. The mouse-like animal, dating from the Jurassic Period about 150 million years ago, lived in burrows to avoid dangerous dinosaurs. Riggs Hill, another notable dinosaur quarry, lies a few miles east of here. Elmer Riggs excavated the first known skeleton of the immense Brachiosaurus there in 1900.

Wedding & Fruita Canyons

The highway bends southeast from the dinosaur site and climbs to Colorado National Monument's west entrance, almost 3 miles from Fruita. Rim Rock Drive begins here at the right turn from CO 340. After passing the entrance station, the paved road crosses the maroon-colored Chinle Formation and quickly reaches steep Wingate sandstone cliffs. The road ascends a tight switchback on the west side of **Wedding Canyon,** with the squat 100-foot-high tower called the Praying Monk plopped east of the loop on the canyon edge. **Redlands View,** 0.25 mile up the drive, offers a look across the Grand Valley and a fault zone below the escarpment.

Past the overlook, the road bends south and enters **Fruita Canyon,** a deep box canyon sliced into the plateau rim. The road swings under towering sandstone cliffs on the canyon's east flank. A turnoff and viewpoint near the canyon's head yield a great view of **Balanced Rock,** a short pinnacle topped with an overhanging block of precariously balanced Wingate sandstone. The improbable 700-ton oddity perches on a horizontal bedding seam. Geologists don't think it will fall anytime soon since the rock still connects to the bedrock pedestal beneath. The rock is one of the few features at Colorado National Monument that climbers aren't allowed to scale due to its limited life-span. Mushroom Rock, another balanced rock in the park, sits on a pedestal in Lower Monument Canyon.

The road climbs steeply past Balanced Rock, passes through two tunnels, and reaches **Historic Trails View** near the cliffed rim. An interpretative sign details the area's early explorations. The drive continues climbing and finally reaches the rim above Fruita Canyon and **Fruita Canyon Viewpoint,** an airy overlook near the head of the canyon. The fenced viewpoint, reached by a 100-foot walk from the roadside parking lot, offers a scenic view of Rim Rock Drive snaking up the canyon below. Look for Balanced Rock on the right side of the canyon. This overlook, like most of the popular ones at the Monument, is fenced to protect visitors from straying onto dangerous cliff edges. Always keep behind the fence for views and photos, and keep a cautious eye on children. A fall from any overlook is usually fatal.

From the overlook, the drive bends south and reaches the monument's **Saddlehorn Visitor Center** after 4 miles from the drive's start. The educational visitor center details the natural history, geology, and history of Colorado National Monument and has a ranger-staffed information desk to answer your questions and suggest hikes. The center also offers ranger-led walks and talks in the warmer months, a video program, restrooms, books, and maps. The 0.5 mile-Canyon Rim Trail runs along the rim of Wedding Canyon from the visitor center to Book Cliff View. Hikers should beware of vertical cliffs and keep children under control.

A paved, one-way side road heads north from the visitor center and loops around Saddlehorn Rock, a prominent monolith of pale Entrada sandstone. Saddlehorn Campground spreads 80 sites in 3 loops along the road north of the rock. The widely spaced sites, offering great nighttime views of the glittering lights in the Grand Valley below, are scattered through a piñon and juniper woodland. The campground, with A-Loop open year-round on a first-come, first-served basis, offers water, restrooms, and nightly campfire programs during the warmer months.

The Window Rock Trail, an excellent 0.3-mile loop trail, begins at **Book Cliff View Overlook** where the campground road reaches the western lip of Wedding Canyon. The short trail winds past twisted junipers and slickrock gardens tucked in alcoves and bays above tall cliffs. The path leads to a magnificent viewpoint poised on the canyon rim above Window Rock, an elongated arch carved by water

Rim Rock Drive spirals up Fruita Canyon beneath vertical Wingate sandstone cliffs.

and ice on the cliff edge. The view encompasses Wedding Canyon and the Grand Valley. The Colorado River uncoils along the valley edge and the Book Cliffs with shale slopes, cliff bands, and forested summits stretching across the northern horizon. The evening is a perfect time to hike to the overlook, with the canyon below filled with silence. As darkness descends, thousands of lights twinkle in Grand Junction and Fruita. Past the overlook is a large picnic area with restrooms.

Rim Rock Drive Overlooks

Rim Rock Drive bends south from the visitor center and after 0.5 mile edges along a narrow bench above an overhanging 300-foot-high cliff. At the canyon head the road turns east and continues along a broad rimrock bench. At the next pullout, **John Otto's Trail** runs 0.25 mile across a narrow promontory above Wedding Canyon to a lofty lookout perched above the Pipe Organ.

John Otto, a trailblazer, promoter, patriot, and outdoorsman, worked tirelessly for the establishment of Colorado National Monument. He first settled in a canvas tent in Monument Canyon in 1906. The next year he wrote, "I came here last year and found these canyons, and they feel like the heart of the world to me. I'm going to stay and build trails and promote this place, because it should be a national park. Some folks think I'm crazy, but I want to see this scenery opened up to all people." Otto devoted himself to building trails, writing the Grand Junction

Chamber of Commerce and President William H. Taft to establish a "Monument National Park" here, and guiding local citizens through the wondrous sandstone canyons of his proposed park. Otto was appointed custodian at a salary of $1 a month after the monument was established in 1911.

Three spectacular viewpoints—Independence, Grand View, and Monument Canyon—lie along the next few road miles. All yield spectacular views into **Monument Canyon,** a wide canyon flanked by sandstone cliffs and floored with ancient bedrock. **Independence Monument View** overlooks 5,739-foot **Independence Monument,** a 450-foot-high monolith that sits atop a soft sandstone cone between Monument and Wedding Canyons. A couple of interpretative signs at the iconic viewpoint describe the formation of the tower and its first ascent by John Otto. This overlook offers fantastic photo ops of Monument Canyon, Independence Monument, and the fertile Grand Valley. Come in the late evening when the sun shafts across the canyon rim, reddening the cliffs, or in winter when white snow contrasts with the rosy rock. Also, bring binoculars to scope the south ridge of Independence Monument for climbers ascending chopped steps up a slab to the airy summit.

Independence Monument formed after water and ice eroded walls that once connected the pinnacle to mesas on the northeast and southwest. Wingate sandstone, a buff-colored sandstone deposited as immense sand dunes 210 million years ago during the Triassic period, forms the park's dramatic cliffs and spires. Atop the Wingate lies the Kayenta Formation, a thin layer later deposited by rivers and streams. The Kayenta sandstone, a coarse, erosion-resistant rock, forms a capstone atop the softer underlying Wingate Formation and slows its erosion. Independence Monument, with a spacious, flat summit, is capped and protected by Kayenta sandstone. By contrast, the nearby **Coke Ovens** weathered into rounded domes with small summits after they lost their Kayenta cap.

Today a moderate rock climb, Independence Monument was first ascended by John Otto in June and July 1910, to celebrate Flag Day and Independence Day. Otto scaled a ladder of pipes laboriously drilled into the tower's west face, a feat that took several months. The Grand Junction *Daily News* reported in an article: "Inch by inch, foot by foot, daring intrepid John Otto, creeping up the giant sides of Independence Monument, the highest and most noble eminence of rock in all Monument Canyon . . . he expects to reach the top before the end of the present week. It is a perilous piece of work he is doing and he should receive great recognition for his feat when he reaches the summit." His first ascent was on Flag Day, 1910. An honor guard carried a flag to the base and Otto scrambled up his pipe route to the flat summit where he hoisted Old Glory. People clapped and hooted both Otto and the flag flapping in the afternoon breeze. Later Otto displayed the 6-foot by 12-foot flag on the summit every Independence Day, giving

An overhang frames 450-foot-high Independence Monument, the tallest freestanding pinnacle in Colorado National Monument.

Independence Monument its name. **Otto's Route,** minus its pipes, is now a moderate 4-pitch rock climbing route. For details on climbing Independence and other towers in the Monument, consult *Rock Climbing Colorado* (FalconGuides).

Grand View Point, another 0.5 mile up the drive, is precisely that—a spectacular view of Monument Canyon, Independence Monument, and the Grand Valley from a fenced overlook. Reach the viewpoint by hiking a 0.08-mile trail from the parking area. Directly opposite the airy overlook is Grand View Spire, a semi-detached pinnacle joined to the cliff below the viewpoint. Grand View is one of the park's best vantage points for photographs, with scenic panoramas stretching to the north. Visit in the morning or evening for the best light on the cliffs and distant mesas.

Past Grand View, the drive twists for a mile along the Kayenta sandstone rim and reaches **Monument Canyon View,** another scenic overlook perched atop tall sandstone cliffs. The sinuous road bends south following the rim of a spur canyon to **Coke Ovens Overlook.** From a pullout on the left side of the road, 3.5 miles from the visitor center, follow a short trail to a fenced overlook with views of the Coke Ovens, four rounded domes shaped like old-time coke ovens in upper Monument Canyon. The Coke Ovens are a lesson in weathering. Once the hard Kayenta caprock eroded, the lower and softer Wingate sandstone was quickly attacked by erosion which smoothed the flanks of the pinnacles and left pinpoint summits.

A quarter-mile up the drive from Coke Ovens Overlook is the upper trailhead for the **Monument Canyon Trail.** This popular 6.3-mile-long trail, built by John Otto in 1910, descends 600 feet from the canyon rim to Monument Canyon's wide floor, traversing almost a billion years of geologic history from Entrada sandstone to ancient Precambrian gneiss and schist. The moderate trail descends to the canyon floor and then winds past rusty sandstone cliffs and soaring towers like the Kissing Couple and Independence Monument before dropping to a lower trailhead on CO 340. Arrange a car shuttle to pick you up at the lower trailhead or hike to Independence Monument and then reverse the trail back to the upper trailhead. Remember that the last trail section is uphill, so carry plenty of water in the warmer months. The 0.25-mile **Coke Ovens Trail** also begins at the parking area and traverses across a wooded bench to a scenic fenced overlook above the Coke Ovens.

Artist's Point sits high above Monument Canyon 0.5 mile up the drive. This lofty viewpoint offers a marvelous panorama of canyons, mesas, and valleys, including the Book and Roan Cliffs to the north and the 10,000-foot-high Grand Mesa, reputedly the biggest flat-topped mountain in the world, to the east. Below the viewpoint is a series of squat pinnacles called the Squaw Fingers. After admiring the view from the roadside overlook, follow a short trail down to a lower viewpoint. In the early 20th century, artists often stopped at this inspirational point to create *plein-air* paintings of the canyons, cliffs, and mountains.

The drive winds upward through a pygmy forest of piñon pine and juniper, passes **Highland View,** the highest viewpoint above Monument Canyon on Rim Rock Road. The semicircular, stone-walled viewpoint, 1.3 miles south of Artist's Point, gives views across Monument Canyon's cliffs to Grand Junction and the distant highland, a barren escarpment of the Book Cliffs topped by the wooded Roan Cliffs. This viewpoint is an ideal spot to study the monument's "wedding cake" geology, with alternating layers of exposed rock. The soft Summerville and Morrison formations cap the top of the opposite plateau. Below them are Entrada sandstone, a rock formation above Rim Rock Drive that forms angled slabs, and Wingate sandstone, the monument's main cliff-forming unit, below the road. Red shale layers in the Chinle Formation below the sheer cliffs slopes down to the canyon floor and ancient black bedrock that once formed the roots of a mountain range over 1.5 billion years ago.

Past the overlook, the road continues to climb and reaches a 6,593-foot-high divide between Monument and Ute Canyons on Monument Mesa. The parkland's scant 11 inches of annual precipitation and an extreme temperature range limits plant and animal life on this high desert. A piñon pine and juniper woodland dominates the monument's mesas and canyons, blanketing the moist, north-facing slopes. Junipers also scatter across the desolate rimrock along the drive, sending sturdy taproots down through cracks in pursuit of water. A sparse under-story of shrubs spreads over the forest's sandy floor, including mountain mahogany, a favorite deer food, and open meadows of sagebrush and saltbush. Late spring and early summer bring a colorful display of wildflowers, including Indian paintbrush, phlox, yellow mustard, evening primrose, and yucca stalks laden with bulbous white blossoms.

Common animals found in the monument include coyote, mule deer, kangaroo rat, bat, porcupine, rock squirrel, bobcat, and occasional mountain lion, black bear, and elk. Bighorn sheep, reintroduced into the monument in 1979, are often sighted along Rim Rock Road and in the canyons. Numerous reptiles and amphibians, including the rarely seen midget-faded rattlesnake, as well as 126 bird species inhabit the monument's varied habitats.

Ute Canyon

Past the divide, the road swings into upper **Ute Canyon,** a broad valley coated with sagebrush and piñon pine. The upper trailhead for the 7-mile **Liberty Cap Trail** lies before the valley floor on the road's east side. The path, a favorite cross-country ski tour in snowy winters, threads across Monument Mesa to Liberty Cap before dropping to the lower trailhead below the monument's rocky escarpment.

A side road, beginning on the south slope of Ute Canyon, heads south and west across Glade Park 5 miles to the small hamlet of Glade Park. Rough 4x4 tracks head west from here to the edge of the 75,439-acre **Black Ridge Canyons Wilderness Area,** a rough desert country seamed by deep canyons and studded with hidden arches. The area, part of the BLM's 123,430-acre **McKinnis Canyons National Recreation Area,** includes 7 major canyons that drain north from Black Ridge to the Colorado River in Ruby and Horsethief Canyons. The **Rattlesnake Canyon** region offers the second largest concentration of arches in the United States after Arches National Park. The canyons 9 arches include Bridge Arch, East Rim Arch, and Cedar Tree Arch with a span of 76 feet. To reach the trailhead from here, drive 0.2 mile to a fork and go right on the Black Ridge Road for 13 miles to the trailhead. A high-clearance, 4-wheel-drive vehicle is required for the last 1.5 miles.

Rim Rock Drive turns sharply east and follows Ute Canyon. The canyon's intermittent stream, flowing only after snowmelt or heavy rain, slowly sliced a V-shaped canyon into the Entrada and Kayenta sandstones. After a mile the canyon abruptly deepens at **Suction Point,** a 350-foot-high drop where the creek cut through soft Wingate sandstone. The drop makes a spectacular waterfall after a summer thunderstorm.

The drive traverses the south rim of Ute Canyon and passes two excellent rimrock viewpoints, **Upper Ute Canyon Overlook** and **Fallen Rock Overlook.** Fallen Rock Overlook looks down-canyon to Fallen Rock, a giant sandstone slab that fell off the sheer canyon wall above. The **Ute Canyon Trail,** one of the monument's best hikes, begins at the parking area and descends 550 feet into Upper Ute Canyon. The path continues down Lower Ute Canyon, swings around Liberty Cap, and steeply descends to a trailhead off Wildwood Drive on the south side of Grand Junction. The 7-mile trail, flanked by tall sandstone cliffs, passes sagebrush meadows, tall cottonwoods that offer welcome summer shade, and cattail-lined potholes alive with spadefoot toads and singing birds.

The road swings around the east arm of Ute Canyon and climbs to 6,640 feet, the drive's highest point. A mile farther sits **Lower Ute Canyon View,** a fenced viewpoint on the east rim of the canyon that looks down the canyon to the distant Book Cliffs. Park on the west side of the road and hike a 0.1-mile trail through a piñon and juniper forest to the airy overlook above a 300-foot-high cliff. The site is dangerous so stay behind the fence for photographs and resist the impulse to walk onto the slickrock rim.

The road turns away from Ute Canyon, traverses a narrow mesa, and after 0.5 mile emerges at **Red Canyon Overlook.** This deep, 2.3-mile-long canyon extends northeast from the viewpoint to Grand Junction. Park on the north side of the road to access the stone wall-lined viewpoint. The short trail to the overlook is wide and wheelchair-accessible. Red Canyon is difficult to access, with no trails entering it. The drive twists along a Kayenta sandstone bench on Red and Columbus Canyons' south rims and after 2.5 miles reaches an intersection with DS Road, a county road that heads southwest above No Thoroughfare Canyon to Glade Park. No Thoroughfare Canyon in the south part of Colorado National Monument offers wild terrain, waterfalls, and primitive trails.

Cold Shivers Point, Serpents Trail, & Devils Kitchen

Cold Shivers Point, a barrier-free overlook, lies north of the road junction. This aptly named overlook, one of the park's most dramatic viewpoints, perches atop vertical cliffs hundreds of feet above the floor of Columbus Canyon. Standing atop the 300-foot cliff below the fenced overlook will send shivers down the spine of every acrophobic traveler. Access the point from a parking area on the west side of the road and walk a short paved trail.

A desert bighorn sheep grazes in Lower Monument Canyon.

The drive begins descending past Cold Shivers Point, and after 0.5 mile switchbacks steeply down the uplifted escarpment of the Ladder Creek monocline. The **Serpents Trail** begins above the north entrance of a long tunnel.

The historic Serpents Trail follows the old road bed of what was called "the crookedest road in the world." The road, built by John Otto and Glade Park ranchers, was completed in 1921 and closed to vehicular travel in 1950 after the lower section of Rim Rock Drive was completed. The Serpents Trail uncoils 2.5 miles down a steep sandstone rib. It's best to hike one-way, with a driver meeting the walkers at the lower trailhead at Devils Kitchen. Rim Rock Drive was built in the 1930s by work crews with the Civilian Conservation Corps, National Park Service, and Works Progress Administration. Some 23 miles of the drive were handmade, with help only from pickaxes and dynamite. Just before Christmas in 1933 a massive rock fall near Grand View killed nine workers.

The drive twists through the dark red Chinle Formation below the tunnel, switchbacking across steep slopes strewn with boulders and twisted junipers. At the base of the descent, **Devils Kitchen,** a collection of tilted Wingate sandstone towers and buttes, makes a fun stop for a picnic and hike. From the Devils Kitchen Trailhead on the right or east side of the road, follow a short sandy trail which climbs 0.7 mile to the rock outcropping. The trail, perfect for families, has minimal elevation gain and ends at a shady sandstone alcove in the formation. A couple hundred feet down the road from the trailhead, turn left to Devils Kitchen Picnic Area with plenty of shaded tables, water, and restrooms. Nearby hides a panel of Native American petroglyphs, or rock drawings, carved onto a slab of Wingate sandstone. The excellent **No Thoroughfare Canyon Trail** also begins at the Devils Kitchen Trailhead, following the canyon floor for 8.5 miles and passing three waterfalls that flow in spring. Hike as far up as you want, then turn around and return to the trailhead.

From the picnic area and trailhead, the drive descends to the monument's east entrance station and the park boundary. Continue northeast down the road to its junction with CO 340. Across the Colorado River lies Grand Junction, US 50, and I-70's business route.

30

Harpers Corner Road

Dinosaur National Monument

General description: This 31-mile-long drive climbs from the headquarters of Dinosaur National Monument over a high plateau to a lookout atop Harpers Corner above the confluence of the Green and Yampa Rivers.

Special attractions: Dinosaur National Monument, Plug Hat Butte, Willow Creek Wilderness Study Area, Bull Canyon Wilderness Study Area, scenic overlooks, Echo Park Road, Whirlpool Canyon, Harpers Corner, Ruple Point, hiking, bicycling, picnicking.

Location: Far northwestern Colorado. The drive begins 1.5 miles east of Dinosaur on US 40.

Route name: Harpers Corner Road.

Travel season: Late spring through late fall. The road opens by late May and closes after the first winter snows, usually in November. Call monument headquarters for information on road closing and opening dates.

Camping: No camping on the drive. Primitive camping is permitted on surrounding Bureau of Land Management lands. Dinosaur National Monument's Green River Campground (79 sites) are located at the Quarry area in Utah, almost 30 miles west of monument headquarters via US 40 and UT 149. Echo Park Campground (22 sites) is below the drive. Check at headquarters for road information and site availability. Deerlodge Park Campground (7 sites) is 53 miles east of Dinosaur off US 40.

Services: All services are in Dinosaur and Rangely.

Nearby attractions: Dinosaur National Monument Quarry (Utah), Deerlodge Park, Gates of Lodore, Cross Mountain Canyon, Skull Creek Wilderness Study Area, Meeker, Flat Tops Trail Scenic Byway (Scenic Route 24), Uinta Mountains, Flaming Gorge National Recreation Area, Brown's Park.

The Route

Dinosaur National Monument spreads across Colorado's Empty Quarter—a remote, wild land of sagebrush-covered valleys, sandstone canyons, and high mesas and mountains. The Green and Yampa Rivers meet in secluded Echo Park beneath soaring sandstone walls in the middle of this 210,844-acre parkland, their placid waters mingling before edging around Steamboat Rock and spinning down Whirlpool Canyon into Utah.

Two distinct natural features comprise Dinosaur National Monument: the unique deposit of dinosaur bones across the border in Utah, and the wonderland of canyons incised by the mighty rivers. Most visitors come only to gaze at the extraordinary bas-relief of ancient life buried in sandstone, but out in the monument's backcountry stretches an equally spectacular natural world.

Harpers Corner Road

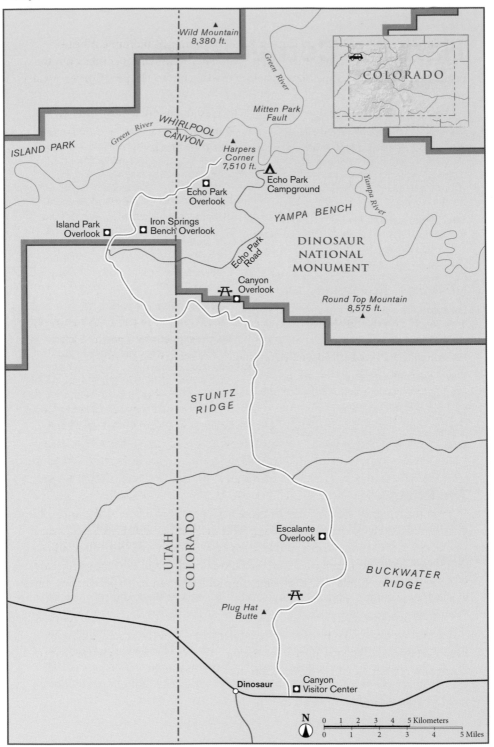

Wild Mountain
8,380 ft.

Green River

Mitten Park
Fault

WHIRLPOOL CANYON

Green River

ISLAND PARK

Harpers
Corner
7,510 ft.

Echo Park
Campground

Echo Park
Overlook

YAMPA BENCH

Yampa River

Island Park
Overlook

Iron Springs
Bench Overlook

Echo Park Road

DINOSAUR
NATIONAL
MONUMENT

Canyon
Overlook

Round Top Mountain
8,575 ft.

STUNTZ
RIDGE

UTAH
COLORADO

Escalante
Overlook

BUCKWATER
RIDGE

Plug Hat
Butte

Dinosaur

Canyon
Visitor Center

COLORADO

N

| 0 | 1 | 2 | 3 | 4 | 5 Kilometers |
| 0 | 1 | 2 | 3 | 4 | 5 Miles |

The 31-mile-long Harpers Corner Road, beginning at monument head-quarters, explores the heart of Dinosaur National Monument. It climbs onto the rounded crest of the Yampa Plateau before twisting out to Harpers Corner, an airy viewpoint perched high above Echo Park and Whirlpool Canyon.

Snow determines the drive's season. The road opens after snowdrifts melt off the higher elevations, usually sometime in May, and closes after heavy snowfall blocks the asphalt, usually in November. Check at **Canyon Visitor Center** on US 40 for road closing and opening dates. Expect hot temperatures in the lower elevations near the town of Dinosaur, with highs reaching into the 90s. Temperatures on the high plateau at Canyon Overlook and at Harpers Corner are cooler, ranging from 60 to 80 degrees. Heavy thunderstorms occur on summer afternoons. Watch for lightning on isolated ridges and viewpoints. Autumn offers warm days and cool nights, with occasional storms that bring rain and snow.

Dinosaur, the Town

The small town of **Dinosaur,** decorated with scattered sculptures of its namesake, including a stegosaurus outside the town hall, is the gateway to northwestern Colorado and Dinosaur National Monument. The town offers visitor services including lodging, dining, and gas. On US 40 in Dinosaur is a Colorado Welcome Center that offers maps, brochures, restrooms, and free coffee.

Dinosaur has a short, interesting history. This town, a scant 3 miles from the Utah border, was first called Baxter Flats for early homesteaders Art and Fanny Baxter and then incorporated with the relatively uninteresting name of Artesia in 1947. For almost 20 years Artesia watched the tourist traffic fly by on US 40, heading to see dinosaur bones at Dinosaur National Monument, before someone got the wise idea that maybe they should change their name to attract those passersby. In 1966 the town council changed to name to Dinosaur and renamed almost all of the streets to reflect its paleo-heritage, with the main drags called Brontosaurus Boulevard (US 40) and Stegosaurus Freeway (CO 64) and side streets labeled with long names like Tyrannosaurus Trail, Brachiosaurus Bypass, Triceratops Terrace, and Ceratosaurus Circle. The east–west cross streets retain more pedestrian names like 2nd Street and 5th Street.

More complete visitor services are found in Rangely 18 miles to the south. The Dinosaur Quarry section of the monument lies 30 miles west of Dinosaur near Vernal, Utah. The national monument's Split Mountain and Green River Campgrounds are along the Green River near the quarry.

The Visitor Center

The drive begins at the monument's **Canyon Visitor Center** (open summers only), 1.5 miles east of Dinosaur, at the junction of US 40 and Harpers Corner Road. The center offers interpretative displays on the area's geology, archaeology, and natural history, a bookstore with maps, books, and brochures, and restrooms and drinking water. The 0.5-mile, self-guided **Cold Desert Trail** begins at the visitor center and explores the natural history and plants of this high desert ecological community.

The Harpers Corner Road heads north from the visitor center, passing an interpretative kiosk. The road corridor, while bordered by Bureau of Land Management public lands, is part of the national monument and administered by the National Park Service. A roadside sign notes that fossil bones are not found in this section. The road leaves the dry Mancos shale country and passes through a gateway chiseled through an upturned hogback of Dakota sandstone. The road ascends Dripping Rock Creek's shallow draw. Junipers, piñon pines, and sagebrush cover the hillsides, and cottonwoods line the dry streambed below. After a half-mile the road climbs onto a broad ridge. Farther up, the drive crosses fire-ravaged hills. Dense grass coats the ground amid blackened tree skeletons from a lightning-caused fire in 1972.

Plug Hat Butte

The road climbs across a divide and winds along the southern base of 6,994-foot **Plug Hat Butte.** A viewpoint on the right side of the road below the butte looks south across broad basins broken by ribbed hogbacks. Rangely and the Rangely Oil Field lie to the south and beyond stretch forested plateaus. Two distinct rock layers form the butte—the Entrada and Carmel Formations. The salmon-colored Entrada sandstone, forming the butte's hat and brim, was deposited some 200 million years ago as windswept sand dunes. Mud deposits on an ancient shallow seafloor form the butte's hatband of red Carmel mudstone.

The road climbs through a break in the cliffs to a broad bench atop the butte. The Plug Hat Butte Picnic Area, 5 miles from the visitor center, sits on the road's north edge, while the 0.5-mile-long, paved Plug Hat Trail begins across the road. This level, accessible trail is easy to walk and offers marvelous views across the cliff-bound plateau edge and the Uintah Basin, as well as exhibits on history, plants, and geology.

The drive bends northeast across a high, rolling benchland. Thick sagebrush and scattered junipers cover the landscape. Sagebrush coats much of western Colorado. This common plant, identified by its gray-green color and aromatic scent, withstands cold temperatures and provides important browse for mule deer in winter. Overgrazing of native grasses by cattle and sheep and the suppression of natural fires expanded the historical range of sagebrush over much of the West during the last 125 years. The piñon pine and juniper woodland also forms excellent animal habitat. Mule deer, porcupines, birds, rodents, and mice use the pygmy forest for both food and cover.

Two BLM Wilderness Study Areas—Willow Creek and Bull Canyon—abut the drive as it ascends above Plug Hat Butte. The Willow Creek area sprawls across ridges and canyons to the east, and Bull Canyon encompasses the cliff-lined drainages below the road on the west. Both offer solitude and good hiking opportunities.

After 8 miles the road swings past 7,710-foot-high **Escalante Overlook** on Buckwater Ridge. Marvelous views unfold west from this lofty point—Cliff Ridge stair-steps up from the desert to the plateau crest, and dry washes and canyons drain down to the Green River's broad shale valley. The road continues climbing past the overlook, swinging through thick sagebrush stands, onto a high upland plateau. Slight valleys, floored with ribbons of water and grass, dip east through rounded ridges. Cattle graze on these high meadows.

Moffat CR 16/Wolf Creek Road is reached after 11 miles. This dirt road twists east over the plateau and through canyons and valleys to US 40. Moffat CR 16S/Blue Mountain Road begins 0.5 mile up the road. This scenic back road drops west into Utah to US 40.

The drive climbs north up a low draw that separates Stuntz Ridge and Round Top Mountain. Here the road crosses the Wolf Creek Fault, where two huge blocks of land slipped against each other. The northern block pushed higher, exposing older rocks than those found on the drive's lower elevations. The road wends north across an undulating plateau, dropping through dry washes and skirting humped hills and sagebrush-strewn plains. Groves of quaking aspen huddle in moist ravines on north-facing slopes, their golden leaves lending bright patches to the dull-colored landscape. Mule deer frequent the roadside on this highland; be watchful for them in early morning and evening.

Canyon Overlook & Echo Park

After a couple of miles the road sweeps onto a wide bench and reaches the turnoff to **Canyon Overlook.** A short side road curves a mile to the overlook and the first view of the Yampa River's sinuous canyon, carved from Weber sandstone almost 3,000 feet below. The overlook perches on the edge of the Yampa Plateau, a high, rounded uplift that is an eastward extension of the Uinta Mountains.

Steamboat Rock towers over the Green River in Echo Park, the wild heart of Dinosaur National Monument.

The Uintas, lifted some 65 million years ago along with the rest of the Rocky Mountains, are North America's only major east–west trending mountain range. Erosion attacked the mountains as they rose, cutting abrupt gorges and canyons into the uplift and sweeping eroded sand and gravel into surrounding basins. Geologists estimate over 25,000 feet of overlying rock washed off the rising mountains. **Zenobia Peak,** the monument high point at 9,006 feet, rises to the northeast above Yampa Canyon. A picnic area sits among firs at the overlook.

The drive crosses into Utah a couple of miles later and drops onto the broad ridge of Harpers Plateau. Shallow draws fall away from the road into steep canyons. The road passes a large corral used in spring and fall roundups, when area ranchers move cattle and sheep to and from high pastures. A parking area and lookout sit alongside the drive at 28 miles.

Two major faults are seen from here. The **Yampa Fault** forms the wide bench below Round Top in a textbook example of step-faulting. The **Mitten Park Fault** drops down and around the east side of Harpers Plateau before bending east at dramatically tilted strata north of Steamboat Rock. Faults formed some of Dinosaur's most spectacular scenery.

Echo Park Road leaves the Harpers Corner drive past the overlook. The 13-mile-long dirt road loops and switchbacks over 2,000 feet down to Echo Park, a sunken hole of looming cliffs, cottonwoods poised on the crumbly riverbank, and the confluence of the Green and Yampa Rivers. **Echo Park Campground,** spread along the bank opposite jutting Steamboat Rock, makes a fine getaway from the world. The 22-site, first-come first-served campground has a handicap site, group site, vault toilets, and water. Besides hiking around the scenic bottomland at Echo Park, visit **Whispering Cave,** a crack in a cliff a mile from the campground on the Echo Park Road, or drive 1.5 miles up Pool Creek from the campground to a panel of unusual dot-patterned petroglyphs created by ancient artists. Another point of interest is the abandoned Chew Ranch along Echo Park Road where Pool Creek and Trail Draw meet.

Echo Park, the lovely secret heart of Dinosaur's backcountry, was named and explored by one-armed Civil War veteran John Wesley Powell, who, with 10 men and 4 boats, floated down the Green and Colorado Rivers in 1869. After running disastrous rapids and making laborious portages through the Canyon of Lodore on the Green River, Powell's expedition lingered in the bucolic hollow for a few days. Repetitious echoes off Steamboat Rock gave the park its name. Powell wrote, "Standing opposite the rock, our words are repeated with startling clearness, but in a soft, mellow tone, that transforms them into magical music. Scarcely can one believe it is the echo of his own voice."

Echo Park later became the home of Irishman Pat Lynch, another Civil War veteran, in the early 1880s. Lynch lived as a hermit in cabins and caves here and in the Yampa River Canyon until his death in 1918. The Echo Park area still bears the name Pats Hole.

The Yampa River twists through a deep canyon east of Echo Park, passing through a rough landscape of sandstone mountains, soaring cliffs, and impassable side canyons. While many adventurers raft down the river, few hikers explore the area, one of Colorado's least accessible places. Those that do, however, occasionally make discoveries. A party of climbers, descending a sinuous canyon above the Yampa's north bank, discovered a previously unknown natural arch in 2006. They named the formation **Outlaw Arch** for nearby Outlaw Park on the Yampa and later returned to measure the arch. It was 206 feet long, the 9th longest known arch in the world and the first major arch discovered in the United States since the 1950s.

Canyon Overlooks

From the turnoff to Echo Park, drive north on Harpers Corner Road and enter Dinosaur National Monument. **Island Park Overlook** lies beyond the monument boundary. This point looks west to Island Park, a broad basin between Whirlpool Canyon and Split Mountain Gorge. The Green River threads across the emerald-colored park between numerous cottonwood-studded islands. Hills and badlands, etched with dry washes and arroyos, fringe the river's floodplain. The 9.5-mile round-trip hike on **Ruple Point Trail,** beginning at the overlook, follows an abandoned road west across Ruple Ridge to Ruple Point, a spectacular viewpoint overlooking Split Mountain Gorge in Utah.

The road bends east and swings past **Iron Springs Bench Overlook.** The point yields excellent views down Pool Creek and across Iron Springs Bench, the historic Chew Ranch, Pearl Park, and Red Rock Bench to Blue Mountain's rounded uplift. The road twists northeast on a narrowing ridge, reenters Colorado, and reaches **Echo Park Overlook.** Echo Park and the mingling of the two great rivers lie far below the east-facing overlook.

Echo Park, now a peaceful retreat for campers, rafters, and hikers, was a battleground in the 1950s. A massive dam, creating a 107-mile-long, 43,000-acre lake, was proposed for Echo Park. The project would have flooded both river canyons; destroyed wildlife habitat; reduced habitat for endangered fish species, including razorback sucker and humpback chubb, which thrive in the Yampa River's muddy waters; and set a dangerous precedent that no national parkland could remain inviolate, undeveloped, and wild. A heated debate between conservationists, including the Sierra Club, and the Bureau of Reclamation resulted in Dinosaur National Monument and its valuable natural values and resources being preserved for posterity.

Harpers Corner

The drive twists through gnarled junipers, becomes one-way, and reaches a parking area 1.5 miles north of Echo Park Overlook. This marks the end of the drive, but not the end of the scenery. The 1.5-mile out-and-back **Harpers Corner Trail** leaves the parking area and threads north along a narrow ridge to 7,510-foot **Harpers Corner,** a jutting promontory high above Echo Park and the Green River. An informative brochure, found at the trail's beginning, explains the area's natural history and geology. As the trail gently descends from the road, glimpses of the canyons unfold below. Finally the path reaches a slight saddle and clambers over bedrock to a magnificent fenced overlook.

Echo Park lies to the east, with the muddy **Green River** making a tight horseshoe bend around Steamboat Rock. Beyond, lost in the ivory-tinted Weber sandstone, hides the sinuous canyon of the Yampa River. The 170-mile-long Yampa River, Colorado's last major free-flowing river, arises from snow atop the Flat Tops on the White River Plateau. In Dinosaur National Monument, the Yampa winds 46 miles through a serpentine maze of pale sandstone cliffs and domes before merging with the Green River in Echo Park.

The Green River plunges through 18-mile-long **Lodore Canyon** above Echo Park. This somber gorge, its stair-stepped upper walls visible northeast of Harpers

The stunning views from Harpers Corner include both the Green and Yampa Rivers and the Mitten Park Fault.

Corner, possesses the monument's oldest rock formation—billion-year-old Uinta Mountain quartzite. A series of frothy rapids, with terrifying names given by Major John Wesley Powell's 1869 expedition like Hells Half Mile and Disaster Falls, challenge river rafters in the canyon.

The Green River changes character below Echo Park, making a wide loop around Harpers Corner. The Mitten Park Fault's upturned rock layers are exposed in a dramatic cross-section above the river. The river enters Whirlpool Canyon at the fault, a spectacular abyss of rocks deposited on ancient seabeds. The cliff-lined river flows quickly through here, tumbling over water-worn boulders and passing secret alcoves and sand beaches.

John Wesley Powell named and described Whirlpool Canyon: "The Green is greatly increased by the Yampa, and we now have a much larger river. All this volume of water, confined, as it is, in a narrow channel and rushing with great velocity, is set eddying and spinning in whirlpools by projecting rocks and short curves, and the waters waltz their way through the canyon, making their own rippling, rushing, roaring music." An earlier passerby, a French fur trapper, etched his name and date, "D. Julien 1836," on a rock panel below Harpers Corner.

Before starting the hike and drive back to US 40, linger atop the lofty aerie of Harpers Corner. Listen to the deep river currents far below, spinning the time-worn music heard by Major Powell. Rivers and time are alike in their relentless resolve and single-minded purpose. To be here now. To hear the flow of the river. That's important. We've left our cultural baggage back in the parking lot and begun to let the consciousness of these rivers and canyons seep in. That's the enchantment of rivers—they're disarmingly simple, yet they teach great lessons.

For More Information

General

Bureau of Land Management
Colorado State Office
2850 Youngfield St.
Lakewood, CO 80215
(303) 239-3933
blm.gov/colorado

Colorado Parks and Wildlife
1313 Sherman St., 6th Floor
Denver, CO 80203
(303) 297-1192
cpw.state.co.us/

National Park Service
Denver Service Center
12795 Alameda Pkwy.
Denver, CO 80228-2838
(303) 969-2100

USDA Forest Service
Rocky Mountain Region
1617 Cole Blvd., Building 17
Lakewood, CO 80401
(303) 275-5350
fs.usda.gov/main/r2/home

1 Santa Fe Trail Scenic & Historic Byway

Bent's Old Fort National Historic Site
35110 CO 194 East
La Junta, CO 81050
(719) 383-5010
nps.gov/beol/i

Comanche National Grassland
Timpas Unit
1420 E. 3rd St.
La Junta, CO 81050
(719) 384-2181
fs.usda.gov/goto/psicc/com

La Junta Tourism
601 Colorado Ave.
La Junta, CO 81050
(719) 468-1439
visitlajunta.net/

Trinidad–Las Animas County Chamber of Commerce
136 W. Main St.
Trinidad, CO 81082
(719) 846-9285
tlacchamber.org

2 Pawnee Pioneer Trails Scenic Drive

City of Sterling
421 N. 4th St.
Sterling, CO 80751
(970) 522-9700
sterlingcolo.com

Greeley Chamber of Commerce
902 7th Ave.
Greeley, CO 80631
(970) 352-3567
(800) 449-3866
visitgreeley.org

Pawnee National Grassland
115 North 2nd Ave.
PO Box 386
Ault, CO 80610
(970) 834-9270
fs.usda.gov/main/arp/home

3 Comanche Grasslands Scenic Drive

Comanche National Grassland
Carrizo Unit
27204 US 287
PO Box 127
Springfield, CO 81073
(719) 523-6591
fs.usda.gov/main/psicc/home

Pike and San Isabel National Forests
2840 Kachina Dr.
Pueblo, CO 81008
(719) 553-1400
fs.usda.gov/main/psicc/home

Springfield Chamber of Commerce
948 Main St.
Springfield, CO 81073
(719) 523-4061

4 Highway of Legends Scenic Byway

La Veta Cuchara Chamber of Commerce
903 S. Oak St.
La Veta, CO 81055
(719) 742-3676
lavetacucharachamber.com

San Isabel National Forest
San Carlos Ranger District
3028 E. Main St.
Cañon City, CO 81212
(719) 269-8500
fs.usda.gov/psicc

Spanish Peaks Country
spanishpeakscountry.com

Trinidad–Las Animas County Chamber of Commerce
136 W. Main St.
Trinidad, CO 81082
(719) 846-9285
tlacchamber.org

5 Sangre de Cristo Scenic Drive

Custer County Chamber of Commerce
Visit Custer County
107 N. 3rd St.
Westcliffe, CO 81252
(719) 783-9163
(877) 793-3170
visitcustercounty.com

Pike and San Isabel National Forests
2840 Kachina Dr.
Pueblo, CO 81008
(719) 553-1400
fs.usda.gov/psicc

6 Los Caminos Antiguos Scenic Byway

Bureau of Land Management
San Luis Valley Field Office
1313 E. Highway 160
Monte Vista, CO 81144
(719) 852-7074
blm.gov/office/san-luis-valley-field-office

Conejos County Museum
5045 US Hwy. 285
PO Box 829
Antonito, CO 81120
(719) 580-4070
museumtrail.org/conejos-county-museum

Fort Garland Museum & Cultural Center
29477 Highway 159
Fort Garland, CO, 81133
(719) 379-3512
historycolorado.org/fort-garland-museum-cultural-center

Great Sand Dunes National Park & Preserve
11999 State Highway 150
Mosca, CO 81146
(719) 378-6395
nps.gov/grsa

Jack Dempsey Museum
412 Main St.
PO Box 130
Manassa, CO 81141
(719) 843-5207
museumtrail.org/jack-dempsey-museum

Rio Grande National Forest
1803 US 160 West
Monte Vista, CO 81144
(719) 852-5941
fs.usda.gov/riogrande

San Luis Lakes State Wildlife Area
16399 Lane 6 N.
Mosca, CO 81146
(719) 587-6900

7 Wet Mountains Scenic Drive

Cañon City Chamber of Commerce
403 Royal Gorge Blvd.
Cañon City, CO 81212
(800) 876-7922
canoncity.com/visitors

San Isabel National Forest
San Carlos Ranger District
3028 E. Main St.
Cañon City, CO 81212
(719) 269-8500
fs.usda.gov/psicc

8 Gold Belt Tour Back Country Byway

Bureau of Land Management
Royal Gorge Field Office
3028 E. Main St.
Cañon City, CO 81212
(719) 269-8500
blm.gov/office/royal-gorge-field-office

Cañon City Chamber of Commerce
403 Royal Gorge Blvd.
Cañon City, CO 81212
(800) 876-7922
canoncity.com/visitors

Cripple Creek Heritage Center
9283 S. Hwy. 67
Cripple Creek, CO 80813
(719) 689-3315
(877) 858-4653
visitcripplecreek.com

9 Pikes Peak Highway

Colorado Springs Visitor Center
515 S. Cascade Ave.
Colorado Springs, CO 80903
(719) 635-7506
(800) 888-4748
visitcos.com

Manitou Springs Visitors Bureau
354 Manitou Ave.
Manitou Springs, CO 80829
(719) 685-5089
(800) 642-2567
manitousprings.org

Pike National Forest
Pikes Peak Ranger District
601 South Weber Ave.
Colorado Springs, CO 80903
(719) 636-1602
fs.usda.gov/psicc

Pikes Peak Highway
5089 Pikes Peak Highway
Cascade, CO 80809
(719) 385-7325
(719) 684-9138 (Pikes Peak Highway Tollgate)
coloradosprings.gov/pikes-peak-americas-mountain

10 North Cheyenne Cañon & Lower Gold Camp Roads Scenic Drive

Colorado Springs Parks, Recreation, and Cultural Services
1401 Recreation Way
Colorado Springs, CO 80905
(719) 385-5940
coloradosprings.gov/parks/page/parks-trails-open-spaces

Colorado Springs Visitor Center
515 S. Cascade Ave.
Colorado Springs, CO 80903
(719) 635-7506
(800) 888-4748
visitcos.com

Pike National Forest
Pikes Peak Ranger District
601 S. Weber Ave.
Colorado Springs, CO 80903
(719) 636-1602
fs.usda.gov/psicc

Starsmore Visitor and Nature Center
2120 S. Cheyenne Cañon Rd.
Colorado Springs, CO 80906
(719) 385-6086
coloradosprings.gov/parks/page/starsmore-visitor-and-nature-center

11 South Platte River Roads

Pike National Forest
South Platte Ranger District
30403 Kings Valley Drive, Suite 2-115
Conifer, CO 80433
(303) 275-5610
fs.usda.gov/psicc

Woodland Park Chamber of Commerce
210 E. Midland Ave.
PO Box 9022
Woodland Park, CO 80866
(719) 687-9885
woodlandparkchamber.org

12 Rampart Range Road Scenic Drive

Pike National Forest
Pikes Peak Ranger District
601 S. Weber Ave.
Colorado Springs, CO 80903
(719) 636-1602
fs.usda.gov/psicc

Pike National Forest
South Platte Ranger District
30403 Kings Valley Drive, Suite 2-115
Conifer, CO 80433
(303) 275-5610
fs.usda.gov/psicc

13 South Park–Tarryall Loop Scenic Drive

Park County
856 Castello Ave.
Fairplay, CO 80440
(719) 836-2771
parkco.us

Pike National Forest
South Park Ranger District
PO Box 219
320 US 285
Fairplay, CO 80440
(719) 836-2031
fs.usda.gov/psicc

South Park Chamber of Commerce
PO Box 312
Fairplay, CO 80440
(719) 836-3410
southparkchamber.com

14 Mount Evans Scenic Drive

Arapaho National Forest
Clear Creek Ranger District
2060 Miner St.
Idaho Springs, CO 80452
(303) 567-4382
fs.usda.gov/arp

Clear Creek County Tourism Bureau
Idaho Springs Visitor Center
2060 Miner St.
PO Box 100
Idaho Springs, CO 80452
(303) 567-4660 or (303) 567-4382
(866) 674-9237
clearcreekcounty.org

15 Guanella Pass Scenic & Historic Byway

Arapaho National Forest
Clear Creek Ranger District
2060 Miner St.
Idaho Springs, CO 80452
(303) 567-4382
fs.usda.gov/arp

Clear Creek County Tourism Bureau
Idaho Springs Visitor Center
2060 Miner St.
PO Box 100
Idaho Springs, CO 80452
(303) 567-4660 or (303) 567-4382
(866) 674-9237
clearcreekcounty.org

Georgetown Gateway Visitor's Center
1491 Argentine St.
Georgetown, CO 80444
(303) 569-2405
georgetowntrust.org/gateway-visitor-center

Georgetown Loop Railroad
646 Loop Drive
PO Box 249
Georgetown, CO 80444
(888) 456-6777
georgetownlooprr.com

Town of Georgetown
404 6th Street
PO Box 426
Georgetown, CO 80444
(303) 569-2555
georgetown-colorado.org

16 Peak to Peak Scenic & Historic Byway

Arapaho National Forest
Boulder Ranger District
2140 Yarmouth Ave.
Boulder, CO 80301
(303) 541-2500
fs.usda.gov/arp

Clear Creek County Tourism Bureau
Idaho Springs Visitor Center
2060 Miner St.
PO Box 100
Idaho Springs, CO 80452
(303) 567-4660 or (303) 567-4382
(866) 674-9237
clearcreekcounty.org

Estes Park Visitors Center
500 Big Thompson Ave.
Estes Park, CO 80517
(970) 577-9900
(800) 443-7837
visitestespark.com

Nederland Visitors Center
45 W. 1st St.
Nederland, CO 80466
(303) 258-3936
nederlandco.org/directory/nederland-visitors-center/

Rocky Mountain National Park
1000 US 36
Estes Park, CO 80517
(970) 586-1206
nps.gov/romo

17 Trail Ridge Road All-American Byway

Estes Park Visitors Center
500 Big Thompson Ave.
PO Box 1200
Estes Park, CO 80517
(970) 577-9900
(800) 443-7837
visitestespark.com

Grand County Colorado Tourism Board
PO Box 131
Granby, CO 80446
(720) 530-1066
(800) 247-2636
visitgrandcounty.com

Grand Lake Visitor Center
14700 US Highway 34
Grand Lake, CO 80447
(800) 531-1019
(970) 627-3402
visitgrandcounty.com

Rocky Mountain National Park
1000 US 36
Estes Park, CO 80517
(970) 586-1206
nps.gov/romo

18 Cache la Poudre–North Park Scenic Drive

Fort Collins Convention & Visitors Bureau
1 Old Town Sq., Ste. 107
Fort Collins, CO 80524
(970) 232-3840
(800) 274-3678
visitftcollins.com

North Park Chamber of Commerce
416 4th St.
Walden, CO 80480
(970) 723-4600
northparkchamber.wordpress.com

Roosevelt National Forest
Canyon Lakes Ranger District
2150 Centre Ave., Building E
Fort Collins, CO 80526
(970) 295-6600
fs.usda.gov/arp

19 Independence Pass Scenic Drive

Aspen Chamber Resort Association
590 N. Mill St.
Aspen, CO 81611
(970) 925-1940
(877) 702-7736
aspenchamber.org

San Isabel National Forest
Leadville Ranger District
810 Front St.
Leadville, CO 80461
(719) 486-0749
fs.usda.gov/psicc

White River National Forest
900 Grand Ave.
Glenwood Springs, CO 81601
(970) 945-2521
fs.usda.gov/whiteriver

White River National Forest
Aspen-Sopris Ranger District
806 West Hallam St.
Aspen, CO 81611
(970) 925-3445
fs.usda.gov/whiteriver

20 Cottonwood Pass Scenic Drive

Buena Vista Chamber of Commerce & Visitor Center
343 US 24 South
PO Box 2021
Buena Vista, CO 81211
(719) 395-6612
buenavistacolorado.org

Gunnison Country Chamber of Commerce
500 East Tomichi Ave.
Gunnison, CO 81230
(970) 641-1501
gunnison-co.com

Gunnison National Forest
2250 S. Main St.
Delta, CO 81416
(303) 874-6600
fs.usda.gov/gmug

Gunnison National Forest
Gunnison Ranger District
216 N. Colorado St.
Gunnison, CO 81230
(970) 641-0471
fs.usda.gov/gmug

Pike and San Isabel National Forests
2840 Kachina Dr.
Pueblo, CO 81008
(719) 553-1400
fs.usda.gov/psicc

San Isabel National Forest
Salida Ranger District
5575 Cleora Rd.
Salida, CO 81201
(719) 539-3591
fs.usda.gov/psicc

21 West Elk Loop Scenic Byway

Crested Butte. Mt. Crested Butte Chamber of Commerce
601 Elk Ave.
Crested Butte, CO 81224
(970) 349-6438
(855) 681-0941
crestedbuttechamber.com

Gunnison Country Chamber of Commerce & Visitor Center
500 E. Tomichi Ave.
Gunnison, CO 81230
(970) 641-1501
gunnisonchamber.com

Gunnison National Forest
Gunnison Ranger District
216 N. Colorado St.
Gunnison, CO 81230
(970) 641-0471
fs.usda.gov/gmug

Gunnison National Forest
Paonia Ranger District
N. Rio Grande Ave.
PO Box 1030
Paonia, CO 81428
(970) 527-4131
fs.usda.gov/gmug

Paonia Chamber of Commerce
136 Grand Ave.
PO Box 366
Paonia, CO 81428
(970) 527-3886
paoniachamber.com

22 Silver Thread Scenic Byway

Creede & Mineral County Visitor Center & Chamber of Commerce
904 S. Main St.
PO Box 580
Creede, CO 81130
(719) 658-2374
creede.com

Lake City–Hinsdale County Chamber of Commerce
800 Gunnison Ave.
PO Box 430
Lake City, CO 81235
(970) 944-2527
lakecity.com

Rio Grande National Forest
1803 W. US 160
Monte Vista, CO 81144
(719) 852-5941
fs.usda.gov/riogrande

Rio Grande National Forest
Divide Ranger District
304 S. Main St.
PO Box 270
Creede, CO 81130
(719) 658-2556
fs.usda.gov/riogrande

23 San Juan Skyway All-American Byway

Cortez Area Chamber of Commerce
Colorado Welcome Center
31 W. Main St.
Cortez, CO 81321
(970) 565-3414
cortezchamber.com
mesaverdecountry.com

Dolores Chamber of Commerce
201 Railroad Ave.
PO Box 602
Dolores, CO 81323
(970) 882-4018
doloreschamber.com

Durango & Silverton Narrow Gauge Railroad
479 Main Ave.
Durango, CO 81301
Reservations: (970) 247-2733
Info: (970) 247-2733
(877) 872-4607
durangotrain.com

Durango Area Tourism Office
802 Main Ave.
Durango, CO 81301
(970) 247-3500
(800) 463-8726
durango.org

Mancos State Park
1321 Railroad Ave.
Dolores, CO 81323
(970) 533-7065
parks.state.co.us/Parks/Mancos

Ouray Chamber Resort Association/ Ouray Visitors Center
1230 Main St.
PO Box 145
Ouray, CO 81427
(970) 325-4746
(800) 228-1876
ouraycolorado.com

Ouray Ice Park
PO Box 1058
Ouray, CO 81427
(970) 325-4288
ourayicepark.com

Ridgway Area Chamber of Commerce & Visitors Center
150 Racecourse Rd.
Ridgway, CO 81432
(970) 626-5181
(800) 220-4959
ridgwaycolorado.com

San Juan National Forest
15 Burnett Ct.
Durango, CO 81301
(970) 247-4874
fs.usda.gov/sanjuan

Silverton Chamber of Commerce and
Visitor Center
414 Greene St.
PO Box 565
Silverton, CO 81433
(970) 387-5654
(800) 752-4494
silvertoncolorado.com

Telluride Tourism Board & Visitors
Center
236 W. Colorado Ave.
Telluride, CO 81435
(888) 605-2578
(970) 728-3041
visittelluride.com

Uncompahgre and Gunnison National
Forests
2250 S. Main St.
Delta, CO 81416
(970) 874-6600
fs.usda.gov/gmug

24 Flat Tops Trail Scenic Byway

Meeker Chamber of Commerce
710 Market St.
Meeker, CO 81641
(970) 878-5510
meekerchamber.com

Routt National Forest
Yampa Ranger District
300 Roselawn Ave.
PO Box 7
Yampa, CO 80483
(970) 638-4516
fs.usda.gov/mbr

White River National Forest
Blanco Ranger District
220 E. Market St.
Meeker, CO 81641
(970) 878-4039
fs.usda.gov/whiteriver

25 Grand Mesa Scenic Byway

Cedaredge Area Chamber of
Commerce
245 W. Main St.
Cedaredge, CO 81413
(970) 856-6961
cedaredgechamber.com

Delta Area Chamber of Commerce
301 Main St.
Delta, CO 81416
(970) 874-8616
deltacolorado.org

Delta County Tourism
655 Grand Ave.
Delta, CO 81416
(970) 874-2115
deltacountycolorado.com

Grand Mesa National Forest
2250 S. Main St.
Delta, CO 81416
(970) 874-6600
fs.usda.gov/gmug

26 Black Canyon South Rim Scenic Drive

Black Canyon of the Gunnison National Park
102 Elk Creek
Gunnison, CO 81230
(970) 641-2337
nps.gov/blca

Visit Montrose
Montrose Office of Business and Tourism
107 S. Cascade Ave.
(970) 497-8558
visitmontrose.com

27 Unaweep–Tabeguache Scenic & Historic Byway

Bureau of Land Management
Grand Junction Field Office
2815 H Rd.
Grand Junction, CO 81506
(970) 244-3000
blm.gov/office/grand-junction-field-office

Bureau of Land Management
Uncompahgre Field Office
2465 S. Townsend Ave.
Montrose, CO 81401
(970) 240-5300
blm.gov/office/uncompahgre-field-office

Gateway Canyons Resort & Spa
43200 CO 141
Gateway, CO 81522
(970) 931-2458
gatewaycanyons.com

Norwood Chamber of Commerce of Wright's Mesa
PO Box 116
Norwood, CO 81423
(970) 327-4288
norwoodcolorado.com

Unaweep-Tabeguache Interpretive Visitor Center
Nucla-Naturita Area Chamber of Commerce
230 W. Main St.
Naturita, CO 81422
(970) 865-2350
nucla-naturita.com

Uncompahgre National Forest
2250 S. Main St.
Delta, CO 81416
(970) 874-6600
fs.usda.gov/gmug

28 Mesa Verde National Park Scenic Drive

Cortez Chamber of Commerce
31 W. Main St.
PO Box 968
Cortez, CO 81321
(970) 565-3414
cortezchamber.com
mesaverdecountry.com

Mesa Verde National Park
PO Box 8
Mesa Verde National Park, CO 81330
(970) 529-4465
nps.gov/meve

29 Rim Rock Drive

Colorado National Monument
1750 Rim Rock Dr.
Fruita, CO 81521
(970) 858-3617 x360
nps.gov/colm

Go Fruita
325 E. Aspen Ave.
Fruita, CO 81521
(970) 858-8373
gofruita.com

Visit Grand Junction
740 Horizon Dr.
Grand Junction, CO 81506
(800) 244-1480
visitgrandjunction.com

30 Harpers Corner Road

Colorado Welcome Center
101 E. Stegosaurus St.
Dinosaur, CO 81610
colorado.com/official-colorado-welcome-centers

Dinosaur National Monument
4545 US 40
Dinosaur, CO 81610
(435) 781-7700
nps.gov/dino

Rangely Area Chamber of Commerce
255 E. Main St., Suite A
Rangely, CO 81648
(970) 675-5290
rangelychamber.com

Index

DISCARD